Practical Cybersecurity Architecture

A guide to creating and implementing robust designs
for cybersecurity architects

Diana Kelley

Ed Moyle

BIRMINGHAM—MUMBAI

Practical Cybersecurity Architecture

Group Product Manager: Pavan Ramchandani
Publishing Product Manager: Khushboo Samkaria
Book Project Manager: Ashwin Kharwa
Senior Editor: Roshan Ravi Kumar
Technical Editor: Irfa Ansari
Copy Editor: Safis Editing
Proofreader: Safis Editing
Indexer: Pratik Shirodkar
Production Designer: Ponraj Dhandapani
DevRel Marketing Coordinator: Marylou De Mello

First published: November 2020
Second edition: October 2023

Production reference: 1121023

Published by Packt Publishing Ltd.

Grosvenor House
11 St Paul's Square
Birmingham
B3 1RB, UK

ISBN 978-1-83763-716-4

www.packtpub.com

Contributors

About the authors

Diana Kelley is CISO at Protect AI. She serves on the boards of WiCyS, the Executive Women's Forum, InfoSec World, and TechTarget Security. She was Cybersecurity Field CTO at Microsoft, Global Executive Security Advisor at IBM Security, GM at Symantec, VP at Burton Group, Manager at KPMG, and Chief vCISO at SaltCybersecurity.

Her extensive volunteer work has included serving on the ACM Ethics & Plagiarism Committee, Cybersecurity Advisor at CompTIA, and the RSAC Program Committee. She hosts BrightTALK's The Security Balancing Act, co-authored *Practical Cybersecurity Architecture* and *Cryptographic Libraries for Developers*, and teaches LinkedIn Learning Security in AI and ML. Her awards include EWF Executive of the Year and SCMedia Power Player.

Ed Moyle is a partner with SecurityCurve and Systems and Software Security Director for Taxwell. In his 25 years in information security, Ed has held numerous positions, including Director of Thought Leadership and Research for ISACA, Senior Security Strategist with Savvis, Senior Manager with CTG, and Vice President and Information Security Officer for Merrill Lynch Investment Managers. Ed is the co-author of *Cryptographic Libraries for Developers* and *Practical Cybersecurity Architecture*. He is a frequent contributor to the information security industry as an author, public speaker, and analyst.

About the reviewer

Eyal Estrin is a cloud and information security architect, and the author of the book *Cloud Security Handbook*, with more than 20 years in the IT industry.

He has worked in several different industries (in the banking, academia, and healthcare sectors).

He has attained several top security certifications – CISSP, CCSP, CDPSE, CISA, and CCSK.

He shares his knowledge through social media (LinkedIn, Twitter, Medium, and more).

Table of Contents

Part 2: Building an Architecture

3

Building an Architecture – Scope and Requirements   79

4

Building an Architecture – Your Toolbox   107

5

Building an Architecture – Developing Enterprise Blueprints   155

6

Building an Architecture – Application Blueprints   197

Part 3: Execution

7

Execution –Applying Architecture Models   251

8

Execution – Future-Proofing   295

9

Preface

Cybersecurity is quickly becoming a make or break topic area for most businesses. We can all cite numerous examples from the headlines that underscore the importance of security: this includes security issues at both large and small companies, breach notifications from the online services we use, and incidents in the companies we work with and for. We all know stories of vulnerable software, scammed users, accidental misconfiguration of hardware or software, and numerous other events that can and do have potentially disastrous consequences for both individuals and organizations.

All of this is happening against a backdrop where **artificial intelligence (AI)** and **machine learning (ML)** are becoming ubiquitous and changing how we do things. More and more, business processes are changing their processes to adapt and accommodate these new methods. They're changing the services they offer, how they engage with customers and partners, how they interact with stakeholders (employees, partners, customers, and others), and numerous other changes.

To help prevent security issues while at the same time best positioning to gain benefits from new technologies such as AI and ML, organizations continue to place increasing importance on cybersecurity. They are making it a higher priority than it has historically been and investing in it accordingly. But how can an organization know whether they are investing in the right places? Resources are finite, which means that they need to be selective about what security measures they implement and where they apply those limited budgets. How can organizations know when they have enough security? How do they know that they've attained their security goals when the necessary steps are dependent on factors unique to them: what the organization does, how it does it, who's involved, and why? Everything from organizational culture to business context to governing regulations to geography and even industry can play a role here.

Cybersecurity architecture is one way to systematically, holistically, and repeatably answer these questions. Much like a software architect creates a vision for how to achieve a user's goals in software or a network engineer creates a vision for how to achieve the performance and reliability targets for network communications, the cybersecurity architect works to create a vision for cybersecurity. This can be for an application, a network, a process, a business unit, or the entire organization itself.

This book takes a practical look at the nuts and bolts of defining, documenting, validating, and, ultimately, delivering an architectural vision. It draws on existing standards and frameworks for cybersecurity architecture, outlining where (and more importantly, how) they can be applied to the architecture process in your organization. This book does this by walking through the architecture process step by step, discussing why each step provides the value it does and how to use it to maximum benefit, and provides tips, gotchas, case studies, and techniques from numerous working architects in the field to supplement our own perspective.

Who this book is for

This book is primarily for cybersecurity practitioners getting started with cybersecurity architecture or those already following a systematic architecture process who would like to build their skills. For the novice, we walk through the fundamental skills and techniques used in the architecture process and, for those with some experience already, we supplement our viewpoint with that of other architecture specialists currently in the field to help them think about challenges in a new way or adapt strategies that have been successful for others into their own toolkit.

What this book covers

Chapter 1, What Is Cybersecurity Architecture?, provides an overview of cybersecurity architecture: what it is, why it's useful, the business value that it brings to the organization employing it, and the role of the cybersecurity architect within an organization. We highlight the history of cybersecurity architecture and important standards, frameworks, and approaches that the architect can draw upon, and lay out the fundamental requirements for the architect before they get started.

Chapter 2, Core of Solution Building, helps the architect assess the important touchstones, contextual background, and goals of the organization. Architecture doesn't happen in a vacuum: the design must be reflective of the organization's needs, its business, and its mission. This chapter helps the architect understand that context – the boundaries around what the organization considers important – that will allow the architect to systematically and purposefully take action.

Chapter 3, Building an Architecture – Scope and Requirements, looks at how, as with any project, the outcome must be dictated by what the organization needs. This chapter presents methods for discovering the scope within which the architect must design as well as the core information about requirements that their solution should address.

Chapter 4, Building an Architecture – Your Toolbox, explains how any project you undertake has a set of tools that will let you do the job successfully. With them, the job is easy – without them, there's nothing harder. This chapter is all about building out the toolbox that you will need as you approach the design process. Getting your tools ready ahead of time allows you to have them when you need them.

Chapter 5, Building an Architecture – Developing Enterprise Blueprints, outlines how to gather, document, and validate the necessary information that will allow you to create a high-level architectural definition. This lets you select a solution approach that is consistent with what the organization needs and is documented in such a way as to protect the organization, streamline efforts, and ensure that technical implementation approaches are optimal.

Chapter 6, Building an Architecture – Application Blueprints, looks at how, in many ways, building a cybersecurity architecture for an application is similar to doing so for the organization in aggregate or for a network. However, because there are different audiences to whom we must present designs and approaches (and that we must of necessity work collaboratively with), there are some elements of the process that are different. To accommodate this, we provide specific guidance on application security architecture efforts within this chapter.

Chapter 7, Execution – Applying Architecture Models, walks through how to implement your design concept technically, walking you through elements of execution and realization of the implementation, as at this point, you will have created a high-level "model": a design that meets the organization's needs. However, the best ideas on paper don't actually provide value until they are implemented.

Chapter 8, Execution – Future-Proofing, goes through the process of ensuring that a design (and subsequent implementation) that you've deployed stays meaningful over time. It discusses ways to ensure that you keep apprised of changes, that you monitor the effectiveness of your solution over time, and that you build in and adapt instrumentation (e.g., metrics) to keep things running smoothly after deployment.

Chapter 9, Putting It All Together, closes the book with strategies that you can use to improve your architecture skills, improve the processes you follow, and ensure that, with each project you take on, you optimize what you do. We present guidance about common issues that architects run into, how to avoid them, and advice for the architect drawn from the experiences of those in the field.

To get the most out of this book

To be as practical in our approach as possible, we've made a few assumptions about you, your skill level, and your needs. First, we assume that you will know the basics of cybersecurity (or information security), such as a working knowledge of common security controls. Second, we assume a baseline of enterprise technology knowledge.

We've also assumed that the organization in which you will be applying the techniques we discuss is like most: one that could benefit from increased architectural rigor but where rigor itself is not an end goal. Larger organizations that systematically follow a highly rigorous process – or service providers with contractual requirements to do so – will find that we have scaled back or streamlined some elements of the process to make it accessible and achievable to smaller teams. In general, we have stated explicitly where, how, and why we have made these changes in the sections where we do so.

Lastly, we suggest (but it is not required) that you have one or more active problems to which you can apply the techniques in this book, meaning that you can apply the process sequentially as you learn it to the real-world challenges in your job. Being able to apply the concepts directly helps ensure that the principles are retained.

Conventions used

There are several conventions used throughout this book.

Bold: Indicates a new term, an important word, or words that you see onscreen. For example, words in menus or dialog boxes appear in the text like this. Here is an example: "Select **System info** from the **Administration** panel."

In some cases, we wish to highlight areas of importance to the reader. Tips or important notes appear as follows:

> **Important note**
> Appears like this.

Get in touch

Feedback from our readers is always welcome.

General feedback: If you have questions about any aspect of this book, mention the book title in the subject of your message and email us at customercare@packtpub.com.

Errata: Although we have taken every care to ensure the accuracy of our content, mistakes do happen. If you have found a mistake in this book, we would be grateful if you would report this to us. Please visit www.packtpub.com/support/errata, select your book, click on the Errata Submission Form link, and enter the details.

Piracy: If you come across any illegal copies of our works in any form on the Internet, we would be grateful if you would provide us with the location address or website name. Please contact us at copyright@packt.com with a link to the material.

If you are interested in becoming an author: If there is a topic that you have expertise in and you are interested in either writing or contributing to a book, please visit authors.packtpub.com.

Share Your Thoughts

Once you've read *Practical Cybersecurity Architecture, 2nd edition*, we'd love to hear your thoughts! Scan the QR code below to go straight to the Amazon review page for this book and share your feedback.

https://packt.link/r/1837637164

Your review is important to us and the tech community and will help us make sure we're delivering excellent quality content.

Download a free PDF copy of this book

Thanks for purchasing this book!

Do you like to read on the go but are unable to carry your print books everywhere?

Is your eBook purchase not compatible with the device of your choice?

Don't worry, now with every Packt book you get a DRM-free PDF version of that book at no cost.

Read anywhere, any place, on any device. Search, copy, and paste code from your favorite technical books directly into your application.

The perks don't stop there, you can get exclusive access to discounts, newsletters, and great free content in your inbox daily

Follow these simple steps to get the benefits:

1. Scan the QR code or visit the link below

https://packt.link/free-ebook/9781837637164

2. Submit your proof of purchase
3. That's it! We'll send your free PDF and other benefits to your email directly

Part 1: Security Architecture

This section gives you an overview of what **cybersecurity architecture** means: what it is, what it includes (and what it doesn't), why it's useful, and what the role of a cybersecurity architect may encompass, depending on their focus and the organization they work in. These chapters work through the origins of security architecture, common frameworks to architecture, and the evolution of the discipline.

By understanding why cybersecurity provides value, the architect can then ensure that they are adding the most value to their organization. The first chapter in this section outlines the business value that the cybersecurity architecture process brings about, while the second chapter helps architects understand the business and, by extension, the differing needs of different organizations. Since the needs and context of organizations differ, the architect should begin with an understanding of the business and adapt their role in it to ensure that the work they do will be viewed as necessary, welcome, and valuable to the organization based on what the organization does, how it does it, and its particular set of needs.

This section comprises the following chapters:

- *Chapter 1, What Is Cybersecurity Architecture?*
- *Chapter 2, Architecture – The Core of Solution Building*

1

What Is Cybersecurity Architecture?

Let's face it – cybersecurity can be a scary, stress-inducing proposition. And it's no wonder. Cybersecurity in modern business is *high stakes*. We've all seen headlines about data breaches, attacks, and even accidental exposures impacting some of the largest companies (not to mention governments) in the world. The truth is, if you do security wrong, you open yourself up to being attacked by numerous potential adversaries, such as cybercriminals, hacktivists, nation-states, or any number of other parties. Even if you do everything perfectly, circumstances can still put you at risk anyway. It's a challenging field – and it can be difficult to get it right.

We want to be clear right from the start that this book is not about a new security architecture framework or a new set of competing architectural methods to what already exists, and it's not a reference book. These already exist and provide plenty of value to those actively using them. In fact, one might argue that the single biggest limiting factor to the discipline itself is the fact that more people aren't actively using, or have detailed knowledge of, that excellent source material.

Therefore, rather than contributing to that problem by muddying the waters or adding competing foundational material, we intend to demonstrate clearly *how* to do the work, which means we intend this book to read more like a playbook designed to build *muscle memory*.

Think about the difference between reading a book on ballistic physics versus working with a pitching coach. The physics book will almost certainly lead you to a deeper understanding of the mechanics, forces, and mathematics of a baseball in flight than you could ever possibly derive from working with a coach. Yet, even with the deepest understanding of the physics, you probably won't pitch a no-hitter for the Yankees. That is, you won't do so unless and until you also build the requisite muscle memory, put in the time to practice and hone your technique, and work with those who can help you improve. However, knowledge of the underlying physics can inform (to great effect) the value derived from working with a coach as those principles can help you hone your technique and realize even greater potential.

Therefore, our intention with this book is for it to act as a sort of *training guide* for those looking to build their skills in the cybersecurity architecture discipline: either because they are in a new architectural role and want to build the necessary practical skills, or because they're an existing practitioner who wants to improve. We will do this by building on the theoretical models, drawing from them, and incorporating them to lay out specific, practical steps that can be followed by anyone willing to do the work. We will focus on one set of steps and techniques – those that have worked for us – and supplement those with techniques that we've gathered from practitioners throughout the industry in architectural roles (either on a large or small scale).

Note that this book also isn't a catalog of security controls. We have purposefully refrained from listing in detail the hundreds – if not thousands – of possible controls, security techniques, technical countermeasures, and other specific technologies that you might choose to adopt as implementation strategies. Consider, by analogy, a primer on the techniques of cooking. Would such a book dedicate hundreds of pages to descriptions of every possible ingredient that a home cook or professional chef might encounter throughout their career? No. Such an exercise would make for boring reading (in fact, it would serve as a distraction from the book's utility), would rapidly become outdated, and would serve little purpose as that material is available through numerous other avenues. Instead, we've chosen to focus on the techniques and principles of architecture, leaving detailed descriptions of specific technical strategies to the numerous standards and guidance that already exist.

Throughout this book, we'll introduce you to many practitioners and provide their viewpoints, their philosophy, their advice about processes, where they've been successful, and where they've made mistakes. We've tried to assemble those who have different perspectives on the discipline of architecture: some from large companies, some from small companies, some heavily invested in formal architectural models and frameworks (in a few cases, those who've authored them), and those that espouse less formal processes. The one thing these professionals all have in common is they've all been successful as security architects. Through interviews with these individuals, we've attempted to capture their viewpoints, the nuances of their techniques, and what they feel is most important. As we do this, you may notice that some of the perspectives differ from each other – in some cases, their advice differs from our approach. This is to be expected. We hope that by presenting all these viewpoints to you, they will help you better synthesize and integrate the concepts, provide you with alternative approaches if the way we've done things isn't the way that's most comfortable for you, and provide a window into the many different strategies that you can use to achieve your security architecture goals.

> **Important note**
> As this is the second edition of this book, note that the titles provided for those we've interviewed reflect their titles at the point in time when we conducted the interview (or interviews) with them.

These short, pointed anecdotes from security architects in the field are intended to provide real-life data and feedback: what worked, what didn't, what the downstream impacts were as a result of a particular course of action, and so on. It won't always be the case that your results will exactly mirror what happened in someone else's experience (since contexts such as industry, organizational factors, regulatory environment, and numerous other elements can play a role), but seeing the cause and effect along with some description of the circumstances can still provide value.

So, to get the most value out of this book, we suggest that you follow along with us. You will still derive value from just reading the words and learning the concepts. However, we believe you will derive even more value if you seek to apply them – as they are presented to you and while they are still fresh in your mind – to your job. If you've never done architecture before, try to develop and implement a plan, working side by side with us as you do so. If you're an existing practitioner, try these techniques as a supplement to your own.

Keeping in mind this philosophy, it's natural to be anxious to move directly into the practical steps of building a security architecture. Before we can get into the *nitty-gritty*, though, there are a few things we need to level set. This first chapter is intended to cover these prerequisites. We believe that understanding the *why* of cybersecurity architecture (that is, why do it in the first place?) is perhaps the most valuable thing you can learn in this book or any other.

This first chapter is almost entirely focused on two things. The first is making sure you understand why cybersecurity architecture exists in the first place (that is, the value it provides, and how and why it helps organizations reach their security goals). The second is teeing up some of the background information necessary for us to leap right into *Chapter 2, Architecture – The Core of Solution Building*. This chapter covers the following topics:

- Understanding the need for cybersecurity
- What is cybersecurity architecture?
- Architecture, security standards, and frameworks
- Architecture roles and processes

Understanding the need for cybersecurity

"I think it's useful to recognize that different stakeholders have different viewpoints. As an example, imagine you are standing on a hill: in front of you there is a valley and mountains to the east and west. Multiple people in that same setting will have a different viewpoint depending on where they are standing and the direction they look. This is similar to enterprise architecture: different disciplines, users, and stakeholders have a different view depending on their focus. The security architect needs to be able to see all these views at the same time. This is because security is a cross-cutting architectural concept that can't be singled out and put into its own, separate box. Instead, it needs to cut across the whole organization and take these different viewpoints into account."

– John Sherwood, Chief Architect, thought leader, and co-Founder of The SABSA Institute

There are numerous unknowns involved in putting the right plan in place for security in a given organization. Creating the right plan involves answering tough questions such as the following:

- What will attackers do next?
- How will their techniques evolve in ways we haven't planned for?
- How will new technologies impact our organization's security model?
- How will new business opportunities impact our security?
- How can we know that we're secure – that we've secured the organization appropriately?
- How do we use our limited resources in the best way possible?

There's no magic bullet, panacea, or sure-fire way to answer all these questions. But some strategies help do so.

Cybersecurity architecture, the discipline of strategically planning out the security measures of the organization, is one of those strategies. As cybersecurity architects, we will work to create a blueprint for security measures in our organizations. We'll plan out what the security profile should look like – and subsequently, work with stakeholders in the organization to make the plan a reality.

Security architecture provides us with a systematic way to guide our organizations to the most effective security measures – to identify where they will provide the most benefit, who they'll provide the most value to, when they should be implemented, and why the organization should select one over another. It can help us know whether the measures we put in place perform effectively and do what we need them to do. It can help us know that the resources we have are being used optimally and efficiently.

All this doesn't happen magically. Cybersecurity architecture takes work. It involves creating the long-term *vision* for security, *selling* that vision to stakeholders throughout the organization, charting a realistic roadmap to move from the current state to the proposed future state, working with subject matter experts and others in the organization to execute the roadmap, reacting to unexpected developments and unforeseen challenges, and ultimately working over the long term to implement improvements.

The reality is that architecture is a craft. And like any craft, it involves a combination of artistry, creativity, planning, and knowledge. Also, like any craft, becoming a master takes time, persistence, and discipline – though it's accessible to anyone willing to put in the time and persistence to learn.

We've written this book for two reasons:

- First, we hope to provide someone new to a security architecture role with a roadmap that they can follow to be successful in their job. To do that, we've tried to outline the methods and techniques that have worked for us and distill down guidance from successful architects in the field about what's worked for them. For someone completely new, this allows them to get started quickly and get a jump on the learning curve.

- Second, for more experienced professionals, we've tried to provide insights and tips that will help them improve. There are as many ways to be a cybersecurity architect as they are architects themselves and there's no right or wrong way to do it (the right way is the way that works for them). By pulling together experiences from an array of practitioners, we hope that some of their techniques can help spark creative new approaches in your practice that lead you to a higher level of proficiency.

Understanding the need for cybersecurity is only the first step in this book. To develop the best, most robust cybersecurity, you need to plan the architecture of your systems. In the next section, we'll gain a fundamental understanding of cybersecurity architecture.

What is cybersecurity architecture?

> *"Cybersecurity architecture is a fusion of architecture and cybersecurity. 'Cybersecurity' is a combination of 'cyber' (from the Greek word κυβερνήτης, meaning 'helmsman') and security ('the freedom from risk or danger'). Putting these all together, it's a model to produce an intended outcome related to freedom from technology-related danger."*
>
> *– Dan Blum, Cybersecurity Strategist, Security Architect, and author of the book Rational Cybersecurity for Business*

The easiest way to understand cybersecurity architecture is through a comparison with the role of an architect in the physical world, such as one who is working on a large structure such as a bridge, tunnel, skyscraper, museum, or new house.

In the physical world, it's easy to understand what an architect does. We all know that you can't just forego planning and *wing it* when it comes to building a safe, durable, and functional structure. Would you, for example, feel comfortable riding the elevator to the 50th floor of a building where they decided to forego planning and *just build it and see if it works? I wouldn't.*

But there's more to it than just safety. There's also ensuring the fitness of purpose – that is, ensuring that the structure meets the various requirements that drive the reason why the structure is being built in the first place. This could include the following for an example skyscraper building project:

- **Financial and budget requirements**: Can we build a structure that meets the intended requirements given the resources available?

- **Aesthetic requirements**: Will the finished edifice meet aesthetic expectations?

- **Functional requirements**: Is the building fit for purpose? For example, can the occupants of the skyscraper get where they need to go with minimal hassle?

- **Timing requirements**: Can we build the structure within the time allotted?

Again, this comes down to planning. In the preceding skyscraper example, can you imagine if someone built it but didn't include elevators? An oversight like that would outrage occupants: no residential tenant would want to walk 50 flights of stairs and no business would hold on to customers who were required to do so. Such a structure would be illegal in many parts of the world for exactly this reason. In this case, the *fitness of purpose* for the building isn't realized – and to remediate it after the fact would lead to tremendous expense, wasted time, and needless impact on the building's occupants.

No – in the physical world, the value the architect brings to the table is obvious: they're the keeper of the *vision* for the structure being built. It is their job to come up with a design based on the requirements of what the structure will do and what it's for, to ensure the fitness of that design for the intended purpose, to make sure the result is realistic in light of the resources available, to work with the many specialists required to implement the vision (for example, to ensure the design is feasible and practical), to ultimately shepherd the project through execution as the final result is brought to life, and to do all the previous things safely.

This, as you might imagine, is easier said than done. It's not a job that exists in isolation. Depending on the type of project, there can be numerous people – or even teams of people – involved: from specialized professionals such as geologists or hydrologists to tradespeople such as electricians and plumbers, to waste engineers and soil specialists, and it even requires in-depth discussions with and input from those for whom the structure is being developed (the ultimate users or inhabitants of the structure).

In the enterprise computing world, the role of the architect is directly analogous to the one we discussed previously. The parallel is so apt that there are often multiple different kinds of architects that can play a role in any technology system. There are system architects, network architects, software architects, cloud architects, data architects, and numerous others. What they all have in common is that, just like in the physical world, they are all the *keepers of the vision* for their particular area of specialization.

Just like the physical architect ensuring that their structure fits the purpose for which it is being built, the technology architect ensures the fitness for purpose of the technological systems in their area. They construct a design based on the needs of the organization and the goals that the organization is trying to achieve, they work with others to vet it and ensure it is feasible, and they craft a plan (in conjunction with other stakeholders and technical specialists) to make the vision a reality.

The cybersecurity architect then is the specific type of technology architect responsible for cybersecurity within an organization. Just like a network or software architect, the cybersecurity architect does the following:

- Identifies the goals and requirements for security
- Develops a *vision* for how to achieve those goals
- Works with other technical specialists to make sure that their vision is practical and feasible
- Works with those specialists to put a roadmap together
- Works in lockstep with other technologists to make the vision a reality

Network versus application security architecture

"There is a difference between network and application security.
They work together, but they are very different: using different techniques and tools.
One is not a substitute for the other."

– John Sherwood, Chief Architect, thought leader, and co-Founder of The SABSA Institute

Just like there are different sub-types of technology architects generally (for example, data architect versus software architect versus network architect), there can also be different types of cybersecurity architects. This can be confusing because sometimes, it is not clear from a person's title what a practitioner's scope, focus, and purview are.

A cybersecurity architect within one company might be focused almost entirely on network infrastructure, while another with the same title and similar job description at another firm might focus almost exclusively on application design. Different types of cybersecurity architects have different scopes and different tools/methods that they use to help them achieve their goals.

In this book, we've chosen to focus on two different *personas* of cybersecurity architect: the application security architect and the network security architect. There are, of course, other specializations beyond this (data security architects, cloud security architects, and so on), and, usually in smaller or mid-market organizations, you can find those with a focus and goals that span both roles. However, we've chosen these two specializations for a few reasons:

- **They are the most common**. While there are potentially as many security architect specializations as there are technologies themselves, most cybersecurity security architect's scope will fall into one of these two groups or (like a cloud security architect) potentially span both.

- **They represent most tools/techniques that you will encounter**. Other specialized sub-disciplines within cybersecurity architecture will likely adapt tools and methods from one of these specializations. For example, a security architect whose focus is on hypervisor deployment in a data center might predominantly leverage tools and techniques from the network security architecture world. Those working on securing a container-driven service mesh architecture might primarily use tools from the application security world.

Ultimately, context will dictate which of the tools and techniques we cover will be most useful to you and germane to your role. However, the versatile architect will have a working familiarity with approaches that address both the application and network side of the technology landscape.

The difference between architecture and secure architecture

"Everything has an architecture – whether you plan it or not. The more actively
you engage with building and shaping that architecture, the more predictable your
system is going to be. By 'system' here I mean it in the broadest possible sense: your
system of getting things done."

– Andrew S. Townley, Chief Executive Officer at Archistry Incorporated

Earlier, we learned what a cybersecurity architect does at a very high level. We looked at a very quick skeleton of what tasks are in the security architect's role. Naturally, at this point, you may be anxious to move directly into the *nitty-gritty* of the day-to-day life of a cybersecurity architect. This temptation to start digging into the weeds is natural, but it's better to begin with understanding the *why* instead of the *how*. This means understanding why organizations have a specific earmarked position of Cybersecurity Architect in the first place.

The fact of the matter is that any organization (including yours) *will* have a cybersecurity architecture. This is true no matter what you do. Even if you do nothing and completely ignore all principles of sound network design, sound application development, and all requirements and principles, you'll still have a *cybersecurity architecture* – just not a planned, thought-out, and efficient one. Instead, it'll be whatever architecture happens to evolve organically in an *ad hoc* fashion over time.

Having an architect at the helm of security design means having someone who is ultimately accountable for ensuring that the overall design and vision are efficient and effective. This is particularly important as human nature tends to favor entropy in design (that is, less mature, considered, and planned out).

> **Important note**
>
> This is generally true, regardless of context; for example, whether you're talking about writing new software, deploying new **commercial-off-the-shelf** (**COTS**) applications, building networks, or adopting new technology (for example, the cloud).

Why does human nature tend to remove focus from planning phases? The reasons why this happens aren't tremendously hard to understand. For the moment, let's imagine a technology project as having three fundamental phases. This is a vast oversimplification for most projects, but bear with us:

1. **Planning**: The process of assessing requirements, marshaling resources to do the work, assigning work to resources, setting key milestones, setting a budget, and so on.

2. **Implementation**: The process of making required investments, setting resources to tasks, writing code, implementing hardware, and taking any other actions you may need to execute.

3. **Maintenance**: The continual process of maintaining the solution you've put in place to make sure that it continues to meet the goals over time.

Represented visually, this would look something like *Figure 1.1*:

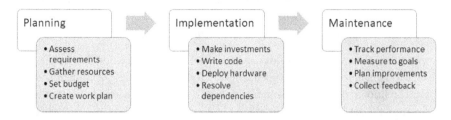

Figure 1.1 – Generic execution process

Now, of these three phases, into which *bucket* does the attention of those doing the work tend to go? Stage 2 (*implementation*), right? Any new project represents an area of need for the organization. After all, if there's no need to do a project, why would they undertake it in the first place? When there's a need, there is pressure to address it. Often, stakeholders will apply pressure to actually *make progress* and sometimes view planning phases as *delays* that gate the organization from getting to a solution, implementing a fix, or addressing the need. The point is that there is often pressure within organizations to minimize the time spent planning.

On the other side, something similar happens with the maintenance and support aspects of the project. Here, there's a similar tendency to de-emphasize maintenance implications and considerations relative to implementation. There can often be a *"we'll cross that bridge when we come to it"* mentality where the focus is on getting the solution to work in the first place (closing the area of need) while leaving the work of sorting out the support and maintenance details until after the immediate pressure to address the need is met.

The point of all this is that most people (and most organizations) naturally feel pressure to move directly to the implementation of a project. This doesn't mean that nobody ever plans – just that there can be pressure to minimize or de-emphasize non-implementation steps relative to implementation-focused ones. Additionally, as time constraints and real-world business needs drive planning cycles to be more modular, it can become harder and harder to see the *big picture*.

The benefits of building secure, resilient architectures

> *"For me, I always look at architecture first from an information asset perspective.*
> *What are the information assets in the scope and how will it be used functionally?*
> *I think of technical architectures as being comprised of the various components and*
> *subcomponents that enable the system functionally. This means that the security*
> *architecture needs to be aligned with the functional architecture to be successful."*
>
> *– John Tannahill, a Canadian management consultant specializing in information security*

All of this highlights why, in a given project, human nature and business pressure work against some of the planning elements of the design. But who cares? Will an implementation that has evolved ad hoc, piecemeal, and organically be substantively worse in every case? No. It does mean though that it can be *more difficult* to optimize over the long term than a more planned, systematic approach.

To illustrate why this is the case, let's consider another analogy: city planning. Most of us know that there are *planned* and *unplanned* cities. Planned cities are those where traffic, zoning, roads, and other aspects are based on human design. Unplanned cities are those that developed organically over time based in large part on the actions of the people living in them. Consider then the experience of driving (and navigating) through a planned city (for example, the Manhattan borough of New York City, Chandigarh, or Dubai) compared to an unplanned one (for example, Boston, London, or Chennai). The planned city might use a *grid* or *ring* approach, while the unplanned city might use road patterns that have evolved over time. For most non-native inhabitants, the planned city is easier to navigate: while they won't know exactly what's on a given road, they will know what direction the road leads in (and likely what other roads it intersects with) based on the planned design.

Likewise, there are benefits from a planned, structured approach to technology projects. Technology projects that are developed and fielded in a systematic way – where detailed attention is paid to the goals of the project, and where future-proofing and subsequent improvements that might be made down the road are accounted for – can have direct performance, operational, or maintenance (supportability) benefits right from the get-go. Likewise, future adjustments to the design or the incorporation of new components/technologies into the mix can be, in many cases, more effectively deployed when existing elements are laid out in a structured, organized way.

What is the point? The technology architect is responsible for coming up with the organizing principles that will be used for the project in scope to achieve this organized, planned result. In the case of a network architect, this means coming up with a design for the network that enables reliable, fast, and secure communications today and that can be most easily extended and upgraded tomorrow. In the case of the application architect, it is the same: they're responsible for coming up with application designs that meet the requirements of users today but that can also easily be updated with new features should the need arise.

In the context of the cybersecurity architect, the same principles apply. The goal in this case though is to create a model and design for security that fulfills today's security needs but that can also be easily extended when new features are needed, when the business context changes, or in any situation where adjustments need to be made to accommodate future activity.

The role of the architect

"When I hear security architecture, two things come to mind. First, there's enterprise architecture: architecture for the whole of enterprise, where you attempt to create one set of documents that cover every possible security scenario. Then, there's the more practical approach where you pick one area to focus on – a narrow set of services or capabilities – and create a well-defined architecture to support

just that. One of the reasons you have these different camps is everyone wants to go straight to the technology. Instead, architecture needs to start with understanding the risk profile: risk should drive the architecture."

– Steve Orrin, Federal CTO at Intel Corporation

The architect then is there to help make sure that technology projects fit into an integrated strategy. An architect comes up with a *vision* for the solution that guides the entire life cycle. Just like an architect working in the physical world on a building or bridge, the technology architect evaluates goals and constraints – things such as the goals and envisioned purpose, support and maintenance requirements, integration with existing technology, the strategic direction of the organization, and budget and resource requirements – to come up with an overarching design that makes the most sense for the organization. Once the architect has a vision in mind, they come up with a blueprint for how to execute that vision.

This is true for any architecture discipline within technology. Application architects, for example, develop and maintain a master vision of one or more applications; they make sure that new software (components, extensions, new features) fit well within the existing ecosystem and are consistent with the direction that the organization is looking to go in with their application portfolio. Likewise, network architects have a vision for connectivity. They create and maintain a master vision of the overall network, ensuring that new devices, new services, and so on fit efficiently and optimally within the larger framework so that service is maximized, and things keep running as smoothly as possible.

Cybersecurity architecture is no different. In a nutshell, security architecture is the process of ensuring the following:

- The approach to security within the organization is well-planned

- Resources are used optimally

- The goals of the organization (both security as well as business and functional goals) are met throughout

- There are measures in place that allow future growth and expansion

A security architect generally develops and maintains a vision of security for the technology elements and components within their scope. The more specialized network security architect is responsible for ensuring the design and execution of the security elements that apply to the network while application security architects do so for the security of applications that may be under development. For each, their role is to ensure that new work in security is performed optimally, that security goals are met, that deployment is efficient, and that the design of new security services advances rather than impedes the overall direction that the organization is trying to go toward.

The scope of the security architect can be narrow or specific. They might be responsible for one or more applications, a network or a set of networks, or the security controls and services within a business unit or the entire organization. A cybersecurity architect in one organization might be responsible for infrastructure controls such as firewalls, anti-malware, and **intrusion detection systems (IDSs)**, whereas the cybersecurity architect at another firm might work hand in hand with developers to ensure that the security needs of a given product or application are met. Formal models and larger organizations might keep architects at a "big picture" level (where implementation and operations are handled by separate folks entirely), while smaller organizations or nimble teams might require architects to be involved in day-to-day operations. Other organizations might have multiple sets of security architects, each focusing on their particular area of specialization. The specific context within which the security architect operates will govern their areas of focus.

Secure network architectures

The role of the cybersecurity architect is, as we've discussed, the chief planner and vision-keeper for security within the organization. As mentioned, though, there are different types of security architects. One of the primary areas where cybersecurity architects will play a role is in the creation, design, execution, and operation of the secure networking and communications infrastructure of the organization.

Historically, most organizations (from the largest to the smallest) of necessity were directly responsible for maintaining their own robust network. The network served as the primary communications medium for employee collaboration (through services such as email, file sharing, collaboration tools, intranet portals, and numerous other avenues of communication) but they also had another role: the substrate upon which internal business applications were deployed. So, in addition to providing internal communication services (a valuable end in and of itself), the internal network also historically played a significant role in enabling business applications that make the organization run.

You might be wondering about the rationale for the repeated use of the word *historically* in laying out the preceding example. This is because, for many organizations, the functional role of the network itself is in a period of transition. Specifically, while the network is still very much the primary conduit for employee communication, much of the use of the network as the *launchpad* for internal services has migrated off the internal network to the cloud. This isn't to say that all internal business applications are now cloud-based; after all, there will always be specialized applications (industrial control networks, biomedical applications, and other specialized hardware/software) that either can't go to the cloud or, for security or functional purposes, it would be foolhardy to relocate there. But for many organizations that don't have these specific requirements, much of what would have been fielded to an on-premises data center, to communicate over internal network channels, has been relocated to cloud environments.

Despite this, the network is critical to the way that business gets done in modern organizations. Not only are there still (despite the cloud migration we alluded to) internal applications that employees need access to, but there are also communication and collaboration tools that they need to use and that require network connectivity for them to reach. There is also an increasing array of mobile and cloud services that require internet access to reach them. Employees, business partners, guests, and others rely on the network for everything from checking their email, sharing documents and files, accessing cloud services and internal applications, conducting telephone calls (for example, via VOIP), and the numerous other activities involved in doing their jobs.

The role of the security architect in a networking context is to ensure three primary goals: **confidentiality, integrity, and availability (CIA)**. Those familiar with security will likely recognize these fundamental concepts, given how critical they are to the discipline of security. However, applying these concepts from a network architecture point of view also means accounting for three other factors across multiple dimensions: *effectiveness*, *resiliency*, and *depth*. **Effectiveness** is very straightforward: are the security measures effective at doing what they need to do in enforcing the CIA goals? The last two require a little bit more explanation. Specifically, by **resiliency**, we mean not that the network itself is resilient (this falls under the existing pillar of availability in the CIA triad) but instead that the mechanisms that enforce those goals are resilient against disruption. Likewise, by **depth**, we mean that the mechanisms need to apply to multiple levels of the network stack.

Throughout this subsection, we'll walk through each of these areas in detail. We'll talk about CIA in general for those who might be unfamiliar with these concepts and then talk about resiliency and depth of coverage. We won't get into the *how-to* (yet) of building a secure design as we just want to outline the specific requirements of what a secure design would entail in the first place.

CIA

The most critical underlying principle to secure network design is to ensure that the network facilitates the security goals of the organization more generally. These will likely be organization-specific to a large degree, but when examined from the highest *altitude* (that is, at their most abstract), they will likely generally align with the tenets of the *CIA triad*, as shown here:

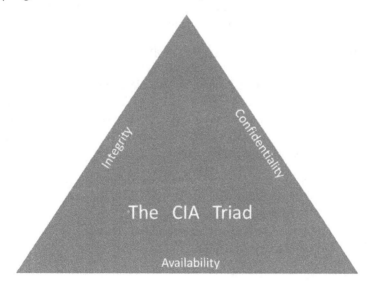

Figure 1.2 – The CIA triad

For those who have some familiarity with the principles of cybersecurity under their belt, they will almost certainly recognize this acronym. For those that do not, it refers to the three core tenets of security:

- **Confidentiality**: The property that information is only disclosed to those that are authorized. This means that data is confidential to all those without a legitimate business need to know.

- **Integrity**: The property that information is reliable: it cannot be changed or modified unless performed by someone who is authorized to make that change.

- **Availability**: The property that resources and information can be accessed when needed.

Each of these elements is important from a network design perspective. Confidentiality is important because the design of the network should mean that conversations between parties who may need to exchange data that needs to be kept confidential should have a way to do so. There are numerous strategies for accomplishing this: using encrypted network protocols (SSH, TLS, IPsec, S-MAIL, and so on), network segmentation (that is, creating sequestered network zones where those not on the same VLAN, segment, and so on can eavesdrop on cleartext traffic), tunneling insecure ports over secure protocols, as well as dozens of other strategies.

Integrity is the capability to ensure data quality is not affected by deliberate tampering or accidental degradation. This can also be facilitated at the network level. Some protocols can help enforce integrity during transmission, applications and hardware can enforce it during storage, and strategies such as blockchain can enforce it against deliberate attack. Once again, even internal segmentation can help drive integrity goals as fewer individuals with access to data, files, or other artifacts result in fewer people who can manipulate them in undesired or unauthorized ways.

Availability refers to the property where services that people need to use are available for use when needed. As a practical matter, natural and man-made disasters can impact availability – for example, when data links are down – as can human agents (for example, denial of service attacks against the network). Just as there are both design strategies and countermeasures that foster confidentiality and integrity, so too can both strategies help with availability. Tools such as DDoS prevention can help mitigate certain types of attacks, whereas high availability, redundancy, and load-balancing strategies can be incorporated into the design to help with natural or man-made disasters.

The point of all this is that it is the job of the network security architect to create designs that account for and preserve each of these properties. More specifically, it is the job of the security architect to understand which of these tenets apply in a given situation based on the business needs and what the relative priority of a given tenet is based on context and requirements, and to craft solutions that address them appropriately given that information.

Designing for resilience

> *"There are businesses that seem to be able to continue to get their job done and function without disruption. This is the primary goal of cybersecurity architecture: to be able to function and continue to perform work functions despite what's going on around you. In general, organizations want to be resilient – to execute their mission with a minimum of disruption; if you can show a track record of value in an organization or point to organizations with a track record of resilience and explain how a robust architecture can get you there, you gain credibility and help pave the way for architecture efforts."*

– Dr. Char Sample, Chief Research Scientist – Cybercore Division at Idaho National Laboratory

One of the primary considerations for the network security architect is designing the network to be *resilient*. We're referring to the ability of resources to remain available and protected despite unexpected events, natural and man-made disasters, attacker activity, and any other unforeseen situation. **Resources** in this context refer to anything and everything employees or the business need to accomplish the organization's mission: everything from the ability to conduct conference or voice calls, to remote working and telepresence, to email and other messaging tools, to internal or external business applications. Even something simple such as access to files or the ability to call a coworker can be a *resource* in this context.

It is an important property of availability that the network is designed such that it continues to operate and provide the right access to the right people, even in adverse situations (such as a pandemic, flood, earthquake, or communications disruption). The way that this is done must, out of necessity, change somewhat depending on what might impact the network and how. For example, ensuring access to services during a natural disaster (something such as a flood or inclement weather) is a very different proposition – using different tools and technical strategies – compared to a situation instigated by human action (such as a human attacker).

However, there is more to the resilience design aspect than just these availability concerns (important though they are). Specifically, it is also important that the mechanisms that enforce CIA are themselves resilient against disruption. For example, should a major catastrophe happen, confidential data is kept confidential, data remains trustworthy, and services remain available. By analogy, think of a bank. Would it make sense to design a vault that would unlock itself and open the door if the fire alarm is pulled? No, right? Even if there is a fire (or threat of fire), we still want to keep the assets protected.

With this in mind, there are a few different individual goals when it comes to the overall design of *both* the network as well as the security mechanisms used *by* the network:

- **High availability**: Ensuring network-based services and tools remain available during natural and/or man-made disasters such as earthquakes, floods, fires, or pandemics

- **Resistance to attack**: The degree to which network countermeasures mitigate or thwart attacks by human or software threat agents

A secure network design will enable both goals. In the case that the architect has direct input into the design of a new network, the security architect will work directly with the engineers and other network architects to make sure that these properties are *baked into* the overall network design; in situations where the network already exists (in many cases, designed and built without these goals in mind or with minimal focus on security), they will work with other stakeholders to build out a portfolio of countermeasures and improvements that help increase resiliency after the fact.

"Depth" of coverage – securing the stack

The last dimension for the network security architect is the need to address security at all layers of the network stack. Security shouldn't just apply to a subset of the network, but instead to all levels.

One of the most powerful conceptual tools in the IT world is the networking stack. Most technology practitioners have some familiarity with either the OSI or TCP/IP stacks. OSI (*Figure 1.3*) divides networking communications into seven layers (application, presentation, session, transport, network, data link, and physical):

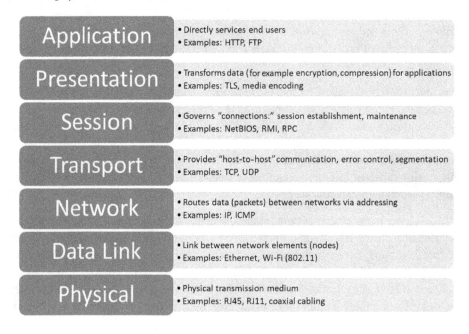

Figure 1.3 – The OSI model

The TCP/IP model (*Figure 1.4*) divides it into four layers (application, transport, internet, and link):

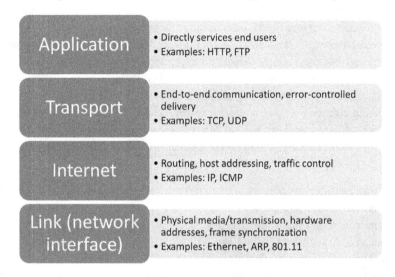

Application	• Directly services end users • Examples: HTTP, FTP
Transport	• End-to-end communication, error-controlled delivery • Examples: TCP, UDP
Internet	• Routing, host addressing, traffic control • Examples: IP, ICMP
Link (network interface)	• Physical media/transmission, hardware addresses, frame synchronization • Examples: Ethernet, ARP, 801.11

Figure 1.4 – The TCP/IP model

As you can see, each layer of the stack is comprised of specific technologies, protocols, software bindings, and other artifacts that accomplish a particular aspect of delivering data between nodes on a network. For example, protocols that encode individual bits as electrical signals on a wire or as individual pulses of light on an optical fiber are defined in layer 1 of both models (the physical and network access layer in the OSI and TCP/IP model respectively). Protocols that group individual bits into more complex structures (frames and packets, for example) occur higher up in the stack, and protocols responsible for delivering those packets to destinations outside the current local network are higher up still.

This network stack concept is powerful because it allows a technology professional to deliberately limit or compartmentalize their scope to only a subset of the network rather than needing to weed through tremendous complexity every time they need to accomplish a particular task. This means that engineers can focus only on one particular layer of the stack at a time; by doing so, they can *compartmentalize* complexities associated with other levels of the stack that aren't relevant to the question they are trying to answer. For example, consider a network administrator looking to understand why traffic is not being read by a given application. They might start by looking to ensure that the network is routing traffic correctly to the destination – looking at the IP protocol at layer 3 of the OSI stack. From there, they can either diagnose and debug the problem or, if they are unable to solve the problem by looking at layer 3 in isolation, expand their analysis to include other layers and consider them each in isolation until they do.

The fact that the network stack is organized in this way adds both complexity as well as opportunity for the network cybersecurity architect. It adds complexity because the architect is responsible for all the levels of the stack and therefore needs to account for all of them in their vision. This means that they need to factor all levels of the stack and how they are implemented in the organization into their planning; it also means that they need to select and apply appropriate security countermeasures in that plan. This adds complexity because, as anyone who's looked at traffic on the network can tell you, there's a lot of surface area when considering all layers of the stack. The fact that the architect's role is so all-encompassing also means that countermeasures they put in can either span multiple levels of the stack or target a different area of the stack other than where the problem occurs. For example, a network security architect seeking to address an application issue (layer 7 of the OSI stack) might target another level of the stack to resolve the problem.

As an example of this, consider an application that might not have a facility for strong authentication of users: maybe it requires a username and password but doesn't use a secure channel such as TLS for transmitting that username and password. The ideal strategy is to address this – a layer 7 problem – at layer 7 itself. But what if that's not feasible? Say, for example, that the application is supplied by an external vendor and they are unwilling or unable to close that particular issue. So, the architect, knowing that there might not be an optimal *layer 7 solution* to the issue at hand, might decide to implement a solution at a lower level of the stack. For example, they might consider tunneling the traffic, using filtering rules to ensure that only users from inside a trusted zone can access the service, and so on.

The job of the network cybersecurity architect is to ensure that the solutions that they create, the network design that they work with other stakeholders to build and hone, and the countermeasures that they deploy protect the network fully and comprehensively – that is, at each level of the stack.

Secure application architectures

> *"There is another value in architecture in that it adds speed to a release process.*
> *Just like writing testing software in code slows down the first few releases but speeds*
> *up all the rest of them, so too does architecture make the first design iteration*
> *maybe take a little longer – but all future design work that leverages it will go more*
> *smoothly and more quickly."*
>
> *– Adam Shostack, President, Shostack & Associates*

From the standpoint of end goals, the remit of the application security architect is like that of the network security architect: ensure the security of the entities in their scope. In this case, though, instead of focusing on the infrastructure that helps enable application delivery, they focus on the applications themselves: ensuring that they are built with security in mind, that the process of building them satisfies security goals, that they have appropriate and strong security features built into them to achieve those goals, and so on.

For the application security architect, the specific responsibilities, actions, and – most importantly – goals depend to a large degree on the phase of the development effort that the organization is undertaking. For example, there are different goals and approaches for projects in the following areas:

- **Requirements**: Outlining and documenting what the scope and purpose of the application are.

- **Development**: While the software is under active development – namely, the period from ideation to release, either for new software or updates to existing software. Note that this includes any interim, pre-release phases such as unit testing, integration, functional and performance testing, building, and any other phases of the life cycle that may apply to a given organization.

- **Release**: The process of deploying the software to production. This includes the release process itself, followed by immediate pre and post-release actions such as shakeout and production deployment.

- **Support**: Post-release updates, support, and maintenance.

This section outlines some of the main concerns and goals of an architect during each of these phases. In addition, just like cloud adoption and externalization have *muddied the waters* in the networking space, so too have evolutions in the software development process added complexity to the application space. As organizations and software development methodologies have evolved, the pace of code release has increased.

> **Important note**
>
> The pace of release has accelerated to the point that now, in many organizations, software release is continuous or nearly so. We've seen new continuous development models emerge along with DevOps (and DevSecOps) alongside breakneck release timelines; Amazon, for example, has reported that they deploy new production code every second (https://www.allthingsdistributed.com/2014/11/apollo-amazon-deployment-engine.html) while Google reports that they conduct over 4 million builds on the average day (https://thenewstack.io/google-reveals-the-secrets-of-devops/).

While the goals of application-focused security architects are the same in models where the delineation between phases is blurred, it may be a little harder to see clearly; additionally, since some of the tools and techniques associated with the architecture process must, out of necessity, be different in this context, we've elected to include a separate discussion in this section about these models specifically.

Requirements and design

> *"The most important ingredient to the security architecture process is understanding what the business (or technology peers) are trying to do. Understanding what a system is for – the broader context and why it exists in the first place – is absolutely essential to ensuring the right security design."*
>
> *– John Kallil, Chief Information Security Officer*

During the earliest stages of planning, the architect is involved in making sure that security requirements are captured and that key features reflect not only important elements of security (for example, authentication, protection of data, data integrity, availability, and so on) but also that *misuse cases* (for example, how the application might be attacked or features subverted) are considered along with the use cases or *user stories* that are used as input in the application design process.

Development

During the period when software is being actively developed, the life of the cybersecurity architect is very busy. At this stage, the architect must create a plan for the application and an overall design that addresses a few different considerations:

- **Security functionality**: Strategies to ensure that any functional security requirements are addressed securely. This includes features such as user account management, administrator and user authentication, logging and monitoring features, secrets management (for passwords, API tokens, cryptographic keys, and so on), availability considerations, and others.

- **Threat mitigation**: Strategies to ensure that the application is resilient against attack or accidental misuse. This includes input tampering or over-run, insecure business logic, race conditions, or any other flaw in the software that could allow or facilitate unauthorized activity.

As you might imagine, each of these areas of focus has its own tools and techniques to achieve the optimal effect; we will discuss some of these tools and techniques in more detail in subsequent chapters as we explore the ins and outs of how to create a cybersecurity architecture for an application. For now, though, the important point is that the design phase of an application provides the architect with an optimal time to make large, sweeping changes to the security profile of an application.

Software engineer and professor Barry Boehm famously pointed out in *Software Engineering Economics, Prentice Hall PTR*, that the cost of fixing a software flaw increases non-linearly over time; in other words, the farther along in the development life cycle a flaw is discovered, the more expensive it becomes to fix. Graphs such as the following one, representing the cost of a software defect over time, are still often informally referred to as **Boehm's Curve** in honor of this insight (*Figure 1.5*):

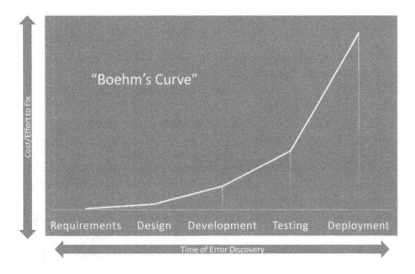

Figure 1.5 – Boehm's Curve (or Boehm's Law)

Just like fixing a defect, changes made to the security model of an application are much more easily and cost-effectively addressed earlier in the life cycle than they are later. Consider a *security defect*, for example: a security vulnerability that could undermine a key portion of the application or that could allow an attacker a method to subvert the application. Should a developer find a bug like this immediately after authoring the code that contains it, fixing it is relatively simple: they just modify the offending code, test it, and call it a day.

But what happens if they do *not* find that bug until much later in the process? Say, for example, they discover it after they have shipped a million units of that software across the globe. At that point, the complexity – and cost – of applying the fix is comparatively astronomical: the developer still has to update the source code and unit test it the way they always would. However, there are other things they also now need to do: integration test the change against the rest of the product, slot it into a release, rebuild the software, release a patch, notify users of the issue and encourage them to patch, and then support the patch (knowing that it will invariably fail for a subset of users). This of course assumes that they can notify users in the first place. As we all know quite well, many times they will not, leaving potentially hundreds or thousands of users vulnerable to the issue.

Therefore, not only must the architect design a *vision* for the overall security of the application during the design and development phases, but they must work extra hard to ensure that they have thought through how the application will be used, how it might be attacked, and any budgetary or resourcing constraints that would be imposed by their design, and they must also socialize and gain acceptance for their design (and the changes that design requires) from the engineers authoring and developing the software. Just like other features, not every security goal, feature, and countermeasure will ultimately make it into the initial release of the application.

Release

During the release process, security is also an important consideration and goal for the architect. At this point, because of their efforts during the development phase, the architect will ideally have a solid design for the application that is implemented (to a greater or lesser degree) within the application as the organization fields it to production. As you might expect, there will likely be some aspects of the security model, vision, and design that will require orchestration during the release process to work and perform optimally.

As an example, consider the situation where the architecture calls for the use of cryptography as part of the application security model and overall design. During the development process, the security architect would work with the development team to create the logic behind this, but reasonable security hygiene would preclude using the same secrets (keys) during development as what will ultimately be fielded into production. Therefore, the process of actually creating those production keys – and storing them in a location where they are themselves appropriately protected – needs to happen during the release process itself.

There are often quite a few tasks like this that will be required when an application enters production. These can include secrets, as in the preceding example, but they can also include deploying new hardware or software security products, reconfiguring existing hardware or software, user training and education, executing scripts, or any other release-related task that the application might require.

The upshot? While during the development phase, the architect will be heavily involved in the planning and design decisions, they may take a more active role as a problem-solver, troubleshooter, and even active participant in development.

Support

Once the application is released, the focus of the architect shifts once again. This is where the work gets the most interesting for the architect as there are multiple areas of focus that they must maintain simultaneously. These are as follows:

- Execute the long-term vision
- Respond to unanticipated behaviors of the application in the field
- Participate in the design of future iterations of the application

As we mentioned during the preceding discussion, it is highly likely that some of the security features, along with countermeasures required to keep the application secure, may not make it into the first release. This can be because those features would require slowing down the release to implement fully and in time for a scheduled deployment. For example, they might be dependent on application functionality which is scheduled for a subsequent future release. It is almost certain that there will be something that will need to be addressed in future iterations. Working with other stakeholders, the security architect will need to continue to work to get these deployed over the long term.

In addition, just like there are *hiccups* in new applications, so too can there be unexpected events that arise in security features and security controls. As part of the support process, the architect will need to be involved in ironing those out. These can be bugs in security features that are intrinsic to the application, they can be emergent behavior that can only be seen once the application usage reaches a certain scale, or they can be bugs or unexpected behavior in security products, tools, or countermeasures that were deployed to support the application.

Lastly, don't forget that it's rare for an application to have one release and never get updated subsequently. It's almost certain that as an application enters the support phase for a given release, the next release will almost certainly be entering (or will have already entered) the design and development stages for new features. So, just like the architect needed to plan security features and protections around the initial release, so too will subsequent releases bring with them modifications and necessary changes that the architect will need to be involved in.

Building security in

Now, you may have noticed that in looking through the lens of these phases, the specific goals and tasks of the architect are clear at each phase when they're laid out in this way. Likewise, you can probably realize how and why the architect changes their approach and focus somewhat on the portion of the cycle that they are in. But the truth is that it is more complex than it seems based on just looking at these discrete, monolithic phases. This is because most new software being built in enterprises today no longer uses such clearly defined phases. Instead, the lines between phases have blurred – or in some cases, they've disappeared entirely.

In other words, under legacy models such as waterfall, development phases were closer to clearly defined, boundary-aligned steps with clear gates between stages, ultimately leading to a developed project. It was never perfect even under waterfall as some phases (for example, testing) were always iterative and not a one-shot, monolithic process. However, newer models have less clear differentiation than even that. For example, DevOps blurs the lines between "development, release, and support" and approaches such as **continuous integration/continuous development** (**CI/CD**) mean that each portion of the cycle may be so compressed as to be almost meaningless.

What's important to note about this is that the goals of the architect – and the scope of what they are called upon to do – don't change substantively even when the development models don't have clearly defined phases. We've described them above through the lens of having discrete phases to illustrate the focus and key aspects of the architectural role in each area, but ultimately, the architect is still focused on developing a clear vision (of the application's security profile, security features, use and misuse cases, and how it might be attacked) for the application, regardless of the underlying model used to author and deploy it.

One additional substantive part of the architect's job that models such as DevOps and CI/CD can help illustrate is the role of architecture in the development methodology and release process itself. Architects often have a stake in how software gets developed in the first place. This means that they can have a role in ensuring a process that fosters reliable, consistent, and secure outcomes. Under a waterfall model, this might mean that they incorporate security design reviews, manual or automated software security testing, code review, or other checkpoints or gates into the release process. Under agile, it might mean that sprint reviews include time to specifically discuss and evaluate security topics and features. Under DevOps, it might mean an automated security testing capability integrated into the pipeline. In all cases, it also likely means a culture built around security: by training developers on security coding techniques, by supplying components (for example, cryptographic modules, authentication components, services, or other software) to encapsulate and provide security functionality, or numerous other techniques.

The distinction between *what is built and how it's built* is subtle, but the outcomes of each are interrelated. Aldous Huxley, in *Ends and Means: An Inquiry into the Nature of Ideals, Routledge*, once famously said the following:

"The end cannot justify the means, for the simple and obvious reason that the means employed determine the nature of the ends produced."

By this, he meant that the way that you derive something ultimately dictates what the result will be. In the context of software development, this means that if you follow a slapdash, disorganized process, then you will tend to wind up with a slapdash, disorganized result – a result that is more likely to have vulnerabilities, security flaws, weaknesses, and other undesirable security properties.

If instead, you follow a process that engenders security – where security is accounted for and actively espoused during the development process – the resulting software will tend to be more resilient than would otherwise be the case. Therefore, ensuring that the result is secure requires an effort to *build security into* the software development life cycle. The tools, techniques, and processes to do this will vary from organization to organization, depending on their culture and context; this means that, for organizations where this is a goal, it is often the remit of the security architect to create a vision for those mechanisms to the same degree that they are responsible for ensuring the security of the software itself.

Case study – the value of architecture

> *"To me, security architecture is a function of building a strong understanding of the resources you have in play and the way that they communicate with each other. This is so that you can properly identify, analyze, and mitigate risk. Remember the 'operators' in The Matrix? They looked at the console and the matrix code and were able to interpret what was actually going on from that. This is what architects do: they read the signals and translate signals from the technology side of the organization to what is really going on – from there, they figure out what will best support the mission and keep everything running smoothly and safely."*
>
> *– Pete Lindstrom, Security Architect and Analyst, Spire Security*

When asked in an interview about the value of security architecture and what it brings to the table, security architect and analyst Pete Lindstrom offered the following perspective. He explained that one of the main sources of value in having a defined and systematically created architecture is that it can highlight unforeseen (or difficult to foresee) risk areas. He went on to describe three related instances to highlight this relationship between risk and systematic planning. Each of the scenarios he described is different, but the *through line* is the impact associated with a lack of planning and the risks that can arise as a result.

First, he outlined an experience early in his career:

"I always used to downplay physical access until one day my desktop computer at work was stolen. In fact, not just my desktop but over a dozen desktops throughout the building. In this case, there wasn't any requirement to physically secure equipment (for example by bolting it to furniture or to the floor). In this particular location, we'd had a few 'smash and grab' thefts in the past – but in general, we were much more concerned about the data center instead of the equipment left on people's desks."

The second example was in a large, publicly traded, highly decentralized, pharmaceutical firm. One day, a new temp (short-term, temporary employee) started working there. Everything seemed normal at first: they were told to expect a temp, and sure enough, a *temp* showed up. There was, however, more to it than what initially met the eye:

"There was a mixup along the way. The actual temp never arrived – but a patient from the mental health facility down the street did. This person left the facility, came into the office, and started working. He also started living there: sleeping in the conference room, eating food left in the kitchen, etc. Due to some unanticipated process challenges, he was accepted right in with no one being the wiser."

The last situation he told us about was a situation where the pipes burst over a data center:

"Another organization I worked with built a new data center but didn't account for the fact that higher floors had water pipes running the length of the building. One day, the pipes burst, bringing about catastrophic damage to the equipment located on the lower floor in the data center. This led to a 'rapid fire' remediation – however, much of the improvements were of the 'lessons learned for next time' variety because of the fact that moving the data center or changing the location would have been so cost-prohibitive."

There are two things to note about these examples. The first is that you'll notice that you don't need to be super technical to understand the challenges here. There's no fancy technology involved to appreciate the risks (this is one of the reasons that we've chosen to highlight these examples now before we start talking about the technology side of the game).

The second thing to note is how these situations all arose – specifically, through missteps in the *security vision*. In the first instance, something as simple as failing to account for physical security challenges led to the loss of some very critical and sensitive information. In the second example, failure to account for possible breakdowns in the authorization and temp employee onboarding process led to a (very) unexpected threat scenario. And, in the last case, unintended consequences led to water damage to critical equipment.

Would a robust architectural approach have prevented all these problems? Since nobody can foresee every eventuality ahead of time, maybe yes and maybe no. However, the chances of preventing a situation like this ahead of time are improved through systematic planning and security architecture.

Architecture, security standards, and frameworks

Knowing what the purpose of the architect is and where/how they might be involved, it's important to spend some time talking about the process that they employ to get there. At the beginning of this discussion, it's important to recognize that much of that process will be unique and adapted to the organization employing it. We've seen that the goals of the security architect, what they're responsible for, and the role that they play within a given organization can vary depending on a few different factors: the organization itself, the scope and focus of the architect's role, and so on. These same factors will play a role in the process that the architect will follow to realize the results the organization needs.

Secondly, we've purposefully refrained from discussing much about the mechanics of *how* the architect approaches these tasks. We'll get there – but for now, we want to make sure that the aspiring architect understands the purpose of the discipline first, before getting into the details of doing it (it's similar to fully understanding the requirements of an IT project – why do it in the first place? – before beginning the implementation work).

One element that does border on execution, but that is useful to tee up early anyway, is the use of architectural standards and frameworks that guide the work that the cybersecurity architect does. Interestingly, there aren't many that directly address security architecture specifically – at least compared to the large volume of documentation that addresses IT system and infrastructure architectural planning more generally. Note that this is not to imply that there aren't any that do so; there are some very solid and helpful frameworks that can provide quite a bit of value to the security architect that we will introduce in this section and discuss how to use in this and subsequent chapters. However, since the cybersecurity architect is likely to encounter concepts, documents, reference architectures, and other artifacts from a variety of sources, it's useful to establish a baseline familiarity with architecture frameworks and models more generally before delving into security guidance specifically.

Architecture frameworks

With that in mind, let's start with architecture frameworks generally. These are formalized approaches to the planning of technology, systems, networks, and related components. It is not hyperbole to say that there are thousands – perhaps even hundreds of thousands – of pages of documentation related to enterprise architecture planning contained in the literally hundreds of enterprise architecture frameworks, supporting reference architectures, standards, and guidance that exist for the enterprise system architect. To name just a few, these include the following:

- **Atelier de Gestion de l'Architecture des Systèmes d'Information et de Commun vication (AGATE)** in *Le manuel de référence AGATE V3*

- **Department of Defense Architecture Framework (DoDAF)**, which in turn superseded **Technical Architecture Framework for Information Management (TAFIM)** in *The DoD Architecture Framework (DoDAF)*

- **Federal Enterprise Architecture Framework (FEAF)** in *FEA Consolidated Reference Model Document Version 2.3*

- **Generalised Enterprise Reference Architecture and Methodology (GERAM)**

- *ISO/IEC 10746: Information technology — Open distributed processing — Reference model: Architecture*

- *ISO/IEC/IEEE 42010: Systems and software engineering — Architecture description*

- **British Ministry of Defense Architecture Framework (MODAF)**; see `https://www.gov.uk/guidance/mod-architecture-framework`

- **NATO Architecture Framework Version 4 (NAFv4)**

- *NIST SP 500-292: NIST Cloud Computing Reference Architecture*

- **The Open Group Architecture Framework (TOGAF)**

- **Purdue Enterprise Reference Architecture (PERA)**

- **The Zachman Framework**

Note again that these represent only a small subset of what's out there. For example, we've deliberately refrained from listing legacy models and frameworks that are no longer in current or active use, models that have an architecture component but that are not specifically architecturally focused, smaller or more limited-scope models, and commercial models behind a paywall.

This is a lot of documentation – more than any one person could be expected to read and digest in any reasonable amount of time. Therefore, the architect incorporating these approaches into their processes needs to be selective: they need to factor in things such as context, applicability, organizational needs, culture, and so forth in determining which of the many that exist might be appropriate for them.

One question that can also provide some insight into the architectural process is the reason why there is so much guidance on the topic in the first place. The reason for it is largely historical, but thinking it through illustrates the value that architecture provides. Specifically, the breadth of coverage isn't hard to understand while considering the role that they've played in the evolution of enterprise computing.

Consider for a moment the early days of information processing – before distributed computing and ubiquitous networking. In that world, organizations were either not using computing at all, or if they were, they had a relatively simple computing footprint. For example, they might have one or two large mainframe systems connected to terminals that didn't have much, if any, computing capability of their own. Under this model, an engineer, analyst, or system administrator can very easily hold the entirety of the computing footprint in their mind or, for a particularly large deployment, with the aid of a few pieces of paper.

As we all know, this is not the situation we're in today. Today, any medium or large enterprise might have thousands or tens of thousands of endpoints, each more powerful than the room-occupying mainframes of the early days. There are server systems in on-premises data centers, at co-location providers, and in the cloud. There are hypervisors running virtual – and sometimes ephemeral – operating system images in addition to application containers such as Docker that further subdivide the landscape. There are mobile devices – some belonging to the organization and some belonging to employees personally – that are used to conduct business and a host of applications hosted all over the world used on a routine basis. It's a world of unimaginable complexity. Anyone saying that they can keep track of even a small enterprise's computing footprint in their head is either lying or fooling themselves.

This isn't a situation that developed overnight. Plenty of smart folks noticed early on that, with the advent and proliferation of distributed computing, complexity was increasing. As scale increased over time, the sheer number of computing devices increased. With this increase in computing footprint, interconnections between devices increased non-linearly. This is both hard to manage and also causes emergent behavior to occur – that is, behavior that occurs at scale in a way that is difficult to foresee based on the behavior of individual systems in isolation.

These architectural frameworks then represent efforts attempting to bring order to the chaos. They emerged as a strategy to help ensure the following:

- Business goals are supported optimally by the technology in use

- Technology is purchased, leased, and/or maintained in support of business goals

- Resources (personnel, budget, time, and so on) are used optimally and efficiently

However, the challenge with so many different architectural frameworks is that you may find enterprises favoring one or another (or in some cases, multiple in parallel) depending on the country you're located in, the business context, the industry segment, practitioner familiarity, and other factors.

Security guidance and standards

At the same time as there are multiple architecture frameworks, there are also several different security frameworks, standards, and regulations that, while not often containing architectural elements in and of themselves, are nevertheless important for the architect to understand. These include the following:

- **Security standards**: Formal standards that govern elements either of security for an entire program or organization or for specific elements of a larger program (for example, risk management and technical standards). Examples include *ISO/IEC 27001* (Information Security Program Management), KMIP for cryptographic key management, TLS/IPsec for transport layer security, the **Payment Card Industry Data Security Standard** (**PCI DSS**), and numerous others.

- **Security management frameworks**: Documents that, while not official standards, nevertheless provide guidance about how to implement and manage security within an organization. Examples include COBIT, the NIST **Cybersecurity Framework (CSF)**, HITRUST, and the CIS Controls.

- **Regulatory requirements**: Governing legislation that contains elements applicable to information security. Examples include national laws such as HIPAA in the United States, the Cyber Security Law of the People's Republic of China, and local or regional laws such as US state breach notification laws.

Don't worry if you're not immediately familiar with all these. We'll spend more time discussing some of them later in this book. For now, just understand that they are important because they provide a backdrop for the general approach to security taken by the organization. They can also influence how and what technical controls are in the organization's security *toolbox*, how they analyze and address risk, processes for the implementation and execution of security measures, goals such as measurement and metrics, as well as numerous other decision points. They may also, particularly in the case of regulatory requirements, dictate what specific security controls are mandatory and which are discretionary.

Security architecture frameworks

> *"In the early days, cybersecurity architecture was almost a 'dark art:' you had to understand a lot of different things all at once: the technology, the organization, the people employing the technology, regulations/standards, and the threat landscape. As we've gained in maturity, the discipline has been moving toward formalization since these early days; for example, there's been a push in the industry to formalize and merge the required skills as well as to introduce processes. These processes are important because, while we still need a number of different skills to ensure a quality job, standardization brings maturity, which lets us ensure consistent, reproducible outcomes from architectural efforts."*
>
> *– Dr. Char Sample, Chief Research Scientist – Cybercore Division at Idaho National Laboratory*

There are also approaches that attempt to unify concepts from both the enterprise architecture world with security, which are likely to be more directly useful for the security architect. There are multiple models (some more well-known and some less), but the primary ones that we will investigate for our purposes are as follows:

- **Sherwood Applied Business Security Architecture (SABSA)**
- **Open Enterprise Security Architecture (O-ESA)** from the Open Group
- **Open Security Architecture (OSA)**

Given their importance to serious security architects, we will briefly outline each of these approaches.

Sherwood Applied Business Security Architecture (SABSA)

> *"The value proposition of security architecture is simple. If you have a security architecture and you're able to understand how that architecture enables and supports achieving the objectives that you want, it gives you, as the owner of those objectives, confidence that you're really going to get them. If you do it with a methodology like SABSA, where you have traceability and measuring your security capabilities versus the risk exposure, then you can show with confidence that you are likely to obtain the result."*

> *– Andrew S. Townley, Chief Executive Officer at Archistry Incorporated*

The SABSA framework provides a generic framework for security architecture efforts. As with many enterprise architecture frameworks, the philosophy of the approach stems from the belief that security architectures, like enterprise architecture generally, should map efforts back to underlying business goals and *harmonize* (that is, be aware of and synthesize) views and viewpoints from different stakeholders in the organization.

It's founded on the recognition that security in an enterprise – and thereby the security architectures that support the security function of that enterprise – do not exist as an end goal in and of themselves. Instead, they exist solely in service of – and to enable – the business. This means that any security effort should map directly and concretely to some business driver, goal, or end state desired by the business.

Originally discussed at the COMPSEC 96 conference in London (called SALSA at the time), the model has been subsequently expanded in more detail over time (see *SALSA: A method for developing the enterprise security architecture and strategy* in *Computer & Security vol 15, Issue 6, John Sherwood*). For those familiar with the Zachman Framework of enterprise architecture, there can sometimes be confusion about the relationship between SABSA and the Zachman Framework. Similar to SABSA, the Zachman Framework is also a matrix-based ontology with an X axis that uses interrogatives (who, what, when, where, why, and how) and a Y axis that uses architectural layers. Despite these superficial similarities, though, the two models evolved independently. The confusion that arises is unfortunate because it distracts from a thorough and utility-based understanding of the models. So, despite a superficial similarity in the ontology, the approach and philosophy of each extend well beyond just the visualized ontology.

The ontology is constructed as a matrix, with intersection points between a Y axis describing the layers of abstraction (from the most general to the most specific). These layers, from the most general to the most specific under SABSA, are as follows:

- Contextual Security Architecture
- Conceptual Security Architecture
- Logical Security Architecture
- Physical Security Architecture
- Component Security Architecture

Running throughout and in parallel to each layer is the *"Security Service Management Architecture"* view. This layer is different in that it applies to all layers rather than applying to only one.

The *X* axis contains the six basic interrogatives:

- What (assets)
- Why (motivation)
- How (process)
- Who (people)
- Where (location)
- When (time)

Laid out as a grid, each cell of the grid contains a unique point that the architecture process must address to be complete. For example, at the intersection of the *Y* axis "Logical Security Architecture" abstraction layer and the *X* axis interrogative "What," you find considerations unique to that intersection point (in this case, "Information Assets") and supporting artifacts (in this case, "Inventory of Information Assets"). Page 16 of the SABSA whitepaper entitled *SABSA: Enterprise Security Architecture* by John Sherwood, Andy Clark, and David Lynas spells each out in thorough detail. You can find it at `https://sabsa.org/white-paper-requests/`.

Note that this book adheres quite closely to the SABSA model in the philosophy and approach that we take to security architecture. We've provided viewpoints and perspectives from many of the luminary voices from the SABSA community (for example, SABSA co-founders, authors, and "power users") to provide perspective on the topics we'll cover (you've seen a few of these already). The reason that we've done so is that the model is lightweight, easily understandable by all with the addition of a minimal time investment, and for the curious is accompanied by detailed supporting materials to supplement the excellent source material. From a process standpoint, though, while we attempt to maintain compatibility with SABSA, we recognize that all SABSA source materials may not be readily available to everyone (some being available only commercially). As such, we will attempt to refer to SABSA where appropriate, but where we can, we will draw primarily on materials freely available.

Open Enterprise Security Architecture (O-ESA)

One of the areas where many more formal security architecture models struggle is in the capacity to handle change within the organization. Recognizing that change in the technology ecosystem is a complicating factor and needs to be specifically accounted for in enterprise architecture efforts, the now-defunct **Network Application Consortium** (**NAC**) created a model for security architecture that specifically accounts for (in fact, presupposes and in some senses relies upon) the fact that change is both inevitable and a natural part of enterprise security efforts (see *Comparing Security Architectures: Defining and Testing a Model for Evaluating and categorizing security architecture frameworks, Rob Van Os, master's thesis, Luleå University of Technology, Department of Computer Science, Electrical and Space Engineering, Luleå, Sweden*, available at `http://www.diva-portal.org/smash/get/diva2:1031560/FULLTEXT02.pdf`).

This model, the **Enterprise Security Architecture (ESA)** model, was absorbed by The Open Group – an industry consortium consisting of over 700 enterprise stakeholders (`https://www.opengroup.org/about-us`), including IBM, Oracle, Philips, Microsoft, Boeing, and numerous others – who took over as steward when the NAC concluded its charter in 2007.

Today, subsequently renamed as the *Open Enterprise Security Architecture (O-ESA): A Framework and Template for Policy-Driven Security*, it continues to provide value to security architects by embracing automation as the primary method to account for continued security in the face of near-constant technology change.

The model stems from a similar premise as SABSA; namely, that business drivers are the fundamental nexus from which all security efforts stem. O-ESA uses *governance* as the starting point and strategy for defining the principles, policies, guidelines, and standards of the organization as input into the architectural decision-making process.

Formally, governance in this context refers to the process of ensuring that IT efforts are in alignment with stakeholder and organizational goals. *COBIT 5: A Business Framework for the Governance and Management of Enterprise IT, ISACA*, an IT governance framework, defines **Governance of Enterprise IT (GEIT)** as follows:

"A governance view that ensures that information and related technology support and enable the enterprise strategy and the achievement of enterprise objectives. It also includes the functional governance of IT – that is, ensuring that IT capabilities are provided efficiently and effectively."

It should be noted that, throughout this book, we will try to attempt to avoid using the word *governance* where possible. This is for the simple reason that the term is used often informally in a way that is contrary to the formal definition and the way that O-ESA intends. This creates confusion and can detract from, rather than add to, the understanding of those confronting the material for the first time. Therefore, while governance (at least in its formal sense) is important conceptually to the architecture process (as its use within O-ESA highlights), we've tried to use specific language in describing what we mean.

O-ESA describes an approach to creating policy, drawing heavily on *ISO/IEC 27001* and *ISO/IEC 27002* to do so. The model goes on to describe elements of *automated policy enforcement* – specifically, automated measures to ensure that policy is enforced throughout the organization. These elements include the following:

- **Policy Management Authority (PMA)**: The central authority responsible for setting policy
- **Policy repository/registry**: A location where policy artifacts are stored
- **Policy Decision Points (PDPs)**: Locations (for example, software or hardware) where decisions are made about whether requests or actions are allowed or disallowed based on the governing policy
- **Policy Enforcement Points (PEPs)**: Locations (for example, software or hardware) where decisions about policy are enforced

Open Security Architecture (OSA)

The last framework that we will look at is that of **Open Security Architecture** (**OSA**). OSA is a community-driven effort to develop a model for security architecture. By *community-driven*, we mean that it is a set of individual elements contributed by whoever has the willingness and acumen to do so, with subsequent peer review by others in the broader community. One way to think about this is along the lines of an open source software project. In an open source project, interested parties contribute to the development of the final work, such as a server (for example, Apache), tool (for example, Wireshark), operating system (for example, Linux), or any other software that might be of interest to the broader world at large. The model for OSA is similar; in this case, interested parties contribute to a repository of information about security architecture "design patterns" for enterprise security measures.

At the highest level of abstraction, OSA provides the contextual backdrop ("landscape" in their parlance) that allows meaningful contributions to take place. This includes a common set of terminology (to ensure that everyone contributing refers to the same concept the same way), actors (personas or roles of stakeholders in the security lifecycle), a controls catalog (based on those outlined by NIST in their special publication 800-53), and a taxonomy – a map of relationships between elements of a security system.

However, the most directly useful element of the OSA effort, at least from the point of view of the practically-minded security architect, is its library of community-authored design patterns. Those with a background in software development (or those who have worked closely with developers) will likely be familiar with the term "design pattern." It essentially refers to a strategy for accomplishing a certain goal that can be used and reused when faced with a given situation.

Design patterns are essentially strategies for accomplishing a certain goal. In a software development context, they are strategies that can be described in a way that is agnostic of implementation and language. Describing these strategies this way allows developers to easily discuss and share those strategies when they are faced with a given problem that they may have never seen before. For example, a developer of an object-oriented program might wish to create an instance of a software object and interact with it via a defined interface; in so doing, though, they might wish to leave the actual mechanics of implementing the functionality to someone else: either another piece of code they didn't write or in a way where the implementation can be dynamically changed at runtime.

To put more specificity on this example, a developer working in Java might wish to create and use a TLS-enabled socket (that is, a "secure socket") to send data but do so in such a way that the actual implementation of the socket (that is, the version of the TLS protocol supported, the cipher suite, and so on) is decided upon at runtime based on the defined policy of the system. There is a design pattern that accomplishes exactly this: in this example, the *factory design pattern*. In Java, this pattern is implemented (among other places) via the *SSLSocketFactory* class, which follows and implements this pattern: it allows a developer to create and use a TLS-enabled socket without knowing the underlying implementation.

These design patterns are very powerful because they provide a concise, standardized way to describe the solution to a problem that others might encounter and describe those solutions in a concise, highly precise way. The landscape and high-level artifacts of OSA allow the creation of security design patterns that do this in a way comparable to the way that software design patterns perform. For example, an OSA contributor can create a design pattern to address any given situation that includes information about the solution (for example, a diagram or schematic), a list of the relevant controls or security measures that implement the pattern, as well as other information, such as challenges and threats that the pattern is designed to defend against.

For example, OSA provides design patterns for securing everything from public web servers (pattern SP-008) to public Wi-Fi hotspots (pattern SP-007), to cloud computing (SP-011), to even a pattern that describes the entirety of a PCI-DSS cardholder data environment (SP-026). These are only a small sample of the many design patterns that are made available through the OSA.

Architecture roles and processes

> *"If your only tool is a hammer, every problem looks like a nail. Meaning, if you talk to a developer or someone who is a product security manager about security architecture, they are going to focus on the software life cycle or how to build controls at various application trust boundaries. If you talk to IT operations, they are going to tell you about segmenting the network and hardening the perimeter. To me, security architecture is more holistic: it's the overall set of processes, policy, people, technology, and controls that ensure security goals are aligned with business goals."*
>
> *– Ted Ipsen, President and COO at Positroniq, LLC*

In this chapter, we've discussed what security architecture is conceptually, describing and providing an introduction to some of the standards and frameworks that are involved in effecting it in an organization. The last topic that we will cover before we get into the "meat" of actually performing the work of the architect is that of roles intersecting the architect's work, as well as an overview of the architecture processes that we will describe in depth and explain how to perform throughout the rest of this book.

First, we'll walk through adjacent roles that the architect will need to work closely with – and that it's helpful for them to have an intimate understanding of – in the course of doing their work. These areas, while not exactly a prerequisite to being an effective security architect, can provide quite a bit of value because they intersect so closely with the work that the architect must do. This means that the more understanding of these related disciplines the architect can develop, the more effective they are likely to be and the more productive the conversations they have with the professionals in the roles that they may need to work with directly in the course of realizing their vision will be.

After that, we will walk through the process (at a high level) that we will explain throughout the rest of this book. While there is no *right way* to perform the work of a security architect (the *right way* is the way that works for you), we will describe one approach that has worked successfully for us in doing so. Our intent in providing it is to give those new to the discipline a starting point that they can follow to do the work successfully and to share our experiences (and, more importantly, the experiences of others in the profession) with more veteran practitioners who may wish to incorporate new or different techniques into their approach.

Lastly, we'll walk through (at a high level) the key milestones and tasks involved in the high-level process that we'll describe. Note that we won't go into much detail yet – at least in this first introduction – however, it is useful to make sure that those looking to adopt or adapt this approach understand the purpose and relative timing of the stages before they undertake it.

Roles

As mentioned previously, there are a few related disciplines that, while not architecture exactly, are nevertheless important for the architect to know about as the work that they do is so closely tied to that of the architect. In fact, throughout this book, we will draw heavily upon elements of each of these disciplines, so it is helpful to understand what each is and why it exists in the first place. The three that we will discuss in more detail are the following:

- Security engineering
- Risk management
- Security operations

Without a doubt, there are more roles than this in many organizations that intersect the role of the architect. However, we've chosen to cover these three specifically for a few reasons. First, most organizations of mid-market size or larger will have these roles either as a named individual who is assigned to them full-time or as a function that is subsumed into another role. Second, they are synergistic and symbiotic with the security architect. Numerous other roles might set requirements (for example, compliance officer, executive management, individual business teams) or that derive benefit from the designs put in place by the architect (business teams, technology organizations, and so on); however, the roles we're drilling into here have a particularly collaborative role to play with the security architect: a "back and forth" and synergy that is different from other roles the organization might have. Lastly, we've picked these roles because, depending on the scope of a particular effort or the organizational makeup, the architect may need to step in to help directly with these other roles.

With that in mind, let's step through what these roles are, what they entail, and how the security architect may be called upon to work collaboratively with them.

Security engineering

Security engineering, strictly speaking, is the discipline of building systems that are resilient to purposeful misuse or sabotage, accidents, natural disasters, or other unexpected events. Ross Anderson, in *Security Engineering: A Guide to Building Dependable Distributed Systems, Wiley*, describes security engineering as follows:

> *"...building systems to remain dependable in the face of malice, error, or mischance.*
> *As a discipline, it focuses on the tools, processes, and methods needed to design,*
> *implement, and test complete systems, and to adapt existing systems as their*
> *environment evolves."*

You might have noticed that this description and definition are similar to the one that we provided earlier in this chapter about security architecture. In truth, there is a significant overlap in focus, goals, and purview/scope. As a consequence, you can probably intuit from the definition alone how closely the two would need to work together in organizations where they both exist (and hence the reason that we're covering it here).

As a practical matter, there is a difference in the execution of both roles – though, frankly, depending on the organization, there can be wide areas of overlap. Just like a system architect is focused on big-picture design and the vision of the system being developed, the security architect is focused on high-level design and the vision of security within their scope of operation. And just like a systems engineer is focused on the implementation mechanics within that system to make sure all individual components perform appropriately in isolation and together, so too does the system security engineer focus on the components within the system that provide security, their implementation, and their inter-operation.

Given the alignment in interests and goals between the security architect and the security engineer, they will need to work together closely. The security engineer can provide important information to the architect such as the feasibility of implementing a particular type of control in a particular location, strategies and designs to allow security controls to interoperate with each other, implementation guidance, and other important information. Likewise, the architect can provide value to the engineer as well; the architect can help provide input and support to the engineer on control implementation, help champion and whip up support for tools or technologies that the engineer needs, and otherwise work collaboratively with them to the betterment of both.

In situations where there is a defined system security engineering role, security architects should be prepared to work closely with them on a day-to-day basis. Where there is not a defined role – or where the function is spread over multiple other departments – the architect will find that they will need to take on some of this role themselves.

(IT) risk management

> *"I think the most important part of the architecture process is risk, informed by data. Nowadays, it's all about the data. We've moved beyond building strategies to protect a given server or service. In reality, what you really need are strategies to protect the data."*
>
> *– Steve Orrin, Federal CTO at Intel Corporation*

Risk management is a key part of most (if not all) of the numerous security frameworks, regulatory requirements, security architectural frameworks, guidance, and other practical security advice you will come across. It is understood to be of such importance that it is near-universally prescribed as a key principle and tenet of generally accepted security practice. Some organizations, particularly larger organizations, will have either a high-level risk management function that cascades in focus to the technology environment or an IT-focused risk management function. Other times, mostly in large and highly regulated organizations, they'll have both.

The function of the risk management team is to ensure that any given risk is identified, assessed for impact and likelihood, mitigated to the extent practical, and tracked over time. What's a risk in this context? It's defined formally by the *International Organization for Standardization, Risk management – Vocabulary*, as the "*effect of uncertainty on objectives*" (see `https://www.iso.org/obp/ui/#iso:std:iso:guide:73:ed-1:v1:en`) or, perhaps more concretely, in *COBIT 5: for Risk, ISACA*, (indirectly referencing the ISO guide) as "*...the combination of the probability of an event and its consequence...*"

In plain language, it's the combination of the likelihood and impact of something unexpected arising. Risk management seeks to account for these risks systematically. Therefore, risk managers are the folks who oversee and implement that effort.

Risk management can be general, applying to the entirety of the business and all risk sources (for example, business risks, financial risks, operational risks, and so on), or it can be narrowly scoped (for example, IT and/or technology risks).

Risk management is absolutely critical to the security architect for a few reasons. First, in keeping with the principle that the security architecture is there to ensure that the business can meet its goals and to enable the mission of the organization, risks to the business are an important part of making that happen.

Second, an understanding of what risks exist is key to the goal of resilience – specifically, knowing what could happen, how likely it is to do so, and what the impact might be as a result is an important part of ensuring that the overall system, network, and applications are resilient to those unexpected events. Risk management is so critical to the process that you will notice that we have included a section on it as part of the process that we've laid out in this book.

In organizations that have a defined risk management function, security architects will find that they are one of the main stakeholders in the work that the architect performs. They will, for example, help the architect prioritize controls, security mechanisms, countermeasures, and other artifacts of their security vision and strategy.

They will help translate underlying business requirements into security goals, they will track residual risks that may exist after countermeasures are put in place, they can help provide and track important metrics to the architect about the function of security solutions post-implementation, and they will, in turn, be a primary consumer of metrics and telemetry gathered by the architect.

Because information about risk is so important to the work of the security architect, if the function does not formally exist within the organization, architects will find that they will need to perform some elements of the risk management process themselves.

Security operations

The last area that we will cover here is that of security operations – that is, the folks who directly use, maintain, interface with, and otherwise administer and support the security controls and tools that the architect fields into production. **Security operations** can be its own team, it can be part of another team (for example, network operations), or it can be distributed functionally based on the tool/control in scope (for example, firewall administration in network operations, application controls with business teams, monitoring tools in the security operations center, and so on).

Operations teams work closely with the architect in a few different ways. First, given their role as the primary interface point for the controls that the architect will deploy as part of their strategy, they can provide valuable input to requirements; they can help ensure that architecture designs are feasible and maintainable. Second, they can provide requirements directly into the architectural process; for example, there may be gaps in the visibility they have into the organization, areas where operations can be streamlined, or other criteria that can become requirements of the security architecture design.

This means that, just like the other roles we've outlined, security architects and security operations teams will need to work together very closely for maximum effect. Likewise, it is not unheard of for architects to take a more active role in the operational side of the designs they put together. This is often the case in smaller companies where security operations may not be a fully realized function – it can happen in situations where security operations are distributed and there is no clear *home* for an operational element in the design, or it can happen for certain areas of operation that are needed by the architect but that the operations team is unable to support (for example, the gathering of metrics from controls).

Process overview

> *"Because security architecture is by nature a 'bridge' or translation, the aspects*
> *of the architecture process that are most important are going to change from*
> *organization to organization. It might be a culture change that is most important*
> *for one organization, just getting things written down in the first place for another,*
> *or the recognition that decisions should be driven by business instead of technology*
> *for yet another. Therefore, be ready to adapt and adjust the process you follow in*
> *light of what's most important to you."*
>
> *– Mark Simos, Lead Cybersecurity Architect, Microsoft*

The last area that we'll cover before we actually dig into the meat of creating an architecture is a brief overview of the process that we'll use throughout the rest of this book. There are as many ways to practice architecture as there are architects – and anyone telling you there is only one way to do it is limiting themselves. Just like there are multiple approaches to writing software, system administration, or decorating your house, there are different techniques and strategies that can be adapted and employed by the architect.

We set out one path that you can follow to design, test, field, and maintain a security architecture. This isn't the only way. It may not even be (for you) the best way. But we believe that the best way to learn something is by doing it. Following the process that we describe *will* result in a functional security architecture. As the architect becomes more conversant with the steps and methods, they can incorporate other techniques, resources, strategies, and methods into their approach.

The process that we will walk through throughout the rest of this book is fairly straightforward. It includes the following high-level steps:

1. **Set scope and requirements**: Determine the scope and direction for your architectural planning. This phase includes validating what will be included in the design you create and also determining the requirements that will guide the solution development.

2. **Prepare your "toolbox"**: Prepare the tools (including documentation) that you will need to undertake subsequent phases and get started on your design.

3. **Build enterprise blueprints**: Design the security plans and develop implementation plans for the organization.

4. **Execute the blueprints**: Put your plan into practice.

5. **Maintain**: Make sure that the goals of the design stay relevant over time by collecting relevant metrics and telemetry.

You'll notice these steps are very high level. There are, as you would imagine, several sub-steps that fall under each high-level step that we will go through in depth when we reach them. This approach is by design. From our point of view, it is more important that you understand the *why* behind each step than it is that you master any specific individual technique comprising a given step. There will be situations when you will not be able to follow exactly the approach we've laid out.

For example, there might be situations where there are process, cultural, or technical limitations that prevent you from being able to follow the process exactly. However, if you understand the *why* behind the step, you can create a path around those roadblocks and ultimately wind up ready to begin the next phase anyway.

An analogy for this approach is that it's like following GPS directions to get to a given destination. If something unexpected happens along the route – for example, there is an extended detour due to construction – it is much easier to stay on track if you know the general direction of the destination and why the GPS was routing you the way it was in the first place. If, on the other hand, you have no clue where you are or why the GPS is taking you down a given road, the impact of an unexpected hurdle like this is much greater.

Key tasks and milestones

> *"What you need to understand first is why you are doing architecture at all. This will inform you as to how much process makes sense. Meaning, if you understand the business drivers for architecture, the value it's providing to you, and why you need it, the answer for how much process to employ and where to apply it becomes self-evident. In some senses, extra process (adopting a process-heavy standard) is the 'lazy person's way out.' It takes more discipline to figure out the actual business needs and apply the creative energy to adapt a model to you versus just adopting something without understanding why you need it or what the value will be."*
>
> *– Ted Ipsen, President and COO at Positroniq, LLC*

Within each of these high-level phases, there are a few important milestones that we'll hit. It's useful to lay out what those are. There are several, but the most important ones to know about for now are as follows:

- **Establishing context**:

  - What is the scope?

  - What is included and what is excluded?

- **Determining requirements**:

  - What are the business goals?

  - What risks should the design mitigate?

  - What threats should the result be resilient against?

- **Assembling the "raw materials" for planning**:

  - What documentation will you need to create?

  - What architectural tools will you use to communicate your design?

  - What exists already in the organization that you can incorporate into your plans and otherwise draw from?

  - What resources are available to you and when?

- **Building your plan**:

  - What controls will you select and how will they be implemented?

  - What areas can you not directly address?

  - What is the timeline for implementation?

  - How will resources be used?

- **Execution/Implementation**:

  - How will you put your plan into practice?

  - How will you overcome the challenges and hurdles you will face along the way?

- **Monitoring**:

  - How can you gather information about the performance of your design?

  - What data can you gather to make refinements?

  - How can you gather additional information to make updates to the implementation in response to external events?

- **Improving**:

  - How can you adjust or adapt your design to optimize performance or improve outcomes?

Note that the execution steps in some areas will depend on the scope. For example, the design documentation that you choose to employ might vary depending on whether you are creating a design for a network, a system, an entire organization or business unit, or an application. With that in mind, when there are differences, we will spell out what they are so that you can ensure the maximum likelihood that the process will work for the situation you are applying it to.

Summary

Throughout this chapter, we've attempted to provide you with information about why architecture exists, the value that it provides, and how it is (at a high level) normally practiced throughout enterprises. We've also tried to lay out some useful background information about what goes into being a cybersecurity architect.

Looking ahead, we will build on this to unpack the specific processes that architects use to do their work and walk through one approach and steps with you that you can use to do so yourself.

In the next chapter, we'll explore governance and why it matters to the security architect; governance structures and their purpose; and learn to cascade from enterprise/mission goals to technology and security goals.

2
Architecture – The Core of Solution Building

In the first chapter of this book, we went through what a cybersecurity architect is, what they do (that is, the functions they perform), and the value they – and the architecture process itself – can provide to an organization. In this chapter, we will build on that to begin the process of describing how to develop an architecture.

Throughout this chapter, we will explore the structures that organizations set up to ensure key outcomes are achieved. The architect needs to understand these elements because the whole point of architecture is to support the organizational mission – to do that, we have to understand what that mission is and the strategies that the organization has put in place to achieve it. This will be the backdrop to all the work we do as security architects.

We'll walk through how organizations derive their goals (including security goals), and strategies they will use to ensure those goals are being met and that resources are used optimally in support of them. We'll go through the *structures* (that is, the processes, documentation, and technology systems) that organizations use to ensure that these things are happening and that strategies to realize goals are performing as expected. Lastly, we'll walk through a process that you can use to tailor such an organization-specific *backdrop*, custom to your organization, which you will use as context and a guide for your architecture efforts.

We'll achieve this by working through the following topics:

- Terminology
- Understanding solution building
- Establishing the context for designs
- Understanding goals
- Structures and documents
- Risk management and compliance
- Establishing a guiding process

Terminology

Before we dive into the meat of this chapter, the first thing we should note is that we have made the conscious decision to use terminology that will be most immediately transparent and accessible to everyone. This, however, will not always be the *same* terminology used by many of the security architecture frameworks, standards, and guidance that you may encounter.

For example, one of the most important concepts in this section is understanding the goals of the organization and mapping those goals to security outcomes and principles, as we stated previously. It is quite literally the case that any security effort, whether architecture, operations, incident response, or any other discipline within security, exists solely to help enable the organization to fulfill its mission. In the case of a for-profit entity, such as a company, this might mean being profitable or providing value to shareholders. In the case of a philanthropic organization, it might mean providing value to the communities it serves. In government, this might mean providing public services to citizens and ensuring transparency. In short, it's whatever is important to the organization to be successful at whatever its mission is.

Formally, this process of ensuring that resources are used in support of the organization's goals and mission is what many frameworks and standards mean when they use the word **governance**. Many frameworks and standardized approaches (both for technical architecture and otherwise) start from the point of view of *governance* used with this meaning.

There are a few problems with this, however:

- The first problem is that not all of the frameworks use this same language – or use it in the same way. For example, the concept of understanding the organization's goals is important in all of them (they have to be for the reasons that we outlined), but they don't all use consistent language to refer to it. For example, O-ESA uses the formal sense of the word *governance* (*The Open Group, Open Enterprise Security Architecture (O-ESA): A framework and template for Policy-Driven Security, Van Haren. Zaltbommel*). OSA uses the word *governance* too, but instead, it uses it as a specific component of the overall **security architecture landscape** (although note that the source material implies a slightly broader definition of the word than that outlined by O-ESA) (`http://www.opensecurityarchitecture.org/cms/foundations/osa-landscape`). SABSA, by contrast, prefers the language of *"business enablement"*(*John Sherwood et al, Enterprise Security Architecture: A business-driven approach, CRC Press*).

- The second problem is that the word *governance* itself can be used differently by different people. Sometimes, though not often, it is used in the formal way we described previously. More commonly, it is used in other ways. For example, one person might use the term to refer to the organizational model of an organization (for example, *the board of directors provides corporate governance*), another about a political body or national government (*the governance of a nation*), yet a third in the formal sense that O-ESA and TOGAF mean it (*technology governance*), and someone else to refer to influence or control (*the king's governance over their realm*).

These factors mean that reasonable people talking to each other can easily speak at cross purposes about this topic in a way that leads to misunderstanding. It is critical to the architecture process that we minimize the likelihood of being misunderstood. As we go through this book, you will see that communication is probably among the most important (if not the most important) skills that an architect can have. We will want to be well understood by others whom we work with, and we want to make sure that we are well understood by you. It is a hard enough exercise to get right without using language that engenders or lends itself to miscommunication.

Therefore, we've chosen language that we hope is unambiguous throughout. If we mean *enabling the mission of the organization*, we will say that. We will attempt to avoid terms (such as *governance*) that might be potentially ambiguous, even when that same terminology is used differently elsewhere outside of this book.

While this is advantageous to us in conveying the concepts clearly to you here and now, we wanted to be clear from the get-go that we're doing this. Why? Because it can get you in trouble if you look at other sources and see the same concepts being referred to in other ways. Should you decide to look into other architectural materials and methods, keep in mind that the same concepts can be conveyed in different ways and that, depending on which material you are leveraging, some of them might use different terms than those we are employing here.

Understanding solution building

To get started developing a cybersecurity architecture, we need to gather a few *raw materials* first. These are the items that will set the context for all the design work that we will undertake in subsequent chapters. Specifically, we need to first obtain a baseline understanding of the organization itself; this helps ensure that the measures we will later incorporate into designs are appropriate, practicable, and in line with the context. This is, in turn, because the nuances and specifics of the organization – everything from its goals to its culture, to its *mission* and unique needs – will ultimately drive the design. Everything about the design – the scope, security measures, implementation, operational constraints, and functional requirements – must account for the context in which it will operate. That context is an extension of the organization itself.

As an example of what we mean here, consider a situation where you decide to plan a fishing trip. There are a lot of tasks you'd need to complete to do so, and several important decisions that you'd need to make along the way. Specifically, you'd need to do the following:

- Acquire the appropriate equipment (tackle, bait, fishing rods, and so on)
- Acquire any provisions that you'd need (food, beverages, hot or cold weather clothing, and so on)
- Organize secure lodging and travel arrangements
- Depending on the type of fishing you want to do, you may need to secure a boat, specialized equipment such as drills (ice fishing), depth finders or radar (deep water fishing), lights (night fishing), and so on

Each of the decisions you make impacts the experience. Some will impact the final experience more than others, but each decision *will* impact the outcome, and you need to make decisions in a particular order. These and other factors govern the circumstances under which your decision-making and preparation make sense – and without them, you have every likelihood of making a wrong assumption, resulting in wasted planning time, wasted money, and bringing about a sub-optimal experience for all involved.

One way to think about it is by drawing an analogy with the laws of physics that govern how our universe operates. We know that light moves at a constant speed in a vacuum ($c=299{,}792{,}458$ *m/s*). We know that the force between two bodies is governed by the product of their masses over the square of the distance between them multiplied by the gravitational constant ($G=6.674\times10^{-11}$ $m^3 \cdot kg^{-1} \cdot s^{-2}$). But what would the universe be like if these values were subtly different?

It would be different – fundamentally different. Even a small change to the underlying laws and parameters of the universe would result in a vastly different universe. If the speed of light were faster (aside from other more pronounced effects), it would impact magnetism, perhaps leading to an Earth without magnetic poles (see `https://worldbuilding.stackexchange.com/questions/10126/what-if-the-speed-of-light-were-100-times-higher` for more details). If the gravitational constant were subtly smaller or larger, the universe as we know it couldn't exist at all. All these values define the context of what we can perceive in the universe.

The point is, even a very small change to the underlying *context* means something vastly different – and a minor change at that most basic level means outcomes that are vastly and fundamentally different from each other. Just like the structure of the universe would be vastly different with even a minute tweak to the underlying constants of gravitation and speed of light, so too will viable designs – even optimal ones – in one organization be total non-starters in others based on the fundamental assumptions and drivers upon which the business is built. A minor, subtle difference, misunderstanding, or *tweak* of the most fundamental contextual parameters means a completely different outcome and set of constraints. So, as architects, it is up to us to identify, understand, and abide by these fundamental assumptions that govern the world in which we operate.

There are the *laws* that govern how your cybersecurity architecture *universe* operates that are just like this: contextual information that governs each decision that we'll make. These represent the fundamental assumptions and constraints under which design decisions make sense and are viable. If you've been in an organization for a certain period, many of them are likely to be so ingrained in you as to be relatively invisible. For example, if I've spent my whole career as a software developer working in a shop that deals exclusively in writing *Java* code, it might not occur to me that it might be advantageous to write in Python.

Either way, we need to know what these things are so that we can design around them and ensure that the designs we're proposing make sense for the organization into which they'll be deployed.

Establishing the context for designs

> *"Bosch (the power tools company) was addressing how to market their products. They started to examine how they market and how they might do it better. They realized in the course of that that they don't provide 'drills,' and that they provide the capability to rapidly and reliably make holes of a certain depth, width, and quality. What their customers want is to make holes: the drill is just a tool to get them there. This way of looking at capability carries across to technology: the 'why' isn't about the technology – it's instead about the business capability. This is what's most important."*
>
> *– John Sherwood, Chief Architect, thought leader, and co-Founder of The SABSA Institute*

This section is all about identifying, breaking down, and systematically cataloging the fundamental assumptions, design constraints, and other immutable factors that will govern what designs are possible. In other words, it's about laying out the *universal laws* that will govern how designs must operate.

Believe it or not, this is uniquely important to the design process. The Roman architect Marcus Vitruvius Pollio, in his seminal 20-volume work *De architectura* (Of architecture), set out three fundamental principles of architecture (see *Hicky Morris Morgan, translator. Vitruvius: The Ten Books on Architecture, by Marcus Vitruvius Pollio, Harvard University Press*):

- **Firmatis (durability)**
- **Utilitas (utility)**
- **Venustatis (beauty)**

These principles are as valid to us today as they were 2,000 years ago when the book was written. They are also almost entirely dictated by the context in which the structure (in our case, the structure of the security mechanisms safeguarding our organization) will be employed. For our purposes, we will be most concerned with the first two of Vitruvius' principles (durability and utility) – both of these are tightly bound to the organization since the *durability* of the solution will vary depending on the context within which the solution will operate, and *utility* will depend on how the solution will be employed and how best it meets the needs of those using it.

So, this chapter will focus on establishing the context for your designs. To do this, we will start by outlining the three most critical areas that will influence your planning:

- **Organizational goals**
- **Existing structures and documents**
- **Risk management and compliance**

The first item, organizational goals, is really what defines this chapter – if there's one single thing that is most critical to architecture design, it's the organization's goals. Understanding the goals is necessary because it is key to understanding what is important to the organization, and this, in turn, informs us what – and how – to defend to best ensure those goals are met.

If it were practical to do so, we might stop and look solely and exclusively at the goals of the organization as the single, pure, and unerring contextual framework upon which we would build our design. This means they would be the sole source of information to guide our design work. We'll explain strategies to do this, but in reality, it is often not practical to do it this way. This is mostly because the time and energy to do so (and do it well) often eclipses what time we have available. This is because a full mapping of all the enterprise's goals, including extrapolating from them the security requirements that will dictate our architectural planning, can take more time than we usually have available to us. Therefore, we employ a bit of a *shortcut* in our approach to understand the organization's goals.

This shortcut entails looking at places where the goals of the organization may already be codified, implied, or otherwise detailed in some written form. For example, *governance structures* such as policy, procedures, guidance, and technical standards provide a roadmap that we can use to better understand the goals of the organization. Because they represent decision points already made by the organization, we can intuit that they are themselves steeped in – and reflective of – the goals of the organization, but exist in a *pre-rendered* format that we don't have to invest time in to discern.

In keeping with the approach that we will follow throughout, we will explain the *why* of these items first. Then, once it is clear why we are examining these things, we will explain how we can use them. By the time we get to the description of *how*, the process will seem, if not entirely self-evident, at least significantly easier to accomplish than would be the case if we merely gave you a prescriptive *recipe* to follow.

Now that we've established the basic philosophy with which we will approach this chapter, we'll move on to the most important aspect – understanding the goals of the company/institution and why they are important when creating security goals.

Understanding goals

> *"The most important piece of architecture is to understand the why: why it is that you are doing what it is that you are doing. Understanding the why leads you to the how. Understand it in the context of the broader business and organization goals context and let that be the guide to when and how you implement security."*
>
> – *Ted Ipsen, President and COO at Positroniq, LLC*

It is a truism that the work of the architect must start and end with enabling the organization to accomplish its goals. Security is not an end in and of itself – it doesn't *operate in a vacuum*. This means it is only useful in furtherance of some other goal that an organization or individual has.

You can prove this is the case by considering what security controls you'd use if there were no threats to defend against. For example, would you use antivirus software if malware didn't exist? Would you hire armed guards to protect an empty room? Of course not. Without a goal – that is, something to protect – security controls have no point.

Therefore, security is only useful to the extent that it is attached to some mission that the organization has: some motivating factor that causes it to be important in the first place. In a business context, the mission (among other things) usually involves the business being competitive, profitable, able to undertake new activities, enabling the workforce, positioning itself the way it wants, and minimizing risk while maximizing opportunity. Other organizations (for example, non-commercial entities) might have different missions that are important to them based on what they do, who they are, their context, and numerous other factors.

Therefore, understanding the mission of the organization is the root from which all security measures and activities spring. Most of us don't think about it in this way often, but we can understand and evaluate the mission of an organization systematically. By this, we mean that we can trace each and every security outcome, goal, requirement, and practice back to the organization's **first principles** – the mission of the organization and why it exists in the first place.

There are multiple ways to do this, but one approach is to start with the enterprise goals and examine them for the **success factors** or **enablers** that are required for those goals to be realized. This means we identify one of many high-level goals, we understand what that high-level goal involves (that is, the reason for it), we understand the implementation strategy of the organization for reaching the goal, and we describe the technology, security, and practical or other factors required for the implementation strategy to succeed.

As an example of what we mean by this, say that I have a goal of learning to play the bagpipes. I can't do that unless certain criteria are met. For example, I'd need someone to teach me; I'd need an instrument to practice on; I'd need a location to practice without disturbing others. If I live on a desert island (without access to an instructor), if I don't have an instrument, or if the only available space to practice is in a busy library, there's fundamentally no path that allows me to achieve the stated goal. In this case, the goal (learning the bagpipes) is supported by multiple success factors that allow it to be possible; those are access to an instructor, an instrument, and a quiet location to practice, in addition to numerous others that we did not list here.

This same principle applies to technology. Specifically, technology itself is only useful to the extent that it serves a higher business goal. Would a company invest millions of dollars in an application that adds no value? No. Would they buy a multi-million-dollar supercomputer and store it unused in a closet? Also no. Therefore, technology itself is an implementation strategy for making possible a bigger plan that is, in turn, a success factor for a larger business goal. You might refer to this as a *technology goal*: a part of a larger plan that feeds into and supports a business goal.

For example, consider Meta (formerly Facebook). Meta as an organization might have the business goal of making money. That larger goal is supported by the implementation strategy of selling advertising on a content-sharing platform. These are true at the broadest level, but how (specifically) will the organization put it into practice? Crafting an answer spawns its own new set of goals that are themselves in support of the larger one. For example, one way that the folks at Meta might conclude that they can achieve the outcome they want is via advertising sales (economic business goal) as realized by them building and providing a website (the Facebook application) where people can share content (technology implementation strategy). This website, which itself is an implementation strategy for the higher-level business, becomes its own goal (technology goal) that's supported by implementation strategies of its own (that is, the implementation that will allow them to create, deliver, and host that website).

You'll notice two things about this. First, this technology goal (a website) is only one of many possible technology goals that stem from the high-level business goal. There are likely to also be others. In the preceding example of Meta and the Facebook application, you'll notice that there are other things they can do to help realize their business goal; they might choose to also have a mobile app, acquire other companies (for example, Instagram), or implement games or other technology that ties into their overarching business goal. The specific technology goal (again itself an implementation strategy for the business goal) of *providing a website to share content* has its own corresponding success factors and subgoals. These get more specific, such as allowing users their own space to upload content, allowing them the capability to access the website from a variety of platforms, and so on.

These technology goals and success factors branch off yet again to be supported by security goals. Specifically, those security goals support technology by describing things that need to be in place to support the usage of that technology securely. Going back once again to the Facebook example, providing a user with space to share content means ensuring that only authorized users can access or edit that content. Therefore, we can see how a security mechanism we're all familiar with (authentication and authorization) supports technology goals directly – and business goals indirectly (that is, by supporting technology goals that are themselves supporting larger business goals):

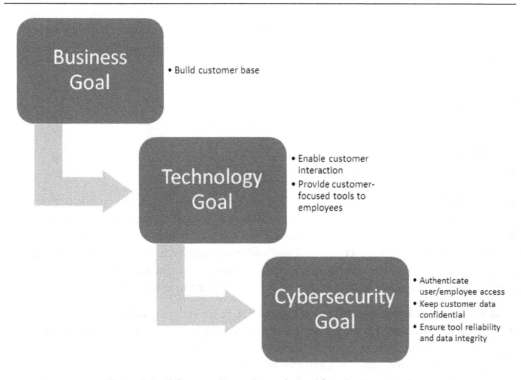

Figure 2.1 – Cybersecurity goals are derived from business goals

Starting from the top down, you could map out most, if not all, of the security goals and necessary functionality that will represent the *universe* of items that are important to us (security requirements) in our security architecture. By *cascading* each of the organizational goals to the implementation strategies that support it, and using the resulting subgoals to provide input to the next layer in a pyramid-like fashion, we would (should we complete this exercise in its entirety) get a complete list of all the technology and security goals that our architectures will need to support.

This is not a new methodology, nor is it unique to this book. Those familiar with it might recognize that this is a security-focused view into the COBIT 5 (and now COBIT 2019) *"goals cascade"* (*COBIT 5: A Business Framework for the Governance and Management of Enterprise IT. Pages 17-20. ISACA, COBIT 2019 Framework: Introduction and Methodology. Pages 28-30*). The goals cascade begins with identifying the high-level business goals of the organization; it derives technology goals from these goals, and then security goals from them. This means that there is a continuous chain from the highest organizational goals down to every technology and security outcome needed to support the organization's mission.

To do this systematically, the process implied by COBIT involves (at least theoretically) the following steps:

1. Understand enterprise goals.

2. Derive organizational success factors (organizational enablers).

3. Derive technology goals.

4. Derive technology success factors (*technology enablers*).

5. Derive security goals.

6. Derive security success factors (*security enablers*).

Now, as you might imagine, you could spend quite a bit of time going through this process completely, fully, and thoughtfully for an entire organization. And there is a benefit to doing so. However, we need to balance completeness and depth of understanding with practicality and the time we can realistically allot to it. This means such an effort – to do it well and completely for the level of understanding we need – would take weeks or even months; for a large organization, it might even take years. This might be a great long-term project if you have infinite time, but we're going to assume that you probably don't.

Instead, we're going to abbreviate this process somewhat. Specifically, any organization you're likely to realistically work with will have documentation already written that codifies – or at least implies – many of these things implicitly or explicitly. This means there will be some documents (usually in the form of policies, procedures, standards, and guidance) that either directly or indirectly state security goals. For example, a policy statement such as "*passwords must be a minimum of 10 characters in length*" tells us something directly about security goals, while a statement such as "*log all access to confidential data*" tells us something indirectly. To the extent that these are recorded already, we can leverage them to save ourselves quite a bit of work in building our baseline understanding of what's important.

Secondly, there are assumptions that we can make based on how things normally work that can also save us some time – that is, we can assume things about the technology landscape that are likely to be true even if we haven't specifically mapped out each and every enterprise goal that they in turn support. For example, I haven't ever been to Montana, but I can assume that people in that state drive on the same side of the road as the rest of the US. I can further assume that the roads there are made of tarmac and that cars in Montana have tires made of rubber. So, while I haven't done the legwork of mapping out the specific mechanics of *why* these things are true, I can (correctly) conclude that they are based on what I know to be true in other regions.

It's important, though, in doing this that we recognize these things for the shortcut that they are. This is true for two reasons. First, there can be times when drawing upon policy documentation can lead us astray. For example, we all know that there are times when security policy is either not followed in practice, doesn't reflect the actuality of what the organization does, or is silent on topics that are nevertheless critical to the organization. Second, sometimes, there can be things that can be almost universally true for most organizations but where *unicorn* organizations exist where that thing isn't true. Maybe there's some unique factor in that organization where what's usually true isn't for them.

So, if we're going to shortcut the work for timing and practicality reasons, we need to do so consciously so that we can be alert for situations where our doing so can lead us astray.

Identifying business goals

For those completely new to an architecture role, it is useful to provide a bit of context around how to identify the business goals of an organization in the first place and how to recognize them for what they are when we come across them in written materials. There are techniques that we can apply to do both.

Essentially, at the highest level, business goals are those goals of the organization that are definitional – that is, the reasons why the organization exists in the first place. For a commercial entity, these might include profitability, shareholder value, or return on financial investment. More tactical goals extend from these as the organization makes decisions about what kind of organization it will be, and how it will realize its core objectives.

The first method that we'll describe to identify what those are begins with a method that is attributed to Toyota as part of quality improvements made decades ago: the **five whys**. The *five whys* technique is essentially a strategy for *root cause* analysis – that is, for determining the root cause of something observable. It operates by asking the question of *why* until the wellspring or source of observation is identified. On page 123 of his book *Toyota production system: beyond large-scale production*, Taiichi Ohno explains the following:

"The basis of Toyota's scientific approach is to ask why five times whenever we find a problem… By repeating why five times, the nature of the problem as well as its solution becomes clear."

For example, say your organization has a policy requiring that personnel be subject to background screening on hire. When we encounter a statement like this one, we can use the *five whys* technique to arrive at the core – the most fundamental organizational goal that causes it to exist in the first place. Take the following example:

- **Observation**. The organization requires criminal background screening for new employees.
- **Why (do we do this)?** So that we know that the staff we hire are free from felonies or other criminal history.
- **Why (do we care)?** So that we can prove to our customers that our employees are trustworthy.
- **Why (does that matter)?** So that our customers trust that they can do business with us safely.
- **Why (does this help us)?** So that we can remove barriers that would prevent customers from hiring/using our service.
- **Why (do we need these barriers removed)?** So that we can better acquire and retain customers.
- **Why (is this valuable to us)?** So that we are profitable.
- **Why (be profitable)?** So that the organization can provide value back to shareholders.

You'll notice that, in doing this, we've identified the root business goal (shareholder value) as well as a host of other subgoals along the way. For example, the organization wants to be appealing to customers (a business goal supporting profitability) and the organization wants to demonstrate its diligence and commitment to customers, and one part of the implementation strategy to do that involves verifying the criminal history of new associates.

The more you do this, the more you will start to realize that you will come back almost invariably to a relatively small number of core things that the organization cares about. They are the kinds of things that are often found in an organizational mission statement. They are usually very high level and speak to why the organization exists in the first place.

Dimensions of success

> *"I'm not going to say that technical skills don't matter, but the skill that will enable all other skills to come out is retrospection. I don't like to use the term 'post-mortem,' because, in reality, nobody has to die for us to learn important lessons. When I teach people to threat model, I tell them to start out with as much time for retrospectives as they spend in their analysis. If you start out cooking and the first time you chop an onion the pieces all come out all different sizes, you can learn and practice until you get better. But often, this might not be the most important skill – a more important skill might be being able to tell if the bottom of the pan is burning, for example. Sometimes, the skills that are most important are the ones that take the least time to learn."*

> *– Adam Shostack, President, Shostack & Associates*

Understanding what the goals are is an important step (arguably the most important step), but it's important to note that it's not the only step in the legwork that we need to do to gather the *raw materials* required to understand the architectural universe. Specifically, we also need to understand how the organization measures itself against those goals. With a goal that is concrete and specific, this is straightforward. For example, a high-level financial goal such as *increase profitability* or *provide shareholder value* is easily measured financially – that is, by looking at revenue, expenses, operating costs, and so on. Other goals (for example, social responsibility, providing non-tangible value, and so on) can be harder to measure.

Security goals are often particularly difficult to measure against as many of them are probabilistic in nature. For example, a goal such as decreasing the likelihood of something undesirable coming to pass (a breach, for example) is based on the probability that the outcome will occur, rather than something directly measurable in and of itself. This matters because, as we discussed earlier, there are often several different implementation strategies to achieve the same outcome. These strategies will not always be equal in how they do so or how they impact other goals.

As an example of what I mean, consider a software vendor – that is, a company whose business is to develop and sell application software. They might set a goal that all source code is reviewed for security vulnerabilities as they conclude that doing so, in turn, supports business goals such as competitiveness, long-term profitability, and so on. One way they might choose to implement this is by using a source code scanning tool (for example, *lint* if they're working in C); another strategy might be hiring a team of experienced C developers to manually audit every line of code for the product. These two approaches accomplish the same thing (vet source code for errors) but perform very differently with respect to cost, efficacy, time investment, and so on. Understanding how each goal is measured informs what strategies are most advantageous to achieving the outcome we want.

There are multiple different dimensions along which we can evaluate a given approach to implementation. It's arguable that there are a near-infinite number of dimensions along which any given strategy can be evaluated, and that each organization might have a different set. However, as a practical matter, there are four that we will consider here:

- Effectiveness

- Maturity

- Efficiency

- Alignment

We'll explain what we mean by each in detail in the following subsections. Again, we are trying to understand how the *organization* measures itself and less so how we might measure in isolation. Thus, as we move through this, keep in mind that we want to understand these dimensions generically but also in terms of how an organization might employ them as a method of self-measurement.

Effectiveness

The first evaluation criteria that we'll look at is how well the implementation strategy performs at doing what it is designed to do. For business goals, this can be straightforward. If the strategy is designed to make money, how well does it do that? How much money does the organization generate? If a strategy is used to reduce development time, how much time does it remove from the process?

Security goals can also be looked at, evaluated, and measured through the lens of effectiveness to the same degree that other types of goals can – that is, how well does the security measure we implement perform at achieving the goal (that is, of protecting the organization)?

With security controls, this dimension is particularly important as controls are not equivalent. Even when security measures are designed with identical outcomes in mind, individual implementations can impact how well they perform. As an example, consider the difference between **Wired Equivalent Privacy** (**WEP**) and **Wi-Fi Protected Access II** (**WPA2**). Both are designed to do the same thing (more or less) from a very high-level point of view: namely, to provide confidentiality of data transmitted over wireless networks. However, they have vastly different characteristics concerning their utility and security.

Those who are familiar with the history of WEP will know that there are serious security vulnerabilities in WEP. These issues are serious enough that they allow an attacker to passively monitor the network and break the encryption that's used in a matter of minutes or hours (*Fluher, Scott, et al., Weaknesses in the Key Scheduling Algorithm of RC4*). By contrast, WPA2 is the current generally accepted optimal protocol for providing robust confidentiality on a wireless network. Therefore, while they both serve the same underlying security goal, they differ vastly in terms of how well they do it. They are not equally effective.

This, in a nutshell, is **effectiveness**: the efficacy security measures have at satisfying the goal/requirement – or, their success at delivering what is intended. Any organization that has conducted a security program review that examined what controls they have in place, and provided feedback on those that were not implemented, has likely been measured along this axis.

Maturity

The second dimension to be aware of is the **maturity** of implementation. This is particularly true when looking at security measures that have a necessary underlying procedural component.

Note that by *maturity*, we don't just mean how long something has existed (that is, how old it is chronologically) or its acceptance in the industry (that is, the *maturity* of a technology or its position in the marketplace). These things can be important in some cases, but instead, we're referring to something else: the reproducibility and reliability of the processes that support the implementation. This is the same sense of the word *maturity* that is used by frameworks such as **Capability Maturity Model Integration** (**CMMI**), which was developed by Carnegie Mellon (now stewarded by the CMMI Institute) for understanding software development process maturity (*CMMI for Development, Version 1.3. Software Engineering Institute, Carnegie Mellon University*).

Two security measures, both designed to fulfill a particular niche and achieve a particular security goal, can have very different maturity characteristics. For example, consider the respective incident response processes at two hypothetical firms. In the first organization, there is no written process, no case management or other support software, no automation, and no metrics are collected about performance. In the second, they have a well-documented and highly automated process where metrics about performance are collected and improvements to the process are made over time based on those metrics.

In both cases, the function is the same: incident response. The two processes might even (on the whole) be equally effective (on average) at servicing the incident response needs of the organization. However, one organization employs an *immature* process to satisfy these needs: it is *ad hoc*, relatively unmanaged, and reactive. Using a scale such as the one contained in CMMI, you might call their process *initial* (level 1) on the maturity spectrum. The second organization has a much more *mature* process: it's reproducible, consistent, and managed. Depending on the degree of ongoing improvement and optimization, it might fall into the *quantitatively managed* or *optimizing* maturity levels (level 4 or 5 in the CMMI model, respectively).

Again, even if the goal is the same – for example, the intent and function are the same and even the efficacy and performance are the same – the maturity of the implementation can vary. There are advantages to using processes that have higher maturity. For example, the more mature a process is, the more likely it is to have consistency in how it is performed each time, the more easily the process can recover from interruptions such as the attrition of key personnel, and the easier it can be to measure and optimize. However, as you might assume, potential budget and time investments may be required to bring a process from a lower state of maturity to a higher one. As a consequence, the maturity of implementation might be valuable for the organization to target in its processes.

Efficiency

Another dimension that matters for control implementation is the **efficiency** of operation. Earlier in this chapter, we used the example of two ways to implement application source code analysis: software testing versus manual code review. We alluded to the fact that these two approaches have different dynamics and characteristics. One of the places where they diverge significantly is in overall cost and efficiency – both in terms of dollars spent as well as in the time it takes staff to perform the tasks involved.

This can be true of any security implementation. Measures might perform similarly – or even equivalently – in terms of effectiveness and/or maturity but still have very different financial cost or time investment requirements.

To make this clearer, consider spam monitoring as an example of how this can be true. Say that, to maximize staff time and prevent phishing attempts, we want to filter out suspicious emails, spam, or other potentially unsolicited or undesirable emails. One approach to do this might be to employ automated filtering (for example, where inbound mails are automatically vetted via software and likely spam emails are quarantined); another approach might be to hire a team of people to read all incoming emails looking for spam. Assuming for a minute that each of these two approaches was equally likely to catch inbound spam, there are advantages to the automated approach. Putting aside the obvious privacy implications of a team of strangers reading your emails, a manual approach would also cost significantly more, both in time and dollars, than an automated one.

This is what we mean by efficiency in this context. Alternatively, you might refer to this as *cost-effectiveness* for organizations such as commercial companies, where staff time and dollars spent are functions of each other. Since this is not always the case (for example, in educational institutions), we thought *efficiency* was a more descriptive word choice.

This is a particularly important metric for the security architect when it comes to implementing security measures. Why? Because any security measure we put in place comes with an opportunity cost. Assuming resources are constrained (that is, that you don't have an infinite budget or unlimited staff), every measure you put in place comes at the cost of something else you didn't do – that is, what you could have done instead but didn't because you went down the specific implementation path you did.

For example, if you dedicate your entire staff to one security measure (having them manually filter inbound email for spam, for example), there are other security measures you can't implement because your resources are engaged elsewhere. Since staff can't do two things at once, the opportunity cost for the path you chose is whatever those resources would be doing instead if their time wasn't completely occupied. Likewise, if you use your whole budget on one very expensive control, you won't have any budget left over for other controls that could also be useful. Again, in this case, the opportunity cost is due to the fact that the entirety of your budget is allocated elsewhere – which prevents you from using those resources to take action in other ways.

Alignment

The last dimension that we'll look at here is what you might call **alignment** with organizational culture and skills. There are times when what you do – or how you do it – will be influenced by other factors about the organization not related to efficiency, cost, or effectiveness. As an example, say that I wanted to watch a little-known, older movie – say, for example, a movie that isn't available for streaming and is only available on the legacy (and almost completely defunct) DVD format. If I (like many others in today's world) don't own a DVD player, it doesn't matter how good the movie is or how much I want to see it. Until I either buy a DVD player or the movie is released in a format that I have access to (for example, streaming), I won't be able to watch it.

This matters with security measures too. For example, if I don't have access to staff with the right skillset to maintain or operate a given security measure, or if, for some other reason (such as culture), the measure would be intolerable or untenable to the organization, it becomes a less compelling choice.

An example that will be familiar to many security practitioners is the forensic examination of compromised systems. As we all know, there is quite a bit of specialized expertise that goes into ensuring courtroom admissibility of evidence gathered during an investigation. We need to preserve the chain of custody, collect evidence in a way that doesn't corrupt the crime scene, be careful to prevent the possibility of writing to source media, and so on. Most organizations, unless they specialize in forensics, don't have the staff to do this themselves. It's not that they couldn't acquire those staff (some larger organizations do), train them, or keep their skills current. Rather, they choose to seek support from outside specialists if such capability is needed because maintaining that skill base can be expensive relative to the amount of time that they will be directly needed.

In this example, a security measure that specifically requires specialized forensics skills to operate would not be a great fit for an organization that has chosen to outsource that specialization. It's not that either approach is right or wrong; it's just a question of whether it aligns with other choices the organization has made. In the same way that purchasing software that runs solely on macOS is a non-optimal choice for an environment that is Windows-only, this security measure requires something that the organization doesn't have access to.

With this new footing in understanding goals and understanding the dimensions of success, we can embark on a quick journey through the policies, procedures, and standards that will help ease the identification of organization goals.

Structures and documents

The dimensions described previously relate both to the goals of the organization (what is important to measure in how it achieves those goals) and also to how well a security measure works within the context of enterprise goals. This is what makes understanding the goals so important. But assuming that going through a full goal-mapping exercise to correlate every organizational goal to technology goals – and map, in turn, security goals to technology ones – represents a time investment that not every architect can afford to make, how can we get to a rapid understanding quickly so that our design work can proceed?

As we implied earlier, one way to do this is by looking at policy, procedure, standard, and guidance documentation that may already exist in the organization. This is because they are the codification of already-made decisions by the organization, which are, in turn, driven by the goals. Sometimes, these items are even referred to as *governance structures* – meaning they are the metaphorical scaffolding upon which governance for the organization rests.

Policies, procedures, and standards

Whatever you call them, let's walk through what these documents are and why they represent a useful shortcut for helping us to define the landscape:

- Policy
- Procedures
- Standards
- Guidance

We'll go through each one, discuss why and how each one is valuable to us as architects, and discuss ways that you can employ them to help distill down management intent to organizational goals.

Policy

> "A mistake people make is conflating policies, standards, procedures, and guidelines. These are all different instruments. Policies are an articulation of the strategic goals of management; they should be high level, and strategic in nature. Technical standards are more closely tied to technologies that you have – or processes that you run in the organization. These may change more often since the underlying technology or processes could change. Procedures are specific actions – step by step instructions – that you take to accomplish a particular goal in achieving a policy goal; these may change even more than standards. Having each of these documents in place at the right level that cover the right things is important for the organization."
>
> – *Ted Ipsen, President and COO at Positroniq, LLC*

The first area we'll look at is organizational policy: both security policy, but also policy more generally. Sometimes described as *"statements of management intent"* (*Wood, Charles Cresson, Information Security Roles and Responsibilities Made Easy. Page 63, PentaSafe*), these are documents that are created by the organization to document and codify the expectations of management regarding a particular topic.

Policies are typically *high-level* in nature, specifically approved by management, and (typically) periodically reviewed to ensure accuracy, completeness, and to ensure they stay current. In practice, though, these things aren't always a given. From a level of specificity standpoint, they can run the gamut between the more and the less technical, and from more to less specific. For example, one organization might have a policy that states *"information should remain protected when transmitted over corporate networks;"* another organization's policy might stipulate that *"data on the internal network must be transmitted using TLS 1.2 or higher."* Both speak to the same underlying goal – that is, keeping information protected from prying eyes when traversing the network – but they do so with varying levels of prescriptiveness and technical specificity.

While practitioners can and sometimes do feel strongly about what the *optimal* level of detail or technical specificity to include in a policy document like this is, the truth is that some are more specific, and some are less so. Either way, because policies are approved by management and are highly visible within the organization (thereby engendering input from relevant stakeholders), they represent a data source summarizing views by management and other stakeholders about the topic the policy addresses.

This means that policy represents a particularly fruitful area for understanding the goals of the enterprise. Why? Because everything contained in that policy is a codification of management intent. The management of the organization putting a *stake in the ground* about a topic means that, at some level, something about that particular topic relates to something the organization wants to do. In other words, there's no reason to write a policy about something if the topic is of no consequence.

So, how do we derive the organizational goals from policy? One method is to use the *five whys* technique discussed earlier – that is, trace the root cause of the policy back to the overarching business goal it supports. Another way is to understand the *intent and rigor* of a policy; meaning what is intended, how much is required, and why.

Procedures

Unlike policy, procedures describe the process that will be used to support a given policy objective. They may or may not require explicit approval by executive leadership, but they are typically very technically specific: at least specific enough to allow constituents within the organization (for example, employees or contractors) to perform the process the same way each time it is executed.

Procedures are useful to security architects in helping us understand the lay of the land, but arguably less valuable in doing this than policy documentation. Why? There are two reasons. First, procedures can be very specific about details, but the area of coverage can be fairly narrow. For example, a procedure for system access log monitoring might outline in great detail the process by which security team members acquire and review system logs, but it probably won't go into much detail about anything else outside this fairly narrow purview. The scope might target logging for a particular subset of hosts, but not logging more generally (that is, on other systems), other types of monitoring beyond logs, or how the logs will be employed or stored outside the narrow scope of the procedure.

Secondly, procedures often offer less insight into management expectations and intent. For example, consider an incident response process. The process might outline who is responsible for what during an incident, how the incident should be handled given various sets of circumstances, what reporting should occur (for example, frequency, format, and to what audience), when the response team will meet, how they communicate, and so on. But the written procedure might not speak to *why* these things are being done. It is possible (though by no means certain) that it could allude to a subset of goals, but it cannot be relied upon that the entirety of the goals surrounding incident response will be addressed within the procedure itself.

So, procedures, while a useful supplement to data gathered through other means, are perhaps the least direct instrument available to the architect in terms of understanding the universe within which our designs will operate. This is not to imply that we can remain ignorant of them; on the contrary, we need to be aware of them to the extent that the designs we implement will need to work with them, enhance them, and not contravene them. In some circumstances, we might be able to intuit broader security goals from procedures, but in general, policy is better equipped to do this.

Standards

Standards, particularly technical ones, help specify how certain goals are to be met. For example, you might have a technical standard that outlines how desktops should be configured, how firewalls are to be deployed, how cryptography is to be used, and so on. Standards are usually narrow in scope/focus and are prescriptive.

Normally, the purpose of a standard is to document the measures required to adhere to a given policy. For example, an organization might have a higher-level policy such as "*encryption should be used to protect data when transmitted*." But what does that mean? How, specifically, can those to whom the policy applies adhere to it? One mechanism that organizations can employ to provide additional specificity and to assist in overall compliance with the policy is to provide details about *how* to accomplish it.

In the preceding example, an organization might have a few supporting technical standards to support the *encrypt data in transit* requirement, such as the following:

- SSH server and client configuration standards outlining the standard for how to employ **Secure Shell (SSH)** and how to ensure that both clients and servers of SSH connections are configured in an appropriate, secure manner

- A web server TLS configuration standard outlining how to enable and configure TLS capability for web servers

- A VPN configuration standard outlining what VPN products are to be used and how to configure them

These are only a subset of the possible standards that could support a policy requirement such as the one outlined. You could also have additional standards governing everything from database connections to proprietary or non-standard communication channels, to secure Wi-Fi and countless other examples.

As was the case with procedures, when trying to understand the *universe* within which our designs will operate, standards have some utility but provide less direct value to us than policies do. The primary reason is that they also don't always provide new information about management intent.

There are two reasons why this is so. First, as you can imagine, standards are only very seldom written by management directly. Instead, they are normally authored by those subject matter experts who are knowledgeable about the topic under consideration. In the preceding example, can you imagine someone on the executive team, such as the CFO, authoring something called the *TLS Configuration Standard*? No. Instead, you'd expect a document such as this one to refer to specific cipher suites (that is, what algorithms should be used), methods of key management, specific software or hardware configuration parameters, and so on. Something this technically specific isn't – and shouldn't be – the primary focus of someone in the executive suite.

The second reason they're not the best sources of management intent is that they already support an existing policy item – that is, a well-written standard will directly support existing policy where the management intent is already spelled out. Generally, standards actualize an intent; they don't specify new intentions not already referred to in the policy.

Guidance

The final type of document we might encounter is guidance documentation. This type of document represents additional, non-prescriptive information provided to those in the organization about policy, procedures, or standards.

Going back to the earlier example about encrypting data in transit, an organization might have a technical standard in place to help support that, such as configuration guides, a list of approved cryptographic products or standards, and so on. They might also provide guidance to be used in certain situations – for example, if they have in-house developers who need to implement cryptographic functionality themselves. In that case, there might not be a direct configuration standard that is applicable, but they still wish to pass along advice that could be useful in achieving the policy.

As with standards, guidance documents usually exist in service to already-existing policy. Therefore, they can help provide additional details about a policy but are less directly useful in ferreting out additional, new information about management expectations that would not already be available in the governing policy.

Applying to architectural frameworks

The very first thing that an architect will need to do is establish what the governing philosophies, needs, goals, and other immutable factors of the organization are that will inform their designs.

In an ideal world, this would come through a reasoned, systematic, and comprehensive analysis of the enterprise's goals – that is, deconstructing every goal that the organization has, tracing out how they intend to achieve these objectives, and then building out the implicit security goals that support their current or proposed use of technology. In reality, though, a complete goal-mapping exercise like the preceding one consumes more time than most practitioners can invest before they begin a security design. So, instead, we begin by looking at what is already codified to begin the process.

This means we begin with the policy, procedures, standards, and guidance that the organization has already written to establish the *rules* for how our security designs must behave and the optimal character of what they should contain. This makes the most sense in light of how the organization already functions.

The most straightforward way to do this is to start by reading the documentation (assuming you have not already done so). By this, I don't necessarily mean that you need to read everything the organization has ever written. An organization (particularly a large one) might have lots of policies and procedures; these might cover everything from time off and attendance to how they handle whistleblowers and ethics violations. However, at a minimum, you'll want to read the security-relevant policy, procedure, guidance, and standard documentation that exists and use them to derive the information about the organizational goals that will inform your work going forward.

This advice isn't exactly rocket science, but following it provides a few valuable things to the architect. First, it lets you get comfortable with the organization's general approach to security. Is this the kind of organization that leaves room for flexibility and creativity on the part of individual employees? Are they risk-tolerant or risk-averse? Do they tend to be more prescriptive in terms of how to accomplish particular goals or do they leave room for individual employees or groups to innovate?

The second thing reading the policy will do is tip you off to the main things that your designs will need to accomplish. It can be helpful to make a list of these things as you encounter them. If the organization requires encryption of data at rest, for example, your designs will need to implement this, so remembering what these things are is an absolute must. Since it is the case that there is often extraneous information in the policy documents themselves, it can be helpful to create a list of *facts* outside of the policy documentation that designs will need to address.

How will you know when you've identified organizational goals? You'll know you've reached one when you get down to a clear, actionable statement that answers the question, "*Why does this organization exist in the first place?*" Examples of foundational organizational goals might be the following:

- **Shareholder or owner value**: A commercial enterprise may exist to provide an economic return to the owners or shareholders
- **Provide value to a given constituency**: A socially conscious organization might exist to provide benefits or value to a given community

- **Impact the world in some way**: Some organizations might exist to bring about a concrete change to the world or society – for example, curing a disease, researching a given topic, contributing to the betterment of humankind, or other specific outcomes

In addition to foundational goals, you might also encounter business goals that themselves spring from these foundational goals, as follows:

- **Maximize efficiency**: An organization might seek to streamline operations. This goal itself is not an *end state* in the foundational sense such as the previous ones. Instead, this goal helps them do something else better. For example, a commercial enterprise might seek to increase efficiency to maximize profitability, or a non-profit might seek to maximize efficiency to have more resources to apply to its core mission. In both cases, the higher-level goal is supported by being more efficient.

- **Reduce greenhouse gas emissions**: The organization might strive to be green in its approach to impact on the climate. Note that this supports a broader goal such as *impacting the world* instead of being an end goal in itself.

- **Expand market share**: Again, this is not an end state in the same way as the foundational goals are. After all, why increase the organization's market if no broader goal is supported?

- **Enhance customer experience**: An organization might seek to improve how it interacts with its customers, either by providing better customer service, a better overall experience with the customer, or through numerous other potential strategies. The motivation might be to make customers *stickier* (that is, less likely to switch to a competitor), to improve market share, or for other reasons.

These are only a few examples of many possibilities. The farther you go down the chain of an organization's goals, the more subgoals you will find. You'll notice, as we outlined earlier in this chapter, that the supporting goals are implementation strategies for how to achieve the broader level goals. In the preceding examples, the goal of improving customer experience is one possible implementation strategy for increasing market share (that is, by improving the customer experience, fewer customers are lost to attrition), which itself is a possible implementation strategy for the foundational goal of increasing profitability.

Additional frameworks

At this stage of the game, it may seem like we're making very slow progress in teeing up the architecture process, but in actuality, we've already taken a few huge steps even at this early stage of the game. Why? Because we've started to build our first (and arguably most important) **view** that we'll use throughout the design process.

A *view* in this context is an important architectural tool – and one that is often misunderstood. But really it just means a way of looking at the overall operation of a system from a set vantage point and the perspective of someone with a certain set of values and priorities. Formally, TOGAF defines a view as, "*A representation of a system from the perspective of a related set of concerns.*" (*The TOGAF® Standard, Version 9.2, Section 3.17*).

We'll spend more time with TOGAF later down the road, but for now, the important part to know is that a *view* is just a shorthand way of describing the point of view – a way of looking at things – for a given stakeholder in the architectural process. It encompasses the set of constraints, concerns, interests, and goals around how a given individual (that is, a person in a particular role holding a particular point of view) might view the system, set of systems, components, environment(s), or any other thing.

This concept can sometimes be hard for people to understand, but it's really not. Let's look at an example to clarify this. Let's say you were building a house. If you're the property owner (that is, the soon-to-be-homeowner at the end of the building process), you have a vested interest in how things turn out, right? After all, you're the one who will have to live there when construction is completed. You, as the homeowner, have a particular point of view about the house. You want it to be comfortable to live in, you want the building expenses to fit within your particular budget, you want the maintenance to be something that you can keep up with, you want it to have good *curb appeal* (that is, have it look nice), and so on.

All of these elements together – that is, your collective point of view about the home – represent your view of the house. There are, however, other people involved – other stakeholders in the building process. For example, there are tradespeople (for example, plumbers, electricians, and others) working on the house, carpenters and masons, landscapers, and so on. Each of these individuals has a different perspective than the homeowner: they have their own concerns and considerations. For example, an electrician might be concerned about wiring connections and placement of junction boxes, a plumber might be concerned with the path of pipes, and so on. And, of course, these folks have a different view from that of a building inspector or code enforcement authority.

All of those folks are stakeholders in the eventual structure that's getting built – they all have an important role to play. However, each of these individuals has a different way of looking at the project with different concerns, considerations, values, constraints, and so on. What we're essentially doing with the goal-seeking exercise described earlier is building out a foundational view of the organization – that is, we're level-setting a certain business-centric view of the organization itself. We will build upon that down the road as we move through the later phases of the architecture process.

Now that we've become familiar with the documentation and how it informs our planning, we are ready to take our work one step higher. The next section will take us through risk management and compliance, in which we will try to plug all the holes in our security planning thus far.

Risk management and compliance

If you limit yourself only to looking at what is already explicitly documented in the organization in the form of policies, procedures, supporting documentation, and other existing documentation (for example, management artifacts), you'll find that you have a good picture but not a complete one. At this stage, the picture can be potentially incomplete in two very important ways. First, there can often be other security objectives that are important to the organization but that are unrealized by the authors of policy and procedure documentation. To see this in action, recall the earlier example where we posited a developer who had spent years working inside a particular technology stack (for example working within the Java ecosystem) to the exclusion of all others. They may potentially take that technology stack so much for granted that the idea of stepping outside of it is a place their thought process just won't naturally go.

The second way that this can happen is when assumptions are so profoundly self-evident that the need to state them explicitly becomes less important. As an example of this, a savvy executive team (who seek to maximize the efficiency of the organization in all ways, including reducing the time spent approving and maintaining unnecessary or redundant policy) might not feel that it's necessary to explicitly mention some baseline assumptions. They may not feel it necessary to mention, for example, that employees should refrain from pouring gasoline on their desks and setting them on fire. Sure, there's probably a broader governing policy about damaging the workplace – but that specific scenario might seem so fundamentally obvious (and unlikely to occur) that there's no explicit mention of it in any governing documentation.

What this means in practice is that starting by looking at policy, procedures, standards, and more is a solid first step – but it may not be the only step. As you work to enhance your knowledge of the organization, you can and should *round out* your understanding based on your own direct experiences, institutional knowledge gained through familiarity, and other documentation that may speak to the organization's goals. You can also, where they exist, look to other sources – in particular, two critical sources – to help round out your understanding. These sources are as follows:

- **Risk appetite**
- **Compliance requirements**

We'll explain what each of these factors is, why they matter, and how to evaluate them in more detail next.

Risk management and appetite

> *"Ultimately, architecture is a risk management process. It tells you what to do based on the priorities of risks that are in your sphere of influence. You use those risks to come up with the right set of controls. These controls go into your architecture all the way down: they drive technology standards, process standards, vendor selection,*

all the way down from the business to the lowest level. Your architecture then becomes an enabler of more effective risk management so that you're maintaining your 'architecture vitality' – the property that, as the business is changing and adapting, you are too."

– Andrew S. Townley, Chief Executive Officer at Archistry Incorporated

Not every organization views risk the same way – just like individuals don't always view risk the same way. As an example, consider your retirement savings. If you're young, you might be fairly accepting of some risk in your retirement portfolio. Why? Because you have time to make up losses down the road if things go south. Since you're young, it might be worth it to take on a little bit more risk now since you know that, over the long term, a potential downtick in the economy will likely be erased by the long-term gains that you will realize from a more aggressive posture. In this case, you are fairly risk-tolerant.

If, however, you are closer to retirement age, it would have a correspondingly greater impact on you if you were to lose a substantial portion of your retirement savings in the very short term. In this case, you might not have many working years left, so you have limited time during which to recoup any short-term losses. Therefore, you are more risk-averse.

Neither approach is right or wrong. However, the circumstances dictate what is right or wrong *for you*. This means that, depending on those circumstances, you are more or less tolerant of incurring risks.

Organizations, just like individuals, can have varying risk tolerance. A conservative financial institution, for example, might be willing to accept less risk than a four-person start-up. Just as with individuals and their relative career timelines, this too is driven by circumstance. In the case of a bank, they might have spent years building a brand image of stability and reliability. They might have invested countless dollars and person-hours over the years in making sure that that image is reflected in everything they do. The start-up probably has less invested in its public image. Likewise, a small start-up might be nimbler than a large organization such as a bank or brokerage and be able to rapidly reposition if they incur a financial loss or impact on their image. In this case, as you'd expect, the start-up is likely more risk-tolerant than the bank.

It is very important to have a solid understanding of the risk tolerance of the organization within which you will be designing your security architectures. Why? The amount of risk that the organization is willing to assume will dictate what your designs need to accomplish in terms of risk reduction, which, in turn, drives what measures you will put in place, how you will implement them, and the amount of money the organization is likely to be willing to spend in doing so.

How can you know what the organization's risk tolerance is? In an organization that has a process for formal, systematic risk management, this will be straightforward. Usually, a statement of risk tolerance is created as input into the risk management process, meaning it will be documented clearly and unambiguously.

This happens because risk tolerance is key to what risk management is conceptually. Risk management is the formalized process of *optimizing* risk. In practical terms, this usually means lowering it – that is, reducing the risk to a level that is within the defined organizational risk tolerances. Therefore, to understand what the tolerances are, the organization will need to have a fairly clear understanding of what level of risk is acceptable to them so that they know whether they have achieved their risk optimization goals.

To accomplish this, risk management techniques usually employ several steps. For example, these are the steps as outlined in *ISO 31000:2018 (the international standard outlining guidelines for risk management) (Risk Management – Guidelines (ISO Standard No. 31000)*, and retrieved from `https://www.iso.org/obp/ui#iso:std:iso:31000:ed-2:v1:en`):

1. **Establish context**: Identify and outline factors to be taken into consideration during the risk management process.

2. **Risk identification**: Identify potential risk sources.

3. **Risk analysis**: Analyze the risk, including developing an understanding of consequences, likelihood, and other factors.

4. **Risk evaluation**: Triage, prioritize, and assign priority to mitigation or other treatment.

5. **Risk treatment**: Address the risk through mitigation (remediation), acceptance, transference, avoidance, or other measures.

6. **Monitoring and review**: Monitor the risk over time to ensure that it stays within acceptable parameters.

These steps can be either quantitative (that is, where numeric values are used to explicitly quantify impact and likelihood) or qualitative (where more *fuzzy* values such as low/medium/high are used). Either way, though, part of establishing the context must involve understanding the risk tolerances (*risk appetite*) that are acceptable to the organization.

Those new to the security profession often question why we don't always just seek to reduce risk to its minimum possible value in every situation. There are a few reasons not to do that.

First, it's not always the case that lower risk is always good and higher risk is always bad. In some situations, risk can be a good thing. Consider your retirement portfolio again. What would happen if you always put your retirement savings in the absolute lowest-risk investment (for example, precious metals)? You'd find that while your retirement funds are certainly safe, they wouldn't grow very quickly. By taking on risk carefully, with due consideration, and in an informed, controlled, and calculated way, you can potentially realize a higher return. This same situation is true in business as well. Sometimes, endeavors are inherently risky: the acquisition of another company, the decision to release a new product, or a provocative marketing campaign. Instead of trying to completely remove all risk, business is about taking careful, studied, calculated risks.

Likewise, there can be risks in not taking action just as there are in taking action. For example, consider what would happen if a business failed to adopt some key technology – email, perhaps – because of the risks associated with spam and phishing. Now, consider what the competitiveness of that firm is likely to be when that firm decides against email but their competitors all adopt it. They would be competing at a handicap relative to their peers.

Second, there is always a cost. Even the most efficient and cost-effective security measures incur some cost. In many cases, the costs involved far outweigh what the organization is willing to spend to achieve a risk reduction goal. Most of us probably wouldn't say no to someone offering us a million dollars. But what if, to obtain that money, we would need to spend the rest of our lives in a sensory deprivation tank with no ability to spend it? Most people would conclude that the price associated with earning that money is way too high. Therefore, trying to achieve "zero risk at any cost" is untenable.

So, the goal of risk management is to understand risk so that the decisions you are making are informed ones.

For organizations that do employ formalized risk management processes, architects will typically interact with that process in at least two ways. First, they will use the information coming from the risk management process – information such as risk appetite, as we highlighted previously – to inform their work. Secondly, though, their designs will themselves be iterative with risk management activities. By this, we mean that they will provide input into the risk management process as they track and manage risk areas that result from their designs (for example, residual risks that may remain in their designs) and also that their designs may themselves be risk mitigation steps for other things resulting from the risk management process.

For organizations that do not employ a formalized risk management process, it is still important that the architect understands the risk tolerances of the organization. In this case, though, it may take some further investigation and analysis to arrive at since it may not have been systematically considered as part of a broader risk planning exercise. In this case, you will want to do some information-gathering to attempt to get an understanding of it before beginning any design work.

In saying this, we should note that it is almost always better to have executive-approved, management-socialized, and documented risk tolerance guidance upon which to base our architectural decision-making. Why? Because it's defensible. There are some people (including some in positions of executive leadership) who will represent themselves as being very risk-tolerant, so long as negative potentialities don't come to pass. If (when) they do, you will find that they are much less accepting. This means that even if we examine, analyze, and document a risk tolerance in the absence of one already existing, we should still work to get it sanctioned and approved.

To help do so, it can be useful to do two things: first, err on the side of being more risk-averse rather than more risk-tolerant. There is a known, well-studied perception bias in people where they tend to view negative outcomes as less likely than positive ones ("*optimism bias*") (*Sharot, Tali. "The optimism bias". Current Biology, 6 December 2011. Elsevier Ltd. Retrieved from*: https://www.sciencedirect.com/science/article/pii/S0960982211011912). Unless organizations are analyzing risk both systematically and quantitatively, this bias can and does tend to cause people to view undesirable, negative outcomes as less likely than positive ones. So, to arrive at something realistic, it can be helpful to deliberately compensate for the bias in our planning. Secondly, it is helpful, even if the organization is not doing any formalized risk management, to document the risk tolerances that we will use in our architectural planning. Even better is if we can get those socialized and approved (that is, signed off) by executive management. Again, this is both for defensibility purposes as well as having a documented artifact to draw on for future reference.

Compliance

"Security architecture in the most general sense is about creating a framework. That framework represents a cohesive model that covers the circumference of the organization's needs to ensure ample coverage for security and compliance concerns. There are obviously numerous dimensions to this, but in essence it's about developing a model that captures what is in the best interests of the organization, aligning organizational discipline to that model, and giving you back something that is measurable, manageable, and provides a solid understanding of the organization's risk posture."

– Dr. Richard Perez, vCISO

The other factor that we will need to consider is compliance. By this, we're referring to any legal, contractual, or other requirements that the organization must adhere to by virtue of the business that it is in, the work it does, or the type of data it processes. Many of these mandates will require specific action on the part of the architect to ensure that they are adhered to.

Let's say, for the sake of argument, that we are working in the healthcare sector for a large, multi-institution health system. Perhaps we have been chartered with developing security architecture for a subset of the health system's ecosystem (for example, a particular hospital in the network) or we are working on security architecture for a healthcare application that will support patients.

In the US, an organization like the one described would be considered a *covered entity* under the **Health Insurance Portability and Accountability Act** (**HIPAA**). This US law outlines a set of requirements that pertain, among other things, to the security and privacy of health information that is used while providing treatment to a patient. The regulatory rules, in this case, contain specific provisions for the encryption of data when it's transmitted over an electronic communications network (*§164.312(e) (2)(ii)* – *"Implement a mechanism to encrypt electronic protected health information..."*) and when it's stored (*§164.312(a)(2)(iv)* – *"Implement a mechanism to encrypt and decrypt electronic protected health information"*).

These two requirements – encrypting data at rest and in transit – are non-optional from a design point of view. Ideally, there will be an organizational policy that stipulates that these controls will be used. In fact, for most organizations, there will be. But we cannot assume this. This means we cannot rely on there being a one-to-one mapping between line-item requirements as outlined by governing regulations and the policy of the organization. As such, it is incumbent on us to understand, remain aware of, and incorporate compliance goals into our designs.

It is not possible in a targeted book such as this one to outline every possible set of compliance requirements for every type of organization in every geographic region. There are hundreds and thousands of potential regulatory requirements that may apply. Therefore, at this stage, some data gathering into the type of operations conducted, and the location where they are conducted, will be required.

For example, an organization that retains information about citizens of the EU will fall under the requirements of the **General Data Protection Regulation (GDPR)** – an EU law governing data protection and privacy (see `https://eur-lex.europa.eu/eli/reg/2016/679`). As in the preceding example, a healthcare provider or insurer in the US will fall under HIPAA – US legislation governing requirements for security and privacy in a healthcare context. A merchant accepting payment cards would need to adhere to the **Payment Card Industry Data Security Standard (PCI DSS)** – a set of rules required by card brands for the protection of payment card information by merchants (see `https://www.pcisecuritystandards.org/document_library/`).

These are only a few examples of the many possible requirements, legal or contractual, that might apply to a given organization. Likewise, multiple regulations could apply to any given single organization. For example, on the surface, it might seem like a US-based hospital would be primarily concerned with the requirements of HIPAA. They are, of course, but there are other considerations as well, including other governing regulations (for example, the *HITECH Act of 2009*) and other potentially applicable standards, such as the Joint Commission Environment of Care standard, rules from the **College of American Pathologists (CAP)** standard governing laboratory environments, and numerous others.

But now, consider other factors that might apply outside of this; for example, how many hospitals also accept credit payments at the gift shop, cafeteria, or for parking? In this case, they would also be beholden to the PCI DSS just the same way that a merchant such as Amazon is (though with a correspondingly smaller scope of applicability). Likewise, consider a publicly traded healthcare insurance provider in the US, a merchant in the EU processing credit card payments, and so on.

Since multiple regulations might apply, it is always a good idea to begin by obtaining a thorough understanding of the various regulatory requirements that are in play, again in a systematic way to ensure completeness. In a large organization or one in a heavily regulated industry, one way to do this is by engaging those individuals responsible for compliance oversight and obtaining a list of focus areas. Chances are, in this environment, they will have put significant thought into what requirements are applicable. In a smaller environment, this can prove more challenging, and you may find that you (at least initially) need to keep track of this yourself.

If that is the case, one way to approach this is to start with what you know based on what the organization's primary business is, but expect that you will need to, over time, add to the list of requirements that are in scope as you learn more. This means begin with what you know and document the various requirements that are likely to impact your architecture but do so in a way that allows you the flexibility to add to the list over time.

Establishing a guiding process

> *"There are 'top down' and 'bottom up' approaches to architecture. Many people start with the highest level of the organization and try to work down; this seems logical at first but what can happen is you lose sight of context as you move down the chain toward more specific usage. What I think is a better approach is to start bottom up: understand the threats, understand the context, understand the risks, and build architectures for the different environments piecemeal while keeping an awareness of the 'macro' – the high level view. This lets you reduce redundancy and normalize, but also create lightweight, modular frameworks that can be reused where needed or improved upon and reworked when needed. Anyone can build an architecture that looks great on paper; but an overly structured approach can be so rigid that it fails when it gets to implementation. You need concert between top down and bottoms up; the best strategies do both at the same time."*
>
> *– Steve Orrin, Federal CTO at Intel Corporation*

Now that we've covered in some detail *what* has the potential to influence your design landscape, the next thing we'll cover is a process you can follow that will result in you having a clear, concise, consolidated view of the important factors that will be used as input into your design process.

Hopefully, having come this far with us in this chapter, you have a pretty good idea of *why* this process is important and what things you will want to look at. Once you understand the why, the *recipe* is probably fairly straightforward. Also, understanding the why means that you'll be able to react if something doesn't go as planned.

So, to gather the information that you will need to set the contextual framework for design, you can do the following:

- Understand the business' high-level goals

- Understand the technology goals

- Draw implied goals from existing documentation

- Capture (or define) risk tolerances

- Account for compliance requirements

Understanding the business' high-level goals

> *"There are two meanings – or perhaps two 'dimensions' – to the concept of risk. One is threat versus opportunity. Remember that security is a business enabler: this means enabling the organization by mitigating potential unwanted impacts (the way we often see risk described), but it also means enabling the organization to seize and avail itself of desirable outcomes. These can be in the form of increased competitive advantage, better ability to fulfill the organizational mission, or better positioning in the marketplace – the specifics depend on the organization's context. Remember*

that the whole point is business use of technology for positive added value: that means minimizing the likelihood and impact of negative outcomes, but it also means maximizing the likelihood and impact of positive outcomes in equal measure."

– John Sherwood, Chief Architect, thought leader, and co-Founder of The SABSA Institute

The very first thing you'll want to do is make sure you understand the high-level goals of the business. What does the business do? What is important to it? What is the mission of the organization? What is the strategy of the organization in pursuit of achieving its ends? The better you can understand this, the better and more complete your designs will be and the less time you will need to spend validating that the approaches make sense later on down the road.

While not required, it can be helpful to document these if they are not already documented somewhere else. Many organizations will have at least some (if not most or all) of the high-level business goals documented somewhere. If this documentation exists, read it, use it, and incorporate it.

Understanding the technology goals

The next thing to understand is the technology goals of the organization. A larger organization might have completed something similar to the COBIT goals cascade exercise outlined earlier in this chapter, or they might have architecture professionals chartered with planning the design for the overall technology footprint. To the extent that you can do so, meet with these folks. Explain to them what you are looking to do, and capture and read any documentation that they have available to help you understand their high-level plan.

As a practical matter, it doesn't really matter that much *how* you capture these goals; you might create a spreadsheet, write a document, or use existing documentation that is already available, assuming it is in a format that is concise and useful. We have found it helpful to document these elements ourselves in a spreadsheet with references to existing documentation, where it exists.

Regardless of how you do it, though, you want to understand any technology goals that are in the scope of the areas where your designs will operate. This may not be the full enterprise – in a large organization, it almost certainly will not be. Remember, you are not trying to *boil the ocean* here (that is, do everything all at once). Instead, you are trying to start small and build a "playbook" that you can refine over time. Plenty of time is built into the architectural process later so that you can validate your designs in case you miss something at this stage.

Drawing implied goals from existing documentation

Read the policy, procedures, standards, and guidance of the organization. Some organizations might have multiple, differing bodies of documentation that vary depending on the region or business unit. Again, you are not trying to do everything all at once here. The goal is just to collect any implied or explicit constraints applicable to the area that you will be designing for (see the *Scoping* section in *Chapter 3, Building an Architecture – Scope and Requirements*).

Capturing (or defining) risk tolerances

Understand the risk tolerance of the organization. Where a documented position on risk exists, read it. Where one does not but there is a formalized risk management process (for example, if there is a chief risk officer or risk function), meet with them to get a feel for the risk tolerance. If no risk tolerance is defined anywhere, write one yourself and socialize it to obtain buy-in.

Accounting for compliance requirements

Understand, and explicitly list, any compliance requirements that may be applicable. If there is governing regulation for a specific type of business (for example, financial services, payments, or healthcare), read it and understand what is required. If there is a compliance office, meet with them to understand what is required and where.

Summary

Throughout this chapter, we've tried to outline the key elements that you will need to account for in any subsequent design work that you perform. Our philosophy is that once you understand why something is important, the specific steps to accomplishing it become intuitive and self-evident. Additionally, since there are any number of permutations in how an organization might be organized and structured, laying it out in this way allows you to adopt methods that will work best in your environment. However, we have attempted to provide a *recipe* that will work in most situations while assuming you understand why each step matters and why it is important.

In this chapter, we've looked at the key dimensions that will inform your planning context: goals, existing organizational structures, and risk management/compliance. These are items that, though not all that you will need data-wise to begin planning, nevertheless inform and direct how your design will proceed. These items are important because they establish the borders within which your design makes sense; using the earlier analogy, they represent the *rules of the universe* (that is, the fundamental set of assumptions, contextual factors, and rules) upon which all of our downstream work will be built. From there, we've outlined a *rapid-fire* process that will get you to a systematic understanding of these items. Note that this is not the only process that you can use to derive this information; for organizations that conduct broader architectural efforts systematically, there might be other approaches that your organization prefers you to employ. However, understanding these items is critical as it tees up the next steps in the process.

Looking ahead, in the next chapter, we will progress to the next phase of design: defining the scope and gathering requirements. This will lay out what your design is intended to accomplish, and where it will operate. Each of these is itself imperative to a solid design, and getting them right will ensure that your design operates as effectively and efficiently as possible.

Part 2:
Building an Architecture

This section walks through how to begin the solution design process: specifically, how to map out the high-level and conceptual design for subsequent implementation. Before we can get to the nitty-gritty of how we will accomplish a given design, we need to first answer the questions of why one design is optimal over another. This, as you might imagine, is unique to the business within which the solution will live.

These chapters begin a learn-by-doing approach that will continue throughout the rest of the book. Beginning with scope and requirements, we unpack how to evaluate the boundaries of our design scope: what needs are to be met, for what areas of the business, and under what constraints. After establishing these key factors that serve as raw materials to ensure business needs are met, we then put together a "toolbox" of the techniques that we will employ as we build the design, marshaling the resources that will help get us there. With those tools in hand, we create, document, and validate the approach that will get us there.

This section comprises the following chapters:

3

Building an Architecture – Scope and Requirements

In the previous chapter, we went through how to establish the *laws of the universe*, which set the context for our architectural design work. Specifically, we examined the nuances of the organization that have the potential to guide or constrain our designs or their subsequent execution. This includes the organization's risk tolerances, goals, compliance requirements, context, business, and anything else that may play a role in the overall approach.

All these things are important to establish context and provide us with a framework to work within. However, on their own, they are not the entirety of what you need to know to plan and field a design. More is required to do that – in particular, gathering and putting together everything you need to know to lay out a full set of requirements systematically. This chapter is all about establishing those important boundaries: what our scope will be, how we can go about establishing that scope, and gathering the other information that we need to move forward.

In this chapter, we'll look at the following topics:

- Understanding scope
- Setting architectural scope
- Scope – enterprise security
- Scope – application security
- The process for setting scope

Understanding scope

"I think it's important to get your scope at the right level of detail and, if possible, avoid scope creep as scope creep is the enemy of project management. Focus then at the beginning on developing the scope, validating the scope, and making sure everyone agrees to the scope. From there, you can get to a point where you can say the scope is frozen for a period of time while you execute. It's a people skill involved with getting a scope that everyone can agree on and work to."

– John Sherwood, Chief Architect, thought leader, and co-Founder of The SABSA Institute

If it sounds strange that we still need more data even to begin the process of design, consider an analogy to a physical building. A structural engineer might tell us that the tensile strength of a high-performance carbon steel beam is 550-670 N/mm² (see *Takumi Ishii et. al, Overview and Application of Steel Materials for High-Rise Buildings, JFE Technical Report No. 14*). A physicist might tell us that the gravitational attraction of the Earth is 9.81 m/s². These are, without a doubt, important pieces of information for folks to know when it comes to building a skyscraper. But those facts alone are insufficient information to design – and subsequently engineer – a building. Why? Because they don't consider what the building is *for*. Is it an art museum, a college, a shopping mall, or an apartment block? Is it residential or commercial? Who will use it, why, and for what?

The purpose of the structure matters as the result will vary significantly depending on what function it will perform and how (where) it will be used. An offshore drilling platform, for example, will have significantly different characteristics when it comes to design and construction than a library; an Antarctic research facility will differ significantly in structure and features from your neighbor's house.

These factors all speak to the *fitness for purpose* of a given design. These, in turn, represent requirements for the building's construction. These are more than just niceties: they matter substantially to the final outcome. For example, determining the location of a building informs the terrain upon which construction will occur; this, in turn, dictates the substrate upon which the building will stand, which influences structural engineering. The usage (how it will be used and why it exists in the first place) of the building influences what features it must have to achieve its goal and be useful.

Failure to account for the usage and purpose will lead to designs that are either unusable or sub-optimal. As we discussed in a previous example, a fifty-floor residential building without an elevator is unlikely to have many residents who choose to live there (at least once you go up a few floors). In the context of security design, requirements analogous to these become particularly important. This is because the security requirements underpin the security model of the system.

Security requirements don't exist independently as *end states* in and of themselves. In other words, they need to exist within a context to make sense; that is, they logically follow from what is being defended – and against what. Just like the thought experiment we posed earlier about hiring security guards to prevent access to an empty room, security measures don't make sense in the absence of a threat. And just as there's no reason to employ protection measures when there's nothing to protect, cybersecurity controls aren't needed for situations where there are no threats to defend against.

This implies that it is necessary to harvest security requirements before any design work can begin, and that they need to be understood in the broader context of what is being defended and against what threats. Said another way, how the result can be *misused* drives the security requirements just as much as how the system will be used.

Those familiar with software development methods stemming from Ivar Jacobson's work, *Ivar Jacobson, Christerson Magnus, Jonsson Patrik, Övergaard Gunnaron, Object-Oriented Software Engineering – A Use Case Driven Approach, Addison-Wesley*, regarding modeling application behavior (for example, UML, RUP, Cockburn, and so on) are probably familiar with the method of mapping *use cases* for application design. For those familiar with this approach, we might say that every security measure corresponds to a *misuse case* or *abuse case*: an inversion of the typical use case – which describes a business or functional requirement in terms of what the end user wishes to accomplish – into some manner in which the application, system, or environment might be misused (by an attacker, by accident, or by circumstance).

The ultimate point of this chapter is to build on the context that we've already established to set the initial scope within which our requirements will be germane. **Scope** is one of the practical realities that governs any design work. For example, consider a large, modular system designed to run (for example) a funds transfer or order entry (stock trading) application. Such a system might leverage components in multiple environments: some components (for example, interface points with backend mainframe systems and legacy apps) running out of an on-premises data center, others (such as those responsible for the frontend UI) running via **Infrastructure-as-a-Service** (**IaaS**) in the cloud, and specialized components built with **Platform-as-a-Service** (**PaaS**) or serverless.

In a complex system like this, it is almost certain that no single architect will be responsible for every component, environment, system, application, and user within it. Likewise, there are different layers: there is the application itself, the software layer upon which it is built (for example, middleware or supporting components such as Docker), the network, and so on. Once any system gets to a certain size, it is no longer feasible for one person to keep all of the implementation details in their head at one time, or to construct a full design in isolation.

This means that any designs we produce, requirements we gather, or work we perform are bounded to some degree by a set, delineated scope. For example, consider the previous example of the funds transfer system. It is almost certainly the case that the physical controls safeguarding the machines hosting that application are important in a situation like this one. After all, there's a reason that law #3 in Microsoft's Immutable Laws of Security is *If a bad guy has unrestricted physical access to your computer, it's not your computer anymore* (see *Ten Immutable Laws of Security (version 2.0)*, retrieved from https://docs.microsoft.com/en-us/archive/blogs/rhalbheer/ten-immutable-laws-of-security-version-2-0).

This means we'd want physical access to machines running portions of the application being controlled, we'd want buildings containing the data centers to employ measures (for example, concrete pylons) to prevent forced vehicular entry, and we'd want to employ appropriate temperature control, fire suppression, track, and record maintenance actions, as well as any other physical-specific security measures.

If we are hosting that application ourselves, we would expect our own data center to implement these measures; if we are using an external provider, we'd want the service provider to do so.

As a practical reality, though, despite how much we might need and want these controls to be in place, it would probably be the case that there would be some portion of those underlying controls that we can't easily modify. For example, the day-to-day operation of that facility is probably already defined with procedures in place, the structure has been built, fire suppression and climate controls are in place, guards have been hired, and so forth.

So, as a practical matter, if we are creating a security architecture for the funds-transfer application that resides in that environment, we might set the scope selectively to presuppose the existing context (that is, the security controls and procedures already employed by the application). It's not that we don't have to care about the underlying physical controls, environmental security design, physical access procedures, and so on. Instead, we are choosing to remove those elements from the scope to allow us to focus better on what we can control.

There are a few advantages to doing this. First, by giving ourselves the freedom to focus on a subset of the broader problem, we make that problem domain more manageable. In a similar way to how the OSI or TCP/IP network stacks allow us to focus on a portion of what is, in total, an astronomically complex feat of engineering (getting data from point A to point B), so too can we derive efficiencies from how we set our scope. Second, being able to systematically and purposefully set scope allows us to delegate, share, or otherwise collaborate on portions of the design.

Additionally, there are situations where we cannot effect change. The reasons why could be many: budgetary challenges, legacy infrastructure, limited available personnel, missing skills, or any number of reasons why an architect may conclude that making changes to a given area would be problematic (at best) or impracticable (at worst). In this case, much like the preceding example, we might choose to remove these areas purposefully and explicitly from the scope. Even though these areas we remove from scope might potentially represent a source of risk to the organization, limiting the scope removes them from consideration within the context of a specific design to allow us to limit focus based on need, the ability to achieve change, organizational boundaries, or for a myriad of other purposes.

The point is that setting appropriate scope is both a necessary and powerful part of security architecture and design.

What's in this chapter?

Throughout this chapter, we outline an abstract process and method for setting the initial scope. We're adding the *initial* qualifier here because, as you'll see, the process of setting scope is iterative. This means that the scope may change to a greater or lesser degree during the design process itself. However, defining an initial scope right from the beginning provides a bedrock upon which to subsequently establish initial baseline requirements.

In this chapter, we will start with this initial scope as a prerequisite to establishing the discrete security requirements that will become input into the design process. This chapter is organized into three sections:

- Understanding scope

- Scope – enterprise

- Scope – applications

We will look at *enterprise* security architecture and *application* security architecture separately in determining the initial scope. It's helpful to treat each one separately because, as we discussed in prior chapters, the underlying tools, techniques, and methodologies for each are a little different. This means that you will, in all likelihood, examine very different criteria in setting the initial scope for a network than you would for a new application.

This impacts scope because it can impact the specifics of what you will look at to determine that scope – both initially and throughout the full design. Once you get a bit of familiarity under your belt, you will find that you can (and will) liberally *borrow* tools and techniques from one approach to apply to the other, but when you're first starting, it is helpful to approach each one separately given this differentiation.

It's useful to point out that we're not referring to process considerations here. At the end of the day, the overarching abstract *process* you follow to set scope is the same (or, at least, very similar) – but we felt it would help to explain the detailed *mechanics* separately. Granted, this is a somewhat artificial delineation; however, we are doing so as we believe it will aid in clarity and understanding.

Setting architectural scope

> *"Be careful with setting scope. If you iterate too much on the scope of what you're trying to secure early on, you may never achieve the first milestone. However, the process and the model by which you create your architecture should absolutely be iterative and the scope will absolutely change. The architectural approaches and models we use need to be able to support these iterative approaches, but very few of the large, monolithic standards will do this 'out of the box.' This is where there is room for the individual architect to exercise their creativity and innovate, adapting their processes to fit their needs best."*
>
> *– Steve Orrin, Federal CTO at Intel Corporation*

Note that right from the get-go, the outcome of this chapter is not about creating documentation. Documentation is an important part of the process and, eventually, we will fully document the scope – both with specificity and in quite a bit of detail. However, we won't be doing so at this point.

There is a solid, practical reason for waiting to do this. Specifically, we expect the scope to remain somewhat *fluid* until requirements are fully gathered – that is, until we've understood from our stakeholders exactly what is expected from us. We will iterate on our scope over time as we learn more and, ultimately, we will use scope setting as a tool as part of the design process itself.

However, we did want to be clear that we are adapting the architecture process in doing this. For example, **The Open Group Architecture Framework** (**TOGAF**) defines a generic method for an architectural design that they refer to as the **Architecture Development Method** (**ADM**). We will draw upon the ADM heavily in this book, but those familiar with the ADM will probably recognize that scope isn't implicitly iterative in that standard. Scope-setting is an important part of the ADM, is systematically addressed during the *Preliminary* phase (see `https://pubs.opengroup.org/architecture/togaf9-doc/arch/index.html`), is an important prerequisite to subsequent architectural planning, and is included in architectural deliverables. However, there's no required *interim* or working scope in the ADM.

The 14th Dalai Lama once famously said, "*Know the rules well, so you can break them effectively.*" Similarly, Pablo Picasso is alleged to have said, "*Learn the rules like a pro, so you can break them like an artist.*" The point of both is that knowingly undertaking a task out of step or according to your own design – breaking the rules, if you will – can be acceptable (even advantageous) to the following extent:

- You are aware that you are doing so
- You have a clear plan and understanding of why you're doing so
- You understand the potential consequences

We are doing this in the way we are because an informal, working scope saves time. It's similar to having a *working title* for a movie or book. While the actual name upon release might vary to a greater or lesser degree from the working title (subject to market research or audience feedback), the *working title* helps ensure everyone is on the same page during creation, helps participants new to the creative process understand what the work is about, and gives everyone involved an easy way to refer to it. Movies such as *Field of Dreams* (working title: *Shoeless Joe*), *Friday the 13th* (working title: *A Long Night at Camp Blood*), and *Alien* (working title: *Star Beast*) all had working titles that encapsulate something about the essence of the project that helps those working on it maintain focus and stay grounded in what the movie is intended to be. A working scope behaves similarly in that it helps those working on the project stay focused on the intended result.

Now that you've been forewarned, we will be looking at initial scope-setting for two different types of architecture design projects:

- Enterprise (network and system) architectures
- Application architectures

We'll explain what we mean by each in this section and go through the *why* first – the reason and value behind each type of scope and its importance – and then, once the rationale is clear, walk through how to arrive at an initial "working" scope that we can use as a foundation for subsequent steps. This will allow us to proceed directly into requirements gathering.

Enterprise security architecture

The first area we will focus on is what we're calling enterprise security architecture. We're using it in the same sense that **Open Enterprise Security Architecture (O-ESA)** and **Sherwood Applied Business Security Architecture (SABSA)** mean it. In TOGAF parlance, we might say that it is the subset of Enterprise Architecture that applies to security. Specifically, we're referring to the selection of controls, countermeasures, operational constraints, and other security-relevant decisions for either the enterprise itself or a subset of it. The focus is on the administrative, procedural, and technical controls that go into securing that portion of the enterprise that we have targeted for design.

To illustrate this by example, say that your organization is considering opening a new branch office. From a security standpoint, there are several relevant decisions that you will need to make to ensure that what you set up meets the requirements that the organization has for meeting its security goals. This might include the planning and layout of the physical space, the network design (to optimize performance and maximize resiliency), the security of the work environment that employees in that location will occupy, the configuration of the workstations they will use, and the services (that is, applications) they will use in performing their jobs.

All of these goals and decisions are important. And, as with anything, these decisions can be approached in either a systematic and workmanlike way or in a slapdash, disorganized way. The systematic and workmanlike way in which we select, apply, operationalize, and subsequently track and monitor these decisions is the domain of the enterprise security architect.

Application security architecture

The second area we'll explore is a little different. When developing an enterprise security architecture, it is not generally assumed that you can directly change the software that employees use to meet business objectives. By contrast, when developing a new application, you can (and will) make changes at the application layer to achieve objectives – both broader business objectives as well as security ones. Arguably, *most* of the changes you will make will occur at this level. Conversely, though you can make changes to the application, you may not be able to directly modify the substrate (that is, the technology stack) on which the application runs.

So, instead of focusing on a portion of the environment, we're focusing on the architecture of the application itself. This is different than the preceding exercise in at least two ways. First, there is the question of exposure. Most of the time, applications will have some *surface area* exposed to arguably hostile conditions. For example, an internet-facing web application not only has a population of individuals who are authorized and credentialed to use the application, but it also has to account for everybody else with a **Transmission Control Protocol (TCP)** stack who might choose to come knocking on the application's door. We can change the application logic to suit security goals and limit that exposure: an option not always available if we're not working directly with the application code itself.

Lastly and most importantly (the real *crux* of the difference), though, is the fact that the application can span multiple environments. Because applications are modular (and likely to become more so in the future), different parts of the application can be run out of different environments. This is true logically, physically, administratively, and geographically.

For example, consider an application with three different components: one is hosted in the cloud with a US-based cloud provider, one is hosted in an on-premises data center in Germany, and another is delivered to end users as an application container that might be run from anywhere in the world. In this case, different laws govern each component, different procedures are involved in supporting the infrastructure required to run them, different technologies are used to support them, there are different technical security measures for each, and so on.

This means that, in a large part, the onus is on the application itself to enforce the security mandates and requirements that the developer of the application sees as important. The application design itself needs to account for this and, to the extent practical, incorporate all these different environments into the overall security design.

This is more complicated than it sounds because application modules can't always be cognizant of where and how they will each be run. A component could be hosted on-premises today and be moved to the cloud tomorrow; it could be on a dedicated host today and in a Docker container tomorrow. Therefore, as a matter of good design, it is helpful to ensure that either the security of the application continues to be functional despite a change in where/how it is run or, if that is not possible, to document and advertise the prerequisites for secure operation.

Defining scope boundaries

It is tempting to view scope definition as a fixed activity that occurs at the beginning of a project and that remains constant throughout the design, execution, and operationalization of an architecture. In an ideal world, this would be true. However, in practice, this is often not the case because scope can change as a result of several factors: organizational changes, design decisions made, and even deliberately as a tool by the architecture team or individual architect.

Therefore, scope – much like the design itself – is often iterative; it can change mid-stream. Again, this is particularly true with smaller, more fluid projects. The architect needs to be able to react to these changes in scope either by growing or shrinking the scope of their design work in response to changes. At any point in the design process, you will need to be willing to question your assumptions about scope. You can amend, update, modify, or otherwise make changes to the scope, so long as you ensure that potential changes or updates are socialized, that documentation is adjusted accordingly, and so on.

One way to envision the iterative nature of scope setting and the process of reacting to scope changes is illustrated here. Note that both waterfall and more iterative processes such as DevOps have scope refinements that are made throughout. *Figure 3.1* illustrates how scope impacts a linear process such as waterfall:

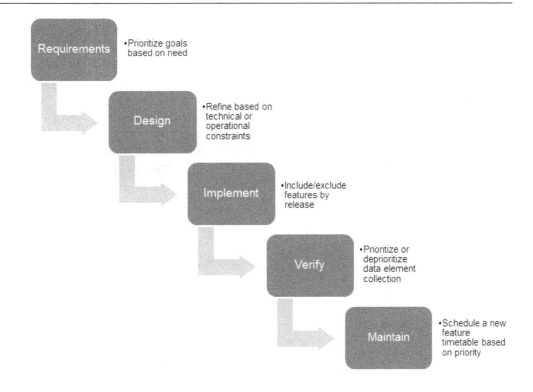

Figure 3.1 – Scope impacts on a linear process (for example, waterfall)

Likewise, *Figure 3.2* illustrates how scope can have ongoing and iterative impacts throughout a continuous or iterative process:

Figure 3.2 – Scope impacts on an iterative/ongoing design process (for example, DevOps)

As you can see, scope is refined and honed throughout the design process. Scope is itself a tool in the designer's toolbox. You can selectively "scope out" certain portions of security enforcement and instead choose to selectively "delegate" a subset of the security requirements to another designer, other teams, existing security measures, and so on. This means that the security requirement stays in place, but the scope of the execution changes selectively based on available time, resources, expertise, existing investments, or any other potentially relevant factor. Removing something from scope doesn't mean that you don't have to account for it or address a concern – instead, it just means that you are choosing not to address those elements as part of the current design context in which you are operating. They might be addressed at a later time by someone else (a different architect or team), or you may be planning around existing measures that you can't change.

Again, for our purposes in this section, what we are most interested in is establishing the baseline, initial scope that we will use as input to gather requirements. Note that, by doing this, we will often be wrong in our initial assumptions. That is fine to the extent that we ultimately drive toward something accurate that we can document, socialize, and get buy-in for. Therefore, we don't have to be 100% accurate at this stage, but rather we must have something that we can analyze, share, and vet as we lay out resources and requirements for our subsequent work.

Critical architectural risks and empty scope

As we pointed out previously, alterations to scope can be useful in situations where what the architect can change is limited or constrained. We used the example of physical security for an existing data center not managed by your organization (for example, a colocation facility or hosting provider). It's useful to note here that there can be situations where what the architect can change is so constrained that the scope of their architecture work is reduced to effectively zero (that is, the null set).

In such a case, the architect faces such an uphill battle that carving out a scope where they can effect change is nearly impossible or impracticable. Likewise, there are situations where the risks involved in arriving at a successful outcome are so high that there is little realistic probability of success for an architectural design. In such cases, the organization may be better off using resources in other ways rather than the currently envisioned security architecture exercise.

Don't interpret this the wrong way: we're not arguing that situations like these mean the organization should abandon security work generally – or security architecture specifically. Quite to the contrary, this is where it is needed most. However, to arrive at a successful outcome, the architect will first need the organization to clear whatever hurdles are standing in their way that prevent them from doing the requisite work.

One of the reasons why we suggest that you start by creating an initial working scope is precisely because it helps you identify these situations in advance – in other words, you can recognize situations where there are *bigger fish to fry* or where the scope of what the architect can change is minimal. When you encounter situations like this, you need to resolve the constraint or challenging situation first before you can proceed through the rest of the scope setting and into requirements.

This situation does not happen frequently, but you should be prepared so that when it does, you can recognize what is happening and work with executives and stakeholders to clear the path first so that your design work will be both productive and useful.

Now that we have an idea of what scope is, what it does, and how we can use it, let's look at how we might approach it through an enterprise security lens.

Scope – enterprise security

"Let's consider the role of an architect through the example of building construction. The role of the architect in the life cycle of designing and building a new structure is to first listen to what the person commissioning him or her wants, and then using their skill and experience to put together a proposal that encompasses best practice, the art of the possible, and their own vision. Security architects do the same – they establish the requirements and create something that combines best practice and the art of the possible with their own vision."

– Andy Clark, Founding Director, Primary Key Associates Ltd, visiting Professor RHUL, trustee of The National Museum of Computing, SABSA Coauthor

With the understanding of scope clearly in mind, let's look in detail at initial scope-setting through the lens of an enterprise security architecture project and an application security architecture project. We'll look at the differences, similarities, generalized process, and prerequisites for moving on to the next phase of design.

Let's begin by looking from an enterprise security point of view. Recall that by this, we mean the process of setting up the security measures that will defend a particular area of the business from attack and that will optimize that portion of the enterprise for resiliency. Most of the time, our main focus will remain on some aspect of the technological ecosystem: the network, employee usage of computing devices, enterprise mobility, or some other aspect of securing the environment that intersects with the technology that a given business uses to satisfy its objectives.

Ultimately, what we're looking to establish are the borders around which our design planning will take place so that we can use this information to know from where to derive our initial requirements set. There are many useful reasons to do this. One is the availability and capacity of architecture personnel to do the work. Some models, such as TOGAF, presuppose a team of architects at the outset of the architecture process. In practice, though, for a smaller design effort (that is, not the entire enterprise but only a subset of it), it can be challenging to allocate personnel until we have a rough idea of the scope of what we're looking to design an architecture for. For example, creating a security architecture for a handful of machines in an IaaS cloud environment probably doesn't require a team of 40 people to accomplish this; in fact, having that many *chefs in the kitchen* could over-complicate the process and result in wasted time and energy.

Another possible reason to limit the scope is due to organizational boundaries. Many organizations have business units that are decentralized enough to have their own IT personnel, their own technology portfolio, their own suite of business applications, and so on. In this case, an organization might choose for each business unit to complete its own security design for its own business unit without interfering with the operational design or strategy of others. Other logistical reasons such as budget timeline, legal or regulatory jurisdiction, type of data to be stored/processed/transmitted, or any other factor can help set this initial scope.

There are countless factors to consider in determining the *final* scope, but for initial scope-setting, we'll look at the three that are the most germane to establishing something to work with and iterate upon:

- Existing capability
- Risk management
- Strategic planning

The subsections that follow outline what we mean by each of these and why they are important.

Existing capability

The first thing that you'll want to consider as you set the initial scope is the existing capability of the organization, particularly the maturity of the technical environment and supporting elements.

Recall that, earlier, we discussed the differences between environments that have evolved *organically* over time versus those that have been systematically planned out. Where your organization falls on this spectrum can be very useful in the initial scope setting. Why? Because the presence or absence of documentation governing the planning will directly impact the setting of the scope. An environment that has been planned will likely have documentation (either using a formal, standardized template or using a "homegrown" format) that outlines what the plan was and how it was implemented, and that provides the rationale and justification for the design. An *organic* environment may have minimal or non-existent documentation about this.

If it exists, this documentation can prove to be a singularly important reference point and a handy way to determine the initial scope. This is true in one of a few ways. If you are layering a security design on an Enterprise Architecture that has been defined while following a formal design methodology (for example, TOGAF or SABSA), you will likely be working within a scope that is already documented and formalized. If you are doing so, it is worth familiarizing yourself with the specific framework that was used to create that documentation.

For example, in a TOGAF or SABSA context, you might refer to The Open Group Guide, *Integrating Risk and Security within a TOGAF Enterprise Architecture*, a joint publication between The Open Group and The SABSA Institute. In particular, *section 5.1* walks through preliminary phase activities (including scope) using an ADM-aligned approach in detail. Given that the organization has invested in a formalized architecture approach already, ensuring that your scope is in alignment with theirs is valuable; following the same process and producing compatible deliverables will better equip you to get buy-in and gain acceptance.

Even if you are not directly overlaying security onto an existing Enterprise Architecture but are instead working within an organization that has defined and formalized scope-setting for another area of the organization, there is value in this. First, you can use the defined and documented scope for other areas as a template and guide for your scope definition. Second, you can ensure that your scope does not overlap with these other areas (unless, of course, it is within the specific remit of your work to do so).

If your organization does not have any of these documents, your work will arguably be somewhat harder since everything from what is included/excluded from the scope, as well as the format and contents of any documentation you produce will be up to you.

Risk management

> "Security architecture is both a function and a means to accomplish effective risk management, and in particular operational risk management. By understanding the organization – why it exists, what it is trying to accomplish, how it is going to go about it, and what its plans for achieving its targets are – you can then understand the business enough to know what the risks are in your sphere of influence that relate to achieving those objectives. However, you need to connect the dots – and you need to connect them based on a thorough understanding of the business. You use the understanding of the business and engagement with business stakeholders and guide the process."
>
> – Andrew S. Townley, Chief Executive Officer at Archistry Incorporated

The second thing that you'll want to consider is the presence or absence of risk management activities already performed by the organization. Formalized risk management activities can help dramatically in setting scope. For example, an organization that has pursued *ISO/IEC 27001* certification will have documentation already in place that outlines the scope of applicability of the **information security management system (ISMS)** – what we might informally call the **security program** (see *International Organization for Standardization, ISO/IEC 27001:2013: Information technology – Security techniques – Information security management systems – Requirements, Section 4.3, Determining the scope of the information security management system*). This is a formal document, required by the standard, that exists to delineate *"…the boundaries and applicability of the information security management system to establish its scope."*

Most formalized risk management approaches – such as those outlined in **ISO 31000**, the NIST **Risk Management Framework (RMF)**, OCTAVE, and so on – will include a definition and documentation of applicable scope (either explicit or implied). For the same reasons outlined previously, this can greatly streamline the initial scope-setting for the architect. In situations where we are working directly within an environment covered by prior work along these lines, it can be helpful to incorporate – either directly or by reference – the existing scope. Even if the environment we're working in does not directly overlap with it, the presence of existing documentation can help us because it marks the *edges of the map* and can give us a clue about how to document what we come up with.

Ultimately, it is easier when we have an existing formalized architecture already in place to use as a reference because we can directly harmonize our design artifacts with those extant in the organization for other purposes compared to existing risk management *scaffolding*, as outlined previously. Both can help inform the scope, but the former is directly analogous, whereas the second is conceptually similar and can help guide. However, the documentation itself is less likely to lend itself to direct incorporation.

Strategic planning

The last area that we will look at is strategic planning that may already exist. By this, we mean business and/or technology planning that may be going on in parallel – or in the background – to the design work that we are undertaking. This may be a little harder to directly incorporate than the previous two we looked at. However, it is important for establishing scope.

The reason why this is the case is twofold. First, it helps us know what portions of the landscape are in flux and which are likely to remain more static during the execution of our design processes. This is more important than it sounds. Not only may it come in handy later (since it's always possible for us to opportunistically *piggyback* design initiatives or security measures on top of changes being made in other places in the environment), but we might choose to consciously and purposefully target scope in light of upcoming changes. For example, it might not make sense for us to design a complete, fully vetted, and long-term plan for a portion of the environment that's going away in 6 months.

The second reason why it is valuable is that it can inform us as to technical boundaries, constraints, or other factors that might exist within the organization that we might not know about otherwise. In subsequent steps (that is, once we get beyond the initial scope-setting), this information can be important to know about for other reasons as it can impact the design, but at this stage, it's useful primarily as a data source to inform the initial scope.

Case study – enterprise scoping

> *"I think scope (and scope creep) is a very important topic for architects. Because architects have such a broad mandate, a pitfall they run into can be trying to solve everything in one go. The temptation is to try to plan years and years in advance and in a very broad way. One of my favorite quotes from Steve Jobs on this though is, 'real artists ship.' I think staying focused on what you can actually ship (deliver) is very important for architects. What can you actually deliver in a productive way given the resources available? Constraint number one then is embracing and staying focused on what your organization can actually deliver and building your designs around that."*

> *– Gunnar Peterson, CISO at Forter*

In an interview, Gunnar described the very real temptation (and potential pitfall) of failing to control scope. He described to us a scenario that happened to him where scope became an issue – specifically, where he went very deep into the technology associated with a design he was working on and, as a result, found that scope was so great as to potentially undermine the feasibility of the design.

He relayed the story to us as follows: *"One of my favorite memories was from teaching a web services security class many years back. This was at one of the earliest OWASP AppSec conferences in New York; it was a full-day lesson where we went through a long list of web services security controls (i.e., which controls to deploy and where) as part of a threat modeling exercise."*

He explained that the timing coincided with a period before **REpresentational State Transfer REST** (that is, web service APIs) was used ubiquitously and where WS-Security and related standards were still in active use in web services architectures. He explained, *"This was back in the WS* days. These were web service specifications originally designed by Microsoft, IBM, and a number of other smart folks to act as a sort of 'checkbox for security.' However, there were a number of different profiles that you could use to deliver security (e.g., WS-Policy, WS-SecurityPolicy, WS-Trust, WS-Federation, WS-SecureConversation, etc.). There were so many that it made you question if the mission of a 'checkbox for security' had really been met."*

> **REST**
>
> For those who are unfamiliar, REST is an approach to application design for creating *web services*. REST was initially defined formally by Roy Fielding in *Architectural Styles and the Design of Network-Based Software Architectures (PhD Dissertation), Chapter 5 – Representational State Transfer (REST), University of California, Irvine*, as an "*...architectural style for distributed hypermedia systems... derived from several of the network-based architectural styles... combined with additional constraints that define a uniform connector interface.*"

"At the end of the class, we did a case study and a supporting threat model for it. We whiteboarded it for about 2 hours, painstakingly distilled the threats we found, took each of the threats, and baked them into the security model, including the WS* standards. At the end, we said, 'Here are all the things you'd need to do for security referencing all of the complex standards and where they fit in the security model.' A person in that class – someone who's gone on to do some very incredible things – said, 'This will never work.' And he was right."

His point was that the scope had become so large and the design so complicated that it was effectively untenable to build and maintain. *"He said that the design was too complicated, that building it (let alone maintaining it) was infeasible, and that the complexity impacted people's ability to actually ship and deliver code. If you go back to the history of WS* and SOAP vs. REST, you will see that REST won by keeping things simpler than others. I myself was seduced by the long list of security standards in WS*. It frankly did deliver what they wanted, but the complexity was so high that it made it harder."*

What's the lesson in this? That scope matters, that it's advantageous to keep things at a size where you can manage them, and that resisting the call to add more to the design can be very helpful when setting the scope of what you intend to build.

Now that we've looked at enterprise scope, let's look at how we might scope within the context of an application security endeavor.

Scope – application security

> "In the requirements phase, you need to ask both what security controls are needed, but also ask what shouldn't happen (account for those things as you find them). During design, threat modeling lets you ensure you understand what could go wrong so that you can design those considerations in. During implementation, incorporate security into IDE, modular code reviews, check-ins, etc. instead of waiting to reach the testing phase for a security-focused discussion to happen. During testing, evolve the security testing program to move from regular intervals to an irregular (unpredictable) or – better yet – continuous manner. Lastly, as you maintain, change the metrics from primarily KPI-driven (for example, the number of critical vulns in production systems) to KRI-driven (e.g. – the number of critical vulns out of SLA in the production env)."
>
> – Phoram Mehta, Director & Head of Infosec APAC, PayPal

Just as we will need to establish the initial scope for an enterprise security architecture, so too is it valuable to do so in designing security architecture for applications. The inputs to this are analogous to those that we would collect for an enterprise security architecture design initiative (conceptually, they fill a similar role), but they target a given application (or group of applications) rather than the broader enterprise.

Specifically, sources of data that we can look at for the application landscape are as follows:

- Development and release processes
- Components, services, and design patterns
- Team/organizational boundaries
- Technology considerations

Let's walk through each to explain what we mean and why/how they can be useful.

The development and release process

The first area that we'll look to for assistance in determining the scope of an application security architecture design effort is the type of development and release process in use for the application or applications in scope. This is analogous to looking at the presence or absence of a mature enterprise design (or, in fact, existing enterprise security designs, if available) when looking at a portion of the enterprise itself.

Most technology professionals – especially those involved in or tangential to software development processes – know that there have been some recent shifts in the way that software development occurs in most organizations. While not explicitly time-bound, we can look at development methodologies along a timeline from their date of inception and extrapolate their rise in popularity and normative use post-inception:

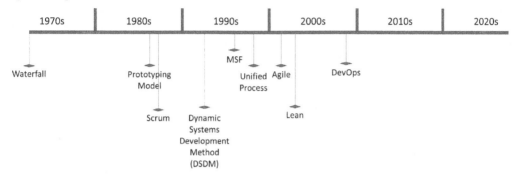

Figure 3.3 – Development model timeline

Any timeline like this one is a vast oversimplification. There are still, for example, many projects that continue to use waterfall development processes. Likewise, there have been iterative, incremental development processes that existed before the formalization of these techniques in Lean, Agile, or the Unified Process. However, looking at the development across a timeline like this one can help us understand the variety of different methodologies in use and their rise and fall in popularity over time.

In the 1970s and 1980s, development often occurred according to a *waterfall* methodology. This model, based on work by Winston Royce, *Managing the Development of Large Software Systems, Proceedings of IEEE WESCON*, described clearly-delineated development phases completed in sequence. These phases are requirements, analysis, design, coding, testing, and operations. Over time, adaptations arose introducing alternative phases as organizations adapted the methodology to their unique needs. One advantage of this approach was the inclusion of "gates" between each phase, allowing specific objectives to be achieved.

In the 1990s, iterative processes such as the Unified Process (based on work from Ivar Jacobson, Grady Brooch, and James Rumbaugh) rose to prominence (*Ivar Jacobson et al, The Unified Software Development Process, Addison-Wesley*). In this model, phases are iterative, proceeding from inception to elaboration to construction, and ending with transition (that is, release into production).

More recently, methodologies such as Agile and Lean have emerged that emphasize the **iterative and incremental** nature of development, allowing developers to refine their solutions flexibly over time and react to changes in requirements or business needs. In today's world, we see the emergence of DevOps approaches that emphasize **continuous delivery**, where many of the incremental processes between development and release into production are fully automated.

From a scope definition standpoint, it matters which model is being employed in the development of the application that you are chartered with creating a security design for. There are several practical reasons why this is the case. First, the type and volume of the documentation produced can vary depending on the model. Each of the various methods has its own set of documentation to describe the purpose and function of the application being developed. A waterfall project, for example, might have a specification document that describes the requisite function points the application will provide – a project developed using the Unified Process might be more likely to employ **Unified Modeling Language** (**UML**) documents such as sequence diagrams or object interaction diagrams. Since much of the initial scope we set will derive from the application scope itself, this means that the relevant documentation that will inform us is likewise likely to be bound to the model in use.

It is also helpful to know how much room for iteration is allowed in our scope – it can be difficult to make changes to the design scope when a development methodology is being employed that is less iterative. This, in turn, informs the desired accuracy of our initial scope. For example, consider a waterfall project. If we are going to set the scope of our application security architecture for a waterfall project, it can be challenging for us to alter it mid-stream. Therefore, it might be better to spend more time upfront in setting our initial scope rather than relying on us being able to adjust that scope downstream.

Components, services, and design patterns

In addition to the model in use, it is also helpful to look at how *modular* existing applications are (or new applications are envisioned to be) in setting the initial scope.

Modularity is advantageous from a developer's point of view as it fosters the rapid development and onboarding of new services with fewer requirements to update, modify, re-release, or otherwise adapt existing components. In short, it can streamline development and increase time-to-market, while also potentially reducing the impact of updates to any individual component.

As you might imagine given recent trends of increasingly iterative, adaptive, and *continuous* development, modularity is heavily favored in modern application design. In particular, REST and other *microservice* building blocks lend themselves heavily to modularity. Likewise, tools and techniques that foster the microservice paradigm (for example, application containers, container orchestration, service mesh, and more) directly support and enable this level of modularity, with REST being the central lynchpin.

In practice, this typically refers to web services: stateless components that use the web (either HTTPS or, in some rarer cases nowadays, unsecured HTTP) as a form of transport for input and output. In this context, by stateless, we mean that they do not maintain an ongoing session with any particular client without some additional, application-layer state-maintenance method (for example, an identifying token, cookie, or another marker to link together requests).

REST is foundational to modularization in modern application design. Nowadays, microservice architecture is the most common development approach; this refers to a software architecture whereby functionality and business logic are broken down into minute, discrete components, with each of those components being fielded independently. Because there's a uniform transport (HTTP/S) and the components themselves are stateless, new components can be fielded easily, moved/relocated, modified either singly or in parallel, and are highly flexible. This lends adaptability and agility to the development process.

The reason why this matters from a scoping standpoint is the greater modularity there is in the application architecture, the more flexibility we have as the architect in scope-setting. For a large monolithic application, there's very little *wiggle room* in what our application security scope must be. For example, consider a very simple *legacy* application that follows a traditional client/server model, such as the one illustrated here:

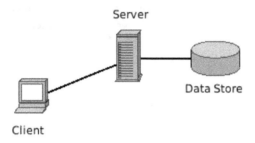

Figure 3.4 – Client/server application

Perhaps, in this application, the client application is a single, client-run executable with both static and dynamic dependencies (*Figure 3.5*):

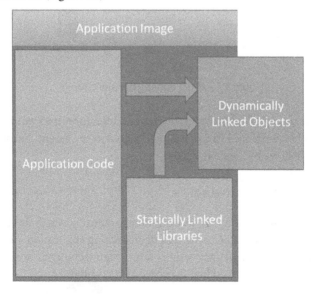

Figure 3.5 – Legacy application "footprint"

In this case, it would be very difficult to *scope out* any individual component: say a static library linked against our client executable. The integration in that case is so *tight* (being, in point of fact, in the same address space as the client executable image) that trying to make an objective case for it being *out of scope* for a security design would be difficult indeed.

As the integration becomes looser – for example, a dynamically linked image (a DLL or shared object, for example), it can become easier to adjust the scope around the boundaries of individual components. Once linkage crosses tiers or cuts across logical components – for example, a database/middleware component in an n-tier architecture application – it can become more practicable to modify scope in such a way as to address only certain components. In the n-tier example illustrated in *Figure 3.6*, for example, we might choose to scope out the database server/data store and focus attention only on UI and application tier components. In the case of a microservice architecture – or any RESTful API or component – it becomes even easier:

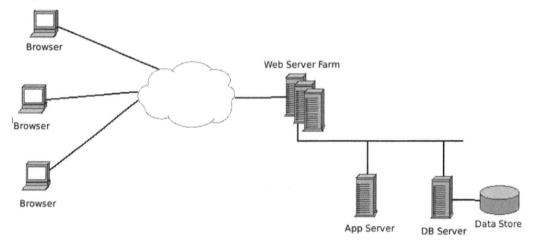

Figure 3.6 – N-tier application (generic)

Therefore, it is valuable to understand the application architecture that's employed (for existing applications) or that will be employed (for new applications) to the extent that such details can be known at the point at which we become involved.

Team/organizational boundaries

Another factor to consider in setting scope is the operational context in which the application will run. This is particularly useful and applicable in the case of an existing application – that is, in situations where we are overlaying application security architecture design techniques over an existing design, such as to improve the security of the product in subsequent revisions.

As we all know, sometimes, multiple different parties – either individuals, teams, organizations, or even business units – are involved in the development, maintenance, operation, or integration of an application. In some cases, we may have the ability to impact security within one portion of the landscape involved but not everywhere. As an example, consider our hypothetical banking example from earlier in this chapter. We might have different business units responsible for different portions of an existing application. For example, we might have developers from a retail banking (that is, consumer-oriented banking) business unit working on an interface to allow customers to see their existing balances and representatives from a brokerage business unit working on a similar interface for a client to see individual positions within their portfolio.

In this case, while both APIs might very well be part of a broader single application, there are organizational boundaries that might provide a strong rationale for separate application security architectural scope between the two groups. In short, the scope of the application security design is selected to align with existing organizational boundaries.

Technology considerations

Lastly, there may be legacy or other technology reasons why you might choose to introduce a segmentation or scope boundary. In the preceding example, we used the example of two different business units participating in the development of portions of a single application. Just like in that situation, organizational boundaries can dictate how we might draw some of our boundaries; there could be technological reasons why that occurs as well.

This is particularly easy to see when viewed through the lens of legacy technologies. As an example, consider once again a hypothetical funds-transfer system. Perhaps this system was designed to follow a structure like that illustrated in the following diagram:

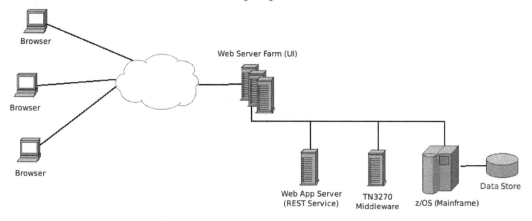

Figure 3.7 – Funds transfer application example (mainframe)

Note that this is a simplified use case; for example, it assumes TCP/IP connectivity to the mainframe. A production deployment might require other components beyond these (for example, a TCP to **Systems Network Architecture (SNA)** protocol translation). Nevertheless, this example is useful as it illustrates a RESTful API allowing funds to be transferred from one account to another, employing middleware to communicate with an application in the legacy backend (that is, 3270 emulation middleware that allows communication with an existing **Customer Information Control System (CICS)** mainframe application). In this case, there are numerous differences between creating the security architecture for the frontend component versus doing so for the mainframe. Here are some examples:

- Operational boundaries that segment the mainframe environment from other technology types

- Organizational boundaries between those responsible for mainframe development and those responsible for development in other environments

- Different mainframe security-specific expertise between teams, including a differing understanding of supporting technologies and tools

Based on this, someone seeking to create a security architecture for the RESTful API might conclude that, based on a combination of these factors, the scope of that design will only cover a subset of the entire application. This means that even though both components are within the same broader application – with both being required to be functional – the scope will be *artificially* constrained down to the level of a given portion alone based on the technology in use. This can be either at a macro or micro level; for example, it could be at the level of *tier*, component, module, or even an individual service. As noted previously, though, this becomes more challenging to do the more tightly integrated the components that comprise the application are.

Case study – application scoping

> *"Mark Twain once said that the difference between the right word and the wrong word is the difference between the lightning bug and the lightning. You don't have to do something big every time: we aspire for the 'lightning' experience – the big impact. What I think every engineer can learn is that we, as security and as architects, can't be in every meeting. We need to figure out which deliverables or tasks to own and which are owned by others. We need everyone to have a common language and a common frame of reference. Because architecture can sometimes move from simplicity toward complexity – toward comprehensiveness and away from comprehensibility. This is a scoping question. Maybe what architects should be asking themselves is 'How little work can I productively do?' Where's the Pareto Principle for this thing that we're building?"*

> *– Adam Shostack, President, Shostack & Associates*

We asked Adam about scope setting in an application security context. He told us about two related (but opposite) situations that each illustrate an issue with scope setting. *"The first happened at a bank. They wanted a threat model that they also wanted to be asset-centric. They're like, 'we're a bank, the money is in the GL (general ledger), and the GL is on that mainframe over there. Let's start our threat model there.' So that's where we started."*

"There were a number of problems with this approach. The mainframe was surrounded by a lot of UNIX servers with read/write access into the mainframe. These servers would manage the complicated business logic, enforce business rules, provide UI support, and many other tasks. They were there to enforce a complex ruleset – but they were an intermediate layer because it was challenging to implement this highly complex business ruleset in the mainframe itself. Surrounding those UNIX devices, there was a fleet of Linux machines doing very similar things, but that were operated by a different division inside the bank."

"So, here you have different devices each owned by different (and siloed) groups. The problem was that nobody was able to accept and review the threat modeling findings as a whole – some of the observations applied to the mainframe, some to developer desktops (since they could SSH into the environment), some applied to the UNIX devices, and still others applied to the Linux devices. The lack of ability to scope made this project effectively undeliverable."

"This is one kind of scoping issue, but let me contrast it with another: making the scope too small. I was doing some work with (at the time) a cryptocurrency startup (they are more established now). They had a very clean architecture with strong controls around a critical server that controlled access to keys. Nobody could SSH into the production devices that owned, stored, and managed those keys. The only way to make something happen (excepting break glass protocol) was via Git (which they used for a variety of tasks). They had me come in to do a threat model on that key storage system."

"The trouble was though that there was a business logic system that controlled this other machine. If I would like to transfer money from wallet A to wallet B, both systems (the key storage machine and the business logic system) were involved. Anything system A tells system B to do, it will do. So, what are we actually threat modeling if only one system (the key storage system) is in scope? In this case, we scoped our analysis too narrowly for exactly the same reason as what made the bank challenging. They had separation of duties in both situations, but both were problematic because, at the bank, you couldn't reasonably track who owned what because of the complexity, while in the second example, the scope was too narrow for it to actually be useful. In both cases, we were unable to redraw the scope down the road. This is why scope is so important."

The process for setting scope

> *"You're going to know some preliminaries about scope when you look at the environment from a data perspective. The data will help give you information about scope, as will your discussions with stakeholders. Data can drive decision-making around scope initially (due to frameworks), but keep in mind that you can expand scope as you go forward with the inclusion of additional data elements, other areas of the organization, or other business processes."*
>
> *– Dr. Richard Perez, vCISO*

So, now that you understand why we are approaching it this way and what factors are driving this (both from an enterprise cybersecurity architecture viewpoint as well as in an application context), the next step is to outline a process or *recipe* that we can follow to make it happen.

Before we get into the details, we should point out that we're in a little bit of a catch-22 situation when it comes to scope. On the one hand, until we can validate with our stakeholders what we intend to accomplish, we are likely to fall short of the mark in what our envisioned scope will be. On the other hand, how can we talk to stakeholders if we don't have even the beginning of a clue of what the borders of our effort will be?

This is the crux of why we've split scope-setting into two phases. The initial scope is a technique that's designed to allow you some room for error as you tee up discussions with stakeholders. Because getting the scope right is so tremendously important to the process, having two passes at it gives you room to be wrong (at least initially) with minimal consequences.

With that in mind, remember that what we're trying to derive at this point doesn't need to be perfect. We must get as close as we reasonably can in our scope where possible, even at these very early phases, but since we will iterate on the scope, we can go into the process with some flexibility, knowing that our output – our initial scope – is almost certain to change as we go through subsequent work. Hopefully, this helps in that it does the following:

- **It lowers the stakes of the work we're undertaking in setting this initial scope**. Since we will often need to get started quickly, having reduced stakes means that we can be more comfortable getting started quickly with the knowledge that we will refine it later.

- **It helps streamline the effort**. Since it doesn't have to be perfect (yet), it's OK if we do it quickly for the first pass.

- **It reduces the documentation barrier**. Since we're not creating documentation (yet), we can place our emphasis on really thinking through the implications of what our scope will be.

With that in mind, the process itself is fairly straightforward. It involves the following steps:

1. Consider high-level goals.
2. Review contextual or other constraints.
3. Set the initial scope.
4. Validate and refine initial scope.

Let's walk through these steps in detail.

Step 1 – consider high-level goals

"One of the issues that I have currently with cybersecurity is the focus people have on buying technology. You go to a trade show and they are filled with vendors trying to sell you on their technology. As practitioners, we get distracted by this. Starting from the solution is the wrong way around: instead, you need to start with the design – with the goals of the system and how it will be used – and, based on those, acquire the tools you need to protect and support it as needed."

– John Tannahill, a Canadian management consultant specializing in information security

It would be unrealistic to assume that you know nothing about what the organization is trying to achieve at these early stages of the architecture process. Specifically, we all know that one of the universal laws of business is that, to marshal resources to work on something, there has to be a point – some goal that the organization is trying to achieve or a problem they are trying to solve. So, by the time architecture personnel are attached to an effort, there will be at least *some* organizational knowledge about what the intent is – what the organization is hoping to accomplish.

So, our first step is to capture as much of that information as we can. At this point, information may be scant, it may be vague or high-level – but there will be at least some understanding (at some level) about what the high-level goal is. If there is documentation already about the goal (for example, a business case, planning document, budget, or other information), read it. Supplement your understanding by *discussing the project with the stakeholders driving it*. This can be business teams, executives, or whoever within the organization is championing the effort. Find out what they want to do, their goals, how they hope to realize the goals, and what *success* looks like for them.

This will give you a high-level perspective on what those stakeholders are hoping to achieve. Depending on the size of the project, this can take more or less time. For a large project, there might be numerous stakeholders and a large volume of documentation. Therefore, you would anticipate that these discussions would take more time than a small project with only one or two internal champions. Take as much time as you need (and that the schedule allows), keeping in mind that you aren't striving for perfect accuracy but instead just a starting point.

When you're at the point where you think you've discussed what you're trying to do with all the stakeholders, that's the cue to look for more stakeholders. Think about all who might be impacted: users, business sponsors, executives, different kinds of users (for example, admins, support personnel), other security team members, internal auditors, corporate counsel, risk managers, compliance teams, impacted business partners or service providers, and so on. Remember that at this point, you haven't committed anything to paper, so it costs you very little to seek out and capture more input.

Step 2 – review contextual or other constraints

Once you have this perspective, the next step is to review any existing constraints, context, boundaries, or other factors that will play a role in placing boundaries around where and what you can design. Take a look at the considerations and other factors that we have outlined here as a starting point, but also think through carefully any that might be unique to you.

If you're doing a design for an application, think through what service boundaries there might be: both those that you know about (for example, in the case that the application will interact with existing components, middleware, services, and so on) but also those that are likely to arise based on the modularity of the application. Think about what technology boundaries and constraints you know about now and what might arise. Think about any organizational, business, reporting, or logical/physical boundaries that might make it impossible (or extremely challenging) for your design work.

If you're working on enterprise scope, think through the business, reporting, structural, and organizational boundaries. Factor in existing information that you know from risk management activities already performed and strategic or business planning that has either been completed or is in flight. Lastly, think through the level of maturity and capability in the existing landscape, factoring that into the overall analysis.

Step 3 – set the initial scope

Once you have put thought into the goals as well as any boundaries that you know about, try to crystalize an initial scope in your head. As we've alluded to several times, the goal here is not about the documentation. However, that doesn't mean you can't use notes. At this stage, I find it helpful to take notes about what areas *must be included* in the initial scope, what areas *should not be included*, and what areas are somewhere in the middle. While you do this, it can be helpful to quickly note why you are including or excluding specific items from the scope. This can be just an informal note to yourself so that, as you learn more information and discuss with more stakeholders, you can update that rationale with the new/better data – or, as the case may be, you can revisit the scoping determinations that you make based on the new input.

The purpose of this is to do two things. First, it can help you work through what you are including/excluding from the scope and why. Second, it can help you socialize and validate your initial scope informally with stakeholders. This way, you will have a discussion document that you can show them to help guide subsequent discussions about the scope, as well as help present to them what you've come up with already.

Step 4 – validate and refine initial scope

> *"As security practitioners, it is very easy for us to view it as an objective good in and of itself. However, security is important in the context of how it supports the organization in establishing its goals. The goal of security is to reach an ever-evolving level of acceptable risk. Even after you have implemented controls to drive*

down your risk, you are still left with a level of residual risk. We don't work in
absolutes: we work in the context of what is important to us as an organization."

– Ted Ipsen, President and COO at Positroniq, LLC

Lastly, validate what you come up with. If you've followed our advice, you've already had conversations with stakeholders about what the goal/point of the work being done is. Go back to those stakeholders and discuss the initial scope that you've come up with based on those discussions. They can help guide you to areas that you've missed, things you haven't thought about, or present you with concrete arguments about why you should include/exclude certain areas.

The feedback from these stakeholders does two things. First, it proves to them that you're listening and being responsive to their feedback. Other teams (especially business teams) sometimes feel like technologists don't listen to their needs or are less responsive than they'd like; this can be particularly true of the security team. By listening to their goals and keeping them involved from the earliest phases, you help demonstrate that this is not the case right from the get-go.

Secondly, it helps make sure that the initial scope you set is on point. No one person or individual team can think of everything; therefore, by working collaboratively with these stakeholders, you get early feedback on things that you might not have thought of. Even just discussing with them where your design *borders* are can help clue you into things that you might not already know. Would you ultimately learn them later in the process anyway? Maybe. But finding them out now saves you that work in the long term and also provides value to you at this stage.

Summary

Throughout this chapter, we've worked through why and how to set an initial baseline scope that will guide our future design efforts. Ultimately, to begin setting our design, we still need to validate this scope. The refinement and validation will come as we work through requirements and other *tools* in the next chapter and will then be further honed down the line as we add specificity and build our plan.

The next step of the process, which we will cover in the next chapter, will be to add the tools that we need to our toolbox that we will use as we create and document our design. We will examine the analytical tools, information-gathering tools, and other validation methods that we will use as we do so. This will allow us to rapidly construct the design and move quickly into execution.

4

Building an Architecture – Your Toolbox

In this chapter, we will introduce you to some of the tools that you can put into your toolbox as you prepare to undertake the design process. These are the tools that an architect can employ to plan, test, and validate their strategy and vision for securing their organization. We'll look in detail at analytical, telemetric, strategic, and other tools that we can employ as part of the creation and validation of a security design, as well as work through how a hypothetical organization might employ these tools as we move deeper into the planning process.

The reason we are introducing this now is twofold. First, the scope that you selected in the previous chapter provides a solid starting point for the selection of what tools and techniques you'll employ throughout the design process. Therefore, sequentially, now is a useful time to discuss these tools and techniques in more detail. Secondly, we will leverage these tools in the creation of our **blueprint**, reference architecture, or other artifacts that codify our design – so making sure we have a robust understanding of the tools ahead of time is paramount.

Specifically, this chapter will cover the following types of tools that we will put into our virtual toolbox:

- Planning tools
- Building blocks of secure design

Introduction to the architect's toolbox

Architects in the physical world don't just have an idea, grab a hammer, and immediately start building. This is for good reason. To do so would fail to account for a large number of valuable intermediate steps that are necessary to ensure the validity of the final product. Missing, eliding, or otherwise deprioritizing these steps violates the generally accepted practices of the profession and would almost certainly result in an edifice that is suboptimal, unsafe, or unfit for purpose.

Security architecture is no different in this respect. There are a number of key steps involved in the development of a security architecture. Each of these steps can be thought of as a specialized tool to validate the end-state design in a very particular and discrete way. Obviously, not every tool will be applicable to every situation. However, building an understanding of what tools there are means that you can select the right one for your purposes as the time to use it arises.

As an example of what we mean, consider scope. In the previous chapter, we talked in detail about scope: why it matters, what you can look at to help determine it, how to take stock of it to help guide your design process, and so on. We even talked about how we can selectively set the scope to make an architecture project more efficient, divide work, allocate resources, and so on. This means scope is essential to the creation of an architect's vision, as well as a primary means of validation for their design.

In this way, scope is a tool in the architect's toolbox: something they can selectively adjust to accomplish the goal of bounding the design work to a size that is maximally achievable and maximally useful. However, there are other key tools beyond scope that will also play a role in what we're trying to do: tools that assist us in the creation of our design or that help us validate the design we will select and implement. Which tools you select will depend on what you hope to accomplish with your design and the culture of your organization, as well as other factors.

You'll notice that, in this context, the definition of *tool* is a little broader than what you might initially think. It includes software tools that can help us with design work of course, but it also includes the techniques, processes, and methods that we can employ to help us with design. For example, techniques such as threat modeling that help provide information about how an application might be attacked and an attacker's motivation for doing so are included. Also included are risk analysis methods that tell us what areas are most risky. We can use these analytical tools – such as gap analysis, risk assessment, and threat modeling – to determine what steps we need to take, where to take them, how to bring them into being, and so forth. Likewise, there are informational tools that provide telemetry back to us to ensure that we're successful, such as effectiveness and economic metrics, **key performance indicators (KPIs)**, and **key risk indicators (KRIs)**, and risk metrics that will make sure that the outcomes of the design process actually function as advertised.

As a practical matter then, part of the preparatory work that you, the architect, will undertake is the selection of the appropriate tools. This chapter is all about assembling the **toolbox** that you will use as you create and execute your plan. To better understand why we are doing this now (that is, as early in the process as we can once the initial scope is set), consider an analogy to a home improvement project. Say, for example, that you are installing a new hot water heater. Probably the least efficient way you could choose to go about this would be to start with nothing and purchase/acquire any required tools in a **just-in-time** fashion – for example, determining what you need serially and responding to the need for new components as each new need arises (see *Figure 4.1*):

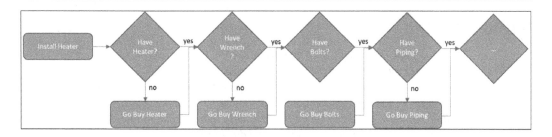

Figure 4.1 – Inefficient plumbing project

In this case, each new tool or part you need will necessitate a trip to the hardware store to buy it – followed by a return trip to actually make use of it. Upon reaching the next step of the process, the cycle begins again.

As anyone who has ever done a task like this is sure to tell you, such an approach would be ridiculous. Think about how much time you would spend driving back and forth to the hardware store to get parts instead of doing the work that you actually care about (that is, actually doing the installation). The best-case scenario using an approach like this one is that you'd (much more slowly and laboriously than is necessary) do the work and complete the job. The worst-case scenario is you run into unexpected delays in the middle of the project that prevent you from completing the job or that significantly delay it. For example, say you discover midway through that you need a part that you need to specially order and that will take several weeks or months for delivery.

Therefore, an approach like this would add effort, delay, and risk to the overall effort. More reasonably, we might choose to follow a process such as this one:

Figure 4.2 – A more efficient plumbing project

In this approach, instead of multiple trips back and forth to acquire tools or parts, you analyze the instructions ahead of time, determine what you need, assemble a **bill of materials** (**BOM**) that represents the full list of all the tools and parts involved, and then – once those tools and parts have been acquired – you complete the work. This is much more reasonable from a planning standpoint: it is more efficient and decreases the overall risk associated with the successful execution of the project.

It is much the same with the tools you'll need when you do your architectural planning. Instead of inventorying tools such as screwdrivers and parts such as nuts or bolts, for an architecture project, you're assembling tools such as documentation and plans. Instead of parts, you're accumulating contextual and constraining factors, such as scope and goals. These are all the *raw materials* that will go into the planning and execution of your vision. In fact, you might think of this as your architectural toolbox.

Planning tools

> *"Every company can benefit from architecture work. For a large enterprise certainly, but even for a small business there's value. For a small or mid-size business, the organization may wish to think through timelines and documentation requirements as, in a small organization, there may be fewer stakeholders to meet with, allowing you to accomplish a lot in a relatively short period of time. Also, while a larger organization might require more documentation of architectural efforts, a smaller organization might be able to make do with less. The process itself though can provide value no matter the size of the organization."*

> *– Dr. Char Sample, Chief Research Scientist – Cybercore Division at Idaho National Laboratory*

From a planning point of view, there are a number of tools that we can employ to help guide us toward a security design. Some are useful right from the get-go; others are useful later on as we get into the execution piece of the project. For our purposes, we're particularly concerned with three types of tools at this stage:

- Analytical tools

- Informational tools

- Modeling and design tools

Again, it bears mentioning that not every tool will apply to every situation and culture. It is part of the planning process to select the strategies that will make the most sense based on the organization's needs, capabilities, culture, and other factors.

We'll go through and explain what we mean by each of these in more detail. As we do so, recall that we're not suggesting you be a master of these tools right away. Instead, we're just laying them out and taking stock – assembling them if you will – so that you know what they are. We will cover each of them in more detail as we go through the subsequent sections.

Analytical tools

> *"A diverse knowledge base is essential to the architect. Not only do you have to understand the technology that's in use – in some cases better than the peers you're working with – but you also need to understand the business and its motivations, how technology supports the goals of the business, and what threats there might be that could impact it."*

> *– John Kallil, Chief Information Security Officer*

It is said that the phrase **know thyself** (γνῶθι σεαυτόν) was engraved in the *Temple of Apollo* at Delphi, making it one of the earliest pieces of human wisdom recorded in the Western world. It's good advice in general, but particularly useful for those seeking to undertake serious security architecture and design work. This is true for more than one reason. First, as we outlined in previous chapters, the design that you come up with will need to fit the context of the organization itself. There's a far more practical reason though: namely, that the design will very often apply to something that already exists.

Now, it's quite possible that in some situations you will be chartered with creating a security model and design for something completely new: for example, if you're working as part of a team that is chartered with creating a new environment completely from scratch. While possible, this is unlikely. In the vast majority of situations, you'll be laying security designs over something – an application, an environment, or a process – that already exists.

For anything that exists already, there will be security properties that this entity (that is, the organization, business unit, environment, application, and so on) already has and that you will need to work within. These can be either the security properties that have evolved organically over time or those that have been systematically designed and architected in. Either way, there is a high degree of likelihood that, whatever security properties already exist, the target state of the design you will put together will differ from them.

Therefore, tools that provide information to you directly about the current landscape that you have in place are directly and immediately useful to you. They're useful because they can provide information about where you are now, and they're useful because they can provide information back to you at the completion of your architecture efforts to let you know whether you've been successful. There are a few that we'll cover in this section:

- Current state assessment
- Risk assessment
- Threat modeling
- Technical validation

We'll walk through each one in detail.

Current state assessment

> "If you're going to take architecture on and do it in-house, you're going to need some help. Getting good consulting support can be helpful. If you're going to do it yourself, what you first need to do – before you do the 'phase 1' of architecture – is a 'phase 0.' Why do you want an architecture? What do you think an architecture is going to do for you? What are the benefits? How will you get there? Who is going to do the work? What will it look like? None of this is about the architecture itself – it's about knowing the context."
>
> – John Sherwood, Chief Architect, thought leader, and co-Founder of The SABSA Institute

In keeping with the sage guidance from Delphi to "*know thyself*," one of the most important tools in your toolbox is a thorough, objective, and detailed understanding of your current state. This means that, from a planning point of view, we'll want to understand the difference between the *design* (that is, the **target state** that you will identify through your design work) and the *current state* as it exists now. Perhaps the easiest way to accomplish this is through a gap analysis. A **gap analysis** lets us understand what separates where we are now and the future state we're building toward. Ultimately, this will be one of the key deliverables of a plan that we can execute to.

That said, there are a few things that we need to do before we can put a gap analysis together – and some sound practical reasons that keep us from doing this analysis first. First, and most obviously, you need to know the target state to assess fully how your existing measures map onto it; for example, the security measures you have in place now could be adapted to play a role in where you'll want to get to. More importantly, though, other details about the environment can influence the planned future state. For example, you might conclude that multifactor authentication is a requirement based on a regulation in scope that you need to adhere to (i.e., that you have a pre-existing requirement to adhere to that regulation). Alternatively, you might conclude that there are pre-existing technology constraints, business constraints, or other forcing factors that will tend to favor certain designs over others.

Additionally, things become more complicated once you move past the purely theoretical and abstract level and introduce implementation details. For example, if you already have the *plumbing* to support a particular implementation, certain ways of accomplishing a security goal might be more advantageous than others. Using multifactor authentication as an example, say you have a RADIUS server with mechanisms to support **Security Assertion Markup Language (SAML)** or **OAuth** (e.g., via **OpenID Connect**). In such a case, practical considerations (expense and speed of implementation) can make it more appealing to leverage those components in your target state, rather than selecting something totally new that you don't have the infrastructure for or knowledge to support. This means that your best fit may not necessarily be the same as another organization's.

Extending the example further, you can see how context also impacts decisions about the overall security model and design – not just implementation. For example, perhaps the existing authentication infrastructure supports some authentication methods but not others. In the preceding example, maybe the existing authentication system supports a one-time code delivered via SMS or a **time-based one-time password** (**TOTP**) but doesn't support other methods such as biometrics or *X.509v3* certificates. In this case, the decision of what authentication method to use is dictated by the existing context; you might save time and money should you decide to use a compatible authentication method (that is, one supported by the existing system) instead of an incompatible one that is not supported.

To begin our planning, therefore, it can be helpful to begin with a current state assessment before you start to envision the end state – or, in fact, before you start to assess the specific security measures you might implement. By understanding the conditions as they stand *now*, you get better information about what existing constraints or areas of opportunity (or efficiency) factor into your planning. This provides an initial baseline that will inform the scope of your planning and provide contextual information that will guide your planning efforts.

We should mention that not all architects – or even standardized architectural approaches – begin the design process with a current state assessment. As with any decision, there are pros and cons to doing so. The primary advantage of leaving a systematic analysis of the current state for a later time (that is, once you've defined a target state) is that it allows you to envision the desired target without bias. This means you can define an idealized *vision* of what you hope to achieve without credence to decisions made in the past.

There are drawbacks to that too, though. First, any opportunities for efficiency that exist in the way the current environment is structured (for example, existing tools, processes, and so on) can be easily missed. Second, dimensions beyond that of effectiveness (that is, maturity, efficiency, economics, and so on) can be overlooked, as you won't have a clear idea of the costs or other impacts associated with the change until much later in the process.

To get the most value from your efforts, then, we recommend you divide the analysis into two phases:

1. Assess the environment using a known, established baseline as a guide.
2. Once the future state is defined, create a gap analysis between the current state and the desired state.

On the surface, this may seem like a wasted effort. After all, aren't we assessing the security posture of the current environment and then analyzing it again to evaluate it against the future state? There would be truth in that, except the difference here lies in how we do it – that is, the practical elements of the execution. Because we are using a known, established baseline to understand the current state – and using that as input into the target state to do the analysis – we are essentially doing the same work, just broken up over two phases.

Doing it this way has two primary advantages. First, we document the current state of the environment in a way that regulators, auditors, and other security practitioners are familiar with. This has immediate and recognizable benefits for those other teams in the immediate term. Second, it allows us to use the knowledge that we gain earlier than would otherwise be the case.

While you can employ several approaches to do this, one approach involves assessing your current environment across three dimensions:

- **Effectiveness**: Do the security measures in use provide risk reduction value?
- **Maturity**: Are the processes that support existing measures reliable and resilient?
- **Efficiency**: Are the security measures in place cost-effective relative to their value?

Effectiveness

The first measure we will look at is *effectiveness*: how well do existing security measures perform at reducing overall risk, complying with regulatory mandates, and so on. This type of analysis is perhaps the easiest to perform since you can reuse existing work. For example, if you've just (e.g., within the past year or so) been through a security program review, ISO/IEC 27001 assessment, SOC 2, compliance audit, or any other type of systematic security evaluation, you may already have documentation that can assist in building out your profile about what security measures you have in place versus which ones you don't.

Really, you can use any catalog or corpus of controls to serve as the baseline to give you information. For example, you might use the controls described in the following references (note that this is only a subset of what exists that you might draw from):

- *NIST SP 800-53*
- *NIST SP 800-171*
- *NIST Cybersecurity Framework*
- *PCI DSS*
- *HIPAA ($164.308-$164.312)*
- *ISO/IEC 27001:2013 Annex A*
- *COBIT 5*
- *COBIT 2019*

The selection of which one to use will depend on a few different factors. If you have a given requirement directly in your regulatory scope (for example, a merchant needing to conform to the PCI DSS for their payment processing or a hospital needing to comply with HIPAA), this might be the one that you can gather information about most easily. Ideally, the framework that you select should be the one that is accepted by – and acceptable to – the organization from a broader context (for example, one that leadership is accustomed to caring about and examining).

If you've been through a security assessment before against any one of these standards or regulations, you will almost invariably have, as a result of that, a systematic breakdown of areas of conformance versus nonconformance for an organized, indexed list of security controls. If it exists already, this documentation is a useful starting point. If it hasn't been evaluated, it is work that extends well beyond the specific task of crafting your security architecture. For example, it can help you track and manage regulatory compliance, manage risk, and numerous other important things. It also will likely have broader utility beyond the specific purpose of architecture evaluation, which in turn can make it easier to acquire and provision resources to conduct the evaluation more systematically.

To produce this type of effectiveness evaluation, work systematically through one of the preceding control catalogs. As you do so, objectively and honestly assess whether or not the controls are in place, whether they are effective in mitigating risk, and whether they meet the intent and rigor of what is intended by the control (security measure).

In doing this, it doesn't really matter how you record successful versus unsuccessful implementation in your analysis. You might use a simple checkmark in an Excel workbook to denote where the control is successfully implemented; you might use the types of nonconformities used in ISO certification audits per the recommendation in clause 6.4.8 of ISO 19011:2018 (*Guidelines for auditing management systems*): that is, major (*systemic*) versus minor (*non-systemic* and *isolated*) nonconformities. In our own work, we've found it helpful to use these nonconformity types (i.e., major and minor) along with the additional categories *in place* (the measure is sufficient to meet the intent/rigor of the control defined in the baseline) and *opportunity for improvement* to denote an area that, while technically in place, the implementation could be improved.

The reason we've found this approach valuable is twofold:

- Since it uses an international standard, there is quite a bit of guidance, interpretation, analysis, and other public documentation to help you make your assessment.

- It forces you to think through exactly why and how a control doesn't meet the intent/rigor of the standard you are using. In other words, in order to evaluate whether a given lack of implementation is systemic or not, you will need to think through how, why, and to what degree what you're doing now isn't sufficient.

In most cases, if you're performing this analysis at the beginning of the design process, it's more important that you be able to get information together quickly than it is that you maintain a high level of assessment rigor and detail. You're neither a regulator nor a certification auditor; therefore, you can save time by being selective in looking at evidence to support what you might learn through other means (for example, interviewing employees).

As an example of what we mean by that, in evaluating a security measure such as *patch management*, you might inquire about the process with the person in the organization responsible for the patch management of the systems in scope. If they lay out a process that, in your determination, is effective at patch management, you might choose to take them at their word and forgo an examination of a sample of the underlying systems, evaluation of patch reports, vulnerability assessment reports, or other evidence to prove that what they say is happening actually is. For a more robust audit such as a certification audit, attestation, or other type of examination, this would never be sufficient. However, for the very specific purpose of this brief, abbreviated evaluation, it can prove workable while saving you a significant amount of time and energy.

We can also creatively use information or documentation that we already have to quickly glean information and draw conclusions. Using the earlier patch management example, this might mean deriving conclusions about the sufficiency of patch management processes based on the output of a vulnerability scan of the environment or other technical evaluation of vulnerability or configuration data. By doing this, we can use data sources that exist already and thereby minimize the amount of time we spend in data collection or the amount of time that we need to spend waiting for key resources to become available to answer questions about the current state.

Measuring your existing posture in this way will give you a quick, relatively inexpensive (in time and money) view into the controls that you have fielded already, what you haven't, and where what you have could be improved.

Maturity

Getting a read on the current environment from a maturity standpoint is likewise a useful endeavor. This means looking at the *implementation* and *supporting processes* for the maturity of security measures: specifically, looking at the maturity of how those controls are implemented and supported in your environment (that is, the processes that support those controls).

Maturity in this case refers to the level of resiliency, repeatability, measurability, and standardization within a given process. According to *CMMI for Development v1.3*, maturity levels represent *"...a defined evolutionary plateau for organizational process improvement. Each maturity level matures an important subset of the organization's processes, preparing it to move to the next maturity level. The maturity levels are measured by the achievement of the specific and generic goals associated with each predefined set of process areas."* (*CMMI for Development v1.3, page 26.*)

Organizations can derive value from examining their overall maturity because it can help them understand how resilient their security measures are and how consistently they are being applied across the organization. Because maturity is concerned with how consistent, managed, or documented a process is (in this case, the processes supporting the security measures we have in place) instead of just whether or not a given control is in place, an organization can get a clearer picture of how well (how consistently and resiliently) a control will operate over the long term.

It's possible (though frankly, much less likely than in the case of a simple analysis of whether a control is implemented or not) that you have some documentation about this already – for example, if you've been through a security maturity review such as a systematic analysis for **Cybersecurity Maturity Model Certification (CMMC)** or the **Capability Maturity Model Integration (CMMI)**. If you don't have this, a relatively easy way to get a *quick and dirty* understanding of maturity is to use the same control set that you used for the evaluation of control effectiveness and assess the same controls through a maturity lens as well as an effectiveness one.

You might, for example, choose to use a scale such as that employed by the CMMI, as shown in the following diagram:

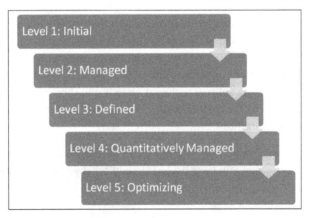

Figure 4.3 – CMMI maturity levels

Under this model, *maturity* is scored along the following spectrum:

- **Level 1 (Initial)**: Work efforts are ad hoc. Tasks may be completed, but little or no process means that work may be delayed, inefficient, or extended beyond budgetary thresholds.
- **Level 2 (Managed)**: Work efforts are repeatable but performed in the absence of a defined process.
- **Level 3 (Defined)**: Work is completed per a standardized, documented process.
- **Level 4 (Quantitatively Managed)**: Work is completed per a repeatable, measured, standardized process. Data and performance metrics are collected about the performance of the task.
- **Level 5 (Optimizing)**: Work is completed according to a *virtuous cycle* of continuous improvement. The data collected is used to guide improvements in how tasks are performed and to optimize.

Note that this is a purposeful simplification of process maturity analysis. In truth, there is significant work that can go into understanding maturity (in fact, there are entire standards and methodologies documented for how to do this). However, as with effectiveness, we are not trying to do everything all at once; instead, we are attempting to arrive at something quickly that we can use to inform our analysis. We want to get to a baseline understanding rapidly and efficiently to drive future planning. This means that celerity is more important than accuracy – at least for our purposes in this immediate usage.

Again, the focus here is on the tasks, processes, tools, vendors, and other components that support the implementation of the security control within your environment. A way to quickly achieve this is to extend the same documentation you created (or that you leveraged) in analyzing the efficacy and include areas to measure the maturity of the underlying process as well. For example, if we were using a spreadsheet to evaluate control implementation according to *NIST SP 800-53*, we could add a `Maturity` column to allow us to record and capture the maturity for the underlying processes supporting each control.

Such an artifact might look like the following:

	A	B	D	E	F	K	N
1	Family	Control	Topic	Control/Enhancement Text	Supplemental Guidance	Observation	Maturity
2	AC	1	ACCESS CONTROL POLICY AND PROCEDURES	The organization: a. Develops, documents, and disseminates to [Assignment: organization-defined personnel or roles]: 1. An access control policy that addresses purpose, scope, roles, responsibilities, management commitment, coordination among organizational entities, and compliance; and 2. Procedures to facilitate the implementation of the access control policy and associated access controls; and b. Reviews and updates the current: 1. Access control policy [Assignment: organization-defined frequency]; and 2. Access control procedures [Assignment: organization-defined frequency].	This control addresses the establishment of policy and procedures for the effective implementation of selected security controls and control enhancements in the AC family. Policy and procedures reflect applicable federal laws, Executive Orders, directives, regulations,policies, standards, and guidance. Security program policies and procedures at the organization level may make the need for system-specific policies and procedures unnecessary. The policy can be included as part of the general information security policy for organizations or conversely, can be represented by multiple policies reflecting the complex nature of certain organizations. The procedures can be established for the security program in general and for particular information systems, if needed. The organizational risk management strategy is a key factor in establishing policy and procedures. Related control: PM-9.	In place	4 - Quantitatively Managed

Figure 4.4 – Maturity evaluation for baseline assessment

As we evaluate and investigate, remember that the intent here is to examine the maturity of the processes that support a given control. In other words, the implementation of a given control within your environment. Ask yourself whether the process is documented, automated, periodically reviewed, and so on. If the process is documented, but not automated, you might choose to assign it a maturity of

3 (documented), whereas if they are automated and such automation collects and records actionable metrics, you might choose to assign it a value of 4 (quantitatively managed).

Efficiency

The last area that it can be helpful to examine is the overall cost-effectiveness and operational efficiency of the controls in place. In essence, this means how much the control costs us to operate. It is valuable to know this because we may choose to factor economic decisions and opportunity costs into the design that we put together. As with maturity and efficacy, this is also not wasted work. Even during the design process for the new model that you seek to build, an understanding of the resource utilization and current investments that you have already made is a valuable exercise.

If you already have access to this information, that's great and it can be a useful part of your design and planning process. If not, we can put something together quickly to address the need just as we did with the prior dimensions we looked at. We might choose to look in-depth at each of the tools and processes that support the implementation of a given control within our environment, in particular their operational efficiency, the ongoing cost to acquire and maintain, the resource requirements to support it, and other items that support the total cost of ownership for that security measure.

There are a few things to note about this. First, it is tempting to look just at the technology tools that we employ to satisfy a particular control. However, it is important that we look both at tools and processes as we approach it. Why? Because bear in mind that staff time equates to money to a large degree; even in situations where it doesn't (that is, volunteer resources) or situations where we don't have visibility into the costs associated with keeping individuals on staff, there is still an opportunity cost associated with their time. By this, we mean that staff members busy doing *task A* aren't available to perform *task B*.

Second, it's important to point out that, sometimes, there isn't a one-to-one mapping between controls and tools/processes. For example, if I purchase a firewall, it's probably pretty clear that this supports a control such as network segmentation. But what about something such as a **unified threat management** (**UTM**) tool that has firewall capability, **intrusion detection system** (**IDS**) monitoring, web filtering, anti-malware, uptime monitoring, and other capabilities built in? In this case, multiple different goals are potentially hit through the use of a single tool and associated processes for that tool. Also, there can be multiple tools and processes associated with a single control. For example, you might have monitoring capabilities on your local on-premises network (an IDS for example), monitoring capabilities built into host operating systems on endpoints, and then additional monitoring capabilities for cloud environments.

One strategy that we've used successfully is to analyze staff time in terms of hours, rather than specific dollar amounts. You can certainly use dollar amounts if you can get them, and there can be value in having this level of granularity in your analysis. However, as a practical reality, very often, this information will not be available to every security architect without significant work. Deriving an actual dollar amount for staff time means that you understand in detail the salaries, benefits, and bonus structures of coworkers (unlikely to be the case), and also that you understand what your organization's benefits packages cost (also not likely). Therefore, while it won't always be entirely accurate due to differences between staff members' salaries, using time as a proxy for dollars when it comes to resources used can help you work around these problems and at least allows you to understand the opportunity costs, even without having a full understanding of the actual dollars spent.

Putting staff time together with the ongoing license and upkeep costs associated with technology tools, we can create a useful economic map by accounting for the following:

- **Staff time (operations)**: The amount of time employed by staff in keeping a given tool or process operational. This can include systems administration, reporting, project management, communications, and other tasks that, while necessary, are focused on maintenance rather than the performance of a process supporting a control directly.

- **Staff time (usage)**: The amount of time employed by staff executing a process or using a tool that supports a given control.

- **Annualized costs**: This includes an annualized dollar amount to maintain and operate a given tool or process. This can include licensing costs, support charges, maintenance, or any other costs required to support the tool on an annualized basis.

The point here is that you want to select the lens for evaluation of the current state that is in harmony with what the organization considers to be important.

Risk assessment

"A business risk assessment provides analysis of risks against the business' objectives. This gives you your high-level strategy for what your security program needs to do. The closer to the business strategy you can make your risk assessment, the better aligned your security program is going to be. From that, you derive a set of capabilities and carve up the world into a set of domains – which in SABSA are a set of elements subject to a common set of risks. And because they are subject to a common set of risks, you can then create a policy that relates to that domain. This sets the scope of what your security program is supposed to do."

– Andrew S. Townley, Chief Executive Officer at Archistry Incorporated

The strategy we covered for current state assessment in the previous subsections may be good enough for small organizations – or organizations that have limited time/budget – but you probably noticed a few things about it as we worked it through. First, you'll notice that it uses as a baseline an existing set of controls that are defined in one of a few different, somewhat arbitrary standards without accounting for what the organization actually does or how it might be attacked.

As an example of what we mean, consider security training and awareness building. Normally, and for most organizations, this is an important security measure. But as a thought experiment, consider a hypothetical organization that is almost entirely automated. Say there are two employees, both of whom have an extensive security background. The rest of the business operations (whatever they might be) are carried out by machines. In an organization like that, how much value in actually reducing risk to the organization would a control such as security training have? Probably not that much.

In fact, one main criticism of a technique such as the preceding is that it doesn't account for how the organization might be attacked; it assumes that all controls are equally important for all situations. We all know that this is not the case. The likelihood of an event coming to pass is an important part of prioritizing which controls to deploy, how much to spend on them, where they should be applied, and so on. In a situation where something is relatively likely to occur, it becomes more important – when it is less likely, it becomes less so.

Likewise, the preceding fails to account for the impact of something coming to pass. For example, what happens if we don't train our employees in security? What happens if we don't employ network segmentation between a critical application server and the internet? As a practical matter, the impact of failing to employ a given measure (or, if the measure is employed, the impact of the failure of that measure) is not constant but, rather, is based on circumstances. For example, the preceding example of the hypothetical, fully automated firm might not see much impact if they fail to train employees in security. Another organization such as a bank's customer service desk might see a much higher level of impact should they make this same decision.

Now, those practitioners who have some familiarity with formalized risk management methods know exactly where I'm going with this – namely, *analysis* and *assessment of risk*. The abbreviated analysis methods that we've discussed so far do not really account for risk since they follow a control-focused perspective rather than one that accounts for the likelihood and impact of how the organization might actually be attacked (or otherwise come to harm).

Formally speaking, risk is a product of two things: the impact of something occurring and the likelihood that it will occur. We all intuitively know this from our daily lives. Something might be a concern if it has a low impact on us but is likely to happen. It might also be concerning if it is relatively unlikely but, should it occur, would be catastrophic. Being involved in an airplane crash is statistically very unlikely, yet the consequences of it happening (almost certainly mass death) are so high that flying makes many people very nervous. By contrast, something with low impact but high likelihood will also cause people to plan around it – for example, catching a cold.

The formal process of evaluating these factors is risk modeling. In other words, the process of systematically understanding the impact and likelihood of a given event. This differs from risk assessment in that, while both include evaluation of impact and likelihood, risk analysis often includes identification and categorization of risk while risk modeling might not. Risk modeling, therefore, is a subset of risk management, the broader discipline of managing risk over that risk's lifetime. This occurs specifically by identifying the risk, assessing it, treating it (either through mitigation, acceptance, avoidance, or transference), and measuring it in an ongoing way.

While both risk modeling and the broader discipline of risk management can (and should) be part of the architect's toolset, realistically, and for the purposes of the preliminary creation and validation of the design, risk modeling is arguably more directly germane at this stage. Here, we systematically unpack and analyze each potential risk area based on the likelihood of occurrence and the impact should it do so.

There are two ways to do this: either qualitatively or quantitatively. Qualitative models include using a *fuzzy* scale (that is, a scale such as low, medium, and high) for both impact and likelihood to derive a risk score that can be used as a way to understand and prioritize risks relative to each other. By contrast, quantitative models (as the name would suggest) seek to derive a numeric score by plugging in values for impact and likelihood.

Economic models

For example, one quantitative risk assessment technique is to calculate **annualized loss expectancy (ALE)**. In this technique, ALE is a product of the **annual rate of occurrence (ARO)** and **single-loss expectancy (SLE)** according to the following formula:

$$ALE = ARO \times SLE$$

ARO represents a numeric value reflecting how often, on average, you anticipate a given event to occur per year. A *100-year flood* (a flood that occurs once every 100 years, on average) would therefore have an ALE value of .01 (that is, 1/100). SLE is a dollar amount reflecting how much that event costs when it does happen. For example, say you live in an area where there's a blizzard once every 10 years on average. In this case, your ARO would be 1/10 or 0.1. The blizzard, when it happens, costs you $2,000 in lost wages from being snowed in. In this case, your SLE would be $2,000, meaning your annualized loss expectancy would be $200: the ARO of 0.1 multiplied by the SLE of $2,000.

The ALE number is useful in a few ways. First, you can compare the cost of mitigation controls directly to the annualized cost of events to determine how valuable a mitigation control is – or whether it is valuable at all. For example, in the preceding blizzard example, if someone offered to sell you an ongoing service at a rate of $55 per winter month to shovel your driveway when the blizzard comes (allowing you to not lose wages), you could use the ALE value to determine whether that's a good deal or not. If there are four winter months, the cost of that service per year is $220. Since the ALE is $200, the mitigation (in this case, the snow removal service) exceeds the expected per-year losses; based on this and barring any other factors (for example, losing your job by not showing up to work when it snows), you might conclude that the use of the snow shoveling service isn't a great deal for you.

The second way that it's useful is that it can help you prioritize mitigations across controls. For example, perhaps you have money in your budget to do only one mitigation – but you have 20 things potentially at risk. Where do you invest? By comparing the ALE of the various options available to you, you can conclude which of the mitigations are the most efficient and select accordingly.

This approach has a long history. In fact, a variant of it is routinely used in the US legal system to calculate negligence in tort law, often referred to as the *Learned Hand rule* or the *BPL formula*. This approach originates from a court decision reached in 1947 by the United States 2nd Circuit Court of Appeals. In the case of *the United States versus Carroll Towing*, the judge (named "Learned Hand," hence the name of the rule) stated that an organization has a duty to implement a precaution if the *gravity of injury* (impact) multiplied by the *probability of injury* (likelihood) exceeds the *burden of adequate precautions*. The name *BPL formula* derives from the mathematical representation of this concept as $PL > B$, where P is the probability, L is the gravity of loss, and B is the burden of due care. As you can see, the BPL formula is an almost direct correlation to the annualized loss expectancy and subsequent control value analysis described previously.

Other approaches

There are several criticisms of this approach. First, not everything can be expressed in terms of dollars. Reputational impacts, for example, are hard to quantify in terms of direct cost. You might argue that a loss of reputation stemming from something such as a data breach would invariably carry an economic cost, but empirical analysis suggests that this is not always the case. In an empirical analysis of breach impact, Alessandro Acquisti *et al.* wrote the following in *Is there a cost to privacy breaches? An event study*:

> *"There exists a negative and statistically significant impact of data breaches on a company's market value on the announcement day for the breach. The cumulative effect increases in magnitudes over the day following the breach announcement, but then decreases and loses statistical significance."*

This means there is a certain immediate impact of a breach on market value (a proxy for reputational loss) in the short term, but this loses significance over the long term. This makes the economic impact of certain types of events very difficult (if even possible at all) to quantify accurately.

Secondly, how do you identify what risks could occur in the first place? A current state assessment of effectiveness using a common index or taxonomy as a reference point can help you understand the degree to which you've implemented (or not) those items on the list associated with the reference you've chosen. But what about things not on their list? By contrast, ALE works well for understanding remediation effectiveness; it also works well as a way to prioritize remediation strategies across multiple risk areas. However, how do you determine the sources of potential risk in the first place?

There are multiple ways to accomplish some level of risk identification; in fact, over the years, quite a few different strategies have been proposed:

- **NIST**: In *Special Publication 800-30 (Guide for Conducting Risk Assessments)*, NIST discusses three approaches: *threat-oriented*, *asset-/impact-oriented*, and *vulnerability-oriented*. **Threat-oriented** means working through threat scenarios to create a list of items to consider, **asset-/impact-oriented** means starting with the critical assets and inventorying systematically what events might impact them, whereas **vulnerability-oriented** means working backward from vulnerabilities to derive the potential risks that could operate on those vulnerabilities.

- **ISACA**: The ISACA Risk IT Framework proposes a scenario-driven approach to risk identification. Under this model, risk scenarios are created either through a top-down approach looking in-depth at business goals to find the most germane sources of disruptions to those goals, or a bottom-up approach whereby generic scenarios are used as a starting point for the creation of a more customized view based on the organization under analysis.

- **ISO**: ISO/IEC 31010:2009 outlines three possible methods for risk analysis: evidence-based (that is, checklists, historical methods), systematic processes (details unspecified), and inductive reasoning.

These are only three of a multitude of documents, standards, methodologies, and approaches that are routinely used for risk assessment. As you can tell, there is a wide range of possible methods and avenues for selecting what specific risks to include in your risk analysis – and a number of possible avenues to derive them. This makes the actual section of risks for consideration more of an art than a systematic, repeatable science.

More complex models have arisen to account for variations in the relative strength and performance of different models servicing the same goal, to address probabilities extant in the likelihood of an attack being successful, and so on. The **Factor Analysis of Information Risk** (**FAIR**) model, for example, introduces concepts such as threat capability, control strength, and primary and secondary loss factors, as well as introduces new ways to measure and model risk.

The point of all this, though, is that there are a number of different approaches that you might select from to introduce risk (i.e., impact and likelihood) into your understanding of your organization's current state.

Threat modeling

> "To the extent that you follow a process to architecture, threat modeling is key to that process. If what you are building is more like one of those Revel 'airplane model sets' where you snap out the parts and glue them together in a prescribed order and paint it, threat modeling is less important – the exact dimensions are known in advance. If, however, what you are architecting is more like an exercise in assembling pieces together (an analogy being LEGO bricks that you assemble together), threat modeling adds the most value because it lets you understand how the final result will adapt and how to protect it. In reality, most organizations are more similar to the LEGO model than the airplane model."

> – Adam Shostack, President, Shostack & Associates

The implicit situation associated with understanding risk presents somewhat of a barrier for those desiring to systematically enumerate risks for consideration, prioritization, and treatment. For example, how will we know how likely something is to occur? How will we know what the impact will be? This information can be difficult to determine once we start to dig into the specifics.

One strategy to help in this analysis is the use of threat modeling to discover how a system, network, application, or other entity might be attacked. It attempts to provide a way to systematically analyze an asset (a machine, a network, data, an application, and so on). We can use threat modeling as a strategy to determine the following:

- **Threat sources**: What are the threats and how will they behave?

- **Attack vectors**: How will an attack occur or a threat scenario play out?

- **Targets**: What are the most compelling targets?

Over time, several strategies have developed to formalize approaches to do this systematically. One early approach developed by and written about by Bruce Schneier in his 1999 article *Attack Trees (Dr. Dobb's Journal)* employs a tree-like analysis technique to provide "*…a formal, methodical way of describing the security of systems, based on varying attacks.*"

To model an attack using an attack tree, you basically map (chart) all of the possible ways that an attacker's objective could be achieved. As an example, consider a situation where an attacker seeks to break into your house. To systematically chart out the paths that the attacker might employ to do so, an attack tree in the format described by Schneier might look like the following:

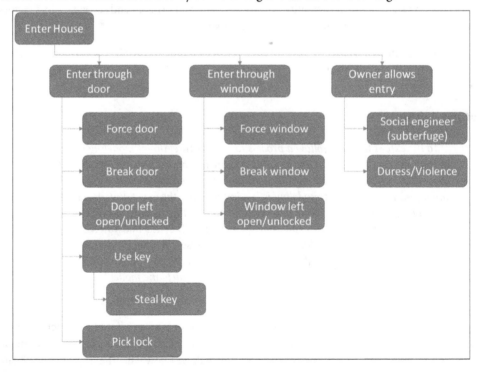

Figure 4.5 – Simplified attack tree (home entry)

Note that this is a vastly oversimplified model used here for the purposes of illustration. A real model would certainly be much larger, even for a relatively simple attack such as this one. For example, a real model might describe various social engineering stratagems, specific mechanisms to place the homeowner under duress (that is, kidnapping, physical violence, threats, and so on), and numerous others.

Building upon approaches such as this, more recent techniques have emerged that attempt to build on this *attacker's view* approach. Application threat modeling, for example, provides a breakdown of threats from the point of view of the threat actor (or threat source, in the case of a threat not having a human agent, such as a natural disaster or pandemic). Applied more broadly, it seeks to help you deconstruct an application into component parts and map out systematically how those parts interact. For example, you might look at component interactions in an application, considering the following at each interaction point or interface, and employ the **STRIDE** mnemonic to look at each of the following for each interaction:

- **Spoofing**: Spoofing refers to the ability of an attacker to spuriously create, replay, impersonate, or otherwise inappropriately generate and/or modify a request. Examples would be IP address spoofing, email spoofing, credential replay, or other attacks that involve the use of fraudulent, inappropriate, or false data to gain access.

- **Tampering**: Tampering refers to an attacker inappropriately modifying data either stored on or sent to a resource to either gain access, manipulate stored data, corrupt or otherwise invalidate information, or for any other unauthorized purpose. An example of tampering would be the malicious corruption of data.

- **Repudiation**: Repudiation refers to the plausibility of denying the legitimacy of a transaction. For example, a situation where a user can reasonably deny having performed an action would allow them to repudiate (that is, to disavow) that the transaction took place under their agency. An example would be a credit card holder disputing a charge.

- **Information disclosure**: Information disclosure refers to the inappropriate leakage of security-relevant information that could be used by an attacker in furtherance of a campaign or to collect data being leaked. An example of this would be providing internal IP addresses on the other side of a network address translation boundary.

- **Denial of service**: Denial of service refers to an attacker bringing about a situation where legitimate, approved usage of a resource cannot occur, is interrupted, or is otherwise degraded. An example of this would be distributed denial of service preventing access to a public website.

- **Elevation of privilege**: Elevation of privilege refers to a situation where an attacker can gain access to functionality that would otherwise be unavailable to them. A system user who can gain root access on a system where they are not an approved administrator is an example of privilege elevation.

We will go into more detail about how to actually perform threat modeling later in this book (in particular, in *Chapter 6, Building an Architecture - Application Blueprints*), but for now, recognize that a systematic and methodical analysis of threats can be a valuable tool in your toolbox.

Technical validation

> *"I think one of the problems with technology and, more specifically, security is the idea that there is a part that is more important than others. We've seen time and again that attackers go after the weakest link, not the strongest part of any product. To ensure that all parts are equally accounted for and done well, there should be an emphasis on security being an integral part of every step in the architecture process. This includes from requirements gathering to design – and from development to testing and the steps in between."*
>
> *– Phoram Mehta, director and head of Infosec APAC, PayPal*

Lastly, and perhaps most obviously, one analytical tool available to the architect is the results of technical information gathering and testing. This can include any instrumentation, telemetry, metrics, or other information about the environment that can be gleaned through the use of technical assessment tools. Such information might include the following:

- Vulnerability scanning results
- Penetration tests
- System update and patch logs
- User access logs
- Authentication logs (for example, successful and unsuccessful login attempts)
- Intrusion detection alerts
- Anti-malware scans
- Cloud access reports
- Application logs
- Web access or HTTP proxy logs
- Data leak prevention logs
- File integrity monitoring logs
- Business metrics
- System uptime monitoring alerts
- Application dynamic or static scan results

This list represents only a subset of possible technical information about the environment that can be collected and that can be used as part of the architect's analysis. What's important to recognize, though, is that this information can be directly and immediately useful to inform you about the status and operation of a given set of controls and the current state of the environment. To assess patch management, for example, what better way to evaluate but to look at the results of vulnerability assessment as a way to empirically observe whether patches are applied?

In addition to these analytical tools that the architect can use to gain information, there are informational tools as well: information resources, sources of knowledge, and other techniques that the architect can apply to the discipline of formulating – and ultimately, implementing – a robust design. We'll cover those in the next section.

Informational tools

While analytical tools can inform you at the outset of a project to help you identify scope and approach, bear in mind that you'll need data too once the design is put together and you move into the execution phase. As such, it can be helpful to lay the groundwork for what information you'll collect and how you'll collect it even before you begin the design process properly. These are what we call **informational tools**.

This is not to say that you can't use the analytical tools we described previously to help you collect information. Quite the contrary, you absolutely can. However, there are also other sources of data available to you that are less about analyzing the environment as it exists now (or is envisioned to exist in the future) but that instead provide data back to you in the form of ongoing telemetry.

These do, however, require some preparation to set up. Ideally, you will want to be thinking about them from the project outset so that the data is available to you once you move into the design and execution phases. As such, getting a start on setting up the channels of information, even before the design process itself begins, can have its advantages.

In this section, we will discuss the following informational tools that can provide value to you as ways to validate your design's implementation:

- Effectiveness measurements
- Economic measurements
- Risk measurements

Once we've laid these out, we'll discuss how to turn this information into metrics: specific performance indicators (KPIs) and risk indicators (KRIs) that you can use to translate the data you collect into actionable information.

Effectiveness measurements

One of the things that will be most useful for you to know is how effective the security measures you will put in place are. Previously, we suggested that you evaluate the current state of the organization's security measures before beginning your security design. This is also a good and timely approach to gathering information that you can use as you begin the design process. It will also prove to be a valuable source of ongoing information as you execute.

Specifically, we're referring here to ongoing measurements and metrics about the effectiveness of security measures and the security posture of the environment itself (even before you start to modify it). For example, if you are performing network monitoring, how well do those processes work? If you're using IDS, has increased use of the cloud undermined its effectiveness? Or is it still performing the way you need it to? Questions such as these speak directly to how well (or how poorly) the measures you have in place are operating. This is different from simple analysis because you are collecting information about the operation of these measures and using that information to guide you as you make decisions.

We also stated that it can be beneficial to begin setting up the instrumentation to collect this information in advance of creating your design. Why? Two reasons. First, it will likely take some time (weeks or even months) for the information you will want to collect to start coming in. This means that if you start now figuring out what data you need – and begin setting up the mechanisms and structures to collect it – you will have that information available to you early in the execution and rollout process, or (perhaps) even late in the design process itself. This information as it comes in can help you select from various implementation approaches based on the data you collect or can inform you on the selection of specific strategies and security models.

Secondly, the earlier you are able to set up instrumentation and data gathering, the more trending information you will have. For example, if it will be 3 months before you actually begin the execution of a design (a fairly quick turnaround), by the time you get to the phase where you're actually putting the design together, you'll have 3 months' worth of historical information from what you've already collected. This trending information can be helpful to you in situations where you will be modifying or adjusting existing processes. For example, if you are using vulnerability scan results as a barometer for how well your patch management and endpoint configuration/hardening processes work as we discussed previously, a few months' worth of data about the baseline performance (that is, before you start making changes to it) can give you useful information about impacts made by adjustments to those processes in light of changes driven by your security design.

In terms of what to measure, there are a few principles to keep in mind:

- Be adaptable
- Don't overinvest
- More is better (within reason)

By *be adaptable*, what we mean is to be creative about the data that you gather and whether/how it provides input about a given control. Looking at the previous patch management example, there are a few data sources that you could tap to give you information about that control's performance. A few options could include the following:

- **Vulnerability scan reports**: Observe to see whether patches are being implemented by looking for the presence or absence of vulnerabilities impacting application software for which patches are available. If you see missing patches, you might find your patch management needs work. If you find misconfigurations, your hardening process might be suspect.

- **Software management agent logs**: Examine logs from software management or inventory agents to view reports on the application patch level. A report about what software versions are installed might give you information about whether patch management systems are keeping pace. Likewise, information about inconsistency in application software deployment or configuration settings might inform you that hardening needs work.

- **Native operating system tools**: Utilize built-in tools within the operating system to collect inventory information about installed software and patches (in Microsoft Windows, for example, you might use Group Policy Inventory). Operating system tools might tell you about configuration and patch management for the operating system software, orchestration agents might give you information about virtual machines or containers, while any of the preceding can be creatively used to deploy scripts to collect information about the application patch level and configuration.

- **System logs**: System logs that show evidence of patch installation. For example, on a Linux system using an **Advanced Package Tool** (**APT**) such as Debian or Ubuntu, you might examine the contents of the update logs (such as `/var/log/apt/history.log`) to ensure that they're being done. Using a script, automate the collection and analysis across multiple machines.

- **File integrity monitoring**: If you have file integrity management tools (for example, Tripwire), collect and examine records of filesystem changes to patched applications. An observation of a change to a critical system file in response to a patch provides you with an indication that patching is working appropriately.

- **Patch management or configuration tool reporting**: If using a commercial patch management platform or configuration management tool, use built-in data collection tools and compliance reporting mechanisms.

These are only a few possible options of ways that you could derive information about whether or not your patch management process or system hardening processes are working as intended. While each one requires separate prerequisites, presents the information in different ways, has its own advantages/disadvantages, and would require an adapted approach to provide the right instrumentation for your use, they all can get you to a useful outcome that tells you what you are looking to determine in a reliable and measurable way.

By *don't overinvest*, we mean stay aware of the fact that the ultimate point of measuring in the first place is because we are likely to be making changes in the operation, implementation, scope, and/or function of what's in place currently. This means we don't want to spawn an onerous, expensive, years-long metrics-gathering initiative at this point. This is not to say that such a program isn't useful; on the contrary, it absolutely can be. However, it's possible that we'll disrupt the data collection mechanism as we design and roll out the new approaches that we will come up with at design time. Remember again to start small to keep things manageable: we just want to collect what information we can from instrumentation that we have in place already (where it exists) or where it can be deployed cheaply/quickly where it doesn't.

Lastly, by *more is better*, we're talking about getting information about all of the controls that you can from the data sources that you have already. This means the more information we can gather about something of interest, the more valuable it can be down the road. Note that we're not suggesting that you fall into the trap of just collecting what's easy or collecting data for its own sake. Rather, we're suggesting that you cast a wide net even if the perfect, exact data that you would like to collect isn't available. There is a little bit of balance that's required here since collecting data can take work, planning, and preparation. Since you don't want to slow down your efforts unnecessarily, you'll want to balance how much data you collect with what you think you'll actually use and need.

Bear in mind as you do this that the same data may serve as a barometer for multiple security measures. For example, earlier, we used the example of vulnerability assessment information providing feedback to us on our patch management approach. That's true – it can. But consider what else it can provide information about, such as configuration, change management, system hardening procedures, user account management (if configured to brute force known weak passwords or using platform-specific tools), and numerous other security goals. Also, depending on the controls list you're using as a baseline, vulnerability scanning itself might be a line-item requirement.

The point? Use what you can creatively to gain the most information you can. Since we're after expediency at this stage rather than the perfect measurement (this will come later), it's more important that you can move quickly and be agile than it is that you take months or years to tailor systems and processes to give you the perfect data.

Economic measurements

> *"One of the things people don't do well is to account for economics in their risk management approach. Someone once told me 'You don't build a ten-thousand-dollar fence to protect a one-thousand-dollar horse.' You want to select controls that are in line with a cost/benefit analysis. This is a key element for me and in the approach I use."*
>
> *– John Tannahill, a Canadian management consultant specializing in information security*

In addition to data and metrics about how well controls perform, it's also useful to keep a handle (when we can) on their total cost of ownership. This is valuable because the economics of security operations can very well be part of why you're making changes in the first place. Depending on what and how you make changes, the economics of operation may also change. This means it can serve as a proof point and validation to stakeholders about the architectural process in addition to giving you information you can use to make informed decisions about future investments.

If you can do so, it can be helpful to set up mechanisms to collect information about economics early. Sometimes, they will remain constant throughout the design and even the implementation. Sometimes, the design itself might lead you to make an investment that, over the long term, will make you more efficient but that will require a short-term outlay. In this case, you want to make sure you're getting your money's worth and that, over the long term, you're actually recouping the value you expect.

Remember that you want to keep track of two things: both the actual dollars invested in purchasing products or services and how staff are spending their time. Both are important elements of the overall financial and economic picture. Keeping track of dollars directly invested (for example, software or hardware purchases) is usually the easier of the two to accomplish; keeping track of the time invested by staff is more challenging, particularly when you might be making a change in how they do their work as a consequence of implementing your security design.

Remember that getting to a high level of accuracy, particularly in keeping track of invested time on the part of staff members, can be intrusive and burdensome if carried out to extremes. Therefore, keep flexibility in mind.

Risk measurements

> *"Generally, my starting point with architecture is risk assessment. If I'm following the NIST SP 800-30 approach, for example, we will end up with residual risk at the end of the risk management process. When the residual risk exceeds the risk appetite, we use controls to mitigate risk to an acceptable level."*
>
> *– John Tannahill, a Canadian management consultant specializing in information security*

Information about the effectiveness of a security measure's operation is valuable, but also valuable is objective information about organizational risk. During the process of implementing our design, we will be making changes to the security posture of the organization, which, in turn, impacts risk. In fact, the risk profile of the organization can change over time due to factors outside our direct control – for example, updates to how business teams employ technology or changes in how existing technology is managed.

As an example of this, consider an existing, legacy on-premises application. An application like this might have been designed around a set of assumptions, and those assumptions can change based on usage, environment, technology in use, and other factors. One legacy application might have been designed around the assumption that communications on the on-premises network are kept sequestered (separated from other environments) and that internal network communications are confidential. Based on this assumption, the application might communicate with backend middleware, an application server, or a database via a cleartext (unencrypted), unauthenticated connection. While modern application design would make a situation such as this less likely to occur, there was a time not so long ago when a design such as this would have been normative and generally accepted practice.

In this example, consider what happens if a portion of the application (either as a whole or portions of it) is moved to the cloud. The backend components are still doing the same thing that they did before. The only difference now is that they are doing it in a different environment: one that you don't control and that might have other tenants on it. If the application was moved in its entirety, cleartext communications containing application data will now be traversing your cloud provider's network (a situation you may or may not be comfortable with). If only one-half of the connection is moved, you may have this cleartext communication happening over an intervening VPN spanning infrastructure both in your environment and at the cloud provider. Again, this may not be desirable depending on the application, its purpose, and other contextual factors (e.g., regulatory compliance).

The point is, being able to measure information about risk, such as impacts that can occur as a result of changing business technology usage, changing context, or other factors, is valuable. Therefore, to the extent that it is practicable to do so, you may wish to account for this in the types of information that you target for collection.

Establishing KPIs and KRIs

> "Metrics are important. It is better that you have one good measurement than fifty rubbish ones – even if the fifty are easy to gather. If they don't actually give you any real information about the success of the mission, it is pointless having them. We love to measure things that are easy to measure. When designers and engineers are asked what a good measurement is, they typically respond with the things they know how to do. As a result, you could end up with a measurement regime where the net result is about as useful as a window box on a submarine. Don't fall into the trap of just measuring things that are quantitative and easy. Think about what a measurement of the effectiveness of the mission is. If you can capture at the beginning what the mission is, measurement is easy. If you find yourself struggling to figure out your measurements, you may need to go back to the beginning and make stakeholders part of the solution space. Ask them to help you design meaningful measurements aligned with the mission."

> – Andy Clark, Founding Director, Primary Key Associates Ltd, Visiting Professor RHUL, Trustee of The National Museum of Computing, SABSA Co-Author

To help you measure the preceding items, it is useful to discuss mechanisms that you can use to accomplish the measurement goals. KPIs can be constructed that will allow you to track a data point over time.

A KPI is essentially a data point about something that you wish to measure. It can be quantitative, reflecting an objective value separate and distinct from the feelings or emotions of individuals (for example, our managed endpoints have averaged 3.4 new vulnerabilities per device in scans). It can also be a qualitative measurement, reflecting overall beliefs or levels of confidence from staff members (25% of our incident response team members are confident or very confident in our incident response process). Both can be useful, though bear in mind that they are actually measuring subtly different things.

As you evaluate your security measures, consider what KPIs you can collect that will give you information about the security measures in your scope. As you do so, be careful to ensure that the metrics you decide upon are normalized for the environment. As an example of why this is important, consider our example from earlier about vulnerability scan information. It is tempting to report an aggregate number of vulnerabilities resulting from scan output – for example, the total number of vulnerabilities in the environment. The issue with this, though, is what happens if the environment changes between scan iterations. The total number of vulnerabilities might increase on the whole, but is that because the patch management isn't working? Or is it because there are now more machines?

To address this, it's useful to normalize KPIs instead of using an aggregate number – for example, instead of reporting the overall number of vulnerabilities resulting from a scan, normalizing the indicator so that it adjusts for population or context. Instead of reporting x vulnerabilities in total, you might instead report a combined metric such as x vulnerabilities per device. This helps establish a consistent score that is meaningful regardless of what happens to the underlying environment. In this example, were you to add additional machines, you may have more overall vulnerabilities, but the vulnerabilities per machine might decrease (if patch management is improving) or stay the same (if it remains constant). If, by contrast, you do not normalize the score to account for the number of machines, obtaining a number of vulnerabilities that is larger than before could be because there are more machines that can and do have vulnerabilities or might be due to actual improvements. Without the contextual information and normalization, it can be hard to know.

Another useful concept here is that of KRIs. Much like performance indicators, KRIs tell you something about the risks to the organization and how they change over time. The only real difference between a KRI and a KPI is the purpose for which you collect it. While a performance indicator will give you information about how well something (a process, a system, an application, and so on) is working, a risk indicator will give you information about how likely an adverse situation is to come about.

For example, say you want to keep track of how likely it is that you will experience a failure in a key system or component. You might choose to keep track of how frequently that event occurs – for example, by tracking the time between failures. **Mean time between failure** (**MTBF**) can give you a window into how likely something is to fail, thereby tipping you off to potential maintenance issues, operational issues, or other issues. In this case, the metric is informing you about a risk (machine failure), which you can use to optimize your planning around keeping that risk managed.

Just like you might use KPIs to ensure that you are collecting and tracking valuable information about the environment (and thereby the operation of security controls), the KRIs can be used to inform you about whether the controls you have in place are sufficient to mitigate risk to the degree you expect and whether things have changed in such a way as to negatively impact your overall risk posture.

Application-specific considerations

When working on security for applications specifically, it bears thinking through a few application-specific considerations and how we'll get data about them during the execution of our design. All of the preceding analytical and information-gathering tools and principles still apply; however, there are a few places where applications, developers, and the development processes supporting them can all benefit from additional or separate collection of data and information.

There are a few places where this is true. First and foremost, as we all know, there are technical tools designed specifically for the analysis of application security issues. **Dynamic application security testing** (**DAST**) can test a compiled binary or web application for weaknesses, whereas **static application security testing** (**SAST**) can analyze source code looking for weaknesses. Special-purpose tools can scan application containers (e.g., Docker) for vulnerabilities in the underlying container image, supporting libraries, middleware, or even the application itself. **Software composition analysis** (**SCA**) tools can look at libraries, dependencies, and other third-party components that the application might depend on. Specialized tools that examine **infrastructure as code (IaC)** technologies (e.g., Terraform, Ansible, etc.) can delve deep into the artifacts that drive deployment and provide security information back.

The point is that, depending on what application you are developing and how you are developing it, data from these tools can serve to provide you with both analytical information during the design process and informational data during the implementation.

Now, if you are working on a security architecture and design for an application and you have access to tools such as these, it goes without saying that you will likely want to incorporate telemetry from these tools into your data-gathering approach. However, even if you are working on a design for a network, environment, business process, or something else, there can still be valuable information to be gleaned from collecting and using information from tools such as these. For example, if you are working on creating a security design to cover a business unit within your organization, and there is a critical business application that is in scope (maybe written in-house or under contract), this data can be important as part of your design process.

Beyond this, there are also considerations about the development process itself. If you're in a shop with a high degree of automation (as might be the case in a DevOps approach), you might consider including information from tools in the DevOps pipeline into the data you collect and KPIs that you track. If you're in a more traditional shop (Agile or even waterfall), you might consider capturing and including data from stage gates or other incremental processes.

Even better is if you can integrate the collection of metrics and information into the process itself. This means that data is collected and provided to you without having to take explicit action.

Modeling and design tools

Of course, in addition to the analytical and informational tools that you can use to gain information that will assist you in the design process, there are also software tools that you can employ as part of the design itself. There are, in fact, numerous special-purpose software tools that can assist with the design process and that you can use as part of your planning process.

Note that the full range of possible tools that you might consider employing to support your work includes hundreds – if not thousands – of individual pieces of software, some open source, some commercial, some cloud-based, and some that run on Linux, macOS, or Windows. Therefore, to provide an exhaustive list of all of them would be impossible. Any tool that can assist with diagramming, modeling, assessing, organizing, and tracking work could be used to support the work that you do. However, there are a few that bear special discussion given how useful they are to a cybersecurity architect's work.

In the following subsections, we will highlight these tools and provide an overview of what they do. Because we are endeavoring to be software-agnostic – and we cannot anticipate important constraints such as the platform that you will be using or the specifics of the tasks you will be applying them to – we will not go into exhaustive detail on the usage of each. Instead, we leave it to you to determine their applicability and suitability to individual projects that you might undertake.

Archi (and ArchiMate)

The very first software tool is the open source Archi tool (`https://www.archimatetool.com/`). **Archi** provides an interface that allows you to create and edit portable architecture models. The Open Group, the stewards of TOGAF, are also the champions and stewards of an abstract architecture modeling language called ArchiMate. **ArchiMate** allows you to employ a standard, visual language to codify stakeholder input, illustrate how those inputs translate to requirements, and illustrate relationships between elements of an enterprise architecture. From there, you can use the language to create views that illustrate how the needs of stakeholders can be met, and also to visually illustrate key decision points (such as, for example, when stakeholder needs are in opposition and one set of needs requires prioritization over another).

The ArchiMate language itself is very powerful: it can be a useful way to organize the design process as well as a useful tool to create illustrations that can be discussed and shared with stakeholders. Note, though, that the ArchiMate specification is not freely available; the Open Group provides a 90-day evaluation copy of the specification for personal use for those organizations that are not ArchiMate Forum members (that is, under a member license).

Microsoft Threat Modeling Tool

For those organizations that intend to make heavy use of threat modeling (which we discussed earlier in this chapter in our discussion of analytical tools), Microsoft provides a free tool to assist in creating threat models (`https://learn.microsoft.com/en-us/azure/security/develop/threat-modeling-tool`). The tool allows you to create a **data flow diagram** (**DFD**) and, from there, helps to automate the analysis process. Specifically, given a set of interacting objects, it helps you analyze (using the STRIDE method) the interactions between components by highlighting potential threats and providing you with a method to categorize, mark up, annotate, and otherwise manipulate the visual representation of the threat model. The software provides generic stencils as well as stencils specific to the Microsoft Azure cloud.

To illustrate this in action, the following is an illustration of a generic, extremely simple web application as shown through the analysis view in the tool:

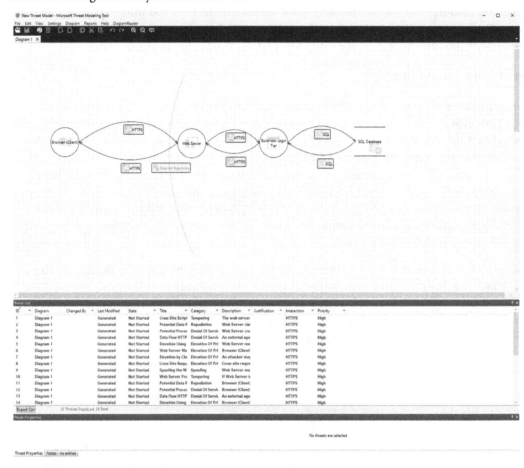

Figure 4.6 – Microsoft Threat Modeling Tool

Threat Dragon

While the Microsoft Threat Modeling Tool has a long history and is in very common use, it is useful to note that it is only supported on the Microsoft Windows environment, which you may not be working in. A similar tool, entitled **Threat Dragon** (maintained at the home page www.threatdragon.com), is being developed by the non-profit **Open Worldwide Application Security Project (OWASP)** as a lightweight alternative.

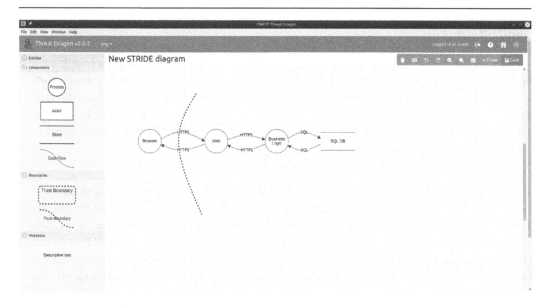

Figure 4.7 – Threat Dragon

Modelio

Modelio (`www.modelio.org`) is another open source visualization tool that can be used to support the design process. In addition to supporting ArchiMate, the software can also be used to create and edit **Unified Modeling Language** (**UML**), **Systems Modeling Language** (**SysML**), and numerous other visual diagramming techniques and standards.

Commercial modeling tools

In the preceding sections, we've focused on free and/or open source software that you can employ to assist in visual representations of your designs. There are, of course, numerous commercial alternatives that you might choose to employ instead. A few examples include the following:

- **ABACUS**: `https://www.avolutionsoftware.com/abacus/`
- **Innoslate**: `https://www.innoslate.com/`
- **Planview**: `https://www.planview.com/`
- **Sparx Systems Enterprise Architect**: `https://sparxsystems.com/`
- **Erwin**: `https://erwin.com/`

Note that this is not an exhaustive list; there are dozens of tools available commercially that can assist with specific aspects of the design and documentation process. In general, recognizing that many commercial tools will be out of reach for some portion of those reading this book (in particular, small teams), we have spent comparatively more time on discussions of free tools. That said, for a larger team, or those with a sizeable budget for architecture efforts, a commercial tool may provide value.

Visualization tools

In addition to those tools that specialize in architecture-specific modeling, there are also a host of other visualization tools that can be used for generic diagramming that are not tied tightly to architectural context and usage – for example, commercial diagramming tools such as Microsoft Visio, the open source Dia tool (`http://dia-installer.de/`), or the cloud-based tool Lucidchart; even (at a pinch) Microsoft PowerPoint or LibreOffice Draw can be used to visually represent your designs.

Mind mapping tools

One special category of tools that bears special discussion is **mind mapping tools**. These tools allow you to organize and categorize related concepts and information graphically. As we get into the specifics of the design process itself (particularly once we progress beyond requirements and high-level goals and move into implementation), we will employ mind mapping tools as one method to help you organize and categorize information about constraints and help you gather together in one place the information required for solution building. Tools such as XMind, MindManager, and Lucidchart can provide this functionality (indeed, as can any diagramming tool if used creatively), as can the open source FreeMind (`https://sourceforge.net/projects/freemind/`).

Collaboration tools

Lastly, you can employ collaboration and productivity tools such as Evernote, Microsoft Teams, Slack, Google Docs, Basecamp, Microsoft Project, and numerous others to help you do the following:

- Communicate with team members and stakeholders
- Capture key decisions
- Record and retain important information and documentation
- Organize and track project work
- Capture and archive discussions with stakeholders
- Create and distribute documentation
- Collect metrics
- As well as numerous other important tasks

In addition to the informational, analytical, and modeling/design tools that we can use as part of the planning process, there are also resources that we can use as input – meaning the specific security measures that we can use and security goals that we can target as we plan out our target state. These are the building blocks that serve as the source material and substrate on which our designs will rest. While there are numerous standards and frameworks out there (a few of the most common that we listed earlier) to help you, it's useful to run through them in detail to level-set. If you are an experienced security practitioner, you may find it valuable to skip over this next section as we will be covering some fundamentals of secure design approaches for those that might be newer to the profession.

Case study – data gathering

"One of the most powerful tools we have is the ability to collect and analyze data. Nearly every organization collects metrics: in many cases, too much. They collect metrics for system performance, system health, and numerous other areas. But not, very often, do they collect the right information. In fact, I have almost never seen an organization collecting and using the right set of metrics. The ones that get closest have a definitive edge."

– Deepayan Chanda, Principal (Cybersecurity Strategy, Architecture, and Governance), UNSW (University of New South Wales)

In an interview, we asked Deepayan Chanda about how important data collection tools and telemetry are to the architecture process. He explained both their importance as well as how he's seen organizations get it right (and wrong):

"Most commonly, I see metrics that are defined and curated in a way that suits the person presenting. As an example, consider members of a SOC (security operations center) team presenting to security management or the CISO. These individuals all have their own frame of reference, and they want to see things from within their own context. They might collect and track information about how many machines are under their management, how many critical tickets there are, how many incidents they've had above a given severity threshold (at or above high criticality for example), etc."

He pointed out that the architect has a strong need to gather information about their current state and how this can directly inform the architecture process. He described how and why via a case study that he observed at one point in his career:

"In a large, multinational organization, they were reporting on coverage for vulnerability management. They were preparing a bimonthly report (every 15 days) where they would report coverage of managed Windows machines; typically, they would consistently report that 95 or 96 percent of Windows devices were managed across the board. This was in every report: 95%, 96%, etc. In seeing this, I was frankly skeptical. My first question was, 'What was your reference point? It says 95%, but 95% of what? Does this represent all the machines we have?' I was skeptical because this is a global organization: the number should have been much higher than what they were showing. Keep in mind that there are desktops and servers, there's on-premise, data center, and cloud infrastructures. When you put all these together, the population should be very high.

The individuals collecting this information described to me how they were only including a subset in this. They had specifically and purposefully tailored their scope such that they were taking a smaller, narrower view into the organization. I investigated why this was the case and was given the answer that they didn't have capacity to include more than this – this was what they were able to collect."

He went on to describe a related situation: *"In this same organization, they had outsourced a portion of the infrastructure within the SOC for security monitoring. In this case, I again asked the same question: how much is being monitored? Just like in the prior example, they were only monitoring a subset: in this case, critical firewalls. Aside from the fact that the idea of 'criticality' in this context is questionable, consider that this was a global organization operating in 50+ countries across the world. The monitoring being done was for about 50 or 60 firewalls. For an organization this size, even if you just count only the perimeter firewalls, 50 is not realistically enough to represent the full picture."*

Deepayan described how the architecture process depends on the ability to know where you stand. After all, if you don't have awareness of where you are now, how can you possibly know what to change and where? He phrased it this way, "*Practically, the question goes back to whether you are collecting and looking at the right thing. If I am not getting the right information in that it's only partial, incomplete, or limited in some way, then I can't make the right choices and create the right strategy. For example, if management sees that they have 95 percent coverage (as was the case in the first example of the Windows coverage reporting), why on Earth would they invest in improvements for that? If instead I show the real number – that it's more like 45 or 50 percent – then they can ask the important questions like how to do it better or where to invest to make improvements. This gives us an end goal, which in turn provides us a path for where to go in our strategy.*"

He went on to describe why this is so very important to the architecture process itself: "*It's very important in architecture to consider whether we need to make a change in the first place. If I'm not able to monitor the entire problem, if I'm only able to get extraneous data, or if I can get the right data but can't process it (for example due to volume), how then can I diagnose what is wrong? How do I assess options for what to do about it? All of these are of strategic importance and represent design elements that should feed back into the architecture process.*"

Building blocks of secure design

Any discussion about the requisite tools in your design toolbox wouldn't be complete without some discussion of the actual security mechanisms that you'll employ as part of your design. These represent specific measures you might use – and specific objectives that you might target – as part of a broader, overarching security design.

It's important to understand what these controls are and what they are not. They are not implementations. Any given control can be implemented in a myriad of different ways. For example, you might have a control objective specifying that any administrative access to production systems (and system components) must be logged and recorded. However, this in itself doesn't outline how you'd do that. Instead, context, circumstances, and the organization itself will dictate how you accomplish the result and how you implement that control within your organizational context. For example, if access to a production system happens via a terminal (that is, a user at the keyboard), you might use the native logging capability of the operating system to log this. If instead, administrative access happens via an application's admin user accessing a web application, you might employ web server logs to accomplish the same thing. The specific mechanism isn't specified when discussing the high-level control objective, the high-level mechanism, the purpose of the control, and so on.

Likewise, controls are not goals in and of themselves – at least not goals that your organization will always have by default. For example, in the case of the system monitoring control we used in the preceding example, you'll notice that the control doesn't specify *why* you would do this. One organization might implement this control because they need to adhere to a regulatory requirement that requires them to do so, while another might do so because of a contractual commitment to a customer. Yet another might be motivated in their decision because they wish to mitigate certain types of risk.

Instead, what these controls represent are *security capabilities*. This means they provide an idealized security-relevant strategy in the absence of a particular implementation to accomplish it. This is why we've chosen to list them along with the design tools that you may wish to employ as part of the design work that you do.

The reason this is valuable to us as architects is that we can examine these controls as strategies that we can consider in response to particular challenges that we might encounter in design. As an analogy to illustrate what we mean here, consider a football playbook. A smart team will select a given strategy from those that the team has practiced thoroughly and that they have drilled on. In response to circumstances (for example, weaknesses in the other team's play, tactics in use by the opposing team, how far into the game it is, the current score, etc.), they might select one strategy over another from those that they have prepared. The playbook doesn't know the circumstances, nor does it specify each individual player by name; instead, it lays out the capability in the abstract and allows the team to select from those capabilities based on the situation and other factors.

Now, we should mention that there is no way that we can cover all the possible security tools (controls) that exist in a book such as this one. Not only would such a list be almost immediately incomplete (as new technologies are always being developed and existing ones added), but it would take more time to go through them at any level of detail than we have space in this book. However, there are some controls that you will encounter time and again (for example, those covered in high-level standards, frameworks, and regulatory requirements) as well as those that you will encounter much less frequently. In fact, you could have a book longer than this one exclusively focused on security controls and still not do the topic justice.

As such, we will provide some background on control categories, but will not go to the level of listing individual controls – or specific tools that allow you to build the capabilities outlined by the controls. This is because of the following:

- They are covered in detail in other sources, in particular the standards/frameworks from which they're derived

- There will always be new methods, implementations, and controls beyond what we can cover (some of which might be only applicable to a small number of organizations)

- Any comprehensive coverage would require a book in itself

- Many of those reading this book will already be familiar with many, most, or all of them depending on background and previous experience

As such, we are deliberately covering these at a high level and leaving the bulk of the exposition to other more authoritative sources. That said, it is productive to walk through some of the high-level categories of security measures that you might have in mind as part of your design for those who don't have years of experience under their belt or those who just find it helpful to have a refresher. We'll walk through some of the high-level categories of measures that you might consider. The purpose of doing this is for those that are newer to the security world and that may have less familiarity with some of the techniques that you might consider employing as part of your security designs.

For the sake of organization, we'll walk through the high-level control areas within ISO/IEC 27001:2013 (*Information technology – Security techniques – Information security management systems – Requirements*) with an eye on describing why they are valuable, how/where you might use them, and some thoughts about integrating them into your security design.

We should note that, as of the second edition of this book, there exists an update to the ISO/IEC standard: specifically, ISO/IEC 27001:2022 (*Information security, cybersecurity, and privacy protection – Information security management systems – Requirements*). While much of the standard is functionally equivalent to prior versions, and the *2022 control annex* (i.e., *Annex A*) can be easily used for this purpose instead of the 2012 version, we have elected to continue to use the organization from the 2013 standard for several reasons:

- Most existing security programs (**Information Security Management Systems** or **ISMSs**) currently continue to use the 2013 version of the Annex due to the relative newness of the updated standard.

- The longevity of the 2013 iteration of the standard (having as it does close to a decade of existing use in the field) means that significant documentation exists addressing the interpretation of the controls and providing additional guidance and resources for those who wish to examine them more closely.

- The organization of the Annex in the 2022 standard has been significantly compressed (there are now 4 categories rather than the 14 categories in the 2013 version). The more granular organization of the prior version assists us in providing the explanation in this section in a more granular way.

Really, we could use any catalog of controls to organize this: in addition to the 2013 Annex, we could use the Annex from the 2022 revision, or we could use another standard entirely such as that found in NIST Special Publication 800-53. The reason why we've selected ISO is twofold. First, alignment. ISO/IEC 27002:2013: *Information technology – Security techniques – Code of practice for information security controls*) is designed to align perfectly with ISO/IEC 27001:2013 Annex A. Likewise, ISO/IEC 27002:2022 (*Information security, cybersecurity, and privacy protection – Information security controls*) is designed to align with ISO/IEC 27001:2022 Annex A. What this means in practice is that, because ISO 27002 provides detailed information about each of the control areas that we'll be covering, there is built-in implementation guidance available within the standards. This means there is quite a bit of information in the source material already for those who wish to gain further information or pursue an individual topic further. Second, because of the use and prevalence of the ISO standard (naturally, given that it is an international standard), many other frameworks and reference materials are already mapped to it (either directly or indirectly).

In so doing, we should mention that we've tried to draw exclusively throughout this book from sources that are freely available to all. ISO standards are not available freely. However, because of the prevalence of the ISO/IEC standards for security, these same controls have been used in numerous other standards and frameworks that are freely available. For example, the NIST Cybersecurity Framework includes controls from ISO/IEC 27001:2013 Annex A in the *Informative References* section of the framework. Likewise, *NIST Special Publication 800-53* includes a list of controls already mapped against ISO/IEC 27001 in *Appendix H* of that document. The point is, by using this standard, additional supplemental information is available both in the ISO standards documentation itself as well as other documentation that is freely available to all. As such, those looking to engage with the material in the standard can optionally do so in a manner that does not require additional expense.

As an overview then, we'll walk through the high-level categories addressed in the standard. For those who have been practicing security for a while and are familiar with the different control areas and how they can be used by the practitioner, feel free to skip to the end of this chapter.

Information security policies

The first items we'll cover relate to information security policy. Policy is important because it establishes the governance structures that demonstrate management intent that security be prioritized.

Management direction for information security

Policies, procedures, standards, and guidance are – as we outlined in *Chapter 2, Architecture – The Core of Solution Building* – an instrumental part of any security program. They have value both in setting the direction for the organization as well as ensuring linkage between security measures and the goals of the organization, as well as any compliance requirements that may be in scope.

From the point of view of the architect, policy is valuable in two ways. First, it can help us effect security measures that are challenging to implement technically. For example, individual employees are a great detection instrument for security incidents: many times, the first inkling that we will have about an attack is from the reporting of suspicious behavior by personnel who are in a position to notice unusual behavior. By codifying a requirement to notify about their observations (for example, in the event of suspicious behavior) and providing a path for them to do so, we can build out our capability for detection. Policy is one way to establish responsibility for doing this.

Second, it is useful because it will underpin many of the decisions that we make about design. We may create designs in order to enforce particular policy goals that pertain to security. So, it is both an input and an output to the architecture process.

Organization of information security

This next area relates to how the information security function is organized within the context of a broader organization. As with any function within an organization, information security should be managed and internally organized.

Internal organization

The internal organization of security is important because it establishes a management framework that can be used by the rest of the organization in responding to security events, managing security, and ensuring appropriate security hygiene. That said, it is also a tool that can be used by the architect as a way to implement specific goals.

There will be times when the assignment of personnel to a task is the only (or at least the optimal) way to bring about what we want. Additionally, we may need to bring about or recommend organizational changes to ensure that what we intend is performed. As an example, say that you want to ensure that systems are monitored – for example, by having analysts review system activity and output from relevant security tools. The organization may not be currently set up to accomplish this. To accomplish your goal in that case, you might need to specifically tap individuals to do so, modifying the organizational structure and personnel assignments in the process.

Mobile devices and teleworking

For those individuals who work remotely, travel, or otherwise need to make use of resources off premises, these controls detail mechanisms for secure connectivity and the protection of systems/data while working remotely. This can include the use of a VPN, **cloud access security broker** (**CASB**), teleconferencing solutions, cloud tools (appropriately protected), and numerous other tools that help extend the work environment off premises. Historically, these were largely focused on providing access to internal, on-premises resources for those that were off premises. However, in today's environment, it can expand to include providing access to cloud resources and other hosted resources that are not necessarily under the direct control of the organization.

From an architect's point of view, we can use controls of this type to enable mobile and cloud usage. This can be a useful way to help accomplish availability goals – for example, when critical business applications can be relocated to the cloud to allow continued access even in the event of a localized outage in our infrastructure. Mechanisms of this type can also help to provide access to resources for particular business processes, applications, or resources.

Human resources security

Personnel management is an important element of security as well. Employee background checks, personnel training, security awareness, disciplinary processes, and numerous other elements are important in keeping the organization protected.

At first glance, it might seem like these elements are outside the scope of the security architect since they do not specifically address technological considerations. However, recall that the work of the architect is about ensuring the security of the environment generally. In other words, there is more to the role of the architect than focusing entirely on technology.

As such, these control categories can absolutely play a role in ensuring the outcomes desired by the architect. As an example, consider an organization that is working on a project for a US federal agency or working in a jurisdiction where personnel working in a certain context are required to be *domestic* (in US defense parlance, *no foreign nationals*) or in a financial services context where felons are prohibited. In such a context, having the ability to vet employees is a goal every bit as important as technological considerations.

Likewise, personnel controls such as training and awareness or hiring controls can help achieve specific security outcomes – for example, reducing the likelihood of an employee clicking on a phishing email. As with other control categories then, it becomes both a potential input (as requirements) and output (as a strategy to achieve specific outcomes) to the architecture process.

Prior to employment

Pre-employment screening includes measures designed to ensure that personnel brought into the organization do not pose a risk to the information that they may have access to. Background checks, employment verification, aptitude testing, credential verification, and other measures to vet the candidate prior to employment can fall into this category.

In terms of our security design, we may introduce pre-employment screening controls in situations where they do not already exist and as a way to ensure that personnel with access to certain types of data (for example, sensitive data, data covered by regulatory and/or compliance requirements, or data that is covered by contractual requirements) are vetted for potential criminal backgrounds or other undesirable behavior.

During employment

While an employee, contractor, partner, vendor, or other associate is working within the organization, they have certain obligations related to cybersecurity. During the course of their employment, we may wish to implement certain measures to ensure that they adhere to these obligations and responsibilities. For example, we might conduct awareness campaigns to ensure that they are aware of certain attacks, that they are on the alert for phishing or other malicious content, and so on.

For the architect, we may wish to either amend, update, or even create new awareness materials, campaigns, and/or training to address issues or to promote certain actions. For example, we might do so as a part of ensuring good mail hygiene through conducting phishing training and phishing simulation.

Termination and change of employment

Just as certain measures are required when a new employee is onboarded to the organization, so too are there obligations that come into play when an employee leaves or changes role. For example, we want to make sure that employees leaving the organization no longer have access to critical resources or confidential data and that they are managed in such a way as to prevent possible violence or retaliation. When changing roles, we want to make sure that we prevent the proliferation of access in specific individuals.

This is obviously good security practice to ensure that accounts are discontinued upon termination. From an architect's point of view, we will want to make sure that we account for the termination of employee access (either because they leave the organization or because they change roles).

Asset management

These controls are concerned with the management of organizational assets. These can be any assets, including the following:

- Servers
- Workstations
- Laptops
- Mobile equipment
- Data
- Environments
- Virtual machines
- Application containers
- Software components
- Applications

As you can see, there are many different types of assets that could be in scope. The specific context will dictate which types of assets you are primarily concerned with.

Responsibility for assets

This relates to ensuring that assets are appropriately managed throughout the organization – for example, that assets are kept track of when they're in use, that they are appropriately commissioned and decommissioned, that there is a process to ensure they stay secure, and so on.

There are multiple strategies to accomplish these goals – for example, we might keep a record of our inventory on a spreadsheet, use a paper record, or use a special-purpose tool built specifically around asset management. We might automate portions of the process to leverage technology components (for example, orchestration tools) that help keep track of entities for us.

As architects, reliable asset management (both of data and devices) is an important consideration for two reasons. First, it speaks to how easy or difficult the environment is to manage – the harder to manage, the more opportunity for accidental mistakes, oversights, or other errors that can open cracks that attackers can use to gain access. Second, knowing what a system, data, or environment is (and what its purpose is) provides a foundational step in knowing how it should be secured.

Information classification

This group relates to separating information into logical groups based on sensitivity. For example, just like you have data that is very sensitive and confidential, so too might you have information that is designed to be public by nature (for example, the information on your organization's public website). These different sensitivities bring about different requirements for how that data is handled, stored, transmitted, and accessed. While the integrity of public information is important (you don't want your competitors to make changes to what your website says, for example), you might have a lower requirement for confidentiality than, for example, your employee salary database or upcoming M&A planning documents. Separating data by sensitivity level is helpful because it helps you apply the right security measures to the right areas.

Media handling

It is important to protect electronic media (any kind of storage – hard disks, tapes, USB sticks, and so on) to ensure that the information on them isn't accessible to those individuals who may come across that media. This means that the media's usage is controlled and that it's stored securely when not in active use; it may even mean that you apply controls such as cryptography to prevent the media from being accessed without the proper key. The entire life cycle of media should be considered in our designs: both at the point that the media is acquired and introduced to our environment, how it's used and handled, how it's shipped, and then, ultimately, how it is destroyed or scrubbed.

It matters to the architect to ensure that media handling does not circumvent or obviate any data protection measures that the architect builds elsewhere, and also to ensure that appropriate diligence is used to secure data wherever it is stored.

Access control

The controls in this group relate to ensuring that the right individuals, devices, or software agents have access to the right things – and that they don't have access to things they shouldn't.

Business requirements of access control

This relates to ensuring that we have the right measures to limit access to information and/or locations where information is stored. This can include logical access controls in the case of logical access to data or physical access controls in the case of a secure facility – it can also include either technical, administrative, procedural, or other measures that help realize this intent. This is important to the architect as a data source – in particular, understanding why access controls are restrictive or permissive in the way that they are.

User access management

This relates to ensuring that individuals within the organization, partners, vendors, customers, and anyone else with whom we have a need to share data have the right access. This means that any authentication information we use to authenticate them (for example, their password) is secured appropriately, that users are provisioned and terminated at the right times, that use of privileged accounts (such as root users, administrative accounts, and so on) are managed, and so on. In essence, this goal is about ensuring that the access that users have is the right access.

For the architect, these controls are important because they define who can get access, how they do so, and under what circumstances.

User responsibilities

This means defining user responsibilities for keeping their access secured. For example, this includes the requirement for users to keep their password appropriately protected and of sufficient quality, and that they refrain from allowing it to fall into the hands of others. For an architect, user behavior can be strategically altered to forward security goals and also to work in alignment with security measures already in place.

System and application access control

This category refers to ensuring that the systems that users will log into (be they operating systems, platforms, network resources, applications, middleware, and so on) appropriately enforce access control measures. This means that they have a robust way to validate the user, that they restrict access to information and features based on roles, that privileged programs are protected based on business needs, and so on. From an architecture standpoint, this is important because it governs access to key systems and applications.

Cryptography

This domain covers controls that relate to enciphering and deciphering data, data integrity, authentication of communications and user sessions, and other security goals that are supported by cryptography.

Cryptographic controls

These controls relate to ensuring that cryptography (when used to satisfy any of the other security goals) is strong, that keys are used and stored appropriately, and that cryptography is implemented in a trustworthy fashion. Cryptography can be a very powerful tool when it comes to ensuring security goals; it can be used to safeguard confidentiality by keeping eavesdroppers or unauthorized persons from seeing data they shouldn't, ensure data integrity by providing mechanisms to validate that data stored or sent was not inappropriately modified, provide proof of the originator of a message or data, and provide non-repudiation. It can also be used in creative ways beyond this – for example, to enforce data spoliation (i.e., crypto-shredding) where data is encrypted with a key that will be purposefully deleted after a defined period of time, thereby ensuring that the encrypted records are no longer available once that time has elapsed.

As an architect (particularly when working on application security architecture), this is one of the primary tools in our toolbox to ensure that data at rest and data in transit is kept secure.

Physical and environmental security

This domain relates to ensuring that the physical locations, facilities, offices, server rooms, data centers, and other locations are protected from unauthorized intruders and are resilient against manmade or natural disasters.

Much like human resource controls, there is a temptation sometimes to assume that physical and environmental controls are outside the purview of the security architect because they often don't relate directly to the technology that we use in our organizations. However, once again, they can be every bit as important both as an input into the security design as well as a potential strategy to help meet specific goals.

Secure areas

This means secure areas remain free from unauthorized access and that they are protected appropriately from disasters, accidents, misuse, and so on. Only sometimes will the physical access to facilities or environments be within the security architect's scope of responsibility. However, there can be times when we might make strategic decisions about what controls to implement based on the physical security of the environment – for example, we might choose to employ cryptography in situations where physical access to devices is unsecured and not do so when they are stored within a data center.

Equipment

This relates to ensuring that equipment stored within a facility is protected – that it is protected from accidental or purposeful damage and also protected from unauthorized access. It also means, though, that the equipment itself is stored, used, and configured in a secure way. For example, this could include cabling requirements for machines within a data center, ensuring that equipment is appropriately maintained (that is, kept in functional working order), and so on.

Operations security

This domain relates to securing the operating environment and operational processes in which critical systems and data operate.

Operational procedures and responsibilities

This group relates to ensuring that procedures are followed to help ensure disciplined, smooth, and reliable operations of technologies and technological systems. This includes change management processes, documented operating procedures, and other controls to ensure that robust and disciplined procedures are followed.

From an architecture point of view, very often the solutions that we design will require amendments or updates to existing procedures, new operational procedures, changes to operational tools and models, or have other operational impacts. Likewise, we might change the operating environment, procedures, or roles and responsibilities to forward a security goal or to otherwise support other security measures that we put in place.

Protection from malware

This group ensures that the organization maintains a robust defense against malware through technical, operational, and other means.

Backup

These controls ensure that systems are kept backed up, that restoration capabilities are functional and will work when needed, and that backups are appropriately protected, free from tampering or spoilage, and are available when needed. The architect may wish to ensure that backup mechanisms are employed in the event of accidental or purposeful loss of data, as a strategy to defend against certain types of attacks (for example, ransomware) or to forward other security goals.

Logging and monitoring

These controls ensure that records are kept about critical events and that the records kept are sufficient to determine what (or who) caused a situation to come about. The specific records to keep will vary depending on the type of system, facility, or application in scope. This includes the protection of log data from tampering or deletion, ensuring that the log entries are sufficient to allow an event to be reconstructed where necessary, and so on. For the architect, this will often be part of a robust design. In particular, to ensure that an evidence trail is retained in the event of an attack or breach.

Control of operational software

These controls ensure that the integrity of system components (for example, the operating system on which an application runs) is protected. This includes limitations on the installation and running of new software on the machine by unauthorized persons, as well as the subversion of installed software through other means. We will wish to limit who can get access to operational software that might subvert the security model that we design.

Technical vulnerability management

These controls ensure that technical vulnerabilities are identified and closed in a timely fashion. This can include the identification of vulnerabilities in critical systems or applications, as well as the prevention of someone exploiting those vulnerabilities (either through remediation or other means). As we construct new designs, we will want to make sure that the security model isn't subverted by means of technical vulnerabilities; we will also want to build in resilience against these vulnerabilities for our design scope.

Information systems audit considerations

These controls ensure that review activities such as audits do not interrupt, interfere with, or otherwise unduly constrain operations (including security operations). From an architecture standpoint, we will want to ensure that systems, applications, and data stay hardened and robust, regardless of other activities (including audits) that may be going on around them.

Communications security

This domain relates to ensuring that communications used by the organization are appropriately secured – specifically, that data is kept confidential, data integrity is assured, and that communications and services remain available when under duress.

Network security management

These controls ensure that networks are appropriately protected. This includes keeping networks hardened against external attack, ensuring reliable monitoring and a robust perimeter, administration of networks, and so on. The architect may need to be involved in helping to ensure this goal and may rely on these controls to underpin the security model in other areas.

Information transfer

These controls ensure that information, when transferred between networks, systems, entities, organizations, or any other parties, is protected up to, during, and after the transfer. This includes formal data exchange agreements with service providers or outside contractors, as well as more informal, lighter-weight exchanges, such as SMS, email, or other messaging capabilities. Architects will want to ensure that the transfer of information is appropriately secured and, as with other communication security measures, may use defenses in this area to underpin the envisioned security model and design elsewhere.

System acquisition, development, and maintenance

These relate to how we deploy and maintain the systems, applications, and other resources in the organization.

Security requirements of information systems

These controls ensure that security is included in the requirements for information systems. This includes the evaluation of requirements during a COTS software deployment, as well as systematic analysis and consideration of requirements during a development project (for example, when we're creating new software). The architect will help define these requirements and work to select and implement the technical, operational, procedural, and other strategies to ensure that they are realized.

Security in development and support processes

These controls ensure that security measures are in place as a system is implemented, developed, and supported. This can include following secure development or implementation processes, ensuring that the help desk or other support staff follow appropriate security measures, and so on. Architects will want to make sure that these controls are in place to ensure reliable, hardened outcomes as a result of development efforts, but also because development and/or support work may be performed to implement security measures that form part of the overall security design.

Test data

These controls ensure that test data is kept appropriately secured, that it does not contain sensitive information, that sensitive and/or regulated information is sanitized, or (in situations where sensitive data for testing purposes is unavoidable) that the data is appropriately protected. Architects will want to secure test data as an outcome of their design work and to the extent that test data is employed as part of operations or testing of their designs.

Supplier relationships

This domain relates to ensuring that relationships with external vendors, partners, and participants in the organization's supply chain are secured. Suppliers form an important part of the security of the organization employing them; for example, consider how important cloud service providers are to the technology landscape of most organizations. Therefore, it's important that we make sure that these principles are protected.

Information security in supplier relationships

Even though our processes might be robust and internal personnel are following the right processes, there are still opportunities for risks to arise as a result of external vendors, partners, suppliers, and other entities within the supply chain. The goal of these controls is to make sure that assets are protected from (or despite) those entities in the value chain. The architect will find these valuable both as an objective to meet with their designs (provided such relationships are in scope) and also since these suppliers may very well support the security model they design and security measures they field.

Supplier service delivery management

This goal is about making sure that the service providers in scope adhere to the defined level of service and security. As with the previous control group, architects will want to ensure that this goal is met and also make sure that services delivered that underpin security are managed appropriately.

Information security incident management

This area relates to ensuring that security incidents are managed appropriately, including breaches or potential breaches, investigations, review of evidence, and forensics.

Management of information security incidents and improvements

These controls ensure that incidents are managed appropriately and that the operational aspects, communication methods, executive decisions, and all other aspects are accounted for and consistent (reproducible) from incident to incident. This helps to ensure that the evidence collected is useful in the furtherance of law enforcement (should it be necessary), that the organization is protected during the incident by following pre-evaluated processes and methods, and that all regulatory, legal, and contractual mandates are adhered to.

The architect will want to ensure that incident response processes are supported by security measures and appropriate procedures, that incident management is fostered by the security design and security models they develop, and that the security model is not undermined during a security incident.

Information security aspects of business continuity management

This domain relates to ensuring that security elements and objectives are met during business continuity planning and that the security goals continue to be met during an outage.

Information security continuity

In the event that business is disrupted, it is nevertheless important to ensure that the security goals that we have are met before the incident (of course), during the incident itself, and during the recovery period after the incident. This goal encapsulates the idea that information security – that is, adherence to our security goals – is important even during a crisis or other unforeseen disruption to business. The architect will want to enable continuity goals and ensure that security measures continue to provide protection in the event of an event or outage.

Redundancies

These controls provide capabilities to ensure that critical services remain available during a crisis situation. This includes both technical resources, such as applications and systems that employees use to do their jobs, and critical systems employed by customers. It provides a mechanism or mechanisms for employees to continue to be productive during an outage or unplanned event. The architect will want to plan redundancies into their designs to meet availability goals and ensure that the security measures they introduce likewise employ redundancy strategies to ensure their continued operation in the event of an outage.

Compliance

This domain focuses on ensuring compliance with legal, regulatory, contractual, or other requirements that may be in the organization's scope.

Compliance with legal and contractual requirements

These controls ensure that all legal, regulatory, contractual, and other requirements are adhered to during the organization's performance of its mission. The architect will want to understand what compliance requirements are addressed in their designs, will want to implement strategies that support compliance objectives, and will want to implement mechanisms that disallow prohibited situations from coming to pass.

Information security reviews

These controls ensure that the security of the organization is periodically reviewed and monitored. This ensures that the security of the organization is kept within defined parameters of operation over time. The architect will want to account for security review as part of their planning and leverage security review where they can gather data about the environment and the operation of the security model and mechanisms they put in place.

Summary

Throughout this chapter, we've looked at the tools that you can put into your toolbox to help you achieve a secure, robust design. This includes enterprise and application analytical and information-gathering techniques, as well as high-level security goals that will become part of your design process. Not every organization can or will establish every analytical or information-gathering tool; likewise, not every goal will be applicable to every organization for every use case. That said, it is important that we understand some of the goals that we might wish to ensure so that we can select implementation strategies to get us there. We'll do this in the upcoming chapters.

In the next chapter, we will begin the process of applying these tools to the creation of designs for enterprise scope. There is still some information that we will need to gather, some questions we will need to answer, and buy-in and validation from stakeholders to gain. However, we can begin the process of putting together the documentation, planning, and other key elements that will support the design – and ultimately, the implementation – of a security architecture.

5

Building an Architecture – Developing Enterprise Blueprints

At this point, you have all the ingredients and raw materials you'll need to complete your design. In *Chapter 3, Building an Architecture – Scope and Requirements*, we went through developing the initial baseline scope that you will use to create your design, while in the previous chapter, we looked at the tools that you might want to have in your toolbox as you ideate, document, and field your design.

This chapter, on the other hand, is all about crafting and documenting your *vision*. This is the information that will let you plan, validate, and document the *blueprint* that targets the security goals you have within the defined scope, as well as plan around any pre-existing constraints.

Throughout this chapter, we'll put those elements together and go through the elements of the enterprise cybersecurity architecture planning strategy in detail. We will cover the following topics:

- Blueprints
- Process
- The vision
- Case study—shared goals, vision, and engagement
- Creating a program
- Documenting your high-level approach

Let's get started!

Requirements

If you've been following along, you'll have a few things already prepared:

- **Informal scope**: You've spent some time thinking about the scope of your planning, but you (purposefully) haven't documented it yet. In *Chapter 3, Building an Architecture – Scope and Requirements*, we went through the process of defining an informal scope. In this chapter, we will build on that to arrive at an actual recordable design scope.

- **Existing landscape**: In the last chapter (*Chapter 4, Building an Architecture – Your Toolbox*), we talked about strategies to understand what you have in place now. This ideally includes an understanding of existing constraints that you'll need to account for and plan around (recall the gap analysis discussion), as well as an understanding of what is in place already so that you can look for areas of efficiency during the implementation process. Some projects will start with a *blue ocean*—meaning a completely new environment, application, or organization/process— where we don't have existing security controls, technology artifacts, or other considerations that we need to plan around. Most of the time, though, you'll be working within a framework of what exists already.

- **Goals**: You should now have an idea of what your organization cares about with respect to security, how it understands security, and what matters to the organization contextually. Recall from the goal discussion in *Chapter 3, Building an Architecture – Scope and Requirements*, that all security measures and elements of the security system trace back to supporting business goals. You will want to refine your understanding of those goals as you create your planning documentation.

As an analogy, imagine that you are working on a craft or home project. There comes a point in that process where you'll have established the scope or boundary of what you're looking to do (for example, that you're going to work on a woodworking project), where you have all your tools organized and assembled, but you have yet to begin doing the work. That's where we are now in the security design process.

Blueprints

In this chapter, we'll take a step forward by building on the elements that we've covered and the work that we've done already to develop the plans that we will execute. This will ultimately result in the creation of a **blueprint—**that is, the design and the artifacts you will develop to encapsulate, describe, and codify the design. Note that the word "blueprint" isn't standard terminology—it's what we're using here to describe a set of related documents that all help achieve a central goal. This is typically analogous to the role and purpose of what a traditional blueprint does in a physical construction context.

So, what's in this blueprint? Several things. At the highest levels of abstraction, we're trying to accomplish two things simultaneously. The first, and arguably most important, is that we want to capture elements of the desired future state that we will be trying to achieve by applying our security efforts. This is the *vision*: what **The Open Group Architecture Framework (TOGAF)** calls the *Architecture Vision* and what the **Sherwood Applied Business Security Architecture (SABSA)** calls the *Conceptual Security Architecture*. The second thing that we are looking to do is create documentation that we can use to execute. Setting the vision allows us to create a buildable, executable design.

Reflect for a moment on the purpose of a blueprint in a physical design context, such as if you were an individual having a new home constructed for you to live in. As a client, the first planning document you would expect to see would not be a physical blueprint if you hired an architect. For example, the architect would likely have a whole host of conversations with you first to explore the *fitness of purpose* before they create a document to build from. This is to allow them to first understand how you will use the space and what your goals are (financial, aesthetic, utility, and so on).

From there, the architect might create intermediate documents—for example, elevation diagrams—to showcase their ideas to you. They might then take you on a virtual 3D view of the house (for example, using design software) or even, in some cases, build a small model of the home that you can view. Only once you've agreed to the design conceptually will they then create a detailed design schematic that someone can actually build to. In other words, only once you and they are in agreement on the end goal will they then turn their initial vision into detailed designs someone can build to.

There's a reason for all this pre-work. From the architect's point of view, they want to make sure that the building is fit for purpose, that you get the aesthetic you want, that there aren't unexpected "gotchas," and so on. For our purposes in a security architecture context, we will need to do the same thing—and for the same reason—to create that more specific, actionable design, meaning that we want to discuss with those who are most impacted by the design to make sure they're getting what they want, that there aren't unexpected snags, that they agree on the end goals, and so on.

Both parts of this process are critical to planning for a few reasons, as outlined here:

- It allows us to socialize the design to stakeholders and decision-makers
- It serves as a template upon which specialized **subject-matter experts** (**SMEs**) can plan the more detailed implementations and logistics that will need to occur for us to realize the vision
- It provides a baseline for the measurement of progress and work-tracking
- It allows us to report to stakeholders and leadership about the status of our design and implementation efforts

As you can see, these are important steps. This in turn means that not only is it important that you *do* the planning work, but also that you *document* that work. This means that you should create an artifact that codifies the design.

As a general rule of thumb, and as we've stated at the outset, our whole goal is to minimize documentation where we can. This is because many architecture documents can become *shelfware*: documents you write that gather dust in the corner and that aren't of any practical use in any ongoing way. Any documentation is only valuable to the extent that it is practical, used, and useful. As such, we'll take a moment to explain the purpose of the documentation we'll create and why we're creating it.

We're not doing this to create *busy work*—instead, it's because there are direct practical advantages offered by creating the documentation that will support your design.

First, it is almost certainly the case that no target state vision can be realized all in one fell swoop. This means your plan will likely take some time (in many cases, this could take years) to come to fruition; it will also likely change along the way in response to business needs, changing circumstances, or evolutions in technology. Likewise, personnel changes can occur. People change jobs: many of those involved in the planning process (even you) might change roles, and someone new will need to step in and pick up where you or others left off. Having a well-documented blueprint allows you and others to stay in touch with the goals as time passes, personnel change, or roles shift. It also lets others pick up the work and carry it forward if key personnel are no longer available.

The second reason why the documentation provides value is that no plan—no matter how well crafted—can be implemented in isolation. This means you will need others beyond yourself to be on board with the execution of your vision in order to make it a reality. This includes the executive leadership who will sponsor, approve, and fund your plan, the technical experts and specialists who will work with you to help refine that plan, and the operations folks who will implement pieces of it directly and oversee it once it's in place. Creating a design means you have something to discuss with them, but the documentation of that design is what they will actually look at and refer to. This means they are more likely to be enabled to make a decision, champion your effort, or otherwise help forward your goals if they have something concrete to look at and evaluate. You help yourself by helping them by giving them better information.

Before we begin, we should note that we're going to take two passes at the design process: once in this chapter and once in the next. Within this chapter, we'll outline how to put together a blueprint for the *enterprise* scope. Recall that this is the context in which we are designing solutions that impact a **business unit** (**BU**), network, or environment. We will draw on existing standards and frameworks (in this case, the TOGAF **Architecture Development Method** (**ADM**)) to develop and document the security *vision*. We'll outline in this chapter why the ADM offers advantages to do this, and we will adapt the ADM to a streamlined, targeted exercise to achieve our goal.

This method is advantageous (in many cases, it's optimal) for working with network security or security measures applicable to the business in aggregate (in fact, it was built for this purpose). However, this method does have some challenges when applied to application design. For example, the model employs documentation types that are not in common use within the application development world, and it does not specifically require foundational steps/techniques that are important to application security and security engineering. While we could, in theory, adapt ADM to accomplish these tasks (ADM is built to be modified—this is one of the reasons why we've found it so compelling as a way to present the design steps to you), there are already other standards that exist to do this "out of the box" and that contain extensive, detailed, and purpose-built supporting documentation that explains how and where to apply them to application security design. Therefore, we will use ADM in this chapter to discuss enterprise scope and use an alternative approach (a systems security engineering approach) in the next chapter to repeat this process for applications.

Our intent in separating it out this way is twofold: first, the difference in the design process at the enterprise/network level and the application level is significant (enough so that we feel it's better to use a separate standard to guide the work effort for each one). Therefore, to do justice to both, we will be approaching them separately. By doing this, we hope that we can provide a detailed description of how you can put your blueprint together, regardless of whether you are working in a network/application context or whether you're working at the level of a particular application.

The second reason why we've separated it out this way is that the documentation for each method will vary, depending on which context you are operating in. If you're creating a design document for an application, it might involve creating artifacts such as the following:

- Data flow diagrams
- **Unified Modeling Language (UML)** sequence diagrams, message diagrams, and interaction diagrams
- State diagrams or state transition diagrams
- Security stories (that is, user stories focused on security)

On the other hand, designing for the *enterprise* or network side of the equation might result in you creating artifacts such as the following:

- Network topology diagrams
- **Architecture Definition Documents (ADDs)**
- Data security diagrams

For these reasons, this and the following chapter are two parallel paths rather than two that occur in sequence. If you're reading through this book sequentially, read both because it's useful as an architect to be familiar with both. If, however, you are reading this book as a guidepost as you work on an existing process, perhaps focus on the one that is most applicable to the type of work you are conducting.

We'll begin by walking through the process that we'll be using for the enterprise scope, with a particular emphasis on why we've chosen this particular method as opposed to the numerous others that are available. We will tee up what you can do from a process standpoint (that is, creating a program for things such as communication, finding resources, identifying stakeholders, and validating goals and assumptions) to help you do this. From there, we will talk about how to use that method to derive the vision of the future state that you are trying to achieve, and then walk through the ways to document this.

Process

"When using a formal model, there can sometimes be a temptation to get too caught up in the details of the model—to the point that people can miss out on areas of significant value that the model provides. Part of the core utility of many of the formal models is ensuring that designers sit down with various stakeholders and learn what stakeholders are trying to accomplish and create pathways to get them there in a way that doesn't compromise security."

– Dr. Char Sample, Chief Research Scientist—Cybercore Division at Idaho National Laboratory

The very first thing that we feel is critical to understand is the process that we're following to complete the design. Earlier in this book, we walked through numerous architectural standards and frameworks—most of which have design processes and methodologies built into them. As you move through your career as an architect, you will need to select from these various approaches, picking the approaches that work best for your particular circumstances and modifying them for how they will best apply to you and your organization.

In this case, we'll be following a process adapted from the TOGAF ADM: the generic architecture process outlined in TOGAF. In fact, if you take a look at the *Preliminary* phase of the ADM, you'll probably recognize many of the activities that we've done so far and see that, while we've laid out the activities in a less formalized way (and in a way that we hope is easier for you to understand), they are essentially similar to many of the fundamental and planning steps outlined in the ADM (though purposefully abbreviated).

We're going to move quickly through several of the ADM phases in this chapter. We will complete a few remaining steps from the *Preliminary* phase because, although we've accomplished quite a bit regarding the suite of goals and tasks outlined in that phase, there are still some pieces missing. We will then move through the *Architecture Vision* phase (*phase A*), through to the earliest steps of what TOGAF calls the *Technology Architecture* phase (*phase D*).

There are a few intermediate phases along the way, though—specifically, the *Business Architecture* phase (*phase B*) and the *Information Systems Architecture* phase (*phase C*). We will spend comparatively less time on these phases. There are a few reasons for this, but the primary one is that the ADM is focused on having an enterprise architecture across a wide swath of an organization, whereas this will only sometimes be applicable to the organizations that we work in and the scale of the work that we're doing. To keep the process lightweight (and therefore accessible to the widest number of folks), we are going to focus on what can reasonably be achieved by a smaller team (or, in fact, even one or two people) in a relatively short period of time. Again, recall that the TOGAF ADM does allow for (in fact, encourages) customization of the process to fit the enterprise context in which it is operating.

Why ADM?

> *"Start with the easiest thing that will deliver value and add complexity only as required. The trouble with a lot of the formal architectural systems is they are heavy weight, complex, and integrated—so it's hard to pick a piece of them and start doing it. In that case, you'd need to reengineer your entire process around them and would be much more likely to fail. At Microsoft, we needed a strategy for delivering secure software that worked within the framework of what everyone was already doing; Microsoft at that point had delivered more software successfully than any other company in history—you can't just uproot every process and install a new one from scratch. A much more useful strategy is to pick what you can do easily, show value, and expand as you need to."*

> *– Adam Shostack, President, Shostack & Associates*

In following this process, it's important to begin with why we're using the ADM process rather than other methods. Since there are multiple approaches that you could choose to employ when developing your architecture—and as an architect, you will be called upon to select from them or adapt one to your needs—it is worthwhile understanding this.

From our point of view, TOGAF generally (and the ADM process specifically) offers a few advantages for our purposes. These are set out as follows:

- **Level of (publicly available) detail and documentation**: The TOGAF ADM is extremely well documented. This means that should you wish to make further adaptations to it beyond what we've described here, investigate any particular step in the process further, or look for more information about a given point, all of the resources to do so are available to you.

- **It's free**: The TOGAF Standard (including the ADM) is available for organizations to use for their own internal, non-commercial purposes free of charge. This means that there's no licensing cost to employ it in your own organization, and the materials to do so are also available at no cost (see the preceding point).

- **Ubiquity of use**: While there are other approaches to creating your architecture, the ADM is well known by many architects and practitioners. Therefore, someone reviewing your design process later will likely be familiar with the steps that you've taken; if not, they can easily find and access the tools to become so.

- **Support for customization**: The ADM itself is conducive to customization (see *section 4.3* of *TOGAF 9.2* and/or *section 1.1* of *TOGAF 10: Architecture Development Method (ADM)*), meaning we are not violating the spirit of the model by doing so. For example, the ADM is often adapted to integrate with the Zachman Framework or other architectural models; the ADM model itself is designed to be modified. Therefore, the fact that we will be modifying it is in alignment with the intention of the model itself. This is aided by the organization of the model as it was built for this purpose.

While there are numerous other systematic approaches to this process, we have elected to use this one as it satisfies all the aforementioned criteria.

In terms of the level of architectural and procedural rigor, you will find that you can and should adapt this to the context in which you're operating. It is often the case that as the scale of architecture scope increases, the more important rigor and discipline become. For a large project and scope, higher levels of rigor can be advantageous because that higher rigor allows you to build in more time for systematic validation and documentation of the design, more time for building stakeholder consensus, and more time to allot to mitigating potential disruption and course correction. In a case like this, you might choose a rigorous process that's larger in scale and scope (whether it's the ADM or another one) and stay relatively close to the defined standard. On the plus side, a larger, slower-moving scope often provides you with more time to create and document designs.

For a smaller size and scope, though, *celerity* and *agility* are often more important than rigor. For example, a start-up probably won't have a year to hold up product releases while you design the perfect architecture. Likewise, an SMB (small or medium business) or mid-market company isn't always best served by waiting for the exact perfect design, especially if they've historically put little or no thought into security until now (meaning you're dealing with a pre-existing disorganized mess) and has yet to see the tangible rewards that architecture can bring to the process. For a context like this one, you might adapt a more rigorous model (for example, the ADM) to your purposes by streamlining the steps and winnowing down the rigor to specifically what you need, what's achievable for your team, and based on the most important outcomes you're trying to achieve.

For our purposes, we are going to assume that you are operating in an environment where you want to gain as much of the value of a robust and disciplined process as possible, but that your organization is still focused on speed and agility. We're assuming that you don't have a huge team at the ready to assist in design work. We're also assuming that you haven't undertaken significant architectural planning work already. We're assuming you need to move quickly—but that you also need to do so in a way that is defensible.

The reason we're approaching it this way is threefold, as outlined here:

1. First, it's perhaps the most common scenario in which we'll find ourselves given that there are (numerically) more small organizations than large ones (and even large organizations often choose to espouse agility).

2. Second, this is perhaps the most challenging situation to operate in. If you can balance the factors of agility and rigor for a nimble, agile organization like this, you will absolutely be able to operate in either a more formal (and more rigorous) context as well as a less formal one.

3. Third, it balances meeting the immediate need in the short term and developing an optimal plan in the long term.

As an analogy, consider how you'd evacuate your house in the case of a fire. Having an evacuation plan is important—and it is prudent to spend time planning it out. But the time to do that isn't when your bedroom is already on fire. When there's an immediate need (such as evacuating a fire or dealing with an insecure legacy environment), get out of danger first, and then (once the danger has passed) invest time in deciding and documenting a better path.

> "Someone taking on a new job will, of course, be focused on what their 30-, 60-, and 90-day reviews look like. If the answer to the question 'what have you done' is 'I've identified stakeholders' or 'I've socialized this project to executive management', that might not cut it. You need to be able to show progress. Picking something small that you can do now and building on it from there through iteration lets you show progress but also achieve something practical and useful."
>
> – Adam Shostack, President, Shostack & Associates

Likewise, it's important to understand that (per the old axiom) *perfect can be the enemy of the good*. This means that in a situation where a larger, multi-month, or multi-year design and implementation effort is untenable, you have three logical options, as follows:

- Apply no architectural design or process at all

- Accept current risks while you work on a larger-scale security architecture design

- Adapt rigor to suit the timeframe, doing what you can now and going back to perfect it (at a potentially higher level of rigor) later

Of these, our belief is that the last point is probably the preferred one for most organizations. Due to this, this is the approach that we've taken here.

Next, we will tee up the starting point for the architecture process: creating the vision that will be your guiding light throughout the work that you will do.

The vision

> "I'm always fascinated by prehistory where we don't have documents about the planning involved. My favorite is Stonehenge. Stonehenge was developed and redeveloped many times: it wasn't developed once and there it is, but instead went through multiple iterations. It's amazing the level of commitment involved in that: you need infrastructure for workers, logistics for moving stone, feeding and housing for workers, and numerous other things to make that a reality. You need people to put all their time and energy into this one project—and you need your children and grandchildren to participate. We have to do this in the modern world: get commitment from all of the stakeholders to accomplish great things. Stakeholder engagement is the key to project success."
>
> – John Sherwood, Chief Architect, thought leader, and co-Founder of The SABSA Institute

The very first thing that you'll need to do is gather enough information about your own organization and its goals. This will ensure the design you will construct will make sense in context. Over the last few chapters, we've gathered information to help you do exactly that. The key elements of *Chapter 2, Architecture – The Core of Solution Building*, and *Chapter 3, Building an Architecture – Scope and Requirements*, were all about building an understanding of the business: what it does, what's important to the business (and what's not), and how the business understands and measures itself. This is, in essence, what SABSA refers to as a *contextual security architecture*—that is, the business needs, constraints, and other *contexts* that will underpin your design.

There are several aspects to doing this and several critical tasks involved:

- Establishing architectural principles
- Setting the scope
- Getting the desired target (future) state

We will work through each of these before we put a program together to help you achieve these critical items.

Establishing architectural principles

As we stated previously, we've done some initial information gathering about the organization. We need to build on that information, document and validate our initial scope, and put together a framework for how we will manage the design process and subsequent implementation. To do this, it is helpful to start with a statement of your vision, as well as what underlies it.

Having a clear understanding of the high-level, simple, business-language statement of what you're trying to accomplish is valuable because it keeps everyone grounded regarding the project's purpose (that is, why do all this work at all) and encapsulates, in an easily understandable way, what the value will be when you're done.

To do this, we need to draw upon the data gathering that we've performed already to derive a few data items. To create this documentation, we will want to lay out several important data items in a systematic fashion. It is useful to do this beforehand since additional thought, analysis, and data gathering may be required to derive them. In general, there are three pieces of data that you'll need to help you with your *vision*. These are as follows:

- **Key stakeholders**: Who will be impacted by the work that we do? This group includes several subgroups:

    - **Beneficiaries**: Who will derive benefit from our design and how? This can be end users or customers, employees, business partners, or any other group, as long as they directly benefit.

    - **Decision-makers**: Who is responsible for giving approval for work?

- **Specialists**: Who are the subject-matter specialists necessary to assist in the work we do? This can include both technical specialists and those necessary to acquire access to resources or gain access to the right expertise in other teams.

- **Key resources**: What budget and other resources are available to us for the design? This might include staff, financial resources (budget), infrastructure, and/or access (for example, to personnel, partners, customers, and so on).

- **Key principles**: What approach will we use to guide our design? What do we hope to accomplish by doing so? TOGAF refers to these as "architectural principles" and provides a systematic way to document them—we likened them to the laws of physics for our architecture work when we discussed them in *Chapter 2, Architecture – The Core of Solution Building*.

As we develop the high-level statement, we will want to put some thought into each of these areas. Also, since each will be part of the initial documentation we'll put together, we should think them through with enough detail that we will be ready to document them on their own. Let's take a look at them in more detail.

Key stakeholders

"The thing that really changed my own thinking and my own practice was, at the time when I discovered it, IEEE 1471:2000, now ISO/IEC/IEEE 42010:2011 ["Systems and software engineering — Architecture description"], the standard for architecture description. From there, I discovered the books Documenting Software Architectures: Views and Beyond and Software Systems Architecture: Working with Stakeholders using Viewpoints and Perspectives. These should be required reading for any architect. It addresses everything about the way that you think about architecture, the way that you talk about the analysis of your architecture, the presentation, and being able to use this approach called views and viewpoints, which is defined by the standard and gives you a lot of value. A viewpoint is a perspective that is relevant to a given set of stakeholders. Within that perspective, you define a number of individual views. This whole concept is about systematically slicing through the architecture in ways that are focused on answering questions people have: the things about the people who are going to build it, use it, maintain it, and ensure that the end result is correct. Architecture is the set of assumptions that you don't expect to change very often. These assumptions that you expect to change least often is what you codify as architecture. The job of the architect is to find out what those assumptions are, document when those assumptions are going to be invalidated, and what they considered and decided against. The job of architecture is to communicate those assumptions effectively, the expected evolutions that you anticipate so that others live within those guardrails. It sets the boundaries of decisions that you can make and defines the constraints, making the best tradeoffs that give you the best chance of achieving what you hope to achieve."

– Andrew S. Townley, Chief Executive Officer at Archistry Incorporated

The first thing that we need to know is why we are doing the work that we're doing. Who benefits and what do they want? Ideally, by now, we have some understanding of this because we've already done quite a bit of information gathering. If you followed our advice in *Chapter 3, Building an Architecture – Scope and Requirements*, when we analyzed our organizational goals, then you should have already had some discussions with stakeholders and talked to them about their needs and important drivers. As you may recall, this helped us arrive at our initial working scope. At the time, we stressed the importance of understanding what various stakeholders' motivations are. Here, we'll build on this understanding and consider each of their viewpoints purposefully and systematically.

We'll want to document a few things as we go through this process. We will start by documenting who the stakeholders are and their concerns. We're doing this because it will inform others of what our design does and (to a lesser extent) how it does it. Documenting the viewpoint of these stakeholders provides valuable insight because it allows you to validate these assumptions with them, as well as help you think them through to ensure you've not left anything important out. As always, it's also valuable because work can be interrupted or staff can change—keeping a record of who the design is for and who is impacted is, therefore, useful insurance against potential disruption. Lastly, doing this is valuable because the process of documentation itself can help you discover other stakeholders that you perhaps didn't realize needed to be consulted.

We do this portion of the analysis first since we will want to find, contact, and subsequently validate the outputs from this phase with the stakeholders we identify. Therefore, even if you didn't reach out to them in *Chapter 3, Building an Architecture – Scope and Requirements*, when you were considering your goals during initial scope creation, be prepared to do so now. Likewise, as we reach out to them, we may discover more that might be impacted but that we didn't know about.

Key resources

In addition to who is impacted, we also want to have an understanding of which resources are available to us. This is important for the design process itself as well as for any subsequent implementation efforts. For example, if we have a team of 10 people that we can draw upon for a group-driven approach to the design and documentation, we will want to know that and also document the participants. Likewise, we will want to understand which resources are available to us for the actual implementation and execution of the design. If we have a large, complicated problem to solve and we only have a 1,000-dollar budget to fix it, we will want to identify that disconnect early on. We will do additional work to understand these constraints down the road, but it is useful to gain an understanding of this here since it can inform even the most basic of the architectural principles we identify and document.

Key principles

We also want to know what the most important precepts are that will guide our design. You'll recall that we spent some time in *Chapter 2, Architecture – The Core of Solution Building*, examining the organization and what's important to it. This should give us much of the information that we need to capture (and document, as we will do together in this chapter) these principles. We'll walk through how to do this in detail, but if you skimped on the work earlier in identifying the most important drivers of the organization, now is the time to go back and complete your understanding.

Documenting

Once you have these items identified, you will document them in a standard format. Note that there is no "right way" to do this (again, the right way is the way that works in your organization and for your purposes), but one option is to use the method outlined in TOGAF for documenting the vision (see *TOGAF 9.2, Section 6.4*, or *TOGAF 10: Architecture Development Method (ADM), Section 3.4*). During the *Architecture Vision* stage of the TOGAF ADM, there is quite a bit of documentation that would typically be produced for a large-scale, enterprise-wide enterprise technology initiative. While TOGAF includes other documentation, as well as outputs for this step, for our purposes, the most important are as follows:

- Architecture principles
- Architecture vision

Given this data, we have sufficient material to create the first piece of documentation: the architecture principles statement(s).

In our experience, it is valuable to create this because it gives you a frame of reference for future discussions with stakeholders. It gives you a structure that you can use to let stakeholders know that you understood the scope of the problem being solved, the reason they need a given problem solved, the drivers, the constraints, and the ideal outcomes. Remember that these stakeholders are the primary beneficiaries and supporters of your design: they represent decision-makers who will authorize it, champions who will help sell it internally, and SMEs who will assist with the implementation. This means that getting the principles right from the get-go is important.

TOGAF recommends following a standardized process to do this. It recommends capturing each of the design principles that you will follow systematically, identifying several key items for architectural tenants that are identified as important. These items are as follows (note that these are consistent between *TOGAF 9.2* and *TOGAF 10*):

- **Name**: A name to describe each principle.

- **Statement**: A concise sentence outlining the principle. For example, something such as *Users will be strongly authenticated* might be useful in a situation where authentication supports a business or technology goal (as was the case in the example we used earlier in this book).

- **Rationale**: The reason or reasons why a given principle is important. TOGAF recommends using *business terminology* to capture rationale, though, for security principles, we might include items that are more technical in nature (since security principles may need to presuppose other, pre-existing architectural or business principles that have already been developed).

- **Implications**: Requirements, impacts, downstream effects, or other items that, while not part of the principle itself, are nevertheless a ramification of the principle.

Should you choose to document your principles this way, you will find that TOGAF provides sample principles (*TOGAF 9.2, section 20.6* and/or *TOGAF 10: ADM Techniques, section 2.6*) that you can leverage to assist you in setting and documenting these principles.

Setting the scope

> *"The biggest mistake I see is people not taking architecture seriously and not actually doing it. If your view of security architecture is 'I'm going to use a checklist to see if I have all the right health and hygiene controls' and you focus on the vendors and the ways those controls fit together—that doesn't buy you much. I see people making the mistake of thinking security architecture is something that it really isn't. This way of looking at it is an isolated island that doesn't give you any value—and doesn't help you demonstrate the value of what you do."*
>
> *– Andrew S. Townley, Chief Executive Officer at Archistry Incorporated*

The second thing we will document is the scope. This represents the borders of the map for what your efforts will include and exclude: that is, what you can change and what you can't. Earlier, we suggested that you should create an informal, working scope with the idea that this will let you have at least some understanding to guide initial discussions. At this stage, we will begin with that initial baseline and refine it in light of discussions with stakeholders and further analysis.

When you looked through the organization, assessed the current capabilities, and determined your principles, it's possible that you encountered areas that impact scope; that is, based on what you've learned about the organization, as informed by your architectural principles, you may find you need to make some adjustments to your initial scope.

For example, perhaps you've learned that systems monitoring is performed by an outside party with its own processes and procedures. Maybe you've discovered that this outside organization is under contract to provide the service for another year and that getting out of this contract would be financially disadvantageous to the organization. If one of your principles, based on the organization's desire to be efficient about expenditures, is to minimize unnecessary costs, you may conclude that alterations to that monitoring capability are out of scope for the following reasons:

- The outside relationship is a sunk cost and extricating yourself from it would have an undesirable financial impact
- The value to you in making a change now is wasteful, relative to the cost and impact that you would incur

This means that while you can include a long-term, aspirational view of monitoring in your vision (you can and should do this), the immediate planning scope might exclude this specific element (monitoring the areas covered by the service agreement) of the overall security program.

Therefore, you should make any adjustments to the scope based on the information that you've already collected and refine your scope. As you do so, document that scope. As we mentioned previously, don't worry too much about being perfect at this point since we will be vetting our design (including scope) with stakeholders as we move through the planning process. This means that if we're wrong about something (including scope), there are mechanisms built into the process to catch those errors and fix them down the line.

Instead, just focus on being clear about what is included in the scope and what is excluded. If you are addressing only a subset of the environment or possible security considerations in only one area, be clear about this so that stakeholders (even non-technical ones) can understand this easily. For example, if you are addressing logical information security elements but not addressing physical security or personnel (HR) measures (since while both may be germane to the broader security vision, aspects such as physical or personnel may be out of our ability to change), be clear about that and where the demarcation point is. Likewise, include information about this if you are only including a certain area of the business but not others, if you are addressing only a given network environment but not others, and so on.

Next, you need to document your desired *target* future state.

Getting the desired future (target) state

In the previous chapter, we put forward the idea of doing a current state assessment. Having this available to you is one of the best ways to help you understand the difference between where you are now (*current* state) and where you would ultimately like to be (*target* state). This is an important element in your planning because the whole point of having a blueprint in the first place is so that you know what to change, where to change it, and what you want to change it to.

A useful strategy is to have this be informed by information about what makes the organization tick. Is security driven by risk management, by compliance, or by something else? Is the organization risk-averse or risk-tolerant? Having an understanding of the organization and its goals will lead you to ensure that the kinds of solutions you pick and the language that you use to express your decisions align with the organization and its culture.

If you do not have this understanding yet, now is the time to derive it. Here, you want to understand the following elements as best you can:

- Current state security measures
- Organizational goals
- Security goals

Hopefully, we've given you enough detail in prior chapters about the purpose of these elements and how to derive them, or at least where you can start looking for information about how to do so. We should note that what's important to your organization will be unique, so there's no *one size fits all* measure here. For example, one organization might be particularly attuned to risk and have security goals expressed purely in terms of risk. For them, it behooves us to use the language of risk to understand our current state (how much risk is mitigated by each security measure, what risks are mitigated, and so on). Another organization might understand their business purely through the lens of economics (what is the efficiency of having security measures and costs being saved by closing security holes?), so for an organization such as this, an economic analysis might fare better.

In the next section, you'll learn how to get more information about these items. You'll begin by understanding the assets of the organization, threats they may be exposed to, and risks that can arise as a result.

Risks, threats, and assets

> *"Once assets have been understood, I generally take a risk-based approach to the architecture process. Together, these give you the asset and the context in which the asset will be used. Key to this is understanding the threats. You need to understand the threats that an asset might be subject to in order to understand how to protect it."*
>
> *– John Tannahill, a Canadian management consultant specializing in information security*

To understand where you want to be, the most important thing to understand is *why*. What are the goals of what you're trying to do and how do they tie back to the goals of the business more broadly? What are you seeking to accomplish with your designs? What are you seeking to protect the organization from? What elements of the business are applicable to ensuring that happens?

These are all good questions, but you'll notice that answering them requires data that we don't have yet:

- What is the organization trying to protect? (Assets)
- What bad things can happen? (Threats)
- What is the result (impact and likelihood) of those things happening? (Risk)

Each question is important in its own way. We'll describe what we mean by each and provide some strategies that will help you derive them in the following subsections.

Assets

Understanding assets is important because these represent the specific things that the business wants to protect. The temptation for many security practitioners to use a word such as *assets* generically is that it often leads us to think of technical assets: things such as workstations or servers. But really, an asset can be anything: it can be a technological component, but it can also be data, personnel, information, files, money, and so on.

Depending on the type of work that you are undertaking, enumerating those assets may be important. This is because while assets do reflect what the organization wants to protect (since protecting the assets is a key driver), this information is also available to us via other means. Specifically, it is also implicit in the organizational, technology, and security goals. This means that being able to systematically understand and inventory assets can be seen as two paths to arrive at the same information—what the organization hopes to protect.

But what's the point of this? The point is that documenting these assets helps you arrive at—and verify—what is important to the organization. As we will see, if you can decompose how security goals can protect specific assets, this can help you understand potential threats that those assets might be subject to.

Threats

> *"There are four basic questions at the heart of threat modeling: What are we working on? What can go wrong? What are we going to do about it? Did we do a good job? People complain about inflexible processes and too much structure; however, my argument is that if you can't answer these four questions, you probably don't actually know what you're doing. If you're doing scooter rentals, you'll get one set of answers to these questions; if you're doing industrial process control, you'll get another. Understand what you are trying to do, what could go wrong, what you can do about it, and how you know if you've been successful."*
>
> *– Adam Shostack, President, Shostack & Associates*

The next thing to evaluate is what you are protecting against—that is, how assets might be attacked or how business goals might be stymied through the actions of someone or something else. There are multiple ways to evaluate this. In the previous chapter, we discussed a few ways to evaluate your threat landscape, including threat trees, threat modeling, and kill chain analysis.

Here, we will consider an approach that combines two of these techniques: *threat modeling* and *kill chain analysis*. We will discuss threat modeling for applications in more detail in the next chapter when we look at using threat modeling as a way to understand, decompose, and analyze application software. However, we can also use threat modeling to evaluate threats outside of an application context.

A full discussion of threat modeling would take up more room than we have to spare, especially since entire books have been written on the subject (with one of the best being Adam Shostack's *Threat Modeling: Designing for Security*). However, in brief, the threat modeling process involves what Microsoft describes in its **Security Development Lifecycle (SDL)** as five main steps:

1. Define the security requirements.
2. Create an application diagram.
3. Identify threats.
4. Mitigate threats.

5.   Validate that the threats have been mitigated.

If you have an understanding of your goals (which you will if you've followed along so far), you already have a proxy for the first step. Here, goals translate directly into requirements, so by understanding the goals, you already have an implicit understanding of the requirements.

Next, you will want to decompose the sum total of what you're evaluating into component parts so that you can analyze them—both their surface area and the interactions between them. For example, you might look at individual assets within the system for analysis and then analyze how they interact with each other and with the outside world. If you enumerate the assets in scope, this will provide you with an atomic unit that you can use to evaluate potential threats.

> *"The way I use the kill chain is that, given a collection of systems, I have a structure for thinking about how someone is going to attack me. For each entity in the system or collection, I can examine what can go wrong through the lens of the kill chain. That, in turn, answers the question 'what are we going to do about it?' A piece of 'what we're going to do about it' is architectural—meaning we, as the organization, can maintain a set of security design patterns informed by the attacks we are likely to see. This allows iterative interaction between requirements, threats, and controls."*
>
> *– Adam Shostack, President, Shostack & Associates*

For each asset, or interaction point between assets, you will want to evaluate how it might be attacked. When we look at applications, we will work through some application threat modeling examples for how to do this using **spoofing, tampering, repudiation, information disclosure, denial of service, and elevation of privilege (STRIDE)**, which is a mnemonic for a taxonomy of application-related threats. In the context of enterprise scope, though, it is perhaps more helpful to use a kill chain approach instead. If we understand the *kill chain* (the steps an attacker takes against your assets) as having specific steps required to accomplish their goal of attacking you, we can examine each asset (or interaction between assets) according to what the threats might be for each.

As an example, say you have identified an HR process as being something that is of high importance for your stakeholders to protect. You might break this process down into the atomic elements that support it (*list A*):

- Infrastructure
- Personnel
- Data
- Applications

For each of these elements, you would systematically examine each of the kill chain phases to assess how they could be used at each stage of an attacker's campaign. The kill chain described by Lockheed Martin in its seminal paper *Intelligence-Driven Computer Network Defense Informed by Analysis of Adversary Campaigns and Intrusion Kill Chains* posited the following phases (*list B*):

- **Reconnaissance**: The attacker gathers data about the target, allowing them to select and hone specific tradecraft to use in their attack

- **Weaponization**: Based on the threat vector(s) discovered during the reconnaissance phase, the attacker creates or customizes a *harness* that they can use to establish an entry point

- **Delivery**: The method by which the attacker transmits their *weapon* to the target

- **Exploitation**: Executing or *triggering* the weapon against the target

- **Installation**: Establishing a "beachhead" point of persistence presence on the target

- **Command and control**: Establishing a mechanism to allow the attacker to communicate with and direct the target's actions

- **Actions on objectives**: The attacker accomplishes their end goals

Therefore, for each item in *list A* (assets and goals), iterate through *list B* and evaluate the applicability of each stage in the attacker's campaign. You'll notice that we selected a very generic set of targets for *list A* in this example. Instead of doing this, you might increase the specificity by using specific machine or data assets, specific categories of individuals (personnel), and so on. Which items you select (and their specificity) will depend almost entirely on the type of work that you're doing. In general, it is a good idea to get as specific as you can within a reasonable timeframe. More specificity (and thereby having a better understanding of the threats) is of value—but more specificity also adds time, which might come at a premium this early in the process.

The point? Get as specific as you can within the time that you've allotted for this portion of the analysis. This will give you a great idea of which threats might be ascribable to a given adversary and the methods by which they might attempt to gain access to the resources that you've mapped out. However, this won't tell you about the risk since you will need to understand some additional information to derive that. Next, we'll walk through how to evaluate that risk and, ultimately, how to use that to guide your initial design context.

Risk

> *"The architecture needs to be flexible to adapt to changing risks and risk appetite. Risk appetite, risks, and threats can change—the architecture needs to change in response. Many organizations start with trying to do the traditional, large-scale enterprise architecture—but smaller, more focused approaches tend to meet with more success."*
>
> *– Steve Orrin, Federal CTO at Intel Corporation*

While a threat-based understanding will tell you where and how you are likely to be attacked, the impact of that attack can still be hard to fully understand without analyzing it systematically. Therefore, a risk-based understanding is also useful to include in your analysis.

This is useful because it helps you understand what really matters from a security point of view (that is, keeping risks within known, defined tolerances) but also because it is relatively easy to go from risk to economics and back again. This means we can understand and express risk as a function of dollars and cents. For example, we can understand how much risk we mitigate per dollar spent by looking at the cost to operate a control versus the economic impacts of risks that the organization incurs. This isn't to say that this is the best way to do things (again, the best way is the way that makes the most sense for your organization and is going to lead to the easiest, most natural comprehension from stakeholders), but if you're struggling with which approach to use and there's no organization-wide cultural standard, this can be a good lens.

> *"The value of cybersecurity architecture is in creating a coherent arrangement of security controls that support information systems delivering capabilities to the business. It has to be aligned with the risks around the use cases for those systems and capabilities."*
>
> *– Dan Blum, cybersecurity strategist, security architect, and author of the book Rational Cybersecurity for Business*

At this point, you can choose to employ a risk-based approach to evaluate how you will protect your assets. You can derive this in part as the output of a threat analysis exercise; likewise, you can undertake a systematic risk assessment exercise such as the ones described in the previous chapter. Either way, you want to evaluate the potential impacts.

As we discussed in *Chapter 4, Building an Architecture – Your Toolbox,* it is important that you understand the risk appetite of the organization in doing this. Specifically, you can't reduce the risk to zero (nor should you try); instead, you want to reduce the risk to what is reasonable and commensurate with risk appetite—that is, how much risk the organization is willing to take on.

In the previous chapter, we mentioned risk assessment, risk modeling, and systematic threat analysis as key tools in your toolbox. In fact, SABSA recommends (see *John Sherwood et al., Enterprise Security Architecture: A Business-Driven Approach, page 189*) undertaking a full risk assessment and risk modeling process as part of developing the *conceptual security architecture* (the level of planning we are entering into now). This is good advice. Understanding how you might be attacked, where you are vulnerable, and what risks the organization should seek to prevent will directly inform you of what security measures are most valuable in preventing these outcomes.

If possible, and if you have not already done so, perform some level of systematic risk examination as you complete this phase of your design. The SABSA process can be helpful in accomplishing this, as can other standards and methodologies, such as those outlined in **International Organization for Standardization (ISO)** *31000:2018,* **National Institute of Standards and Technology (NIST)** *SP 800-30,* **Operationally Critical Threat, Asset, and Vulnerability Evaluation (Octave),** and others.

Information from your analysis of current measures that have been employed by the organization informs you of this, so draw this in to aid your analysis.

Next, we will outline how you can put this data into a set of documents that you can use to validate assumptions with stakeholders. This documentation will be useful to you throughout the rest of your architecture efforts within the organization.

Documentation

Using the information that you've collected, the next step in the process is to identify your target state. After you've made changes (that is, implemented your design), what will the security of the organization look like and how will it operate within the scope you've identified?

The answer to this should logically follow from three things that you've already identified from the work you've done in this section:

- The goals of the organization

- What you are protecting against (the threats and risks that the system will be subject to)

- The architectural principles that you've established based on what's important to the organization

Using these as a guide, it is helpful to think through these two follow-on questions:

- How can security forward the goals of the organization based on the criteria of most importance to it?

- How might a threat agent (attacker, natural disaster, malicious or accidental insider activities, and so on) potentially bring about unwanted outcomes?

The first question is straightforward. This essentially involves deconstructing the goals of the organization, as well as the stakeholders within it, and crafting your security model around them. Where there are business goals, how can you support those goals with security measures? Where there are technology goals, how can you advance those goals—and what security measures would help you do so? You can analyze these questions systematically by looking at each of the enterprise goals you identified and iterating through a catalog of control areas, security measures, or control objectives, such as those you might find in *ISO (27001 Annex A or 27002), NIST (SP 800-53)*, or other frameworks (for example, **Control Objectives for Information and Related Technologies (COBIT)** or even the NIST Cybersecurity Framework). It may take some time, but analyzing this in this way will help you see which security outcomes and measures support your business goals (or indirectly support them by forwarding technology goals).

The reason why we suggest that you employ a control catalog (for example, NIST, ISO, and so on) when doing this analysis is that it helps you think through the applicability of security controls that may not otherwise be at the front of your mind. These frameworks are intended to be generally applicable to large segments of industry. This means that most of the controls they detail are likely to be applicable to you and your environment; they may not be applicable to the specific scope or to the specific goals you have, but they have a chance of being so given their purpose and applicability. Now, it's important to point out that we're not saying you should target every security measure in a guidance catalog such as NIST or ISO just because it happens to be listed there. Instead, what we are saying is that if, at first, you don't see a direct correlation between a business or technology goal and supporting security measures, working through them systematically and considering the applicability of each in a workmanlike fashion can help. In other words, the controls are listed there for a reason—and even if you don't see a connection at first glance, there may be a subtler one that isn't obvious from the get-go.

The second question is particularly important, as well as unique, to security architecture. The reason why is due to how technology in the organization can be misused. This is almost as important (maybe more important) as how it will be normatively used. Here, we want to fold together the attacker's-eye viewpoint and look at how they might attempt to achieve outcomes that we don't want, including stealing resources, obtaining data, preventing access to critical resources, modifying data, harvesting account information, and so on. These threats help inform you about what you will want to prevent; this, in turn, will provide input into what you will want your security landscape to look like.

Based on the output from the risk assessment process, you should evaluate what areas are most risky for the organization while paying particular attention to areas of unmitigated risk—that is, areas where risk exists but where existing measures don't address those risks. Recall that risk is fundamentally the product of impact and likelihood; as such, resist the temptation to defend against all possible threats. Here, you should factor in the principles that you have outlined, as well as your business goals, economic considerations, and all the data that you have collected thus far in doing so. There are some resources that can help you do this; we've mentioned threat modeling as an option, we've talked about kill chain analysis, and there are even frameworks such as MITRE's **Adversarial Tactics, Techniques, and Common Knowledge (ATT&CK)** framework (`https://attack.mitre.org/`). You can use any of these sources to help inform this adversarial viewpoint and, much like how you used the control catalog to help identify control areas, you can use these approaches to catalog how an adversary might attack the environment.

The outcome of this process should be goal-focused (for example, you might identify high-level goals such as *maintaining the confidentiality of data at rest*). Implementation will come next, but at this stage, we just want to make sure that we have a clear (again, unvalidated and *draft*) understanding of what we think the goals are. An analogy for this is drafting a **statement of work** (**SoW**) for a consulting project. Initially, you might meet with a potential client and discuss their needs. Based on that, you put together your thoughts about how to achieve their goal(s). However, you will still need to validate the SoW with the client to hone and refine it before they hire you. You need them to agree with you that the work you are doing does, in fact, achieve what they want. As you might expect, it's much easier to have a conversation (both in creating the SoW and validating it with them) if you come in with a goal-focused statement of your understanding as this will help drive further conversations.

Remember that as you do this, you're not trying to get to a very high degree of specificity yet. This will come later. At this stage, you just want to have a general goal-focused idea of what the target state for the environment will look like. We will revisit this and validate it time and again throughout the subsequent work that we do, so don't worry if your view isn't perfect from the get-go. Think about it this way: you haven't talked to the stakeholders yet to validate what you envision, so there's only a certain level of accuracy that you can expect to achieve here. Much like how we approached scope, what we are shooting for is a starting point—something that we can use as a guide for discussions with stakeholders and feed into further analysis so we're not starting from scratch in subsequent work, and something that will give us a scaffolding for setting up processes that will allow us to move on.

Once you have an idea of this at a high level, you can start planning the overall approach.

Planning your approach

> "A diagram isn't architecture. A diagram is a slice through architecture, but the architecture is the connections and the way that elements in a system work together to achieve an objective. The shape and the structure of that set of connections—that graph—that's what architecture is."
>
> – Andrew S. Townley, Chief Executive Officer at Archistry Incorporated

Based on the information we've gathered, you have a strawman (currently unvalidated), idealized view of what your organization might or could look like (from a goal point of view) based on the higher-level business goals of the organization and the threats that it might encounter. At this point, at least at a high level, we've thought through which measures will provide the most value and mitigate the most risk.

It is also useful to spend some time thinking through how you might achieve the target state goals. It bears saying again that everything is still an unvalidated draft at this point. You will need to validate and vet with stakeholders—you will need to turn the work you've done into something more *collaborative*. There are two reasons for this. The first is that you will want to make sure that the initial vision is accurate and does what you want. You can't do this on your own. Secondly, even if you are 100% right out of the gate about everything you've put together (which rarely happens, if ever), you will still want to work with stakeholders to make them feel invested in the outcome. When those stakeholders have ownership and agency over these fundamental decisions, you will get much more internal support down the road.

Next, we want to put some work into taking our *goal-oriented* view and deriving a *capability-oriented* one. The example we used earlier was one of ensuring the confidentiality of data at rest. That is a goal. But what capabilities do we need to support it? That is what this portion of the process is designed to help you analyze. There are multiple capabilities that could help you achieve this: file encryption, disk encryption, database encryption, access-control measures, network segmentation, and more. (As always, do not overinvest in these examples: these techniques serve different purposes and can be used in different ways to accomplish potentially vastly different outcomes.) The scope, resources, and other information will guide you to the capability that makes the most sense to support the goal.

There is a bit of a balancing act that you'll need to maintain here: having some idea of how you will accomplish a particular outcome helps you ensure that what you're coming up with is feasible, while too much detail at this stage is counterproductive since it is a draft and work in progress. As you think through how (at a high level) you might put the target state into practice, think about (again, at a high level) how you might achieve a target state security goal itself but also which other things you might need to have in place to support that. For example, say that you identify that encryption of data at rest is a capability that supports the goal you've identified. What else is required to achieve this?

The reason why we are doing this step is that we want to make sure that the capabilities we use as input to the discussion process are realistic. Coming up with desired outcomes without regard for implementation can lead us to ideas that—could they be implemented—would be great, but that are impractical, infeasible, or economically problematic given current realities and circumstances.

For example, if we were an organization that fields extensive workloads into an IaaS cloud provider (that is, a virtual slice on a hypervisor hosted outside our organization), a risk analysis might lead us to conclude that encrypting data everywhere is advantageous: we might conclude that we want to encrypt data at rest and in transit. In fact, without considering technical feasibility, we might even conclude that encrypting data in volatile memory (RAM) is something we want to do. After all, couldn't this help mitigate side-channel attacks or segmentation information leakage such as *Meltdown/Spectre* (https://meltdownattack.com/)? Couldn't it help ensure protection against integrity-undermining attacks such as *Rowhammer* (https://en.wikipedia.org/wiki/Row_hammer)? Maybe. But depending on the scope and context, it may be totally impractical to attempt to actually implement this. How would key management work? Would we need to recompile all our software where data is manipulated directly? Would we need to modify the operating system? Thinking through these capabilities helps us weed out strategies that sound good on paper but realistically can't be achieved.

We also don't want to go too far *into the weeds*. In particular, you absolutely do not want to start the implementation phase yet. There are good reasons for this. First, bear in mind that you haven't validated anything yet other than (maybe) initial scope. You could be wrong about key assumptions, which would cause all your work designing the ideal mechanism for some security control to be completely irrelevant. Also, keep in mind that architects are not the sole arbiters of everything technical in the organization. Just as an architect of a physical building (a museum, for example) isn't solely responsible for doing all the interior design work, laying out the electrical wiring for the entire building, and mapping out each pipe for the plumbing, so too will the security architect need to rely on skilled engineers from other areas and disciplines to design and vet the implementation. This must be a collaborative process—and because we are just trying to make the subsequent collaboration easier at this stage, overthinking it isn't useful.

Try to keep to a middle ground. You want to think about implementation enough so that you can weed out anything that is untenable, but not get so wrapped in it that you slow yourself down or do wasted work. In doing this, it is better to err on the side of worrying less about implementation versus more. This is because, when we validate our design, we will catch anything untenable that sneaks through when we get to that step. The advantage of catching these things earlier is that we increase our efficiency in bringing "non-starter" items to stakeholders.

Documenting

Once you have an idea of what you want to accomplish, you will want to document it. Later in this chapter (in the *Documenting your high-level approach* section), we will talk about strategies for how to do so, but for now, we'll focus on what you're documenting. Specifically, there are two important elements that you'll want to include:

- **What you are trying to accomplish and why**: This represents the key security measures needed for the organization and the rationale behind them. This includes the business, technical, or security goals that the measures support. Be specific about how what you intend to do forwards the benefits that you want for the organization; that is, how will the organization be enabled by virtue of what you intend to do?

- **Contextual assumptions and additional required effort**: Include any key assumptions or areas where the plan will need to include input from others. This could include requirements for additional layers of implementation detail from the various SMEs. Again, try to balance ensuring feasibility (by thinking through and providing some information about the implementation assumptions) with going into too much detail.

There are two things you accomplish by doing this. First, remember that at any point in time, personnel could change (including you). Therefore, making sure that you're clear about why your plan includes what it does—and excludes those elements that it doesn't—means that new folks can come in and pick up where you or others left off. Second, early in the process, we are going to assemble a program around the design you construct; we are also going to vet the design past all stakeholders (we will do this in the next section). By thinking through additional effort that may be required and the contextual assumptions, we have some idea about candidates for representation in that program and of personnel to vet the plan.

Next, we're going to start assembling the program we will use to track implementation and form the pillars of "governance" (that is, how we will govern and manage the process) for the transformation effort.

Case study – shared goals, vision, and engagement

> *"Planning and processes need to include all stakeholders, ideally in the same team, but where everyone needs to be working towards the same goal, which is secure design, development and maintenance of an application. A critical architectural principle for streamlining DevOps efforts therefore is a shared understanding of goals."*
>
> *– Dr. Wendy Ng, Principal Cloud Security Architect, OneWeb*

In an interview for this book, Principal Cloud Security Architect Dr. Wendy Ng shared with us a particularly insightful anecdote. Though the context overlaps somewhat with application development (coming as it does from a DevOps perspective), we thought it was particularly apropos to share here as it illustrates unambiguously the value that is brought about through documentation efforts and communication exercises (for example, communication with and validation of goals/precepts by stakeholders).

She told us a little about the history to set the context: *"For a large travel services company, I had the opportunity to work with software development teams in different business units, which developed and maintained several thousand applications and APIs. As an organization that partly grew through mergers and acquisitions, business units involved had different ways of working, and different tools and processes (including software development processes). This provided an opportunity to observe practices and how well they worked."*

She went on to describe the value of having a systematic and well-understood set of architecture principles such as those outlined earlier in this chapter:

"Empirically, we found that development teams which follow good architecture principles had higher output and better code quality. Most code lines, ~80%, in commercial applications consist of leveraging open-source libraries, rather than bespoke code. In one of the most mature secure software development business units, they heavily leveraged libraries as microservices, which are then called upon for product offerings. They worked on a public cloud environment and the teams made use of templates to ensure consistency in the development process."

From this, we see the value associated both with establishing robust principles, but also the advantage of building rigor into the way that information is exchanged and communicated (that is, via templates). So, too, for our efforts can this documentation provide tremendous value, ensure consistency, and improve outcomes.

She went on to describe the value of communication and interaction with stakeholders and how important those lines of communication and feedback were. She told us:

"They worked in small scrum teams that had daily stand-ups to communicate issues and potential blockers on progress and then throughout the day through collaboration tools, which are integrated into their CI/CD pipelines, so team members are notified of potential issues, thus providing visibility and metrics for the development and deployment process. As part of the application development process, they also integrate code quality and security assurance checks, in the SDEs, where possible, to further streamline the development process. This helped with early detection of issues. Despite the best will in the world, in the modern software development environment, it is often infeasible to resolve every issue. This is where a good understanding of the application, its goals and architecture will help, particularly for triage and remediations, specifically prioritization. Finally, the application is maintained and reassessed particularly for security vulnerabilities for the entire lifecycle of the applications at a cadence specified by industry and corporate product requirements."

Creating a program

> *"John Kotter has a book called Leading Change. At a meta level, all of the frameworks and processes for architecture boil down to the eight steps he outlines: create a sense of urgency, build a coalition, form a strategic vision, enlist others, enable action by removing barriers, generate short-term wins, sustain acceleration, and institute change. One of the primary sources of value for architecture is reducing technical debt. Stay focused on that: how can we make our lives easier in the future based on what we do today?"*
>
> *– Adam Shostack, President, Shostack & Associates*

You'll note that at this point, we still don't have any fully realized documentation for our goals, capabilities, or target state. We've done quite a bit of thinking about these things and maybe created some informal notes, but we have yet to put pen to paper to document this officially. To do that, we find it helpful to set up a structure within which we can have collaborative discussions that we can use to set and capture important process elements such as communication plans, project management artifacts, and so on. In essence, this will be an architecture program that will provide the operational and structural framework within which our efforts will take shape.

Note that by this, we don't mean the project or program management structures that you will use while implementing the designs you construct. This will come later. For now, we just mean the processes that you will establish to make your life easier during the design process itself.

The ordering of this may seem unusual to you: after all, why not set this up earlier (before we start doing any work at all)—or why not wait to do this until after we have a document that charters and governs our efforts? In fact, TOGAF's ADM positions this earlier in the process (in the *Preliminary* phase of the ADM—see *TOGAF 9.2, section 5.3.3*, and/or *TOGAF 10: Architecture Development Method (ADM), section 2.3.3*), as does SABSA (see *John Sherwood et al,. Enterprise Security Architecture: A Business-Driven Approach, Chapter 8, Managing the Security Architecture Programme.*) So, why are we doing it now instead? As always, there are a few practical reasons why we are deviating (slightly) from the explicit or implied order of operations established by other approaches. The primary reason relates to assumptions around how the effort gets initiated in the first place.

In a large, top-down architecture initiative, there is no question that establishing the program as early as possible has advantages. Why? Because bringing in representatives from all stakeholders early means they are available to you as you do the design work, they can work with you to help ensure accurate and complete reporting to executives, and they can help ensure accountability for the efforts undertaken. Likewise, there is a high bar of accountability and oversight for a large, enterprise-wide architectural effort. However, these larger efforts all imply that there is some level of internal executive support for a broader effort, which means that executives have already recognized the value and have given the go-ahead to assemble a program around it. This isn't always the case. In many cases, architecture efforts start as small, individually championed efforts: almost like "skunkworks" (a small, focused, informal team operating within a broader organizational context).

If support isn't already there, a *top-down* approach means selling executives on the value in order to gain the support that you will need. This means waiting to begin until you have that support and until the effort is officially sanctioned at the highest levels. In the case that you don't have buy-in already, you need ammunition to get it. The thought you've put in then becomes, in essence, the ammunition that you will use to get the support you need.

Put another way, it is much harder to get internal support if you don't have a clear picture of what, specifically, the business value will be at the end of the process. If you are in a smaller shop or a larger one that hasn't yet realized the value that can come from a systematic, workmanlike planning of security architecture, you cannot presuppose that management will support it without a clear value proposition. Getting internal champions on board—and demonstrating to decision-makers how you will realize business value from your efforts—means being able to explain (with at least elevator-pitch specificity) what the value is and what you are hoping to accomplish. This is why you do the preliminary analysis first: because you can do it relatively quickly and use it to marshal internal support to put the project team and resources together.

If you already have executive support and internal champions, by all means, put the program together as the very first thing you do. In that case, there's no reason not to do so. However, if you do not (as is most often the case) but you still want to approach your security architecture in a disciplined way, gaining support is much easier once you've put thought into the value that you will derive. Trying to sell the concept of security architecture *cold* based on generic platitudes is much less compelling than a specific, detailed recounting of the business goals it supports, an accounting of how it will help you achieve those goals, an itemization of the threats that can be mitigated, and a clear explanation of the risks it can mitigate. You'll be able to discuss these elements with specificity if you put in the *bare minimum* analysis that we've outlined so far.

> "The 'idealized' architecture process starts with a top-down approach—where you get business sponsors at the executive level to buy in and really participate in the overall process, where you identify key business functions, determine the technical assets they rely on, and get executive commitment and sponsorship. The reality though is that most organizations have been in business a long time—in some cases, decades before cybersecurity was relevant to them. So, the architecture process often happens piecemeal from the bottom up, with point-solutions deployed by operations staff who work to solve problems with the budget they have, and in the absence of unified security policy. For example, folks in technology operations—when there's a mishmash of product and there's no central alignment—work from the bottom up to establish principles and socialize them while implementing discrete security products that don't work well together."
>
> – Ted Ipsen, President and COO at Positroniq, LLC

With this in mind, let's start putting together the program that will support your architecture effort. Recall that to do this, you will likely need internal support since the work now extends beyond what you can hope to accomplish alone. Marshalling that support is important but is a much more individualized exercise—meaning the approach will vary from organization to organization. Therefore, the specific guidance that we can give you about how to approach this is limited. Suffice it to say, though, that at this point, you will want to obtain the internal support and buy-in that will allow you to structure the architecture program and put it in place. Part of the program development process that we'll outline includes checkpoints and steps for finding and cultivating internal champions. However, you do need the green light from management to at least begin. This is because this will enable other teams and individuals to help forward the work and give you the mandate to proceed.

Discovery, identification, and validation

Putting your program together starts with doing four main things:

- Resource discovery and project management
- Identifying executive supporters and internal champions
- Validating goals and assumptions
- Establishing feedback/reporting mechanisms

You will want to do these things early in the process. For practical reasons, it can be helpful to at least start them (as we are now) before you have put your full architectural definition and supporting documentation together. This is because you will want to include the results of this in the documentation that you create, as well as because the output of these items will directly inform what that documentation contains.

We will walk through each of these in detail in the following subsections.

Resource discovery and project management

For the first item, you will want to identify the resources that you will need throughout the rest of the planning phase and when executing your vision. This is, in essence, a project planning exercise. Therefore, if you have project management personnel available to you, including them at this point yields tremendous value. For practical reasons, we can't really give you a full *play by play* (detailed walkthrough, itemization, and accounting) of how to bootstrap project management for your effort; the reason why is that each organization will have a different process and a different way of doing things. Even in situations where the organization follows a standard methodology, it is likely to have adapted the specific steps in light of organizational context and nuances.

If you do not have a formalized approach to project management in your organization, SABSA (Sherwood, 156) offers a summarization of the key elements of the process for a security architecture project. Alternatively, resources such as the **Project Management Body of Knowledge** (**PMBOK**) can be brought to bear to help provide guidance on how to oversee the effort from a project management point of view.

From a tactical point of view, an important consideration as you do this is to identify the resources that will be involved in the program for it to be successful. I'm referring less to budget here (though this is important too), but instead to the specialists, engineers, and other points of view that will bring you from a high-level, abstract understanding to a specific, technically buildable one. For example, if you need an identity and authentication infrastructure (that is, the components and tools that will enforce your **identity and access management** (IAM) strategy) and you have specialists in-house that focus exclusively on identity, note this. Identify them as people to include as validators of your design, as potential internal champions who can help you in your efforts, as resources to help do the technical design work, or any combination of these.

Identifying executive supporters and internal champions

As you do this, pay particular attention to those individuals who could be your champions and executive supporters. These are the individuals who will help you get the traction you need as you seek to finalize, validate, and roll out your plan. They will also give you the organizational impetus to bootstrap project management and get the attention of—and prioritization from—key resources that you will need as you go through this process.

You will want to get these folks involved as soon as you identify them. You will need their support to get the right folks throughout the organization to invest the time in reviewing and vetting your designs. For example, consider the case of the hypothetical application identity management specialist. In many organizations, they have an in-demand specialization—they are likely requested to be involved in multiple groups to assist in multiple different projects. They likely have their own efforts underway, too. In this case, you will need their participation, but how will you get it as they are probably already overtaxed?

One strategy to obtain this is to bring them on board directly; that is, to approach them and enlist them yourself. Ideally, they will see the value and participate. However, that happening is contingent on two things:

- Identifying them so that you can approach them
- Having them prioritize the effort

Neither of these things is a given. In a large organization, even identifying them in the first place can require significant work in research, as well as making the efforts apparent to others in the organization. Even after you find them, they are likely to be busy with other things.

This puts you in a bit of an uncomfortable situation that can be challenging to resolve. You need them to be involved, but you need to either make it so compelling to them (for example, by using the architecture process itself to meet pain points they have) or make it so compelling to their management that they free up time by reprioritizing other work. Both approaches require that you identify that this person exists in the first place (discovery) and that you can enlist someone (either that person directly or senior management) to help you.

Taking time to identify internal supporters and champions does two things to help. First, it helps find these folks in the first place. Second, it helps you empathize with them. By understanding who they are, what they do, and what their goals are, we can create a message tailored directly to them to help win them over to our cause.

Validating goals and assumptions

As we bootstrap the program, we should spend some time doing additional validation of the informal goals and assumptions we've pulled together. It is particularly useful to do this as we identify new individuals to participate. New eyes can help you spot and refine issues that you may not have already discovered, so as you identify stakeholders and those that can help you support the planning phase, share your informal view with them and get them to help you validate it. In fact, one of the reasons why we're doing this now—that is, prior to full documentation—is so that we can iron out any kinks and therefore be as efficient as we can be with our time. So, make sure you are leveraging this as best as you can by modifying assumptions now while they are still formative.

As we mentioned previously, don't worry if you are not 100% precise. Recall that this process is iterative. As such, we will validate the design in its documented form, as well as refine it while getting it into a documented state. Engaging with newly discovered stakeholders as they come on board (before the design is finalized) helps you get their buy-in. This means those stakeholders can feel as if they are part of the design process before it's complete. This gives them ownership and, in the long term, will help you ensure that the work is viable and that you have the right resources in place to achieve what you want.

Establishing mechanisms for feedback and reporting

Even from these earliest phases of doing the work, it is important that there's accountability. As such, as you engage with executive decision-makers, stakeholders, resources, and specialists, you need to establish a common methodology to provide feedback to them. Discussing this with them as you identify them and bring them on board helps you ensure that you are putting visibility in place according to what they need and want. Some, such as executive sponsors and champions, will want feedback on implementation progress. In this case, they might be interested in project management oversight—perhaps using whatever status tracking and reporting methodology is otherwise used for projects in the organization. Others might be more interested in the way the implementation meets security or risk goals. In that case, they might be more interested instead in having visibility into metrics that inform you of whether you are on target from an outcome point of view.

Either way, establishing a mechanism to provide them with information at these earliest stages is advantageous because, in situations where you need additional telemetry or visibility beyond what you've identified in your own measurement set, you can build those into the plan to make sure they are addressed. In other words, you have the best opportunity to think through how you track, collect, and manage metrics.

At this point, you know enough that you can complete what you started earlier in this chapter: the documentation of your high-level approach. This is what we will do next.

Documenting your high-level approach

> *"In documenting your architecture, you need to have the consumer in mind. I don't mean end customers here—I mean the intended audience for the documentation itself. The CEO needs a different level of understanding about the architecture than a system administrator. The right way to approach this is to figure out what is the most useful format of the documentation for the audiences in the organization that need to consume it. To do this, you need to understand why they need it, how they will use it, and what their goals and interests are."*
>
> *– Ted Ipsen, President and COO at Positroniq, LLC*

As we mentioned previously, in this section, we'll be putting together the initial documentation that will guide our work. We'll be creating this in two stages:

- **Phase 1**: A high-level roadmap that provides an abstract, business-facing view of the design
- **Phase 2**: An architecture definition that provides a complete package outlining the design and codifies the analysis that went into it

Realistically, we could compress this all into one large effort. However, we are modularizing it so that we can do this in stages. The reason for this is that we need to vet the plan past stakeholders; this includes individuals on the business side (often the direct recipients of our efforts) and executive decision-makers. To ensure that our assumptions are valid, we will want to socialize and present our efforts and adapt in light of their feedback.

Our experience has been that changes often arise in response to feedback from these groups. So, no matter how carefully and fully we have informally vetted the design with them beforehand, there are likely to be changes that arise upon more systematic consultation with them. Therefore, the roadmap is designed to present a "business view" of what we're hoping to accomplish. Only once this has been understood and fully explored will we then complete the work that depends on this clear understanding. This way, if there are mistaken assumptions on our part, issues with scope, additional unforeseen constraints, or other changes that arise as a result of those discussions, capturing and addressing them iteratively—that is, against the comparatively more lightweight roadmap—helps us operate efficiently. This means that if we discover issues, we can adapt to avoid them before we invest in creating the full documentation.

In the following subsections, we'll explain both of these phases and walk through how to create them.

Creating the roadmap

As we outlined previously, the purpose of the roadmap is to document the business-facing view of the security goals and desired outcomes. Since the roadmap is primarily designed for business stakeholders and executives, it is important that we cover the business aspects thoroughly.

From a process standpoint, we will basically be compressing and documenting the outputs that are analogous to *phase A* (the *Architecture Vision*) of TOGAF and the contextual security architecture (the *Business View*, as described in SABSA). The primary focus will be on the business-focused elements that we can discuss and vet with business stakeholders who may not fully understand the technical elements.

From the work we did previously, we will want to include and document the following:

- **Charter or goal statement**: A brief (one or two sentences) description of the effort. Focus on the value provided from a business point of view.

- **Scope**: Put the working scope that you developed earlier into writing with appropriate modifications based on subsequent stakeholder discussions and analysis. Document what is included and why, as well as notable areas that are excluded and why.

- **Principles**: Document the architectural principles. Which approach are you using and what are you basing it on? These are the principles that you put thought into earlier in this chapter.

- **Goals and outcomes**: Discuss the goals you are supporting, focusing on the value to the business that will be realized from achieving these goals. Ideally, by this point, you have put thought into what those goals are and should have some experience in articulating them systematically.

- **Transition "mileposts"**: Explain (at a high level) how you see the outcomes being realized; that is, how you will achieve the goals and outcomes you've listed. If there are transformative changes that you will need to make (that is, a sequence of events that can be staged over time), outline what each of the stages is and what is important in each one.

- **Project management artifacts**: Include any project management artifacts that may be relevant to business stakeholders. This could include a high-level summary of forecasted timelines, a communications and reporting plan, key metrics that you intend to hit, and so on.

- **Impacts**: Any impacts that you foresee occurring to business areas as a result. Keep this business focused rather than technically focused.

As you create this roadmap, focus first on brevity. The goal isn't to get to 100% out of the gate or produce unnecessarily thorough documentation. Instead, recall the purpose. What we are trying to do is provide a structure that you can use to validate assumptions and initiate discussions. Ultimately, what we are building is an **architecture definition document (ADD)**—this is the document that will outline your design fully at what the SABSA model calls the *Architect's View* (the conceptual security architecture) level.

We're not there yet, though. First, we need to validate that the material we are putting into our more thorough documentation is accurate. Therefore, think about this roadmap as the *elevator pitch* version of the full ADD document.

Since it's an *elevator pitch*, brevity trumps detail. You'll want it to be as long as it needs to be to provide sufficient information to the business, and no longer. However, you'll want to avoid it being so long, detailed, or technical that readers either a) don't read it thoroughly or b) get bogged down in the details. You want them to focus on and validate the principles, scope, assumptions, and process that you used to derive your high-level goals. If you include technical details beyond the minimum required for them to understand the business value, you will shift their focus away from what you need (validating the assumptions, scope, and process) and toward items that will still need to be validated anyway (for example, technical or operational elements that will still need to be vetted past the SMEs that oversee them). The worst-case scenario at this stage is to end up in detailed technical discussions with business stakeholders, spending time answering questions about and explaining detailed technical concepts, or otherwise wasting their (and your) valuable time on things that are irrelevant to their needs or will change. To help avoid that, you might socialize the document first with a particularly trusted stakeholder and ask them for feedback about whether the content is at the right level, ensuring it's not overly technical.

Since we are doing this in two stages, we will roll the results of the validated roadmap directly into our ADD document to not waste work. This means that, as you create the roadmap, make the effort to do it in a way that, though concise, is still accurate and clear (remember **ABC**: be **accurate, brief, and clear**). This provides the advantage of being easily understood by those that you will validate it with but is also valuable in that it will require minimal rework to be used within subsequent more comprehensive, detailed documentation.

Also, don't feel you need to do this all on your own; leverage the resources that you pulled together to get others on the project team to help. For example, you might work with the project management representation so that you can pull together any project management information executives or business partners will want to see, and (if there are multiple individuals working together on the architecture itself) leverage others that might also be on the project team to help put this together. Another example is you might leverage stakeholders in communications, marketing, or PR to help you express the concepts clearly and crisply.

Validation

Once you have a version of the document pulled together, the next step is to socialize it and gather feedback. This sounds easy, but there's more to it than you might think. Ideally, you'll have most of the stakeholders identified from work that you've done previously (for example, when defining scope, putting together your analysis, and so on), so reach out to them and get them to validate your approach and your assumptions, review the architectural principles, and so on.

As you work through this documentation with them, be sensitive to any areas where what you're proposing impacts existing processes or areas of the business that they oversee or deal with directly. Where there could be impacts, be direct and forthright about these. Focus on the following:

- What impacts there could be

- Why these changes are necessary

- The business value associated with making these changes

- The scale of potential changes and impacts

- The transition effort and time where things will be in flux

- Measures that you can or will take to ensure that impacts to the business are minimized

The purpose of this phase is to validate (and, based on that validation, modify) planning in light of stakeholder feedback. Therefore, resist the urge to be combative about feedback. Have a *"customer is always right"* approach in how you treat them, recognizing that resistance may stem from the fact that they don't have access to the same details and information you do. Even if they are wrong about a technical detail or assumption in expressing feedback to you, the fact that they cared enough to point it out means that there is a real concern there that you will want to hear, understand, and be empathic about. Refining things now just makes it stronger down the line.

This vetting exercise is your opportunity not only to solicit buy-in but also to increase the quality of the output. Therefore, view each piece of feedback with acceptance and act upon it. There may be feedback that you don't entirely want to hear. For example, stakeholders may introduce challenges and cause you to rethink your planning; they may point out the impracticability of an approach, or even invalidate a key assumption. When this happens, this is a good thing. Why? Because the problem would have arisen anyway—finding it now just means that you have done so at a point in time where addressing it is significantly less work than it would have been later down the road.

Once you have received this feedback, account for it by updating the document to reflect what you have learned. If time allows, it is a good practice to send updated versions of the document back to stakeholders with changes made. Where you are unable to address a given piece of feedback—either because there's no way to do so and still meet risk/economic targets or for logistical reasons—spell out why. Going back to the stakeholders to tell them that their feedback has been accounted for gives them agency and ownership. It also demonstrates that you are willing to accept their feedback, treat it as valuable, and respond to it.

Architecture definition

Once you have a vetted roadmap, the next step is to incorporate this into an ADD. This document includes areas in the roadmap but also includes the next layer down in terms of technical detail. It is at this level that you will want to spell out how things will operate post-transition, as well as, from a timeline perspective, how you will implement these changes.

Per TOGAF, a typical ADD includes the following items (source: *TOGAF 9.2, section 32.2.4*; sub-bullets removed):

- Scope
- Goals, objectives, and constraints
- Architecture principles
- Baseline architecture
- Architecture models (for each state to be modeled)
- Rationale and justification for the architectural approach
- Mapping to the architecture repository
- Gap analysis
- Impact assessment
- Transition architecture

You will note that we have collected most of this information already (though yet to be documented in some cases) from work that we've already done. The scope, goals, principles, impacts, and rationale were already included in the roadmap document that we vetted earlier in this chapter. By using that document as the core of this one, it becomes relatively straightforward to either insert that material directly or incorporate it by reference.

This then leaves us with three new things to include:

- **Architecture models**: Modes of business, data, application, and technology architecture.
- **Gap analysis**: An analysis of the difference between the current state and the goal state.
- **Transition architecture**: Intermediate phases (that is, *transition states*) between where we are now and the ultimate goal state. These represent the intermediate phases we will go through to reach the target.

Now, let's discuss some strategies we can use to put these together.

Architecture models

> *"The most important thing about the architecture process is the outcome. Each one of the formalized architectural frameworks are big—probably too big for someone new to the job to consume and really understand the consequences. Even just reading the formal approaches can represent days of work, let alone selecting one in full awareness of the subsequent implications. What's most important is that you start light: start with what's manageable, look at the most important elements, and do a retrospective at the end to learn how you can refine over time."*
>
> *– Adam Shostack, President, Shostack & Associates*

TOGAF includes phases you can use to model a few different elements of the end-state design. At the stage in the ADM process where you are creating the ADD, several of these models will have been created:

- **Business model**: What the end state looks like from a business point of view. This focuses on business processes, functional areas of the business, business organizational elements, and external services that support the business.

- **Data model**: How and where data will be impacted, as well as changes that will be made to data based on the architecture design.

- **Application model**: A view of the architecture that highlights application impacts and transitions in application delivery.

- **Technology**: A model that includes any new technologies that may be included in the end state or modifications to technology. This mostly focuses on communication, hardware elements that allow applications to communicate, and the business processes so that they can interact.

You'll note that each of these artifacts looks at the end state through a different lens. If you choose to include each of these in your document, The Open Group provides a modeling language (**ArchiMate**) that helps in the creation of these models. ArchiMate provides a standard methodology and language for capturing these design elements, as well as a common methodology for documenting and modeling them. Generally speaking, ArchiMate is a useful tool, and one that we, in security, can leverage should our efforts be of a scale where we have the time and scope to do so. In fact, open source tools such as **Archi** (https://www.archimatetool.com/) can assist in the creation of these designs and be used free of charge to assist in the development of these models.

For most projects, though, we will probably need to deviate somewhat from the *typical* process and supporting models employed by TOGAF for documenting an ADD. The reason why is twofold, as explained here:

1. First, we are focused specifically on the security elements of the end state rather than the entirety of the technical architecture (that is, the rest of the technology landscape). Our ability to directly change the rest of the environment is often limited (unless we are working within a broader effort where other architectural design processes are going on in parallel), so while we can model these other areas using a standard mechanism such as ArchiMate, our ability to effect change to them isn't always there.

2. Second, because we are an *overlay* on the rest of the technology landscape, it can be helpful to adapt modeling strategies already in use elsewhere. So, for example, if your organization uses marked-up network topology diagrams to document the current state, there are advantages in using that for our purposes too. If, instead, they use another standard (such as the **Ministry of Defense Architecture Framework** (**MODAF**) or the **Department of Defense Architecture Framework** (**DoDAF**)), using those mechanisms becomes advantageous.

Using the already established mechanism for documentation and/or modeling means that others in the organization will be immediately familiar with the mechanism you're using and will know how to interpret it. This means that you limit and constrain time spent explaining the documentation methodology and can instead immediately focus discussions on what the artifacts themselves contain. Likewise, adapting an existing diagram can provide speed advantages in its creation. Because we will only rarely be able to directly make changes at other layers (for example, to business processes or how applications are fielded), modeling these elements so that they're included (in parallel) for a security architecture can be somewhat counterproductive. This is because you have to keep them synchronized, it makes you dependent on methodologies and processes you can't necessarily control, and so on. Again, your organizational needs, scope, and required level of rigor will inform you of this.

Reference architectures

In some cases, a useful strategy (where it is applicable) is to incorporate any reference architectures that have informed your design. A reference architecture, as described by the **Organization for the Advancement of Structured Information Standards (OASIS)** in *Reference Architecture Foundation for Service Oriented Architecture Version 1.0*, is "*...the abstract architectural elements in the domain of interest independent of the technologies, protocols, and products that are used to implement a specific solution for the domain. It differs from a reference model in that a reference model describes the important concepts and relationships in the domain focusing on what distinguishes the elements of the domain; a reference architecture elaborates further on the model to show a more complete picture, which includes showing what is involved in realizing the modeled entities, while staying independent of any particular solution but instead applying it to a class of solutions.*"

Creating a reference architecture is a common way to outline generic solution strategies to common problems. This can be particularly helpful when you're creating a security model in the abstract without extending that design to specific implementation details that you will actually execute. This lets us document how we will achieve a security goal in an abstract way. You can either directly refer to reference architectures created by others or develop your own generic approaches and incorporate them by reference into your ADD.

Creating a reference architecture can be very useful in situations such as the following:

- A large project that will have multiple, similar entities within it

- Decentralized environments where technology decisions are made locally; for example, a holding company where each property within the portfolio has its own technology culture

- Situations where we are handing off a generic architecture to someone else for execution

It is not necessary to create reference architectures; instead, it is a tool in your toolbox, should you need it. In cases where there is a reference architecture that you can refer to, it saves you from recreating that work for your own use; likewise, it helps minimize work in situations where you envision architectural design patterns can be reused. It is a useful documentation strategy that can help you reuse your work over time, as well as incorporate other strategies that have been documented—and are available—externally.

Gap analysis

If you've been following along, then you will likely have the core of a gap analysis already. Recall that we suggested doing an assessment of the current state in *Chapter 4, Building an Architecture - Your Toolbox*. If you've already done this, then the gap analysis consists of describing the difference between where you are now (current state) and where you intend to be post-implementation (target state). This should be a relatively rapid exercise as you have already put effort into your current state analysis and have spent time thinking through your end state in detail.

Transition architecture

TOGAF generally assumes that you will have multiple states between where you are now and where you intend to ultimately be. Some people find this concept a little confusing, so it's useful to look at it through the lens of analogy. Consider the phases of building a house, for example—you don't just go from nothing to a completed, fully realized edifice in one fell swoop. No—instead, there is an order to the building process: you plan and prepare the site, you lay a foundation or slab, you erect the structure (for example, a frame), then add internal cosmetics, then finishes, and so on. The steps are ordered such as they are for a variety of time-proven logistical reasons. Each phase represents a transition along a spectrum that starts with nothing and extends through a variety of transitional states to a completed structure.

This portion of the document provides you with the opportunity to describe these intermediate states. It is useful to include these when time allows, but keep in mind that, from a security standpoint, we have a bit less flexibility in transition states than would be the case in a broader enterprise architecture project. This is because the security goals don't change, even during the project's execution. For example, a transitional state where *login is disabled* (that is, users go unauthenticated) is itself unacceptable from a security point of view. Therefore, you will find that the path from the current state to the goal state is actually more constrained in terms of security architecture effort, which means it needs to be more iteration focused rather than having large, monolithic transitional states. This can make this portion of the documentation easier in some respects, but also means that you must carefully think through how you can get from A to B without compromising security along the way.

Additional materials

TOGAF also specifies a separate document called the **Architecture Requirements Specification** (**ARS**) that lays out a *quantitative view of the solution*; that is, the metrics, **key performance indicators** (**KPIs**), and other measurable goals that you will use to measure success. While you absolutely can create this as a deliverable in its own right, we often find it helpful to fold key elements of measurement into the ADD itself. The primary reason is that the more documentation there is, the more intimidating it is for those outside the project and the less likely it is for others to know about and read this documentation. We absolutely address measurement in much more detail later as we get more into the mechanics of planning and validation. However, at this stage, you will want to take note of and document any important measurements that will inform you of whether security goals are being met.

For our purposes, we will include this material in the actual ADD itself when we know it. When we don't, we will instead lay out our measurement and metric strategy (that is, our plan for how we will derive key metrics) within the ADD rather than specific metric items themselves.

There are a few ways to approach this. One way you can represent this information is as a subsection of the document; that is, one that describes how we will measure and quantify the performance of the final goal state across dimensions that we can cross. On the other hand, you may choose to have it encapsulated in an accompanying document (outside the ADD) that you use for reference. This could be, for example, a website dashboard. In fact, the format doesn't really matter as long as it is a) focused on validating the outcome (that is, it gives you information about whether you achieved the goal or not) and b) reviewable and can be validated by stakeholders.

Ideally, the metrics will align with how the business measures itself, which will, in turn, align with the planning work you've done so far. For example, if you've used a risk lens to create your goals, this might be a description of your risk modeling and risk metrics, including **key risk indicators** (**KRIs**) and other measurements. If you used a maturity or capability lens, it might include strategies for how to measure that. Expect to receive feedback on these metrics and incorporate that feedback as it is raised.

Accompanying documentation

In addition to the ADD, it can be useful to capture your thinking in a few other areas as well. As we move into the execution phase, it can be helpful to document the following:

- Key decisions
- Risk management artifacts
- Requirements

Let's walk through each of these and discuss why they matter and how we might ultimately use them as we transition into the next level of planning and, ultimately, the execution phase of the design.

Key decisions

The first item we must capture is the set of important decisions that will be made by the architecture team over and above those explicitly laid out in the ADD. For example, say that we intend to employ a *zero-trust* approach to our design (that is, the assumption that all entities in a given scope are untrusted and potentially compromised). For example, we might decide that internal resources (that is, employee workstations, on-premise servers, and so on) are untrusted and that we intend to treat them as such for the purpose of the architecture's scope.

In this case, we would almost certainly specify that this is an architectural principle. However, recall that architectural principles are designed to be concise and focused on the desired outcome. Making this decision, while useful as a one-liner, might be based on numerous other factors, discussions, considerations, and justifications, which is much more material than is conducive to include in one architectural principle statement.

In this case, a key decision document can help supplement the material in the ADD with this additional detail. The format of the document is less directly relevant than the fact that you are capturing the information, recording it for posterity, and aligning it with the relevant architectural principle.

Risk management artifacts

One of the most reliable ways to arrive at your end state design in a security context is through a systematic analysis of risk. In almost every case, risk management will be one of the most important (if not the most important) instruments to allow you to do this. It is so important, in fact, that it is a foundational component of both the SABSA and **Open Enterprise Security Architecture (O-ESA)** methods. So, document those artifacts. This will prove useful as we move from the high-level definition we have now and into the actual implementation phase.

Recall that we still need to bring the model down a few layers of specificity to actually implement it. Doing this in the presence of the original risk management artifacts is significantly easier.

Documenting requirements

Where you can, explicitly document your security requirements. You'll notice that, while the design was based on the requirements that we gathered, it does not specifically itemize them. This is good and bad. It's good because it keeps the ADD focused and concentrated on the elements that directly fulfill its purpose, but it's bad because, while the architecture principles are the direct result of analysis of requirements, there can actually be more to it than can be stated in a brief principle as we've captured here. This means that documenting requirements explicitly is valuable.

Recall that there may be a time lapse between when we document the ADD and when we can begin its execution. This is because we will need to get other groups to weigh in on the document, provide their input to ensure feasibility, and so on. The *worst-case scenario* is that, in that interim time, we forget a requirement. Documenting requirements explicitly while they are fresh in our minds prevents that.

Summary

Throughout this chapter, we have created and vetted the documentation that we will use to execute our architecture project. There is still some refinement to do before we can fully begin that execution, though. For example, we will need to work with the various SMEs to create detailed implementation plans for subsets of our blueprint, and we will also need to make sure we vet the plan with technical stakeholders. We will do this iteratively as we move into the implementation phase in *Chapter 7, Execution – Applying Architecture Models*.

In the next chapter, we will cover the steps required to do the same pre-implementation artifacts for applications. Because the application architecture is different enough from the enterprise architecture that it has its own standards, deliverables, design, and modeling languages, we will discuss how to integrate security into those types of projects in a manner parallel to what we've done in this chapter. From there, we will move into the execution phase, where we will create our technical implementation strategy, deploy our work efforts, and transition closer to our identified target state.

6

Building an Architecture – Application Blueprints

In the previous chapter, we discussed the process of creating a high-level design document for a segment of the enterprise architecture. As you may recall, we employed several steps, many of which are elements of the architecture definition document described in the TOGAF **architecture development method (ADM)**. While none of the actions we took were necessarily specific to TOGAF, we did employ their concepts and process in a way that we hope will allow you to glean existing information, should you need it from those resources.

In this chapter, we'll go through the same process but using a slightly different method for applications rather than the enterprise scope. Specifically, we'll go into the details of creating a baseline, high-level design framework for applications. You'll probably find the specific steps of this process analogous to the exercises we went through in the previous chapter. However, as we go through them, you will realize that the tools and techniques that we'll use to do so are, in many cases, different. As you'll see, there are some good reasons why these are different: software developers have their own mechanisms for gathering requirements, diagramming designs, managing the development process, and other tasks. Where possible, we want to leverage the methods and techniques that are most familiar to these stakeholders.

In this chapter, we will cover the following topics:

- Application design considerations
- Life cycle models
- Considerations for Waterfall projects
- Considerations for Agile projects
- Considerations for DevOps projects
- Process for application security design

Let's get started!

Application design considerations

"There are three kinds of security defects in the world. At the network level, most problems are just configuration errors: you set it up wrong, you didn't block the right ports, you accidentally put your firewall behind the thing instead of in front of the thing. Those are configuration errors, the first generation of security problems, and the ones we've been dealing with the longest. The second kind of defects are bugs. These are implementation errors in code: you use the wrong system call in C or C++, or you used Java incorrectly and now you have a bug that can be tickled from outside by a smart attacker. The third kind of security defect has been generally-speaking ignored by everybody, which are design issues.

When you have a software architecture, you can do an analysis of it. Some people call this a threat model; others say it's architecture risk analysis. The idea is let's look for flaws in our design or our architecture. There are many advantages to doing that. The main one is economics. Because if you're dreaming up an architecture and you need to make some changes, all you need do is change your mind, which is cheap. If you need to change a fielded system that's already out there and you need to change the code, that's going to be really, really expensive. So in the design phase, if you can do this analysis and make the changes you need to make, it's going to be the cheapest way to get good security fundamentals. It's easier to do that when you have an architecture."

– Gary McGraw, Ph.D., Founder, Berryville Institute of Machine Learning.
Best selling author of Software Security and 11 other books

As we mentioned previously, the approach we used in the previous chapter works well when constructing designs at the *enterprise* scope – for example, designs for a business unit, an environment, a business process, or a set of related business processes. However, this is only a subset of the type of architecture efforts that we might become involved in – and only a subset of the specific situations within which we might need to create a design. We might need to perform design tasks for security elements, security-relevant features (for example, authentication, logging, and more), protection mechanisms, and other important security considerations within a software application.

Creating a security design for software and applications is a little different than it is for selecting the right controls to use within an organization or a portion of an organization. There are a few reasons why this is the case, but the primary ones have to do with two things:

- The communication methods used with software development resources and stakeholders

- The impact of (and alignment to) the software development method in use (that is, the **software development life cycle (SDLC)**)

Specifically, just like we needed to communicate and engage with stakeholders from business areas (including executives) and throughout the organization when creating our initial documentation and architecture principles, so too will we need to do so in an application design context. In addition, for an in-house developed application, we will also need to communicate with the development teams actually building the application, as well as project management, product managers, integration teams, and other support teams.

Recall that when we discussed communicating with stakeholders previously, we suggested that you should employ the same language and methods that stakeholders use to communicate with each other – and we recommended that you use the same prioritization strategies and measurements for how the business evaluates itself. In other words, the way you communicate with stakeholders should ideally be optimized around how they work and how they perform their jobs. So, if those in your target audience evaluate business decisions financially, it is advantageous to us to express our intentions through an economic lens. If they communicate primarily in the language of operational efficiency via metrics, we should do so too. We selected the engagement strategy that was the most likely to engage our audience. Likewise, we codified the information we collected during the information-gathering process using the "lens" (that is, method of documentation, framing, viewpoint, priorities, and language used) that they would respond to best.

This same principle applies to a software and application context too. In this case, though, many of the stakeholders that we will communicate with will be those who are a part of – or interface directly with – the software development process. This means that they will likely communicate in such a way and through channels that have been optimized around software development. Due to this, we'll want to communicate with them and employ their language, so we'll need to use that style and those methods, and then create deliverables that can be understood by them and are useful to them.

Another factor is that the process of software development has its own *rhythm*, depending on the life cycle approach that the organization uses. One organization might employ a modified waterfall approach to development (this is less likely nowadays but still a possibility), while another might employ a DevOps approach where production releases occur continuously. The point is that the cadence and rhythms of that life cycle will vary – and these can and do impact us when it comes to how we approach our architectural process, as we will discuss throughout this chapter.

To see why this is the case, consider how using the process we used in the previous chapter would play out in two different software development approaches: the first using a linear, *serial* development process (that is, the waterfall method) and the second using a continuous DevOps style model. Under the linear model, the process we outlined would probably work fairly well. We would set principles, design an approach, validate it with stakeholders, analyze risks and threats at the beginning of the effort, develop a gap analysis that describes the difference between where we are now compared to a goal future state, map out anticipated evolutionary changes that would impact our design over time, and so on.

So far, so good. But what happens when we are using a more iterative approach or one where we are releasing code into production on a nearly continual basis? In this case, the application itself is fluid: vectors of attack that were not possible yesterday might be nearly unavoidable tomorrow; likewise, risks change constantly as new features are introduced, old ones are modified and adapted, and new usage scenarios are introduced that change how the application is used from a business perspective. The overall design principles for the application might stay the same, but items that logically follow from the design and implementation – for example, gap analysis, risk, threats, and other key variables – are not constant. How well would the approach we outlined fare? Probably not very well, right? Unlike something slower-moving such as the technology footprint of the organization itself or a slow-moving software release process, we have a situation where underlying assumptions are revisited and where modifications can happen quickly that impact fundamental assumptions. The process from the last chapter works well when things are not changing too often, but when things are constantly changing, our design process must adapt as well.

Consequently, we need to adapt our process somewhat to account for different methods of development. This is because the way we develop the software will dictate "when," "how," and "how frequently" key activities will occur. As we go through this process, you will notice that we are capturing all the same (or similar) information that we did in the previous chapter when designing at the enterprise scope – and you'll notice that the underlying principles of why we're doing what we're doing haven't changed either. What has changed is how we apply them. This is because it is a principle of good security architecture that what we design must ultimately service the needs of the organization in which that design will operate. Therefore, the process we follow for our software security architecture must operate well within the context of the development processes in use.

For both these reasons, we have chosen to approach the security architecture process for software differently from how we approached it in the enterprise context.

Life cycle models

> *"Start small. Don't try to boil the ocean. Start with a small, manageable size and 'follow the bit.' By this, I mean follow data from creation, through usage, to transmission, to storage, and ultimately to end of life. A good security architecture should be fluid; it needs to be a living document. If you try to make all decisions at once, they will tend to compete. Narrowing the focus is step one. Understanding the full life cycle is step two."*
>
> *– Steve Orrin, Federal CTO at Intel Corporation*

Typically, the development model in use ties to the security architecture for a given application at a fundamental level. There are a few reasons for this. The first is that the way software is developed will likely influence the security of the result. We stressed this previously: if you follow a disorganized, slipshod development process, you'll increase the likelihood of producing a disorganized, slipshod result. As a result, it is often the case that software development methods and life cycle considerations find their way into the work of the security architect. We will see numerous places where this is the case as we work through this chapter.

Second, consider what the architect is applying their talents to in the first place. Ask yourself why an organization would have a security architect involved in application design and development processes at all. The answer, almost universally, is that the organization seeks to create a secure result in the software being developed. Specific rationales, processes, and contexts may vary, but it is almost always the ultimate and fundamental point of having security engaged in the process that they seek to ensure a secure result of those processes. By this, we mean that they want to ensure that the software that's being developed by the organization is robust, resilient, and resistant to attack, that it protects any application data that might be stored within it or processed by it, and so on.

How can an architect influence these things? In many cases, this will be done through two methods:

- By making modifications to the software design and/or implementation
- By making additions or modifications to security controls outside the application's code but within the substrate or environment in which it will be used

To accomplish the former, security designs will often find themselves implemented within the software in the same way that other elements of the application are – or included as elements of the substrate or as underlying support components. Because modifications to software (and changes to underlying components) all go through the same life cycle – including those adjustments that we might require to implement security design goals – they need to be accounted for within the release process as well.

For the latter, you will notice that we're making security changes that impact security without modifying the application itself directly. While this could "free" us from the practical necessity of going through the release process directly to make implementation changes, there are still practical reasons why the release process matters. This is because relevant security features need to be cognizant of underlying application features and usage. Specific security strategies – as well as threats and risks – will likely change based on the release. A new feature might introduce new risks or close old ones. Since those features are tied to the release, this means (as we outlined) that the release process matters.

As an example of this, consider what happens if you identify an issue in an application where input filtering is less complete than we might like, thereby exposing the application to issues such as cross-site scripting or SQL injection. Perhaps the application is written in such a way that this lack of filtering makes certain types of attacks much more likely – for example, reflected cross-site scripting. There are a few ways to potentially mitigate this. One strategy would be to change the application itself so that there is input filtering (and thereby protection against cross-site scripting is built into the application). In this case, the filtering code would need to go through the release process, just like all other production code.

Alternate strategies that do not involve changing code, such as using a **web application firewall** (**WAF**) in front of a web application to ensure unexpected input (such as cross-site scripting attempts) is filtered, still require synergy with the release process. This is because the issue you are addressing (in this case, the lack of input filtering) is bound to a given release. The developers of the application might fix the root issue in a subsequent release, they might make another change to the application code that would obviate the issue (for example, removing the form field in question), or they might make other application changes that cause the issue to be overcome by events. Also, the specific context of the application, how it performs, its features, how it is used, its business scope, and the business processes it supports can change with new capabilities (implemented via the release cycle), new features (developed and fielded per the release cycle), and in response to other code changes (bound to the release cycle). Therefore, even if you're not changing code directly, the release cycle still matters.

So, whether you choose to adjust the application software itself for security reasons or whether you choose to implement something outside of the application itself as a control or countermeasure, the release cycle – the SDLC – plays a key role.

Because of this importance, we will start by walking through the most popular approaches to software development at a high level. Here, we will discuss how and why the process will play a role in your security planning. As we do so, we will focus on locations where you can inject security processes into the life cycle. But lest you think we are suggesting that you proceed directly to injecting security features, process updates, or controls into the development process right away, we're not. Just like other architecture activities, you will want (or need) to create documentation that reflects your strategy, stakeholders, transition effort, and so on. You will also need to validate assumptions and get buy-ins from stakeholders.

We are deliberately choosing to present the development process overview first for a few practical reasons. Understanding the development process and your role in it helps you do the following:

- **Identify stakeholders**: In addition to the business stakeholders, users, and developers, there are likely numerous others. Integration teams, performance, and functional testing teams, build teams, operations teams, engineering teams, third-party relationship managers, and numerous others can be important stakeholders.

- **Identify gaps**: Understanding the development process can help you identify potential gap areas that represent weak points in your security approach.

- **Build process understanding**: The more you understand the development process in use, the better you will be able to empathize with developers and other key players in the release process.

Because of this, it is useful to think about the development process first before you put any documentation together. Also, keep in mind that there are two different *control panels* available to you; that is, two different contexts in which your architecture efforts may be germane. First, there is the architecture of the development *result* – the software that is developed by the organization as the output of the development pipeline. You will be called upon to apply design effort to the applications that are being constructed. In this way, you participate as part of the development process and are a key collaborator in it.

In addition to this, though, you may also be called upon to apply security design and sound architecture principles to the development process itself – the *method* by which output (in this case, business-enabling application code) is produced. Just like any other business-enabling process, you – the architect – can and will be called upon to make adjustments to fulfill the organizational mission – in this case, the element of that mission that is supported by the development of the software. Note that in doing so, you will need to use caution. The process of software development can be intrinsic to the organization. This means that there can be potentially significant impacts to the organization resulting from changes to how software is developed. Due to this, we will need to approach changes here holistically while taking the larger business impacts into account.

We will also need to make a few minor adjustments to the way we approach our design process and documentation efforts to effectively support both use cases. However, since both require a concrete understanding of the development process itself to be successful, we can accurately say that having knowledge of this process is the most important key element to understand. Therefore, we'll start there.

Environment

As we begin the process of looking at development modes, bear in mind that there are two distinct "lenses" that we want to consider. The first is the design process around the software itself – that is, what changes can we make to the software (or how it's deployed) to help accomplish security goals. This is very important, but it's not the only thing that we need to consider. The temptation is often to limit the focus to just the application source code, the application design, component interactions, the interface points with the user, and so on. However, environmental considerations also play a significant role. There are numerous elements to this: the platform that the application will be deployed to, the operational context that it is to be fielded in, the technology substrate that the application rests on, and so on.

This matters because the application and the environment that it lives in need to operate synergistically to be secure. This is true both beneficially and detrimentally to security. On the beneficial side, we can influence the environment so that it addresses limitations at the application level; for example, we might deploy monitoring tools to supplement a deficit that the application has in logging. Alternatively, we might introduce application-level controls or security mechanisms to overcome limitations in the environment. For example, if we are deploying to an environment that is less trusted (for example, a multi-tenant public cloud), we might implement additional features within the application to help us ensure that we accomplish the same outcome, such as encrypting data in the application itself if the underlying platform or environment doesn't provide that capability.

On the detrimental side, problems or limitations of the environment can enable avenues of attack that would otherwise not be there. For example, a weak environment could potentially allow interpreted code to be leaked (and thereby analyzed by an attacker for flaws), manipulated, or otherwise subverted. Likewise, issues in the application might put elements of the environment at risk; for example, an application that employs CGI scripts or PHP in an insecure way that allows untrusted code to be run on a server.

The point is, as we walk through each of these development models, keep in mind that just because we're talking about application development, the scope needs to include both the application code as well as the operational context in which that code is fielded. With that in mind, let's walk through the most common development methodologies and look at what they are and how the architect may play a role in them.

Considerations for waterfall projects

"For applications, you need to make sure that pieces align correctly and that the application itself is secure. The architecture process is there in part to ensure that developers don't do things that will wind up in the application being successfully attacked; for example, to ensure that logging is enabled, that authentication is in place, that secure session identifiers are in use, and so forth. Failure to do these things can often result in an attack because they weaken the application. The architect, seeing this, can design solutions that ensure the application's original goals are satisfied while at the same time closing these issues."

– John Kallil, Chief Information Security Officer

Nowadays, not many software projects are built using the traditional waterfall development process. It is useful as a starting point because it is still sometimes used – notably for special-purpose software (for example, industrial control systems) – and because the waterfall process is linear, making security integration into that life cycle very intuitive and easier to understand. This is because the linear nature of the process allows us to concentrate on describing interactions linearly first so that when we start looking at iterative and continuous models, we already have a frame of reference and point of comparison.

As you may recall, we discussed waterfall approaches at a high level in *Chapter 3, Building an Architecture – Scope and Requirements*. There, you learned that waterfall models are generally thought of as having a set number of linear development phases that proceed serially from project inception through to production release. The specific number of steps varies from model to model, but for the purposes of our explanation, we will use the five-stage model shown in the following diagram:

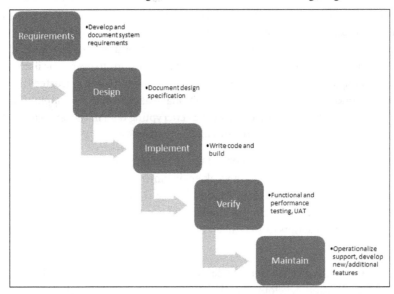

Figure 6.1 – "Typical" waterfall process

As you can see, there are five principal stages:

1. **Requirements gathering**: The development team gathers and documents application requirements.

2. **Design**: The application design is developed, including the application architecture and the application's overall structure. The design is usually created to address the requirements that were identified in the requirements gathering stage.

3. **Implementation**: Developers author application code, create supporting libraries if needed, and unit test functionality. This stage also usually includes application build steps (for example, compiling and linking) to the extent that they are required.

4. **Verification**: Personnel are engaged to test application functionality. This can include ensuring there's conformance to documented requirements (user acceptance testing), testing to ensure the features operate appropriately through functional testing, as well as validating that the application adheres to performance objectives (that is, performance or load testing).

5. **Maintenance**: This stage includes the ongoing operations tasks associated with the application, as well as improving the application through the development of new features.

A common approach that's used to help ensure the security of the application being developed is to include a *stage-gate review* (sometimes referred to as a *phase gate*). This reflects a project management approach whereby the project (in this case, our application development) is divided into clearly delineated phases (or stages) with an oversight function being introduced prior to transition between those phases.

At each stage or phase under this model, there are opportunities to introduce security measures to ensure a resilient application at the end of the development process. In the next section, we will outline each phase, with a focus on some of the more commonly appearing security techniques that are sometimes employed within each phase and their intent.

Requirements phase

The waterfall process begins with a systematic and workmanlike gathering of the business and functional requirements that are germane to the system's functionality. These requirements include the following:

*   **Business requirements**: This represents the objectives that the application must complete to satisfy the business needs that are causing the software to be developed in the first place. These answer the question of *why* the software is being developed.

*   **User requirements**: Sometimes codified together with the business requirements, these represent the set of mechanisms by which users of the application will interact with it. This answers the question of *what* the software must do for it to be useful and who it will be useful to.

*   **Functional requirements**: These are the things that reflect what the development team will need to do to deliver the solution. These answer the question of *how* the solution will be built to achieve the specified goals.

- **Transition (or temporal) requirements**: These are the things that reflect the intermediate or evolutionary stages of application development that will be obviated once development is complete. This includes requirements that are needed to move from a legacy system to a new one. This helps answer the question of *when* the software will be available (and used) and how.

- **Non-functional (solution or system) requirements**: Sometimes codified together with functional requirements, these include all the ancillary-but-important items that aren't directly related to building the system but are nevertheless important. These can address elements of *where* (for example, specific localities or geographies that might be germane to business continuity or compliance), *when* (for example, specific timing and delivery time frame requirements such as meeting a particular timing milestone), *how* (for example, system performance and throughput requirements), and so on.

The requirements phase can be a good time to gather and document any security-specific requirements that the application might have. In general, these will often stem either implicitly or explicitly from the user requirements. For example, were we developing a system that facilitates file transfers between users, implicit in the requirement that "users can share files," there are a number of security goals. These might include the following:

- Others can only access a user's files if they have authorization to

- Users are authenticated to ensure that they are who they claim to be

- File content is protected while stored and in transit

- Files are deleted from transient locations (for example, a cache) when they're no longer in use

- A record of files accessed by users is kept

Of course, these are only a few examples of security requirements that might stem from just one single functional requirement. Should we partake in a requirements definition exercise in earnest, we would likely find and isolate many more. Just like you would author and validate functional requirements, it can be helpful to do the same with security requirements. As you go through the phase gate, validate that security requirements exist to support the user and functional requirements and ensure that they are complete.

Design phase

The next phase is designing how the application will be written to satisfy the requirements that were discussed in the previous phase. During this phase, the application itself might be systematically mapped out using techniques such as flowchart creation and pseudocode or through the creation of various other design artifacts. Once the design is complete, the application will typically go through a design review process before transitioning to the next phase.

At this stage and from a security point of view, there are numerous ways to get involved. First, it is important to get an idea of how the application may be attacked; that is, how an attacker might use the application to do something that would be explicitly precluded by the security requirements.

We're in a bit of a Catch-22 as we do this. On the one hand, when we can identify potential issues with the application early in the process, the cheaper and easier it will be to address those issues (recall our discussion of Boehm's Law way back in *Chapter 1, What Is Cybersecurity Architecture?*). However, potential issues that may impact our application are heavily dependent on the design of that application. This means the way in which the application is constructed will impact what attacks it might be subject to, how those attacks will be conducted, and what the impact of a successful compromise would be. In other words, we won't know what the threat context will be until after the application is at a certain point of development.

Therefore, since it is during the design phase that the overall high-level design of the application will be authored, it's also the soonest that we can undertake a systematic examination of that design for potential issues (since, prior to this phase, there is no design to examine). This means that systematic examination of the design (for example, using application threat modeling or other techniques) is best positioned to happen contemporaneously with the application design. This presupposes a close working relationship between application security staff and those designing the application. Where such a relationship does not exist, as a stopgap, we can perform the evaluation process as part of the phase gate handoff between design and production. However, practically, it is optimal if we can do this examination while creating the design itself to allow for back and forth (iterative design) with application developers and software architects working on the design.

Implementation phase

The implementation phase is the point where the design is executed, where software is written that meets the requirements identified, and where the application takes its ultimate shape. There are several opportunities for the participation of security resources during this phase.

First, there are opportunities in coding the application. Some application vulnerabilities such as input validation issues, authentication state maintenance issues, and others can arise as a byproduct of the way the application itself is authored. For example, failure to validate input from users can lead to issues such as SQL injection; issues around how memory is allocated and managed (along with input verification) can lead to buffer overflows. Because of this, there is often value that can be provided by engagement between security and the developers themselves. What level of interaction is appropriate will depend on the organizational context, the language and technologies that are employed, other processes and standards (for example, coding standards), and other factors.

In addition to this, there is also a role to play for security staff in validating and reviewing application dependencies. It is tempting to think about developed software as a unified, cohesive *whole* since this is how it is often discussed and how we often perceive a finished application. However, most applications have numerous dependencies: static libraries, dynamically linked libraries (or shared objects), middleware, and other software that supports the application. Likewise, the application may be running inside an extant ecosystem of software, hardware, and middleware.

For example, consider an application that is built as a container designed to be fielded into a container-centric cloud environment (for example, Amazon's AWS Fargate). In this case, not only do you have the application itself (including any supporting libraries that might be statically or dynamically linked against it for it to run), but you also have the container environment (the container engine), the cloud service that it will be fielded into, and so on. The point is that the implementation can have other dependencies (from a security standpoint) outside of the code that's been written by the organization itself.

Security can engage with the development process along any or all these dimensions. They can engage in ensuring that the code is authored using secure practices (for example, bounds checking), that appropriate techniques are employed to validate user input, that underlying components and middleware are recorded and tracked so that vulnerabilities in underlying code don't accidentally introduce issues to your application, that components lower in the stack (for example, container runtimes, hypervisors, and so on) are secured and configured robustly, and so on.

Verification phase

Once the application has been implemented and subjected to phase gate analysis, review, and approval, the application will move into the verification phase. At this stage, the application is validated (tested) along a few different lines:

- **User acceptance testing**: This is designed to ensure that the system fulfills the needs of the users. Typically, this involves a period whereby users employ the application and provide feedback on what features were successfully implemented and what still needs additional work. User requirements are compared to the result of the implementation to validate that the users achieved what they want – that the features that they desired exist and that none are overlooked. If this is not the case, they will note areas of deficiency so that the implementation team can get those issues addressed.

- **Functional testing**: This is designed to ensure that features work as expected. On the surface, this sounds like it might or could be part of user acceptance testing; that is, if a feature doesn't work, then it won't be accepted by the users, right? This is true, but keep in mind that some issues might be more subtle than an entire feature failing to work. For example, a situation might arise where there's a bug in a given feature that can only be observed once every hundred times the feature is used. An issue like this one, while not undermining the feature in its entirety, is nevertheless an issue that should be caught and addressed.

- **Performance testing**: In a situation where an application might be used by many different users all at the same time, this process might include ensuring that all the users are able to use the application at the same time without causing performance issues. For example, a web application that can handle 10 simultaneous users is great – unless you have a population of 100 users that you are trying to service with that application and that are all accessing the application at the same time. The point of performance testing is to ensure that applications can handle the volume of usage that's expected.

As you might imagine, there are opportunities for security teams to participate in the testing process as well. For example, we might introduce security-specific test scenarios to existing test measures. We may do this to ensure that security features perform as expected and that they enforce the security properties that we want.

We may also introduce security-specific testing during this phase; we might employ automated scanning, static or dynamic application analysis, penetration testing, or other testing techniques to validate the security of the application. For example, in addition to testing security features using the testing types described previously, you might incorporate security-specific tests into each testing type. The following are some examples of how you might incorporate security testing into each testing area. Note that this is not intended to be an exhaustive list – you are limited by your imagination, your needs, and the available resources for what specific test situations to include:

- **User acceptance testing** (**UAT**): UAT can be a good time to incorporate testing for several security elements. You might choose to validate access control measures by making sure that user roles are assigned appropriately, that the session state is maintained in a secure way, that roles perform as expected (that is, they gate access to resources appropriately), and so on. You can also choose to test monitoring and auditability features such as logging and alerting.

- **Functional testing**: In addition to employing methods to test security-relevant features within the application, you might also perform application scanning (for example, using an automated web scanning tool), dynamic or static application testing, or application penetration testing. This helps establish that security requirements are addressed and that the mechanisms put in place to do so are implemented in a reliable, functional way.

- **Performance testing**: Because the application is under load during performance testing, load-heavy testing scenarios such as brute-force testing (testing numerous username/password combinations to find hardcoded or development/test credentials left within the application) fit well here, as do testing techniques such as parameter fuzzing (repeatedly testing large permutations of input to look for unexpected behavior). Due to the ability to monitor the application under load and with a high volume of requests, difficult to find, timing-based issues such as race conditions can be observed easier during this phase of testing.

There are numerous avenues to explore here and there's a significant role to play for the security team during the testing phase of a development project.

Maintenance phase

The last phase of any waterfall process is the maintenance phase. Once the application has been designed, implemented, tested, and fielded into a production environment, it is time for the ongoing *care and feeding* of that application. Depending on the application, this might include there being ongoing upkeep of underlying components (for example, supporting libraries), such as maintaining the underlying components that keep the application running or numerous other important elements.

From a security perspective, there are ways to stay involved in this as well. For example, we might keep tabs on security vulnerabilities that appear in underlying libraries or components so that they can be addressed. We may also look out for security issues in the underlying substrate that support the application, flagging them for remediation when they occur. We can also, of course, periodically test the application for new issues and vulnerabilities as they are discovered to make sure that the applications themselves stay hardened over time in light of new attacks and techniques. Let's look at a case study describing waterfall development considerations.

Case study – waterfall development

> *"The biggest challenge by far in both waterfall and agile is when nobody writes the architecture down or nobody uses a consistent manner to describe it. Maybe somebody scribbled it on a whiteboard, used UML, or some other way. It's really hard to tell what an architecture document ought to be. There's no hard and fast rule for that. A lot of people do it differently. However, it's more likely that you're going to have an architecture document in waterfall approaches. Why? Because in waterfall there are phases. And each phase is supposed to waterfall one after the other. And you're supposed to create documentation to get from one stage to the next.*
>
> *In agile, sometimes people start coding first and thinking later. It can, in the worst cases, lead to an absolute lack of engineering rigor and discipline. And so it's very easy to skip the part where you write down the artifact. Someone can say, 'The architecture is in the code; just read the code?' But that's naïve -- and it's wrong. Another factor is how often do things change and what does it take to change it. In Agile you're supposed to change things. You get new requirements and you're changing features throughout development. This can actually change the architecture in many cases. In Waterfall, it's much harder to make fundamental architectural changes."*
>
> *– Gary McGraw, Ph.D., Founder, Berryville Institute of Machine Learning. Best selling author of Software Security and 11 other books*

In an interview for this book, Gary McGraw explained to us some of the benefits that can be realized from evaluating architecture systematically in a waterfall context. He explained how security considerations played out in a large payments company that employed a waterfall approach.

"When we were working on a smart card project for a large payments company, they had this platform they built using a Java card. This was just an operating system basically with a filesystem, and built on top of that was a way to do credit card transactions securely. But the threat model with something like this is very tricky because you are basically giving your attacker a copy of the whole platform. They can take it with them in their pocket wherever they want, whenever they want. They can take it to the lab, put it under a scanning tunneling microscope, glitch it, interact with it, and do all sorts of things that make life difficult because you just handed a copy of the entire security apparatus (barring cryptographic keys) to the attacker."

He went on to explain how they were able to apply analysis to the model within the context of the development model and use that to harden the result against attack.

"They were counting on the Java virtual machine to encapsulate attacks against the machine by having the virtual machine in between the attacker and the application logic. It was a typical sandbox model. And the problem was that in the design of some of the systems, there were calls that went all the way down to the hardware to talk to files directly. They didn't go through the virtual machine at all in those cases. So it was not possible for the virtual machine to go, 'whoa, wait a minute. You're not supposed to do that.' That was a bad design. We pointed out that you can't do it this way if you're going to have a virtual machine: it has to encapsulate everything and be an unavoidable block everywhere."

He described how one of the reasons why this was possible was due to the security review. In turn, that security review was facilitated by how they adapted the waterfall approach to include a security review.

"They believed us and they changed the fundamental design. That came about as a direct result of architecture analysis and architecture review. We weren't trying to make things perfect. We knew that we couldn't get perfect security design, but we knew that we could design things so that we could hold fraud down to an acceptable level and give knobs to the business on the back end to reduce fraud to where we wanted it to be. In this case, there were design documents and there was a specification. The good thing about specifications is without one, your software can't be wrong – it can just be surprising. When you have a specification, you know when it's wrong."

Considerations for Agile projects

"Recently, I've been doing more work with Agile and DevOps environments. One problem in how these models are used is that stories are often used to lay out requirements [for example, 'user stories']. In security, though, many of the architecture requirements stem from stories that are not 'functional stories' – instead, they might be invisible or taken for granted from a user point of view. This makes it harder to account for security in the design process, which, in turn, makes architecture even more important in these models."

– John Tannahill, a Canadian management consultant specializing in information security

As we walked through the various phases of the waterfall architecture, you probably noticed that the stages in a waterfall development approach aren't very *iterative*. As illustrated in the *typical waterfall process* shown in the previous section, there are *stages* of development with gates between phases. Anyone who's been involved in software development knows that this isn't always super realistic. There will always be some iteration – some need to reach backward into prior phases to accomplish a particular task.

As an example, consider testing. Imagine a software development project that goes through the requirements phase to identify and document what the application needs to do, then goes through the design to identify a way to do this, and then goes through implementation to make it a reality. All these things can happen serially and in sequence. What happens though if, during the testing phase, users point out that there was a fundamental misunderstanding on the part of the development team about what the application's purpose is and what the application needs to do?

In that case, the development team will typically do one of two things: either go back to the design phase so that the design, implementation, and subsequent testing of that feature can be redone or, if the feature is not critical, schedule that feature for delivery in a future release. Either way, the process becomes iterative. In the first case, an iteration of prior phases occurs so that the issue can be addressed; in the second case, the entire release cycle becomes iterative to accommodate a future update. It can be hard to understand that this level of iteration is possible (in fact, expected) just by looking at a typical flow diagram of the waterfall process.

The agile technique attempts to account for the iterative nature of issues like this within the process itself. An agile process, rather than having linear stages, is built upon the premise that certain phases of development operate best when they are iterative. The specifics of this can vary from approach to approach, but at its most basic, the development phases of the project are iterative in nature and designed to be so.

In some models (for example, Scrum), there might be short time intervals (*sprints*) that provide time-constrained windows in which tasks can be performed, such as the development of features. Features are fed into a *backlog*, where they are worked on within the context of a particular sprint. At the end of the sprint, the team comes together to review progress, make adjustments, and prioritize what features will be completed next.

While not a perfect depiction of this process, the following diagram illustrates an iterative development process ("construction") occurring within an overall project framework:

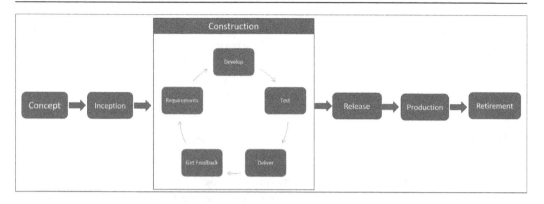

Figure 6.2 – Iterative development process

The project management framework in the preceding diagram includes a conception and inception phase. These are the phases where budget is allocated, resources are assigned, and so forth. The concluding steps include turnover to production and, ultimately, the retirement of the application.

Within an individual sprint, developers gather requirements, design and develop the software, test it, and deliver it. At the conclusion of each sprint, feedback is gathered so that future iterations can refine and improve upon the progress that was made during the sprint. This informs any future development of the lessons that were learned from prior sprints. Though the previous diagram does illustrate the conception and inception phases, these might be better understood as being an ongoing series of *loops*, whereby the output of each loop is provided as input into the next.

Within the construction phase, you might have something that can be represented as follows:

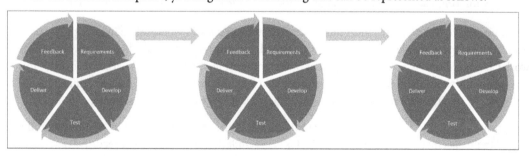

Figure 6.3 – Cascading information through iterative sprints

While the preceding diagram is not a perfect representation, what you'll notice is that each sprint (represented by circular pie-shaped processes) is iterative in and of themselves; however, they feed into each other as design decisions, requirements that have been harvested, and user feedback that's been "passed forward" into future design iterations.

An agile process requires more reactivity on the part of the security practitioner around when and how they integrate security measures into the process. The reason for this is that, unlike a waterfall or other linear development approach, there are no set *stage gates* that mark the transition of the project from one development phase to the next. In the next section, we will highlight some of the key places where security teams might consider integration with the development process.

Conception phase

At some point, even in an iterative and ongoing process, someone needs to start with an idea. This means that there is an initial moment when someone says, "*we could really use an application to do* _____." The earliest phases of many agile processes start with this moment of initial conception or pre-planning. This stage represents the pre-work that allows the project to get off the ground in the first place. This includes doing things such as the following:

- **Identifying business opportunities or needs**: Identify what the drivers behind needing to develop an application in the first place are. For a commercial product, this could be exploring the market niche and end user pain points that will be addressed by the project; for an internal application, this could be an itemization of the business needs that necessitate building a solution for the problem in the first place.

- **Establishing context and assumptions**: Determine what the scope of the effort will be, the context in which it will operate, any assumptions that will impact how it is developed (this could include a "build or buy" decision), and identify any hidden drivers, assumptions, or other data points that will influence the work.

- **Evaluating viability**: Ensure that the work is technically, operationally, and financially viable.

In the normal course of events, it is unlikely that most organizations will think to involve the security team at this stage of the development project. Instead, security teams typically become involved once work has started on the actual development of the application. This is not to say that security teams can't or shouldn't be involved at these early phases (in fact, this can be very beneficial) – it just means that security involvement may be overlooked at these early stages as a practical matter.

The primary integration point for security at this stage is in the arena of notification; that is, becoming alerted to the fact that a new project or product is being undertaken. From there, a security team might choose to *embed* a representative into the project team (allowing them to stay apprised and plugged into future work). Alternatively, they might choose to track the evolution of the project from these earliest phases so that they are not surprised later on down the road.

A related approach involves appointing a *security champion* from each development team; in this model, the champion serves as the single point of contact for security matters for each team. In this model, the security champion serves a similar function as an embedded security resource but may have budgetary advantages since it does not require additional security staff since it leverages existing development staff.

Inception phase

Once the project has been *envisioned* – that is, once the feasibility and general context have been established – there are still a few steps required before developers can sit down and start cranking through sprints. Specifically, resources (both staff and funding) need to be secured, a general approach decided, risks identified, scope determined, the work environment structured, and so on.

These things represent the logistical and procedural prerequisites to getting a development effort off the ground. The inception phase (sometimes referred to as *sprint zero*) represents the time in which these items are completed, and work is begun. Depending on the approach that you're following, you may also elect to do some preliminary modeling of the application, harvest the initial high-level requirements, or do other work that will let you develop the business case for the project, socialize and gain approval for that business case, secure resources, gain internal support, and ultimately kick off the development work in earnest.

From the point of view of the security practitioner, this phase is very important. It is at this point that initial decisions about the project are made, and the work environment is created. And more to the point, this is where we start to see the requirements and initial modeling take place.

These artifacts – the initial requirements and models – are as important to the security practitioner in an agile context as they are in a waterfall model. Of course, it is to be expected that new requirements will be identified as iterations progress; likewise, it is a given that new modeling will occur as new features are added to the backlog and new plans are put together for how to address those features. However, from this point in the process and beyond, the security team can add value by participating in the requirements gathering process.

The reason for this is twofold:

- First, security practitioners will tend to pay more attention to misuse and abuse cases during requirements discussions; that is, those situations outside of an application's *happy path* (the normal, expected application usage flow without error conditions or exceptions).

- Second, having a better understanding of user stories, requirements, and use cases translates directly to having a better understanding of attacker motivation and how the application might be attacked. This can translate directly to the use of techniques such as application threat modeling as modeling artifacts are developed.

Lastly, core decisions such as what platforms will be targeted, what language the software will be written in, and so on are likely to coalesce at this phase. This means that security-relevant guidance can be introduced at this point. For example, if you have a project that will be written in C++ and will run on Windows systems, you might introduce C++ coding standards; likewise, if the outcome is intended to be a web application, you might introduce requirements for input validation at this stage.

Construction phase

The construction phase of an agile project is the point at which the application comes together. Each sprint will consist of gathering new requirements for features in the backlog, designing features that address those requirements, developing the software that implements those features, testing that software, and ultimately gathering feedback about the implementation for input into the next phase.

There are a number of ways that security teams can influence the process of each sprint. For example, as new designs are crafted, they might employ threat modeling techniques to ensure that the overall design addresses the ways in which the application may be attacked. As the application is expanded and each new sprint adds to the vision of the entire work, those threat models can be built upon and expanded with feedback provided to future iterations in the same way that feedback from users is.

Also, like in waterfall approaches, bear in mind that security requirements are important. Just like you would introduce security requirements to the overall functional specification or requirements list for a waterfall project, so too can you introduce security-specific outcomes to the goals and targets for an agile project. Because each sprint is (more or less) self-contained, you will likely wish to do this on an ongoing basis – introducing new security requirements into the mix as they become germane to decisions that are made by the project team.

Lastly, keep in mind that software will be developed during each of the iterative sprints that are conducted during this phase. Testing is often partially encapsulated into the sprint itself, with testing being conducted in an ongoing way as the project moves along. Therefore, just like you could introduce testing scenarios such as vulnerability scanning, penetration testing, static or dynamic application testing, and other methods to the testing phase of a waterfall project, so too can you implement those tools here.

Release phase

At some point, you will need to stop developing new features and put the ones that you have developed into production. This phase signifies releasing the software into a production context. It should be noted that the whole process itself can be (and often is) iterative. This means as you move some portion of the application into production, you begin a new cycle of development targeting the next release of the software, which includes additional features, new users, or other goals. However, it can be useful to view the transition of software from a limited audience, rapidly changing context to a user-facing, less changing one as a milestone in and of itself.

As you move software into a production context, the security team can be involved in multiple ways. First, they can introduce controls and security measures designed to underpin the security of what was built and is currently being released. For example, consider an application where weaknesses in input validation are discovered. Should this be discovered early, the introduction of security requirements detailing the need for input protections could very well be introduced back into the backlog and thereby address the issue. However, if time does not allow for this, one approach to accomplish a similar goal could be to ensure that the application is fielded behind a web application firewall. We used this example previously, but it is a useful one for understanding how you might address a known issue at another level of the stack and, in this case, at a different time in the development cycle.

The release phase includes testing the system, developing the system manual or other documentation, as well as releasing the overall software to the production environment. Depending on the approach you employ, security testing activities can either be done as part of individual sprints, as suggested previously, or they can be folded into the release process, along with any final QA activities that may occur during this phase.

Production phase

This phase represents the long-term operational support of the software in a production context. In addition to security measures that you may have included during the release to production (the prior phase), there are also additions that you may incorporate in the long term as the software lives within a production context. The security team can evaluate lessons learned from the release process, such as by analyzing metrics and the results of security testing, and then incorporate these lessons learned back into the development process to improve the process in the future. Likewise, any open risk areas that were not resolved during the release or in software can be addressed by how we support it in production, as well as the operational processes that have been employed.

Retirement phase

The last phase, retirement, represents the ultimate decommissioning of the software as it is removed from production and is either replaced by something new or removed entirely. There are three key security tasks involved here. The first is ensuring that any security measures or goals that have been propped up within the software itself continue to be performed once the software is decommissioned if necessary. Second, we need to ensure that the software is decommissioned in a secure way (for example, by purging sensitive data from production systems, monitoring the decommissioning processes, and so on). Finally, we need to ensure that if the software is being replaced by something else, a secure design and deployment process is followed in rolling out the new alternative.

Case study – Agile development

"You must have enough discipline to write down the architecture. Agile, waterfall, or DevOps doesn't matter to me, but you better do the architecture risk analysis, and you better do the threat modeling. The book I wrote 16 years ago in 2007 (that book is old enough to drive by itself now) used this notion of software artifacts, not methodologies, to talk about touchpoints and to say 'if you've got code, use a static analysis tool; if you've got design, do some architecture risk analysis; if you've

got something to ship and execute, do some security testing; and if you're putting something out in the world, do some penetration testing.' Those touchpoints were agnostic to the development model; meaning the notion of waterfall or agile (or something else) doesn't matter. For that reason, architecture, risk analysis, and threat modeling are both directly applicable, regardless of your methodology."

– Gary McGraw, Ph.D., Founder, Berryville Institute of Machine Learning. Best selling author of Software Security and 11 other books

In the same interview as the prior case study we outlined, we asked Gary McGraw about where he's seen effective strategies in agile development. He described the following scenario to us.

"We did an analysis of this one company (that doesn't exist anymore) that made a platform for day traders and was developing using an agile methodology. They had a direct connection to the ATM network so that they could do wire transfers, they had an interface for trading execution and order entry -- all potentially very dangerous functionality in the wrong hands. They asked us to do an analysis of this: not really a penetration test, just a security analysis and design review."

He went on to describe that there was an almost complete absence of documentation.

"We told them that we could do the work, but we asked if they would first send their design documentation to us so that we could estimate how much effort it would take. Their response was basically, 'Oh yeah, we've been meaning to write all that down, but we haven't yet.' So instead of being able to work through it, we went to them to walk through their design since they didn't have any documentation."

He described what they found through their examination.

"They had this one person an agile designer who sat in the same room with the developers and implementers of the system. This one designer had the whole design in his head. We pointed out that one serious security risk was that this one person was a single point of failure. They agreed with that. As a consequence, we spent a lot of time and money writing their architecture down for them because that was their number one risk. The code was designed, but because there wasn't a hard and fast need to write it down, it was all in one person's head. The design itself was very good. But the lack of documentation in this case was a risk because loss of that one personnel (through attrition, accident, or some other circumstance) would have been catastrophic. To get them to a state where we could perform an analysis, we needed to build that documentation from the ground up."

Considerations for DevOps projects

"Things such as DevOps, DevSecOps, and all of the 'infrastructure as code' and all that doesn't change things. With the risk environment, if you understand it and have done it in a systematic way, you know what the risks are. Yes, there are new vulnerabilities being discovered every day, but they're not new potential things that could go wrong, they're just in different places. 'There's a buffer overflow in the web browser instead of the email client.' Who cares; it's still a buffer overflow – what

you're trying to do is protect access control to the underlying platform.
The particular way in doing this or the method of attack used doesn't change the
impact – though it might change the likelihood."

– Andrew S. Townley, Chief Executive Officer at Archistry Incorporated

The last model that we will walk through in detail is DevOps. Remember that there are as many software development life cycle variations as there are software development teams themselves (since everybody has their own needs) – but we are only covering the major model types here, so expect your process to deviate somewhat from what we've covered.

DevOps seeks to move away from an iterative approach to software development to a continuous one. The ultimate goal, as posited by Len Bass et al. in *DevOps: A Software Architect's Perspective*, is to minimize the time between *committing* a change and placing that change into a production context while ensuring that quality goals are met. This happens via several mechanisms:

- **Mechanism 1**: The first mechanism is an interdisciplinary approach to the development and operations process. The term DevOps itself, a portmanteau of *development* and *operations*, reflects the unification of the two disciplines into a whole, whereby the work done by both amplifies and assists each other. This interdisciplinary approach helps ensure that the software that's developed can be maintained, that it lends itself well to disciplined and reliable operations, and that operations processes enable better, more rapid development. And, as should be no surprise, just like silos between development and operations are broken down, so too are silos between development teams, and between other stakeholders in the development process such as QA, build, product management, source management, and other teams.

- **Mechanism 2**: While useful, just breaking down silos is not sufficient on its own to ensure an optimally rapid release of software into production. Instead, the second mechanism – automation and tooling – is used to create the requisite channels for rapid release. Automation is used to enable rapid transition from development to production, and from ideation to release. The automation steps that exist between the development world and release to production are referred to collectively as the DevOps pipeline. The point here is to remove the friction associated with manual intervention throughout the process, which means less "*lag time*" throughout the process as time spent waiting for human intervention is minimized.

Every pipeline is different: they will use different tools, have different phases, have different stages of maturity, and so on. This means that trying to lay out a "*generic*" pipeline is a very difficult exercise. However, at a high level, you might envision an abstract development pipeline as having seven steps, as shown in the following diagram:

Figure 6.4 – Abstract development pipeline.

At first, it is natural to want to think of these as "*stages*" along a serial, sequential process. In fact, if we were to superimpose the stages of a waterfall process against the preceding diagram, you might see quite a few similarities. Thinking about it this way is a bit of a "*trap*", though. The reason why this is the case is because these stages aren't intended to reflect a linear process at all. Instead, they reflect stages that each individual code push might go through – but these are not "*stages*" in the same way that they are in a waterfall approach, for example. Instead, you could potentially have a thousand different individual features or units of code going through the process at any given time. In fact, different code can be (and often is) in different stages of the process at any given time while other units are in another. Because each segment along the release pipeline is automated, there's often minimal need for manual intervention along the pipeline, meaning that multiple different changes can progress through the process simultaneously.

With that in mind, let's walk through what's involved at each stage of the pipeline and how/where we can integrate security measures. Note that we're focused on the pipeline itself; there is, as you would expect, a number of different processes that happen outside that. For example, design activities, feature selection, product ideation, and more all need to happen just the same way that they do in other models. However, we've chosen to focus here on the more definitional aspects of DevOps/DevSecOps.

Develop

The first step of the pipeline involves creating and committing code. It is here that developers author the code that will ultimately make its way through the pipeline. Typically, this involves design elements – integrating the code into the existing, high-level application design, as well as storing and archiving the source code that implements the functionality that's developed.

For example, in a service-oriented approach, a developer might author a new RESTful web service and commit that code to source control using a tool such as Git, Mercurial, or Subversion. In this example, a scaffolding already exists that defines how individual elements of the application interact with each other (RESTful web services, in this case). Likewise, there is an automated framework in place to handle updates to existing code, new code, and other elements of source control.

From a security point of view, we have a few options of how we can interact with this stage of the process. Since developers are (usually) working within the context of a set of assumptions (language choice, application scaffold, and so on), we can provide input to those elements in the same way that we would under other development models. As an example, if developers are working in C++, we might consider coding standards, training, bounds-checking tools, and elements of language safety in the same way that we would in other development models.

Also, depending on the skill set of the security team, we can author security components to help the development team accomplish critical tasks. For example, the architect might identify design goals, work with the development team to design the software to implement those goals, work with other team members to develop the software, and deliver and support it. You may see the term "DevSecOps" in some cases – this term refers to integrating security into the DevOps pipeline in this way: either operationally or as a co-equal pillar of the software creation process.

Build

Once the code has been checked in, the next step is *building* it. In many cases, code must be compiled or linked for it to be functional in the environment and for the architecture in which it is to be deployed. For example, if you had code written in Java, you can't just take the arbitrary source files, run them, and expect anything to happen. Instead, you need to compile and package it first such as by compiling Java files into bytecode class files using a tool such as javac. If you're building a Windows executable or DLL in C++, you'd need to compile the source/header files into object files and then link (combine) those object files in the appropriate format to allow them to execute (in this case, into **Portable Executable** (**PE**) format).

The point is that there is some work to be done in-between authoring the code and being able to execute – and thereby test – those files. In a DevOps pipeline where this stage is necessary (for interpreted languages it might not be), typically, this process is heavily automated, much like other aspects of the release process.

From a security point of view, the automated nature of this stage can provide a useful location that will introduce compiler-aware code validation tools. For example, you might choose to add automated instrumentation, apply static analysis tools as a prerequisite to build completion, and so on. Because the build stage itself is automated, you too can automate security testing as part of the auto-build process.

Unit test

Once the code has been built, the next step is to ensure that the code performs as expected. Typically, most developers will *unit test* software as they develop it to ensure that, when they commit a change, it does what they want. A developer might write a test harness to perform unit testing on the code that they write before they ever check it in and commit it. That being said, they might not test every possible situation that the software might encounter once it is released into the field. As such, they may also author test scenarios that can be automatically run for their code to ensure that, should they change it in the future, the baseline functionality performs the way they expect every time it is run. For any future changes to that code, they can rerun the tests to ensure that they haven't broken anything accidentally as they made a modification to the software. Again, this process can be automated so that, should a test fail, the developer is notified that they need to make a fix.

Alternatively, some languages and frameworks will support the direct creation of test cases as part of the development process. For example, Django (for those who are unfamiliar, Django is a Python model/view/controller – or in Django parlance, a model/template/view – open source web framework) strongly recommends the creation of test cases for modules written in that platform. Upon deployment, these

test cases are run to help ensure that new changes do not inadvertently have unexpected functional side effects on the existing code base.

For security-relevant features and functionality, there is a good opportunity for the security team to participate in this process. They might, for example, ask for certain test conditions to be introduced that exercise functionality such as encryption, authentication, or other security measures in modules where such things are relevant. They might also help develop automated test cases for security-relevant functionality such as logging mechanisms, authentication, encryption of data at rest or in transit, or other functionality. That way, not only is the functionality tested for new changes but so too is the security functionality exercised.

Deploy (integrate)

Once the code has been unit tested, the next step is to put it on the platform in the format where it will ultimately be run in production. This phase of the process involves validating the software in the conditions that you expect it to be in within a production context. Again, this is typically performed in an automated fashion. Using the same example of Django we used previously, we might rerun the test cases that have been built into the existing modules to validate that new changes do not break existing functionality.

From a security standpoint, depending on the environment, there are steps that we can perform here. Since the code is now packaged into the format and context that will be used in a production context, we can introduce tools such as vulnerability assessment scanning, configuration validation, and others into the process to ensure that the entire package, as a unit, has the level of hardening and resiliency that we expect. When it does not, feedback can be provided to the developer to let them know that they have unintentionally broken something that is critical to the security of the application. In situations such as application containerization, we can ensure that the underlying container has the properties that we want – for example, that it's not using known vulnerable versions of middleware, software libraries, and so on.

Quality assurance

Much like the unit testing stage, we can now run test cases against the software as if it already exists in a production context. The main difference at this stage is that the software is now in production-ready form. This means that it has been packaged and deployed in the same way that it will be in production. Once again, we can now perform tests to validate that updates have not broken anything in ways that we didn't expect. Also, this stage allows us to test its interoperability with other software that is already in production. Here, we can validate that modules/services/components can still communicate with each other, that the behavior is as expected when they do, and that subtle errors haven't been introduced that would compromise how the application performs as a whole.

Again, as with unit testing, the fact that this stage is automated allows the security team to inject security testing scenarios into the process. We might, for example, build on automated test cases introduced in unit testing to further and more extensively test scenarios such as user logon, data protection measures, monitoring and logging capability, and other security-relevant functionality in an automated fashion. We may also incorporate testing tools such as **static application security**

testing (SAST) tools or **dynamic application security testing (DAST)** tools, which help find and flag security problems that may be present in the software.

Production

Once QA has occurred, we can then move the software into a production context. This step of the pipeline triggers any steps that are required to move the software from QA to the production environment, where it can then begin servicing users.

Validate

Once the software is in production, we can measure and validate that everything works. Sometimes, it is possible for subtle bugs to be introduced that weren't flagged during the automated unit testing and QA portions of the pipeline. When this happens, the ongoing monitoring processes are there to help flag and provide feedback to development about potential issues.

As you might expect, this is a very rich area for security involvement, particularly since it pertains to security metrics, operational validation, and monitoring. We can introduce collectors to gather information about security-relevant events (for example, valid or invalid login attempts, data access, privilege use, and so on). This can help us both with operational security monitoring but also as we seek to gather information about the performance of security-specific features.

Case study – DevOps/DevSecOps development

"Security architecture is as applicable to DevOps as it is to other models. In this context, I find it helpful to think of security as a special flavor of quality control, because the nature of a security defect is simply to cause a system to do something it was not designed to do in the first place. If having unintended operating or failure modes is generally considered to be undesirable in a product or service, why would we think of security any differently?

Take, for example, segregation of duties, which is a key concept underpinning many aspects of security architecture. This same concept exists in all sorts of other contexts dealing with quality control: crash safety testing is a separate function from engineering vehicles, large banking transactions require four eyes (i.e., multiple approvers), mass destruction weapons require different individuals to launch, bank safety deposit boxes require two keys held by different individuals, and so forth.

DevOps makes it possible to establish a model where a developer can do everything from coding to triggering deployment. Although this might be tempting, we have to consider (security inclusive) quality issues, as it is entirely possible to leverage DevOps while simultaneously separating duties in order to improve quality while reducing risk.

Ultimately, organizations care about quality because quality directly drives profitability. If we realize that security is just another kind of defect affecting quality, and utilize the frameworks that exist to mitigate risk (in this case security architecture), managers can begin to quickly draw a line directly from better security architecture to increased profitability."

– Iñigo Merino, Founder and CEO of Cienaga Systems

In an interview, we asked the CEO of the AI security firm Cienaga Systems, Iñigo Merino, about his experiences in DevOps organizations and where he saw successes or challenges related to security architecture. He told us about two parallel experiences that illustrate the value of secure design in the application space. For the first example, he referenced the highly sophisticated DevOps process used by a leading cloud services company. He told us, *"In this company, developers had a high degree of autonomy: they could create code and the code was automatically deployed to the entire customer-facing fleet consisting of thousands of servers – a process that could take months to complete because the changes were rolled out in waves for logistical reasons, as well as to be able to detect issues. This process was one key source of inefficiency and quality control issues for the company."*

He went on to describe some of the unique process considerations in an environment like that and how they had to adapt processes to ensure security goals were met.

"Continuing on the segregation of duties example, the issue here was that there weren't traditional segregation of duties. The architecture initially didn't account for that initially and eventually, the team grew to 500 or so developers who all had access view and edit the entire code base and they could (and did) change each other's code without fully understanding the implications to the complex code base. This created a problem for productivity as well because developers would 'parachute in and make changes to other people's code, causing it to break -- not on purpose, but because the engineer making changes didn't understand it well enough. They would leave the code in a broken state, meaning it now became the other person's job to fix. This created outages for customers and impacted revenue for the company."

There's an important lesson here. Specifically, just because you have a highly sophisticated and automated pipeline, doesn't mean that there isn't room for traditional security goals and controls. Even something simple such as which users have the permissions to access specific code files can have very significant impacts on quality, productivity, reliability, and even profitability. He went on to describe another situation within a large global pharmaceutical company that faced similar challenges but addressed them in a much different way.

"By contrast, at a large pharmaceutical company also in a DevOps context, I've seen a high degree of success be achieved through assigning ownership to a 'DevOps provisioning' or change management type role: an individual whose job it is to take delivered code and ensure that all the right processes are followed, that the right approvals are in place, that the right documentation exists, and that the code is deployed within the right time window. What's ironic about this is that reliability, quality, and productivity were all improved through the addition of something that was less automatic; less continuous."

In outlining how they were successful at improving productivity, security, and quality in this context, he described that it's not just about increasing or decreasing automation, but instead making sure that the right levels of automation exist to ensure secure/reliable outcomes. Many organizations would shy away from adding new manual process steps to a DevOps release pipeline such as this. But the point Iñigo made is that this type of thinking can be counterproductive and limiting. Like any architectural undertaking, it's about understanding the outcome you want to achieve, drawing upon your entire toolkit to build strategies to get there, and putting those strategies into practice. Said another way, automation for its own sake is not the essence of DevOps. Instead, building pathways to realize the most desirable outcomes for the organization (for example, by automating intelligently where needed and drawing upon human expertise where needed) is. He went on to describe the impact of this change.

"Prior to separating duties, developers had direct access to production. They would release code, there would be bugs, customers would see the bugs, and the developers would fix those bugs overnight. Magically the next day, the code would be working again – it was almost like elves coming in overnight to make everything work. This created a ton of confusion and management overhead as it was impossible to reproduce problems to find root causes. Sometimes, developers would run things in a dev or test environment and move the data output over to production in an uncontrolled way to 'prop up the solution. The goal of the organization was to increase the reliability, stability, and overall quality of outcomes associated with this process. Improvement came about in two ways. First, automation helped make removal of developer production access possible. Second, the introduction of a new role whose job it was to make sure that all changes to production had undergone the right controls provided huge benefits. This person made sure processes were followed: they would track user stories, ensure changes were approved, ensure release windows exists, ensure documentation exists and is reviewed, etc. By using a blended strategy of automation, design patterns like microservices, continuous testing, and continuous integration, and an accountable oversight role, automated platforms were able to test the code and thereby reduce the likelihood that things were going to break when pushed to production."

Process for application security design

> *"On the technical side, one has to focus on the conceptual architecture. Cloud, for example, is a whole new concept with tremendous implications. At the detail level, there are many aspects of the cloud; you need people like that to know those details and do that work. But the really creative architecture work is at the higher level, the conceptual level: how businesses use the cloud, not how the cloud itself is implemented."*
>
> *– John Sherwood, Chief Architect, thought leader, and co-Founder of The SABSA Institute*

There are, of course, other approaches beyond the three software development methodologies and life cycle archetypes that we have highlighted here. However, hopefully, the integration strategies we've looked at that are associated with these different models has shown some of the logic behind where we've chosen to integrate. If not, that's OK: we will work through how and where the development model plays a role as we work through the rest of this chapter. Ultimately, it will be up to you and your creativity to work within the context of your development process (since no two approaches are identical), but we trust that understanding why the life cycle matters – coupled with understanding the fundamental purpose of what we are trying to capture – will make the legwork of connecting the two together more or less straightforward.

To create a security architecture for an application, we must approach the design from two angles:

1. First, we need to keep integration within the development life cycle that's in use in mind.

2. Second, we need to ensure that we come up with an architectural description that is relevant and that accomplishes the same goals that were covered in the previous chapter.

In the previous chapter, we drew heavily from the stages and concepts of the TOGAF ADM to create our architecture definition. We chose this for a few reasons, including the fact that the source material is freely available, it is comprehensively described, and so on. However, one place where we can get hung up with that approach in applying it to a software development use case is in the chronology of key tasks; that is, were we to attempt to do a threat analysis once at the beginning of the development process, we might very well wind up in a situation under a continuous development model whereby threats change and we have little or no mechanism to account for it. Therefore, in this section, we've elected to draw upon an alternate process strategy for application scope.

Specifically, we will draw upon some of the principles of system security engineering – in particular, those elements outlined and described in *NIST Special Publication 800-161, Systems Security Engineering: Considerations for a Multidisciplinary Approach in the Engineering of Trustworthy Secure Systems.* There are several reasons why we are using this particular method as we tee up how we will create the documentation for our application security architecture:

- **Level of detail**: The information provided in the special publication is comprehensive, which means the approach is extensively documented. Should you wish to delve deeper into the guidance, you will find extensive documentation and supporting materials (there are over 200 pages in just the special publication alone, not including additional materials on the topic outside of that provided by NIST).

- **Documentation is freely available**: This is not the only material available that covers the discipline of system security engineering. In fact, there are numerous excellent forms of guidance and standards out there. However, NIST special publications are freely available to any who wish to use them. Therefore, they will be accessible to all practitioners without additional fees or licensing costs.

- **Emphasis on views and viewpoints**: One of the key elements of the architecture definition, as outlined in this document, is its emphasis on views and viewpoints. Throughout this book, we've often highlighted the importance of different viewpoints in the architecture process (viewpoints of stakeholders and so on). This is the language that is used within *SP 800-161*, which, in turn, helps it be philosophically compatible with other architecture models and design approaches such as *SABSA* and *TOGAF*.

- **Abstraction of process order**: Despite providing extensive guidance about critical outcomes from the architecture definition process, the publication itself is agnostic about the order in which they occur. While there is an *implicit* order of tasks, the outcomes are not structured in the guidance in such a way that they must follow a particular set order. This is useful from an application architecture point of view because it allows us to reorder elements in light of our software development approach, or even make elements iterative to match how we develop software in our organization.

With this in mind, let's look at systems security engineering in general, discuss why it makes a useful backdrop for software security architecture, discuss the key elements of the architecture definition process as outlined by the guidance, and then put them together with the techniques we've covered so far to produce a process-aware architecture definition.

Systems security engineering

> *"I'm a person who reads books about the philosophy of cooking. That's great, but there comes a time when I want to actually make a dish. I don't usually go back to those books when I want to make a specific recipe; instead, what I want are recipes where it spells out exactly what to do. I want to understand the philosophy and build my skills, but I also find it useful to have a specific list of things to do in a particular order. As I understand the philosophy better, I can adapt and make more changes."*
>
> *– Adam Shostack, President, Shostack & Associates*

NIST SP 800-160 defines systems security engineering as follows:

> *"...a specialty engineering discipline of systems engineering that applies scientific, mathematical, engineering, and measurement principles, concepts, and methods to coordinate, orchestrate, and direct the activities of various security engineering specialties and other contributing engineering specialties to provide a fully integrated, system-level perspective of system security. Systems security engineering, as an integral part of systems engineering, helps to ensure that the appropriate security principles, concepts, methods, and practices are applied during the system life cycle to achieve stakeholder objectives for the protection of assets across all forms of adversity characterized as disruptions, hazards, and threats."*

As you can imagine, this is a broad, expansive discipline that addresses the development and implementation of secure systems down to the most fundamental levels. Like security architecture, the goal is to ensure a secure, resilient outcome for the organization. Likewise, its ultimate purpose is to ensure that the organization is better equipped to achieve its organizational mission.

At this point, you might be wondering what the difference is between security architecture and system security engineering. To answer this, it is useful to look through a process lens. Namely, the goal of system security engineering is to ensure there are security-aware *processes* that are designed to achieve secure *outcomes*. This means that development processes, when followed, are optimized around secure results. This is a little different than the exercise of manipulating the outcome of a process to ensure a particular set of characteristics. The difference is arguably subtle and nuanced, but it's there.

As an analogy, consider the job of a zookeeper. The organizational mission of the zoo might include better preservation of animal species, promoting ecological awareness, educating the public about animal welfare, ethology (animal behavior), and so on. These are all worthy goals. As part of that mission, you might choose to make structural modifications to the zoo – its visitor and veterinary facilities, its organization and staffing, and so on – to allow zoo employees to better achieve those goals. This is somewhat analogous to the architectural approach we covered in the previous chapter.

By contrast, if you wanted to optimize the zoo's *processes* to best support these goals, you might choose to make different decisions and investments. For example, you may decide to focus on the processes used for veterinary care, animal feeding, breeding programs, and enrichment so that the processes themselves reinforce and engender the intended outcome. This would mean optimizing the existing processes so that you favor the outcomes that support the organizational mission (in this case, the goals listed previously). Perhaps in so doing you also make investments and structural/facility changes as well. The optimization of these processes is analogous to an engineering approach.

Obviously, the goals are similar and the techniques that are used are complementary. But there is a little bit of a different focus because you are looking to optimize processes in support of the goals. In the case of system security engineering, you are tailoring the processes you use so that outcomes are *secure by design*; that is, security is "*baked in*" to the outcomes that you develop. When applied to engineering a software endeavor, you are optimizing processes around a secure outcome.

From just this explanation, you can probably tell why system security engineering techniques are advantageous when applied to a software development exercise. This is largely because we've already discussed why software development is so dependent on the processes and development life cycle used to create that software – in other words, how the outcome from the software development process is inexorably linked to the process used. Therefore, optimizing the software development process (regardless of what it may be) to achieve secure outcomes is *exactly what we are trying to accomplish*.

Now, it goes without saying that how we will apply these concepts is a comparatively narrower scope than something like what the NIST special publication guidance covers in its entirety. That being said, as a framework for our software development security architectural endeavors, there are many concepts that can provide tremendous value. It is certainly worth reading the entirety of the guidance, but for the purposes of this chapter, we will be looking primarily at the **architecture definition process**, as outlined by the guidance (in the current version of the guidance, this can be found in *section 3.4.4*, which starts on page 101).

First, we'll walk through the process as outlined, adapt it so that it is compatible with the legwork that we've done already, and work through creating a definition artifact. Then, we'll look at adapting your development approach to incorporate elements that can help you refine the development process itself in a way that helps reinforce secure outcomes.

Architecture definition process

The architecture definition process in *NIST SP 800-160* contains a list of activities that are designed to achieve the following outcomes (paraphrased from the guidance for brevity):

- Address stakeholder security concerns

- Define secure functionality for the system level

- Develop views, viewpoints, and models

- Set security domains, boundaries, and interfaces

- Identify security-relevant system elements

- Align the architecture with security requirements

- Ensure any enabling services for security are available

- Trace architecture to stakeholder security requirements

- Identify security-related metrics

To accomplish these goals, the guidance outlines several key tasks that support them. The following list recounts the key supporting tasks (also paraphrased for brevity.) Each of these tasks directly supports, and by completing them, results in, the attainment of each of the goals. For example, by identifying security drivers (*AR-1.1*) and stakeholders (*AR-1.2*), you help ensure that stakeholder security concerns (the first bullet in the preceding list) are appropriately addressed:

- **Prepare**:

  - Identify security drivers (goals) [*AR-1.1*]

  - Identify stakeholders [*AR-1.2*]

  - Define a security architecture definition approach and strategy [*AR-1.3*]

  - Define evaluation criteria [*AR-1.4*]

  - Identify and enable enabling systems/services [*AR-1.5*]

- **Develop viewpoints**:

  - Define a secure function [AR-2.1]

  - Select viewpoints based on stakeholder security concerns [AR-2.2]

  - Identify security architecture frameworks [AR-2.3]

  - Record the rationale for the selection of frameworks that address security concerns, viewpoints, and model types [AR-2.4]

  - Select modeling tools [AR-2.5]

- **Develop security models and views**:

  - Define a context and boundaries [AR-3.1]

  - Identify entities and relationships between entities [AR-3.2]

  - Allocate concepts, properties, characteristics, and behavior [AR-3.3]

  - Select security models [AR-3.4]

  - Compose views in accordance with viewpoints [AR-3.5]

  - Harmonize models and views [AR-3.6]

- **Relate views to design**:

  - Identify security-relevant system elements [AR-4.1]

  - Define interfaces, interconnections, and interactions [AR-4.2]

  - Allocate system security requirements [AR-4.3]

  - Map system elements to security design characteristics [AR-4.4]

  - Define security design principles [AR-4.5]

- **Select a candidate architecture**:

  - Assess each candidate architecture against requirements [AR-5.1]

  - Assess each candidate architecture against stakeholder concerns [AR-5.2]

  - Select a preferred architecture and capture all key decisions/rationale [AR-5.3]

  - Establish security aspects [AR-5.4]

- **Manage the security view**:

  - Formalize a governance approach, as well as roles and responsibilities [AR-6.1]

  - Obtain acceptance from stakeholders [AR-6.2]

  - Maintain concordance and completeness [AR-6.3]

  - Organize, assess, and control security models and views [AR-6.4]

  - Maintain the definition and evolution strategy [AR-6.5]

  - Maintain traceability [AR-6.6]

  - Provide information for the architecture definition [AR-6.7]

> **Important note**
>
> Note that we have pared these descriptions down (quite a bit, in fact) and we have (on purpose) not excerpted the detailed descriptions of each that the guidance includes. We have done this both for readability purposes and since the source material is available to you for your perusal at any time. However, by purposefully paring back some of this information, we have likely lost valuable nuance along the way. Therefore, we encourage you to read the relevant sections of the guidance as time allows (or better yet, read the entire guidance) so that you have the best and most complete perspective.
>
> However, since we are adapting the process to err on the side of a more lightweight approach that can be practiced by a small team (or even an "*army of one*"), we will leave out the formal descriptions from the guidance. We will also explicitly call out those elements that are the most germane to the work that we will cover here and that we will adapt in our approach.

Architecture definition

In the previous chapter, we employed steps from the TOGAF ADM to create an ADD that encompassed the following elements:

- Scope

- Goals, objectives, and constraints

- Architecture principles

- Baseline architecture

- Architecture models (for each state to be modeled)

- Rationale and justification for the architectural approach

- Mapping to the architecture repository

- Gap analysis

- Impact assessment

- Transition architecture

If you compare this list with the elements outlined in the NIST guidance, you will notice a significant amount of overlap. You will find that most of these items have a corresponding counterpart with the items included in NIST (at least they do when viewed at a high level of abstraction).

Because we are attempting to use a similar overall model for the prework (*phase zero*) tasks of identifying scope, stakeholder validation, assessing current state, and so on, we will purposefully use a similar documentation format as we create our documentation for the application scope. That being said, there are some items in the NIST guidance that aren't covered that we will want to include in our documentation set. There are also some elements that we have left out because we are attempting to *scale down* what is otherwise a very complex, time-consuming, and long-term endeavor to a lightweight one that can work within the context of a small team.

As such, unless you have a large team and many resources at your disposal, it might be advantageous to abbreviate those items for now, recalling that you can always optimize, iterate, and improve as you build maturity and marshal organizational support. Others beyond these will need to be addressed since they form a foundational element in adapting our approach to the software life cycle we're using. We will discuss the latter in detail later.

Therefore, just like we did in the previous chapter, let's pull together the *prework* that will form the core of our document. As we stated in the previous chapter, even if you are trying to be nimble, it is still a good idea to document these items. Hopefully, by now, you know that we strive not to create documentation for its own sake; however, this document is so crucial, so potentially valuable down the road, that we strongly encourage you to take this documentation seriously. It won't take long, but it creates a record that can be critical.

Ultimately, what we are trying to do is produce a document that is compatible with our overall approach – one that serves the same purpose as the ADD we created in the previous chapter but that does so in a way that recognizes our emphasis on process adaptation. The *format* of the document and the way that the concepts are presented might not change all that much, but the *focus* of it will.

Now, because we are potentially operating at one of two scopes (the development process and its controls or the development outcome and its controls), we will need to be able to select which focus to employ based on scope as needed. It's important to bear this in mind as we undertake each step in laying out our approach.

Establishing architectural principles

Just like we did in the previous chapter, first, we will pull together "raw materials" using a few different methods before assembling and integrating them into the documentation that we will socialize with stakeholders. The first of this prework involves documenting the following:

- **Key stakeholders**: Who will be impacted by the work that we do? This group includes several subgroups:

  - **Beneficiaries**: Who will derive benefit from our design and how? This can be end customers, employees, business partners, or any other group, so long as they directly benefit.

  - **Decision-makers**: Who is responsible for giving approval for work?

  - **Specialists**: What specialized personnel and subject matter experts are required for us to interface with or that are needed for us to perform the work?

- **Key resources**: What personnel, budget, and other resources are available to us for the design? Pay special attention to method of engagement: how we can get access to teams, individuals, budgets, or resources when we need them.

- **Key principles**: What approach will we use to guide our design? What do we hope to accomplish by doing so? TOGAF refers to these as "architectural principles" and provides a systematic way to document them – we likened them to the laws of physics for our architecture work when we discussed them in *Chapter 2, Architecture – The Core of Solution Building*.

As you can see, these are the same elements that we collected and documented in the previous chapter as a starting point for our documentation exercise; in fact, you'll notice that these are the same foundational bullet points (with some minor variation) we used in describing these items previously. We will assume that you have read and understood the material from the previous chapter, so we won't explain each one again.

We should note that process plays a larger role this time around so that it's in keeping with a systems security engineering process-aware approach. In the previous chapter, the assumption was that we could develop plans that impact portions of the organization and that we did not necessarily need to constrain ourselves to any defined timeline in doing so. This is not necessarily the case any longer (this is mainly why we are covering applications separately). By this, we mean that, as you distill your architectural principles, stakeholders, and resources, you always have the SDLC model, which will be used to develop the application at the forefront of your mind.

You might set principles based on the SDLC model; for example, a principle might be that all code is security tested before being released into production. The implications of how and where to do this will vary significantly between a waterfall versus agile versus DevOps approach, but as we discussed, we should keep implementation specifics out of the principles as best we can. However, the *implications* and *rationale* can vary quite a bit, depending on the development methodology.

For example, the implications of requiring testing for all code prior to production release might be that we need to introduce new automation components to a DevOps pipeline to accommodate this requirement, or that we retool an existing integration or release step to do so. Likewise, the SDLC process can drive the rationale: for example, a rationale for *why* to security test all production code might be precisely because developers aren't always as disciplined as we'd like when it comes to validating "misuse cases" (or "abuse cases") in unit testing, and existing functional test harnesses might not already fully address security issues.

The point is to retain an awareness of the SDLC model as you enumerate the principles, document your known stakeholders (bearing in mind that a stakeholder can include process owners for individuals or teams in the release path), and the resources available to you (again, automated processes or the involvement of other teams can be resources available to you in support of security goals).

The most important element of this is identifying stakeholders. What are you trying to accomplish, for whom, and why? What does the application that you are looking to protect do and who benefits? Who are the users? Why does the application matter to the organization and who will make use of it? Who are the folks responsible for creating the application and how do they do so? Who will oversee the application once it is developed and out into production? The answers to each of these questions represent stakeholders that you will want to engage with. They each have a different view of the application, a different set of interests, and so on. The more diverse the interests represented, the better.

Just like we outlined in the previous chapter, we should always be on the lookout for more stakeholders. Remember that at the point in time where you think you've found all the stakeholders, that's the time to look for more. As we mentioned previously, we will want to establish connection points with stakeholders to understand what their goals are, how they prefer we interact with them, what security concerns they have, and so on.

Setting the scope

> *"Try to employ the same philosophical practices in the architecture as you would with software development: modularity, software-defined, agility, rapid change, and automation. All of these concepts are ones that you can integrate directly into your architectural approaches."*
>
> *– Steve Orrin, Federal CTO at Intel Corporation*

Just like we did in the previous chapter, we will want to codify our scope so that we can validate it – and also so that we can record it as part of the ADD. Recall from *Chapter 4, Building an Architecture – Your Toolbox*, that we have an initial working scope to start from. However, one of the key differences when working with applications is that our scope can be time-constrained to align with the SDLC (for example, we might set the scope to cover a particular release in a non-continuous development model) or we might be constrained in coverage scope to include only a subset of the release process (though this is less common). The point is that we refine our scope at this phase in the process while paying particular attention to the SDLC and how it might impact the scope that we derive.

Desired future (target) state

Once again, we want to define the goal state of where we want to end up. There are two ways to approach this, depending on the scope that you derived previously:

- **Goal application state**: This is the goal state that you hope to achieve for a given application – that is, the security capabilities that you wish the application to have either through the introduction of new security-relevant features or by making modifications to the underlying application substrate (that is, the production environment, supporting infrastructure, ancillary tools, and so on) that support the application.

- **Goal development process state**: This is the goal state that you hope to achieve for the development process itself – that is, the security properties of the development process itself and how you wish to change it so that it's optimized for secure outcomes and secure software.

You can choose to target one or the other – or both together. Again, this will depend on the scope that you have established. Typically, when first becoming involved in an existing application, we tend to start with the first one and then expand to the second once we have a clear vision of how we'd like to improve the security of the application design itself. However, your organization's needs might call for doing this the other way around – or for doing both at the same time. For example, if it is a new application being developed, you might find that it is easier to start with the process first and create smaller, more targeted evolution pathways for individual releases once the process and the initial application parameters have been set.

Just like in the previous chapter, you will want to capture relevant information about the current state, risks, threats, and assets to determine what your future state will look like. There are a few differences regarding how this is done in an application context. We will run through some of these options in the following sections.

Application threat modeling

> *"Threat modeling is a way to think about the security of your system using models. The reason why it is important to use models is that you can do analysis before any other engineering work. When the system is in a 'back of a napkin' state, you can make changes more easily there than at any other point in the life cycle of the system. If your security approach is to have a list of static 'checkboxes' that are always the same regardless of context, then really what's the point of involving the security team in the discussion? To adapt security measures to usage, threat modeling allows you to answer the right questions, work collaboratively with other teams throughout, and providing meaningful value along the way."*
>
> *– Adam Shostack, President, Shostack & Associates*

In the previous chapter, we talked about using threat modeling as a technique for understanding the threat context for the work that you do. Application threat modeling provides the same value but is specific to an application context. In fact, in our experience, the method that we have had the most success with in evaluating applications from a security perspective is the threat modeling approach.

Now, before we get into the meat of how to do this, we will call your attention once again to the fact that a full treatment of threat modeling techniques would take its own book. There are already several excellent books on the topic (for example, Adam Shostack's *Threat Modeling: Designing for Security*). Therefore, we don't have sufficient space to cover it exhaustively. However, we will give you a "quick and dirty" synopsis of the approach and how to accomplish it in an application context.

At a very high level and in brief, threat modeling an application consists of three steps:

1. Decomposing the application.
2. Iterating through threats at interaction points.
3. Mitigating any issues that have been identified.

The threat mitigation piece is ultimately what we will feed back into our future state. The first two steps codify a process that we can use to determine what the threats are in the first place. We will run through this approach quickly to illustrate how this can be done.

The first step seeks to identify interaction points between components or modules in the application. For the sake of illustration, say that you have a rudimentary n-tier application, similar to the one we had in *Chapter 3, Building an Architecture – Scope and Requirements*. This might look similar to the following:

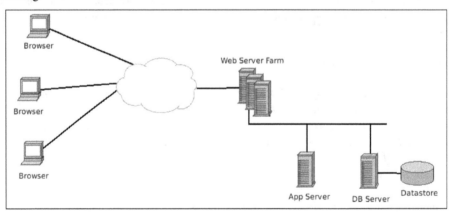

Figure 6.5 – Rudimentary n-tier application

Now, it is a given that most new applications will not be structured this way, as modern applications are much more likely to be service-based (for example, REST-based) instead of employing dedicated application middleware. However, we are using this model since it illustrates different kinds of data connections and how they can be modeled.

In this example, perhaps the service in question is a simple video streaming application. For simplicity's sake, say that the flow of the application is as follows:

1. The user connects to the UI via their browser, where they are presented with a list of available videos.

2. The user selects which video they would like to see from a movie catalog stored in the database.

3. The system hands off a user request to the application server to validate the user's credentials (these are stored in the database, along with the user's viewing preferences).

4. If the provided credentials are valid, the video is streamed directly from the server farm.

Given an application like this, we can create a **data flow diagram** (**DFD**) that maps out how these components interact between each other and traces the data as it is exchanged between the various components of the systems in scope, between the various software elements in scope, and so on. Such a data flow diagram might look like this:

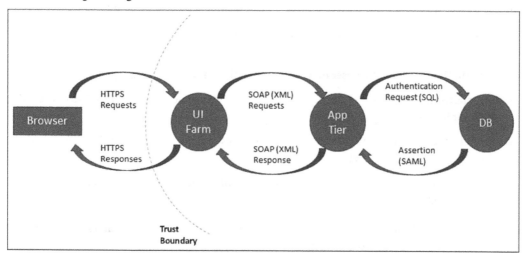

Figure 6.6 – Simple DFD illustration

The reason we selected this example is because it has a relatively small number of interaction points and can therefore be explained and understood easily. It is advantageous to use a method like this one because you can have multiple components per device. This means that you might have different data flows between separate components on different boxes, or even inter-process or inter-module communication between different components on the same box.

Typically, you create the DFD by systematically tracing and documenting how the application's components, services, systems, and other system elements interact for the application to function. This diagram serves as a sort of *roadmap* by which you can understand the interaction points and how the components of the application interact. You'll notice that this DFD is roughly analogous to the asset-level view that we used when applying threat modeling concepts to our technical ecosystem in the previous chapter. The key difference lies in the fact that the atomic units of the DFD are components instead of systems or other assets.

You'll find that there are different styles for creating a DFD. The *"canonical"* method uses a dashed line to illustrate trust boundaries and arrows to illustrate data interactions between components. In reality, though, you can adapt your method to whatever is conducive to your analysis and – in some cases – based on what is easy to create in light of existing documentation. If, for example, you have an existing **Unified Modeling Language** (**UML**) object interaction diagram, you might choose to employ that and overlay security information to existing interactions. The advantage of this is that, since you're using documentation that already exists, the burden of adapting it is reduced, should it change. As a practical matter, there are numerous possible documents that you can potentially use here: network topology diagrams in some cases, object interaction diagrams, sequence diagrams, message diagrams, data flows, and more.

Using the DFD as a roadmap or guide, examine each interaction point and evaluate how it might be attacked according to the STRIDE mnemonic. Let's take a look at what STRIDE stands for:

- **Spoofing**: How might a message be replayed or manipulated between components?
- **Tampering**: How might a message be modified to the detriment of the application between components?
- **Repudiation**: How might a user disavow a transaction or message exchange?
- **Information disclosure**: How might information be leaked or exposed in the course of communications and/or operations?
- **Denial of service**: How might access to key services or components be stifled, constricted, degraded, or ceased entirely?
- **Elevation of privilege**: How might a user be able to increase their level of access in unauthorized ways?

Here, we should walk through each interaction point between components or modules and consider each of the elements of the STRIDE mnemonic for each of those elements. As you do so, consider how such a threat might occur and what the impacts of it would be.

> *"STRIDE and kill chain are roughly substitutable in the threat modeling process: they are both models of what goes wrong. Think about it like a nested 'for' loop: for each item in a collection (systems, components, processes, and so on), we're looking at each attack outcome, stage in their campaign, and so on. STRIDE is advantageous for the inner part of the loop for an application context, whereas the kill chain model can offer advantages in the inner loop for enterprise IT."*
>
> *– Adam Shostack, President, Shostack & Associates*

Threat modeling is a useful technique for examining an application to be used as input for the architecture process for a few reasons. First, it informs us of what the software should be designed to be resilient against. Second, as you go through and evaluate impacts, it gives you a few of the risk elements for the application.

We should note that risk elements, in the context of an application, are arguably more complicated than in a broader context. The reason why this is the case is due to the dimension of likelihood. Recall that risk is the product of impact and likelihood. When evaluating risk, you want to understand what the impact of an event would be but also the likelihood of such an event coming to pass.

For an application, though, the likelihood dimension might be exaggerated somewhat. A public-facing application such as the one in this example will likely be always available (or nearly so) to anyone from anywhere. This means that while likelihood is still important in the risk equation, most threats – over a long enough time horizon – have a high probability of being relevant.

This is not to say that you can't or shouldn't account for risk in your planning efforts when it comes to applications. It does, however, mean that it is significantly easier to focus analysis efforts and mitigation/remediation planning on threats directly, rather than attempting to quantify or qualify likelihood, which, as we discussed, can be challenging to do.

> **Important**
>
> Note that this is only true when it comes to applications themselves; controls and capabilities that underpin the development process (that is, the life cycle) can still be (and absolutely should be) evaluated from a risk standpoint along the axes of both impact and likelihood (in much the same way that we did in the previous chapter).

From the point of view of the desired future state for your architecture, consider how you might mitigate the threats that you discover in your application and fold them into the future state. Just like you did in the previous chapter, pay attention to the expected evolution of the application, which might be codified in the application feature backlog, use cases/user stories for upcoming releases, system requirements and roadmaps, and so on. You want to understand not only how you want the security profile of your application to be after your architecture is in place, but also how the application might change as it evolves.

Misuse case development

Another strategy involves the creation of specific "*misuse cases*" (sometimes called "*abuse cases*"). This is analogous to the process of use case (or user story) development, such as use cases employed in the Unified Process of software development (https://en.wikipedia.org/wiki/Unified_Process). However, instead of describing how users will interact with the application, they describe how the application might be misused by an attacker. If this sounds similar to threat modeling concerning the outcome and goal, it is. The key difference lies in how the misuse cases are developed.

Typically, much like you would author and diagram use cases through brainstorming and asking users how they will employ the application, you might use a similar approach; that is, brainstorm attack methods and examine the methods of potential attackers. You might, for example, look to guides such as the **Open Web Application Security Project (OWASP)** testing guide (https://owasp.org/

`www-project-web-security-testing-guide/`) to explore the specific methods that an attacker will employ in subverting an application. You might look to models such as MITRE's ATT&CK framework (`https://attack.mitre.org/`) to help understand and evaluate for applicability: specifically by looking for attacker tradecraft (that is, tools, techniques, and procedures) that can be brought to bear on your application or its supporting technology stack.

Defect prediction, defect analysis

While threat modeling and misuse case analysis provide quite a bit of useful information about the application, they are by no means the only way to gather data about an application's potential security issues. Another technique that can be used in a complementary manner to these approaches is defect prediction and defect analysis. This technique involves attempting to forecast the number of defects (bugs) in a given application.

There are actually numerous strategies you can follow to accomplish this. The most common approach is *empirical defect prediction*, which involves using statistical models to determine the number of potential latent (undiscovered) defects in the software. For example, if an organization routinely authors software and has observed that the software contains, on average, 10 security defects per 10,000 lines of code, they can estimate the number of defects that would occur in an application containing 100,000 lines of code (100), one million lines of code (1,000), and so on. These are, of course, unrealistic numbers, but we've chosen them merely to illustrate our point. In addition to defects per line of code, you may instead choose to track the number of defects per "*function point*" (feature), per unit of development time, or other baseline values.

From a security point of view, this is useful to us since it's tracking a different thing than threat modeling. Threat modeling attempts to take an attacker's point of view to map out how an attacker might attempt to subvert an application and what their motivation might be in attacking it in a particular way. This is very useful from the point of view of understanding the resiliency of the application and for control/mitigation planning, but less directly useful for understanding other things that might be of interest to an application security architect. For example, recall that at the beginning of this chapter, we discussed why the architect might wish to modify the SDLC to improve security. Will threat modeling provide input back to the team to help them determine whether the SDLC that were changes made were beneficial? Not really, right? However, tracking defects does provide a metric that can be used to help ascertain if SDLC improvements were beneficial or detrimental to code quality. Over time, this can help hone and refine the development process to optimize for secure outcomes.

Composition analysis

The last technique we will cover in depth is **composition analysis**. Note that we're not referring here to the specific product category known as **software composition analysis (SCA)** here, but instead the broader technique of analyzing the components in an application (though we can of course use SCA tools to support the goal) from a software supply chain point of view. This involves looking at what supporting libraries and components are employed in the development of a given piece of software. Most technologists who are not (or who have never been) application developers may not realize this, but most applications heavily incorporate existing code to operate. Developers can make use of existing code in one of several ways:

- **Direct incorporation**: Directly including existing source code into their applications. For example, a developer might find example code on the internet that accomplishes a similar task to what they are looking to do. Rather than write the code anew, they might directly integrate that example code (for example, by copying and pasting it) into their source files. They might consult an *oracle* such as a peer network (for example, Stack Overflow) or large language AI models (for example, ChatGPT, GitHub's Copilot, Google's Bard, and so on) and incorporate that code into their work product.

- **Static linking**: A developer might use a packaged library as part of their application. In the case of an interpreted language such as Python, they might use a packaged module that provides the capabilities they want, whereas, in the case of a compiled language, they might incorporate a static library such as **Java Archive (JAR)** or another library into their application.

- **Dynamic linking**: Developers might make use of dynamically linked libraries, shared objects, COM, or other packaged modules that can be dynamically linked to the application at runtime.

- **Web services**: Developers might employ outside services such as REST APIs (web services) to incorporate additional functionality hosted outside the organization.

Regardless of how they do so, however, composition analysis attempts to examine the supporting libraries, objects, dependencies, and other artifacts of the application to obtain information about what underlying software is required for operation. By understanding what modules comprise the application, information can be gleaned about the security of the resulting application. There are multiple ways to go about this. There are SCA products, **software bill of materials** (**SBOM**), manual methods, component inventory, and more.

Documentation

From here, you have enough raw materials to start *documenting* your architecture. As was the case in the previous chapter, you want to pay particular attention to the future state of the application itself (that is, once threats have been mitigated sufficiently and security features are in place), as well as the process by which applications themselves are developed. What will be the most important depends on the scope. Is the scope just a given release of an application? Is it the underlying development process itself? Is it a series of releases? Or is it all three? This will dictate which areas you focus on.

Based on the work that we've done so far, we can already document the following:

- **Charter or goal statement**: A brief (one or two sentences) description of the effort. Focus on the value provided and focus it from a business point of view.

- **Scope**: Put the *working scope* that you developed earlier into writing. Document what is included and why, as well as notable areas that are excluded and why. Refine it based on any new understanding you've developed in light of your threat analysis and additional research.

- **Principles**: Document the architectural principles. What approach are you using and what are you basing it on?

- **Goals and outcomes**: Discuss the goals you are supporting, focusing on the value to the business that was realized from achieving those goals.

- **Impacts**: Any impacts that you foresee occurring to business areas as a result. Keep this business focused rather than technically focused.

Note that each of these was a line item in the list of pre-materials that we prepared in the previous chapter. From an application point of view, these are valuable too. We've left out a few items this time, though, specifically the following:

- Transition "mileposts"

- Project management artifacts

The reason why we have done so is probably not overly surprising. Specifically, in the previous chapter (*Chapter 5, Building an Architecture – Developing Enterprise Blueprints*), transition mileposts represented how the overall migration from the current state to the desired future state will be brought about over time. From an application point of view, though, you may have a less direct say over this in an application context.

Specifically, this is because of the way that application features (even security ones) are developed and released. Consider an agile project, for example, where a feature backlog is prioritized and spread out across multiple sprints. In that case, it might be hard to know exactly when a given feature will find its way to production. Therefore, it can be difficult to ensure that security feature targets will be introduced in the order that you specify. So, instead of well-defined mileposts here, it is more useful to focus on adding dependency information and associating it with transition activities.

In much the same vein, we also didn't include the project management artifacts that we pulled out as ingredients in our ADD in the previous chapter. The reason for this is related to what we mentioned previously; namely, that project management artifacts are likewise tied directly to the development model in use. In an agile environment that incorporates elements from the Unified Process, these might be codified best in backlog entries that derive from use cases (and abuse cases); in a DevOps environment, it might be more fluid deriving from a feature map and work schedule. The point is that the specific artifacts will vary, depending on the model in use.

In addition to removing these elements, there are a few that we will want to add to the list; these are as follows:

- Life cycle process artifacts

- Mitigation dependencies

Let's look at each in depth.

Life cycle process artifacts

The first items that we are including in our documentation are any specific artifacts that help provide understanding to stakeholders in the language of the development model we're using. This will be highly situation-dependent. In a waterfall model, we might use flowcharting techniques and requirements specification documents to codify the security features and capabilities that we envision. For the Unified Process, we might author security use cases (and abuse cases), as described previously. For agile, we might author security stories that spell out what we envision.

The point is that the method that you use to convey your security goals should use the language of the process in which you operate. So, if your developers use UML 2.0, convey your ideas using UML 2.0; if developers initiate new features using user stories, use user stories; and so on. You'll likely need to do a bit of "translation" to achieve this; this is to be expected. But at the end of the day, we want our work to be as transparent, available, and clearly articulated for the stakeholders that we will need to partner with to achieve our desired outcomes. This means that we acknowledge, respect, and integrate with the way they do their work.

Mitigation dependencies

The second thing we must document (regardless of the specific method of documentation we're using) is to understand what dependencies exist in the specific outcomes we want to accomplish. As an example, say that we decide that the way we mitigate an elevation of privilege attack is, in part, through the use of an enhanced login (for example, multi-factor authentication) for administrative application users. To implement that feature, perhaps there are other specific features that we need to implement first. Because we are limited in our ability to dictate the order in which individual features are implemented (depending on the process), this means we need to separately capture what these dependencies are as input to the process. Take the time to understand what is required for each feature or what needs to be changed for it to operate correctly. Document what you learn.

Validation

> *"There are two schools of thought: 'how can something go wrong?' compared to 'how do we make sure something goes right?' Both are important, but building an architecture so that the 'right way is the only option' actually makes it easier because we can preclude entire classes of attacks that would otherwise have the potential to arise. Think both about what could go wrong but also about how (for example, through processes or technical means) you can ensure that the secure outcome is the one that's arrived at."*
>
> *– Dr. Char Sample, Chief Research Scientist – Cybercore Division at Idaho National Laboratory*

Once you have this information pulled together, document it in a similar way to how we did it in the previous chapter. As in the previous chapter, it is less important (in our opinion) *how* you do this than it is *that* you do it and, more importantly, that you *validate* it. What we mean by validation here is that you engage with the stakeholders and state that your efforts ultimately serve to verify that the information you have captured is accurate, that the scope is appropriate, that you have thoroughly addressed their requirements, and so on.

Validate these items with the stakeholders and make updates based on their feedback and input. Recall that demonstrably responding to their input ensures that they have a sense of ownership of the work that you have done, that they have agency (since, again, they are the beneficiaries of the work that you're doing), and since they can help guide you, should you have mistaken assumptions or other problematic areas in your documentation.

Modifying the SDLC and development processes

From here, you've created and validated a document artifact that serves a very similar purpose to the ADD that we created in the previous chapter. This is an important element for ensuring you have a robust design of the specific application for which you are currently creating a security design. However, earlier in this chapter, we talked about the strategies we can use to adjust our overall development processes to self-reinforce secure outcomes. Just creating a document won't do that on its own. Instead, you will want to be thinking about how you can tailor future iterations of software development to ensure these outcomes.

The question then becomes how to make changes to your development processes to achieve these outcomes. The NIST special publication we discussed earlier (*SP 800-160*) is one such approach to "building security" into the application development process. However, this is an extensive document (about 250 pages). To do it justice would take a book bigger than this one. So, while we do recommend that you read the guidance to fully appreciate and understand what's involved in optimizing your software development for secure outcomes, we will explain the techniques that are available to you using a different resource.

To help the architect understand what is involved, a useful resource to employ is the **Building Security In Maturity Model (BSIMM)**. The BSIMM (`https://bsimm.com`) is a framework that is used to empirically benchmark application security processes in the industry. It's freely available and was released under the *Creative Commons Attribution – Share Alike 3.0 License*. It is organized into 4 domains encompassing 12 practices; each practice is further broken down into specific activities aligned to the maturity level in furtherance of the practice.

We should note that the purpose of the BSIMM isn't necessarily to give organizations specific guidance about how to implement any particular method or process – or even necessarily to dictate what practices they should have in place. Instead, it's designed to allow objective benchmarking of processes as used within the industry and to allow a more detailed industry-wide understanding of what measures drive secure application development outcomes. However, to allow that benchmarking to occur, they have done extensive work in categorizing the various processes and techniques (for example, those described extensively in *NIST SP 800-160*) into discrete, organized units that are reflective of possible measures that organizations can employ to help drive those outcomes. Due to this, we are leveraging their excellent work to help convey these concepts succinctly and to illustrate what tools and techniques are available to an architect seeking to optimize their processes.

Here, we have listed the domains and the supporting practices within each domain, along with an explanation of how you can employ each as part of your process refinement.

Domain 1 – governance

The first domain, governance, encompasses three practices, as follows:

- **Strategy and metrics**: Strategy and metrics involve establishing an optimization loop – a *virtuous cycle* of continuous improvement for secure software development. Metrics gathering helps you ensure that you can track how changes or investments perform over time, while the strategic elements involve everything from goal establishment to resource assignment.

- **Compliance and policy**: Compliance and policy is about meeting any contractual, legal, industry, or regulatory requirements that might be in scope for your organization. This encompasses both the validation that processes are equipped to do so and that there's ongoing verification of conformance over time.

- **Training**: Training is about ensuring that those in the development process – for example, the developers, system engineers, operations staff, and even project managers – have the appropriate training on security techniques, security considerations, resilient design and development approaches, and so on to safeguard the applications they develop.

Domain 2 – intelligence

This domain encompasses three practices:

- **Attack models**: Attack models refer to the development and cultivation of a systematic understanding of how applications will be viewed by an attacker. It can encompass the methods we described earlier in this chapter (for example, threat modeling, misuse case development, and so on), as well as other modeling techniques and data sources about how attackers may attempt to subvert the application.

- **Security features and design**: Security features and design refers to the processes you employ when designing and engineering the application itself. This includes establishing review processes to validate designs or security features, selecting secure design patterns (for example, authoring tested, hardened, and robust design patterns in a central library), or employing secure data structures, objects, or underlying libraries/components in furtherance of security goals.

- **Standards and requirements**: Standards and requirements refers to the systematic creation and dissemination of security requirements, as well as development and design standards for organizational use. For example, you might author software coding standards and socialize them or publish them to developer stakeholders. You may also employ specific configuration or hardening standards for the technologies you use as part of your application development substrate.

Domain 3 – software security development life cycle (SSDL) touchpoints

The practices for this domain are as follows:

- **Architecture analysis**: Architecture analysis refers to using techniques such as diagrams, documentation, design review, and others to evaluate software architecture systematically.

- **Code review**: Code review involves establishing ongoing processes to validate that the code that's been developed is free of security defects, for example, through the use of manual peer review of code, the use of automated tools, composition analysis, and other methods.

- **Security testing**: Security testing refers to including security-specific testing and integration of security with the QA process. This includes testing misuse cases, using automation tools within QA to help test for security issues, communicating and exchanging data between security and other testing types (for example, functional testing, UAT, and so on), and so forth.

Domain 4 – deployment

The last domain includes the following practices:

- **Penetration testing**: Penetration testing involves simulating an attacker's campaign against your application. You might actively attempt to exploit the application using the same or similar methods as those used by an attacker as this helps determine the degree to which the application is susceptible to those same methods. It also involves the processes in place that have been designed to ensure that any discovered issues are remediated.

- **Software environment**: The software environment practice involves the underlying substrate on which the application runs. For example, in the context of a web application, this involves the underlying web server, any application middleware, modifications or changes that have been made to the underlying technology, and so on.

- **Configuration and vulnerability management**: This practice involves ensuring that both the configuration of the application and the supporting artifacts are managed, controlled, and auditable. This also includes managing vulnerabilities as they are discovered and communicating with customers, partners, or other parties that rely on the software about issues.

Again, note that we are not suggesting that you do all these things right out of the gate. We only wanted to provide you with a brief overview of what specific elements of the development process you might choose to invest in, as this will help you refine your software development processes and optimize them for security outcomes.

Summary

Throughout this chapter, we've built on the techniques that we've teed up in prior chapters and extended them to the application space. We positioned the key tasks through the lens of a process-based systems security engineering methodology (or at least the architectural elements of that discipline), rather than a purely enterprise architectural one. This lets us work within the constraints of the SDLC that our organization uses.

From here, we will start executing our architectural vision. Whether you created a vision at the enterprise scope in the previous chapter or created one at the application scope in this chapter, the next step is to lay the groundwork to put it into practice. This includes engaging subject matter specialists and engineers in key supporting areas and mapping out a technical architecture to support the higher-level, business-focused ones. We will do this in the next chapter.

Part 3: Execution

This section continues the theme of how to execute, describing methods of execution and how to integrate architectural designs into ongoing work. We begin by creating an implementation that fits into the model of the high-level solution that we've put together based on the organizational requirements and within the target scope. From there, we build in mechanisms such as metrics and instrumentation that allow us to optimize and improve the solution over time, and since no project is ever perfectly executed out of the gate, we work through the various issues that can arise during execution, such as scoping failures, misaligned requirements, and technical hurdles. Lastly, we look at the design process itself as an iterative cycle that can be optimized and improved over time.

This section comprises the following chapters:

- *Chapter 7, Execution – Applying Architecture Models*
- *Chapter 8, Execution – Future-Proofing*
- *Chapter 9, Putting It All Together*

Execution –Applying Architecture Models

The last two chapters have focused on creating the high-level designs associated with what you're looking to build. By now, with not that much time investment, you have a fairly good idea of what you're looking to build and why. You've also validated that direction with the individuals who will be most impacted by what you'll be doing. These are all important things, but there are still some critical steps involved in actually bringing it down a level of abstraction in preparation for doing the necessary work.

In this chapter, we will create and document the detailed technical design schematics that will guide us throughout the execution process. Specifically, we will cover the following topics:

- Process steps
- Technical design
- Operational integration
- Telemetry

Let's get started!

Process steps

As we go through this chapter, you'll notice that this phase of the design process is very tightly bound to the execution of our vision. This is by design. At this level of specificity, the execution of the design and the design itself are tightly intertwined. Therefore, as we move through this chapter, we will be concentrating both on the creation of the design itself and on the process of how we will achieve this. Due to this, we will also present two examples of how to effect the technical strategy through two hypothetical situations, both drawn from real-world business challenges that organizations are currently struggling with. We believe that breaking these examples down best illustrates how to overcome the technical design challenges that we might encounter.

Before we get into the meat of this, though, it's important to talk about how we will approach this. As an analogy, consider once again a traditional architect (that is, an architect in the physical world) who's been hired to design a house for a client. The architect will meet with the client to find out what's important to them and what they're looking for in the end result. Then, they'll typically create sketches – for example, floor plans and elevations – that illustrate what the final outcome will be. This is the point that we're at right now: we have a goal in mind, and we have a conceptual understanding of how we will achieve it.

There's still one more step that is required to bring the design process to a point where someone can actually build what the architect envisions. Specifically, you need the diagrams and schematics that can be read by the folks who will actually do the building – those who will erect the edifice. For the architect of a house, this takes the form of the buildable drawings that will be shared with the construction crew, engineers, and others responsible for doing portions of the building work. For us, we need those same elements. This is what we're going to do next. It's important to note though that, just like an architect working on a house will not be solely responsible for the work of all the tradespersons involved (e.g., plumbing, wiring, landscaping, etc.), so too is it not the role of the cybersecurity architect to create the detailed design themselves. Instead, this can and should be a collaborative process.

Using the preceding example of the home architect, we're at the stage now that is analogous to them having created the floor plan and elevations of a finished house. This is analogous to the level of understanding that we've been carefully building over the course of the past few chapters. These elevations and floor plans are useful for the purpose of confirming with the architect's customers (our stakeholders in this analogy) that the design the architect envisions meets the criteria important to the customers: in the case of designing a house, the usability and aesthetics the customers have in mind. This is, in fact, how we used the documentation created in the previous chapters: for validating design concepts and discussions with stakeholders. But just like you can't just grab a front or side elevation sketch of a home and start digging a foundation, so too is there a step missing in the documents we've created so far. Namely, you need something that the engineers, builders, and other specialists can read at a level of specificity that lets them do their part. Not surprisingly, this is also what we need to do next: create more detailed *drawings* (or documentation) that will be used to guide the execution of the project.

There are a few reasons why we need this:

- First, we will need to involve various subject matter experts so that they can leverage their skills and expertise in the process. Remember that the architect is not expected to be an expert in everything – therefore, the folks who will need to perform specialized tasks in the adaptation of the design will need something to work from so that they can understand how to perform their role(s).

- Second, this stage helps ensure that everyone stays on the same page. We are going to pivot from this portion of the design directly into execution, so it's important that we have a master framework that everyone can use to stay coordinated and on task.

- Lastly, there are solid practical reasons to maintain a written record. There will almost always be unexpected events that arise during the execution phase – due to this, we'll want a way to keep track of changes and any unanticipated modifications that we will need to undertake. Creating a lower-level, more detailed iteration of the design helps us do this.

Let's begin with the technical design as we bring our high-level designs to a higher level of operational specificity.

Technical design

> *"Successful architecture needs both structure and agility. You need just enough structure to where that structure is useful, but anything beyond that is bad. The way I started thinking about security controls and applying them to the rest of the organization is through the lens of healthy friction versus unhealthy friction. Healthy friction is friction that makes the developer or IT person pause, ask, and genuinely answer a critical thinking question such as 'should I be doing this differently?' or 'can I do this better?' By contrast, if you get to the point where the security measures are onerous – for example, by adding thousands of false positives to a developer's queue or adding repetitive tasks to a user workflow – it becomes unhealthy friction. I view architecture the same way; introducing a process that makes people ask the right questions, talk to the right people, or do the right things is good. Adding structure that slows folks down or processes that makes others less likely to engage can actually damage security as it rewards people for bypassing security processes."*
>
> *– Mark Simos, Lead Cybersecurity Architect, Microsoft*

The very first thing we need to do is create the technical design that will guide us. The previous chapter gave us a high-level "*conceptual*" design, but as we explained, this is not enough. We still need to go from there to a more detailed understanding to actually execute it. In TOGAF **architecture development method (ADM)** parlance, this would be the "*technology architecture*" step; SABSA describes this as "*physical security architecture*." Specifically, we want to translate the high-level security and functional design goals that we identified in the previous section and now think through the specific mechanisms that we will use to implement those goals. We'll need to focus both on *what* we need these mechanisms to accomplish as well as *how* they will do so.

The outcome of this process will be a set of approved, vetted documents that will encapsulate the technical architecture of the solution that meets the goals that we outlined over the course of the last two chapters. To put this into context, let's take a look at the phases of TOGAF that we are attempting to accomplish. Again, as we've stated throughout, we're adapting the elements of the TOGAF ADM for a somewhat more lightweight approach. The goal is to still ensure enough discipline in the process to provide consistent, quality outcomes while making the approach workable for small, agile teams. For the technical architecture phase, section 11 of TOGAF 9.2 ADM outlines the following steps:

1. Select reference models, viewpoints, and tools.
2. Develop a baseline technology architecture description.
3. Develop a target technology architecture description.
4. Perform gap analysis.
5. Define candidate roadmap components.
6. Resolve impacts across the architecture landscape.
7. Conduct a formal stakeholder review.
8. Finalize the technology architecture.
9. Create the architecture definition document.

We will work through each of these steps, albeit at varying levels of formality. This is because we've made some assumptions about the environment that you'll be working in. In the event that you are working in a context that requires additional rigor beyond what we have assumed here, you may wish to stick closer to the ADM (or other architecture standard customary for your organization) in putting these elements together. However, if you are in an environment (like most) where agility is preferable to increased rigor, we find that the approach we've described here provides a good trade-off by being relatively lightweight while still ensuring that good design elements are incorporated.

To understand how we will approach this at a high level, it's useful to use the analogy of solving any other, non-security technical challenge. Say, for example, that we wanted to enable remote access for employees in our organization. If we wanted to do this, we might go through steps analogous to the ones we've gone through so far in this book to identify the business and functional requirements. Using those and validating with stakeholders, we might identify that – given how users do their work, what resources are available to them (and us), and other operational factors – a usable and cost-effective solution is a cloud-based virtual desktop (i.e., cloud VDI).

That's a great start, but there are a ton of residual questions that need to be answered to actually implement that. These might include the following:

- What specific provider do we use to do this?
- Do we need additional infrastructure (VPN, access points, etc.)?
- What client software do users require (if any)?
- What procedural elements do we need to support this (for example, training for the helpdesk, users, and so on)?
- What edge cases do we need to support and how do we support them (for example, BYOD, mobile access, high latency connections, and so on)?

These are only a few of the possible items we'd need to investigate, overcome, and design solutions around. Recall that, at this point, we've already collected and analyzed the business and functional requirements for what we need. This is what led us to select the solution we did in the first place. Also, to the extent that there are technical and security requirements, we've had the opportunity to discuss and validate those too. However, to answer each of the preceding questions, there are additional facts and answers that we need to know before we can proceed. Along with others, those might include the following:

- What specific provider do we use to do this?

- Do we need additional infrastructure (VPN, access points, etc.)?

- What client software do users require (if any)?

We will detail these in the next few subsections.

What specific provider do we use to do this?

Since we have decided that we are going to use a cloud-based service, we need to know the following:

- Do we have an existing provider relationship that will be leveraged?

- If so, can we get advantageous pricing if we use them?

- What features do we need to support the various use cases?

- What connectivity is required (for example, IP/SEC VPN? TLS? SSH? Other?)

Do we need additional infrastructure (VPN, access points, etc.)?

Before we can be sure that the provider in question is suitable, we need to know the following:

- What does the rest of the environment and network look like? How will we interface with it from the remote provider?

- What resources are employees accessing and where on the network are they located? Will this method of access allow the right folks to reach those locations?

- What monitoring capabilities do we have in place already and will they extend to this new usage?

What client software do users require (if any)?

If client software is required, the following questions would apply:

- Will this software be installed only on managed devices, or do we need to support a blend of different platforms?

- Do we need to support specialized situations such as developer access, alternative platforms, and so on?

- What authentication methods are we using internally and what authentication factors are we using for external access?

There are other questions that can apply here. We've only blown out the first three questions since we think that's sufficient to make our point, but you could continue to do this for the rest of the example questions we've listed, as well as potentially dozens of additional questions that you can envision that we haven't listed here.

You'll notice two things about the sub-questions that we've listed:

- First, you'll notice that many of them relate to items that are unique to your organization. In almost every case, the answer is almost entirely dependent on some element of your existing technology ecosystem, your organization, your goals and requirements, and so on. In fact, you could present these questions to 10 different organizations and get 10 different answers back. This means that you need knowledge and analysis about the organization *above and beyond the high-level design* to account for them.

- Second, you'll notice that many of the questions are dependent on each other. For example, the provider you select to provide your VDI might be influenced by the type of authentication methods that you need to support, whether you need to support ancillary technologies, what type of protocols are in use, and so on. This means that trying to answer any individual question in isolation can "lock you in" and limit your options in how you approach the other questions.

We are pointing this out for two reasons:

- First, you will need to do additional work beyond what you've done already in order to answer these questions. This should not be done in isolation. Just like you engaged with stakeholders to derive the high-level vision, you'll need to once again engage with them to craft and validate the strategies that you come up with at this level to implement the target future state. In fact, you may have a broader set of stakeholders at this stage because the audience will include other technical specialists who will help answer these questions.

- Second, because the questions are dependent on each other, you will likely want to approach the design process in an iterative fashion, which means creating a draft approach, validating it, responding to feedback, and so on. Doing this in iterations while always keeping an eye open to the possible need to revisit, amend, or even completely obviate design elements gives you freedom to select designs that work well with each other, and helps you avoid "painting yourself into a corner" by answering a question in a way that closes the door on a viable design somewhere else.

Some might naturally question why we didn't do this work at the same time that we were gaining information about the high-level goals from the last two chapters. The simple answer is that each phase answers different questions. In the last two chapters, we laid out what are essentially design goals. In this chapter, we are creating implementation strategies to achieve those goals technically. Looking at the goals separately from implementation means you are both unbiased and (ideally) holistic in your approaches to solving those goals. This means you can know, at a high level, all of the things you need to accomplish at once without having a preconceived idea of how you will implement them. This in turn lets you be more flexible and creative in your thinking and lets you view related challenges together (potentially coming up with one solution that addresses multiple needs).

From a process standpoint, what we ideally want to do is as follows:

1. Create technical implementation strategies for functional elements.

2. Assess constraints, synergies, and areas of opportunity.

3. Validate implementation strategies against likely threat paths and create a skeleton solution document codifying those strategies.

4. Validate implementation strategies with subject matter experts and technical stakeholders.

5. Finalize the documentation.

While each of these steps does require potentially significant work, the high-level process is relatively straightforward. We'll walk through how to do each one while using the example of remote connectivity (enterprise scope) and application containerization (application scope) to illustrate this process.

Creating technical implementation strategies

> *"My advice to new architects is don't fall too in love with your ideas. It is good to love your ideas: you need that passion and connection to them in order to sell them and to weave a strong story around them. But you also have to be willing to rethink them and even walk away if you need to. I've learned this lesson the hard way. I have a plaque on my wall from a project that I worked on in 2011 where I created a very successful model that helped a number of organizations. I let that success blind me to how the world was changing over time and I made the mistake of being unwilling to listen to the sage advice of others about improving it, making it more accessible, and moving on from it. I eventually did move on, but it was so much harder to unwind this because of how late I started the process. What I've learned as a result is to always be willing to change approaches in light of new information. The discomfort of swallowing your pride at the time is nothing compared to the effort to fix it later (much like fixing 1-degree error in spaceflight is much cheaper at the beginning than it is later). In a way, this is the shift left principle that's applied to your learning process."*
>
> *– Mark Simos, Lead Cybersecurity Architect, Microsoft*

The very first thing that we'll do is create the technical implementation strategies to support the high-level design goals that we created over the last two chapters. In the last two chapters, we created documents that specifically outlined the security goals that we want to achieve. Recall that in *Chapter 2, Architecture – The Core of Solution Building*, we discussed various business goals where we established how each business goal is supported by specific implementation strategies; these strategies represent the mechanism the organization will use to achieve the outcomes they want (the goals). At the time, we emphasized how those implementation strategies *cascade* to technology goals, their implementation strategies, and ultimately, security goals. Now, though, we are developing the implementation strategies that support the security goals we've established and vetted as part of our architecture definition.

Doing this isn't necessarily hard. However, those new to the profession can sometimes find that there's not much detailed, practical guidance out there about specific steps. This can prove frustrating to new practitioners. Moreover, it can sometimes make it seem like more experienced practitioners are deliberately making learning the ropes more difficult. Instead, the opposite is true; sometimes, even with the best of intentions, it can be challenging to verbally explain (or explain in writing) the process involved. This is because the *way* we learn it doesn't always lend itself well to transmission.

As a thought experiment to understand why this is the case, imagine how you'd respond if someone asked you to teach them how to whistle, or how to ride a bike. If you agree to teach them, you would probably employ a few different methods encompassing both demonstration and guided feedback for the learner on their own attempts. But could you teach them effectively if you could only explain verbally, without demonstrating to them how to do it? It'd be hard, right? You've established (through trial and error over the course of many years) a method that works – but that is also, in many ways, unique to you. It relies on "muscle memory" rather than rote memorization of facts or a singular technique. Many things are like this: learning a musical instrument, learning a language, learning to play a sport, and so on. You need to know conceptually how to do it, but you also have to practice, try things out for yourself, and build your own muscle memory for the skills involved.

We're pointing this out to you for one very important reason: we're going to carry out exactly the approach of walking through (verbally) the design process. But haven't we just said that that's limiting? We have, and it is. This means that it's important that you build up muscle memory for yourself in addition to being presented with a workable process – meaning, you need to practice it to really internalize it. Therefore, you should expect your mastery to build as you undertake design projects of your own – and be alert when discovering the strategies that work best for you and the way that you work.

Caveat aside, we'll try our best to break this down into steps that you can follow. Let's start by working through an example together. Then, we will break it down into the salient factors for consideration and some tools that you can use to help you as you undertake it. Keep in mind that, for any given scope, there will likely be multiple high-level goals. You will want to have an implementation strategy for each one, but in some cases, you can use the same implementation strategy to accomplish multiple things.

For example, consider the following separate goals that we might have identified as we did our analysis in prior chapters:

- Record successful user login attempts

- Record unsuccessful user login attempts

- Record system events

- Record use of administrative privileges

At first glance, we might conclude that the same implementation strategy could address all these items. And, in fact, in many situations, we'd be right. However, it is still useful (in our experience) to assess each goal independently, even though a cursory and initial view might suggest the same solution will fit each.

There are a few reasons for this. First, looking at each set of constraints and requirements in isolation before deciding on a solution is valuable. This is because situations can arise where edge cases, unique constraints, or specific requirements necessitate modifications or adaptations to a design. For example, given the preceding set of goals, what if we are working with a **commercial off-the-shelf** (**COTS**) business application? In this case, recording login attempts, as well as application administrative privileges, might happen via an application log, whereas recording system events might happen outside of it. This means that even though some portion of the implementation strategy might overlap, there are components of it that might not.

The second reason why this is beneficial is that the first pass in identifying constraints and requirements takes minimal time to do – at least using the process that we will articulate here. Likewise, documenting them takes even less time. Ultimately, we will want to document our implementation strategy in full (with the assistance of various engineers, subject matter experts, and others), but in keeping with our overall philosophy, we tend to do this in an iterative way where the first initial pass is "low stakes." This means that we can do an initial analysis quickly and delve into more detail later. Since we do that *before* identifying synergies, we can fully analyze the constraints associated with each element before concluding (or not) that multiple goals share a single implementation strategy.

Approaching it in this way saves time in the long run. Minimal time is wasted by addressing each item separately, whereas the reward for doing so can mean significant time savings down the road – for example, in situations where what seemed like the same solution at a cursory glance really needs to be addressed separately.

For our first example, let's consider an organization that has identified a need and a strategy for multifactor authentication to support a portion of its ecosystem. It has created a definition document and has determined that multifactor authentication is required – in this case, for a given cloud-hosted COTS business application. They know *what* they want at a high level (multifactor authentication); they also know *why* they want it, since they've done an analysis of the threat landscape and determined that this goal will help them prevent a subset of the threats that they might encounter, such as spoofing user credentials, the delivery phase of the kill chain, and so on.

Understanding this goal is important – and by this point, we've done a significant amount of work to understand why we'd want it, how it ties to the business, and what threats it will mitigate. However, this is a far cry from being able to directly construct an implementation strategy and implement it. We need to know a bunch of other things as well, such as the following:

- What specific technology elements and components we need to support what we want to do

- Who will interact with it directly from user, administration, ownership, and other points of view

- Where components will sit in the technical landscape, including what logical (network) infrastructure it will live on, what substrate is required to support it (for example, OS and middleware), and so on

- How it will operate – that is, what protocols it will use, to what effect, and how it will interact with the existing ecosystem

- When it will be used and under what circumstances

We need to know all these things, in addition to a host of other factors that are specific to the thing itself being protected. For example, the fact that the thing being protected is a SaaS application (that is, cloud-hosted software) means that some strategies may not fit the use case. An on-premise RADIUS server, while potentially being a perfect solution in a different context (that is, an on-premise business application), might not fit the bill here.

Therefore, we need to select a strategy that will work. There are a few ways that we can approach this and a few options for us in how we approach the design process. First, we can look for a compatible and applicable reference architecture or design pattern. For example, remember that the **Open Security Architecture** (**OSA**) project maintains a corpus of community-provided design patterns that can help practitioners easily reference abstract solutions that apply to a variety of situations.

Alternatively, standards bodies, analyst firms, and in some cases, individual vendors, supply reference architectures that can help with designing solutions. This is one approach that you might choose to potentially leverage to help bolster the work that you undertake. However, in many situations – either because of the unique circumstances around what you are trying to plan for, because of circumstances unique to your organization, or because of the presence of newer technology that might not fall into a pre-existing model – these may not align perfectly. Therefore, they are useful to consult for reference and ideas, but perhaps in many situations will not fit the bill as written. It is useful, nevertheless, to look for existing artifacts as they can help inform what you ultimately decide to do.

In addition to a pre-existing solution, as just described, a second path to potentially solving this problem would be to create the design yourself. Doing this involves looking at the goal across a few dimensions. As a starting point, we'll want to distill the implementation strategy by asking and answering the basic interrogatives: who, what, when, where, why, and how. Here, we look at the following:

- **Who**: Who needs to use it and what constraints do they have?

- **What**: What does it need to do? What components are required? What does it need to interface with?

- **When**: What are the time constraints around its performance, both in terms of chronological factors (that is, how long it will need to operate for) and temporal factors (whether it needs to operate all the time or only during certain situations)?

- **Where**: Where will it need to reside (both logically and physically) in order to be useful?

- **Why**: Why does it need to perform a certain way? What factors influence how it will perform?

- **How**: How will it operate?

This is, of course, not a new approach. In fact, it's arguable that both SABSA and the Zachman Framework are built on the systematic application of these same fundamental questions at various levels of design specificity. However, for the exercise that we are undertaking now, these basic interrogatives are very useful when creating an implementation strategy. In fact, in most cases, by the time you have answered all these questions, you have narrowed the solution space down to an extremely narrow and tailored subset.

It is useful that we spell these things out in detail and work through them in a systematic way. This is because, often, we can *think* we have a viable solution only to find out that some critical factor has been overlooked. Had we put in the time and energy ahead of time, we would have discovered this flaw early on and been able to take action.

As an example of this, consider a situation such as the global COVID-19 pandemic. At the beginning of the pandemic, many organizations found that social distancing requirements meant more employees working remotely who had not done so before. This translated to an *overnight spike* in teleworking. Business leaders, many of whom were initially confident in their teleworking strategies, discovered that their remote access strategies were suboptimal. This included organizations that relied heavily on on-premise VPN solutions to allow employees access to internally-hosted services. From their point of view, because existing teleworking arrangements had worked fine before, why would they fail to do so going forward?

This trouble came about in many instances due to dissonance between what the prior solution had been designed to do compared to the actual conditions encountered. In many cases, for example, prior to the introduction of social distancing restrictions, only a small subset (perhaps 10 or 20%) of employees used VPN technology to work remotely at any one time. After social distancing, 100% of them were doing so. What is the logical outcome of this? Not only were VPN concentrators overwhelmed by the volume of traffic, a volume that they were neither designed nor scaled to accommodate, but there were emergent properties that further eroded performance.

For example, what happens when a new operating system or application patch is released and every remote employee attempts to download that same patch over the corporate VPN at the same time? The current VPN infrastructure, already overloaded by the sheer volume, is now further overloaded by these contemporaneous, high-bandwidth requests. This turns what's already a problematic situation into a potentially unworkable one.

This example illustrates the point of why systematically capturing, analyzing, and addressing each of these elements is valuable. Had we systematically looked at capacity – that is, who will be using the system, for what, and when – we would have a clearer understanding of what the solution is designed to accommodate and what it is not. We still might continue to scale the solution in the same way for cost reasons, or because our strategy intends to shift much of the usage to the cloud anyway, in time – but should we do so, we go into that situation with our eyes open, understanding the potential ramifications should the usage context change.

Who

In the case of the prior example of multifactor authentication in a SaaS application context, we could proceed as follows. We might start by enumerating *who* it is that the implementation strategy applies to. In the case of that example, end users are of course impacted, since they are a large portion of the folks doing the authenticating, but other stakeholders could be impacted as well. This could include auditors, security operations teams, managers, administrators, and really anyone else who will be impacted by the solution. In the case of our example, we might conclude that the most impacted parties are as follows:

- **Application users**: Those individuals who need to log in and use the application

- **Administrators**: Those who will need to perform various administrative tasks, such as new user creation and configuration of application settings

- **Auditors**: Internal and external auditors who need to review and assess the application

This is only a subset of individuals and could, depending on usage, include other people as well, such as executives, line managers, technicians, vendors, business partners, and numerous others. You'll want to consider each because, depending on who the impacted individuals and users are, you may need to adjust your design, since this could impact what answers you have to the other questions.

What

From here, we analyze the *what* – *t*hat is, what it is that the solution needs to accomplish. These are, in essence, functional requirements for the implementation. It is helpful to be as descriptive here as we can be, listing any constraints that we have in terms of the operation of the implementation. In the case of our SaaS business application example, we might have constraints introduced to us by the service provider – for example, the method for identity federation (that is, using the same access credentials to access resources across logical domains) uses **Security Assertion Markup Language** (**SAML**). Other SaaS applications might have other constraints (for example, another might support only OAuth while another may allow you to choose either OAuth or SAML). There may also be constraints that are unique to us; for example, perhaps the primary source of user identity for our organization is a Microsoft Active Directory hosted in Azure – this makes **Active Directory Federation Services** (**ADFS**) more compelling because it is built for the express purpose of allowing us to do this. The point is, we want to capture all of the constraints that we can while also making sure we have a solid understanding of the requirements that are driving the effort.

When

Once we have these constraints listed, we will want to examine *when* the solution needs to be deployed. There are two aspects to this. The first is when, chronologically, it will need to be available. The second is when – on an ongoing basis – it will need to be operational. For example, we might conclude that we need a solution within the next 6 months and that the solution will need to be available on a continuous basis. At first glance, it may appear that understanding the timing is less important than the other questions that we are asking and answering. In reality, though, there can be hidden constraints involved in answering the *when* question that, while subtle, influence what we do.

As an example, say that we identify that we need a solution that will be operational in 3 months (a very rapid turnaround). This can often be the case when addressing issues that arise from a regulatory enforcement action or audit where we don't have multiple years to plan, or, thereby, enough time to go through a complete budget cycle. In that case, our design might include multiple phases: an interim stopgap measure and a longer-term strategy. Likewise, while most modern applications will need to be available continuously, opportunities for cost reduction can be achieved if this is not the case. Therefore, we should systematically examine this as we go through the questions.

As applied to our example SaaS scenario, we might conclude that, since users will need to make use of the system throughout the day – and given that we have business users all across the globe (due to remote office locations and also due to mobile remote employees who travel extensively) – we need to have the service operate continuously. Likewise, we might conclude that users are not dependent on the solution to get their work done, so time constraints are somewhat flexible; in this case, an optimal deployment might occur within the next year (12 months).

Where

The next question to evaluate is the *where*; namely, where will the solution reside, both logically (that is, what infrastructure) and physically (that is, what physical location)? The answer to this is very important as it can have downstream impacts. For example, in the case of our hypothetical SaaS, the infrastructure that our solution will live on is dictated in part by the usage (since, in this case, it needs to be internet-accessible to accommodate users outside our office network), in part by our existing technology landscape (maybe, in this case, we are heavily externalized), in part by our strategy (maybe our strategy favors cloud deployment for new services), and by potentially numerous other factors. Therefore, it is important that we think through where the solution can live (and where it should live, based on threats, risk tolerances, and other factors) as we map it out.

Why

The *why* is probably the easiest question to answer at this point in the process. This is for two reasons. First, we've put quite a bit of thought already into the goals that we are looking to achieve before we even got this far. Therefore, the rationale for why we want to do this (from a business and risk perspective) is likely already well understood both by us and the stakeholder population. However, in addition to this, we want to move down one level of abstraction and analyze why we might need to approach the solution in a particular way versus others. In the case of our SaaS, for example, perhaps we want to mention the constraint about being "boxed in" by the cloud vendor since they only support SAML for federation of authentication between their service and our identity provider. Anything that influences or moves the design in one direction versus another should be considered at this point.

How

This is the meat of the analysis and there is a good reason why it occurs last. At this point, you've identified all the constraining factors that will cause you to narrow the scope and direction of the implementation strategy you come up with. In answering the *how*, you will want to account for these factors and find a path through the constraints that satisfies the *why* and accomplishes the *what* for the *who* within the constraints of *where* and *when*. You'll want to account for a few things as you do this:

- Consider what components and portions of the solution are needed. In some cases, there will be dependencies that are unsatisfied. In this case, you will need to satisfy those dependencies for your solution to operate.

- Consider how data will be exchanged between components and systems that comprise the solution. What format will the data be in? What protocols will be used to communicate? These items are important for making sure that the solution is functional and that any required adjustments to configuration, network paths, or other required items are addressed.

Putting them together

> "When I started out, there was a very traditional view of how applications were fielded. Things were very monolithic: for example, you had a web tier, an application tier, a database tier, and so on. We would deploy controls around these models, which meant you had to build security measures into each new project separately. From my perspective, though, this approach ceased to be the norm about 7 or 8 years ago. Now, threats don't originate within the DMZ – instead, they can come from – or target – anywhere across the entirety of the infrastructure. Before, you could layer on controls as you discovered new types of attacks; now, particularly because of the cloud, you need to think defenses through ahead of time and often have less room to add new layers. This increases the value of architecture but does change how we do it."
>
> – Anand Sastry, Director of Cyber Operations USA, Barclays

Once you have all these dimensions and answers in mind, it can be helpful to write them down. There are still a few factors that we need to consider and design around, so having a record of our thoughts and analysis while we complete those steps is useful. This is advantageous for two reasons: so that we don't lose our place in the interim, and so that we can add to the list as we think of new things that will impact the implementation strategy.

The manner in which you document these things isn't super-important at this stage because we are going to build on it later to create something that can be validated, assessed, and improved upon by subject matter specialists – and that is more formal and thorough. Therefore, you might choose to record your thought processes in a simple list, spreadsheet, mind map, or whatever approach and format is most comfortable for you. For example, for the SaaS application that we've been discussing throughout, you might document a list such as the following in Excel or another spreadsheet software:

Interrogative	Answer
Who	Needs to authenticate business users and application administrators. Needs to provide reportung to internal and external auditors. Needs to provide monitoring information to the security operations center.
What	Needs to support SAML integration with active directory via Active Directory Federation Services (AD FS)
When	Needs to operate at all times, peak times 9AM to 5PM Eastern time, non-peak access 24/7.
Where	AD FS hosted via Azure; business application hosted at cloud services provider.
Why	SaaS service supports only SAML assertions for federation with existing user stores.
How	Federation accomplished via SAML assertion. Communication pathway happens over HTTP POST (ideally) or HTTP redirect binding. Leverages built-in capabilites of SaaS authentication federation model.

Figure 7.1 – Simple spreadsheet

If you have the capability to do so, a mind map can also be a useful vehicle for capturing your thoughts, reasoning, and justifications. A mind map can be created quickly and can be added to easily for capturing new data points as you discover them, as others suggest information, or as you learn more in the course of the validation and analysis process. In addition to easing the creation and editing processes, a mind map offers the advantage of letting you see key details at a single glance. It also allows you to add information in an *out-of-band* way – for example, attaching comments/notes/documentation, modifying colors/symbols, or applying other formatting elements to individual nodes to denote importance, factors that are still under discussion or evaluation, critical constraints that impact design elements, and so on.

Again, this doesn't have to be complicated. For example, we might capture the same information shown in the preceding Excel spreadsheet in a simple mind map, such as the one depicted here:

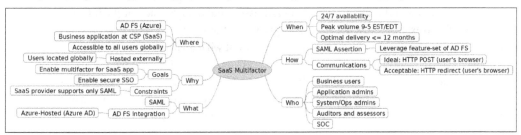

Figure 7.2 – Simple mind map

As you can see, this is just a different strategy for capturing and representing the same information. Since you are the primary audience for the information that you are capturing at this point, select an approach that is comfortable for you and that you can edit easily. Ease of editing is a useful thing to ensure at this stage, since you will likely want to iterate over the information that you capture several times; therefore, you want to pick a format that is conducive to that, and that won't deter you from iterating (for example, using a tool you're unfamiliar with or that is difficult to use, or including information that requires significant work to keep updated).

To the extent that you can, incorporate any requirements necessary for the solution to operate over time. These can include the following:

- **Staff requirements**: What personnel do you need to keep the envisioned design operational?
- **Technology "stack"**: What supporting technologies will be required for it to operate?
- **Systems and hardware**: What hardware, operating systems, network infrastructure, or other elements are required?
- **Partners and third parties**: What partnerships or other relationships are required to support it?
- **Budget requirements**: What budget will you need, or what budget constraints exist?

Understandably, you will not know all these elements with a high degree of specificity at this point. However, some will become known (even if only in estimated terms) as you create the initial conception of the implementation strategy. When you can, capture these assumptions. We will refine them when we get into the more detailed solution design portion later in this chapter. The reason that we're starting to capture them now is that understanding these items will help us evaluate the synergy between implementation strategies, as well as select the optimal solution where multiple approaches are viable. Keep in mind that this is iterative. We will build upon our understanding of these elements and gain a deeper understanding later in this process.

Again, the important part here is not how you analyze and capture the information, but that you put some thought behind it and that you systematically assess and analyze each of the interrogatives in turn. You should also examine how the answers to given questions influence available answers to others. This is because the answers to a given interrogative can limit what answers would work in other areas. For example, in the case of the situation we analyzed previously, you'll notice that the answers to the *what* and *how* questions are directly related. In this case, the SaaS application supports only SAML for SSO. This limits how we can accomplish what we hope to achieve. There might be dozens of situations like this where the answers to a given question influence possible answers to others.

And perhaps the most important thing to keep in mind as you do this is, once again, that this should be an interdisciplinary and team approach. We are absolutely not advocating that you do the entirety of this work yourself. To the contrary, you absolutely should not. The best resource you have at your disposal is the team of stakeholders and specialists you've curated. Leverage them to help you formulate the right questions in the first place and leverage them again to get the answers. You might, as a purposeful, tactical choice, elect to perform some of the planning in a limited-audience manner (for example, to respect stakeholders' time, operate more efficiently, etc.), but do not forget that you have a whole team available to help answer questions and that we need stakeholders to have ownership of the solutions being developed.

Factors outside your control

In going through this, you'll notice that the organization (and by extension, the architect) has some degree of direct control over the answers to the questions that we ask in doing this exercise. This means that the answers to many of the questions may be somewhat malleable, depending on the goals and intentions of the organization as well as their willingness to adapt in particular ways. For example, economic, contextual, cultural, and technological factors are, to a large degree, representative of the goals that the organization has and the strategies that they've put together for how to achieve them. However, it bears noting that there can be situations outside of the direct control of the organization that we will want to include, such as constraints and/or answers to these basic interrogatives that have little or no flexibility.

As an example of what we mean here, consider geopolitical impacts such as regulatory requirements within the region in which your business will operate. If you are designing a (securities) order entry system for a US-based broker/dealer (that is, a brokerage house), SEC rules require that you precisely record information about given transactions; if you're developing an email infrastructure in the same context, you may have to work within the rules of requiring storage and archival of messages (including emails) to or from a financial consultant and/or branch office.

It is imperative that we capture these constraints clearly and directly as we lay out these parameters. The reason for this is that there is less *wiggle room* in how we address them and they should factor directly into planning. Ideally, these will have been raised as requirements, but this is not always the case and should absolutely be systematically analyzed at this stage.

Assess constraints, synergies, and areas of opportunity

> *"Knowing when to walk away from a design is important. This is where metrics can guide you. If you are trying to build an automated response to 'low-hanging fruit' incidents, you might set a goal to measure how many tickets get reopened that receive an automated response. You might decide that a 25% reopen rate is acceptable but a 50% rate isn't. As you get to the threshold, it's time to reevaluate what you're doing."*
>
> – Samantha Davison, Engineering Manager, Robinhood

In capturing these constraints, we deliberately aren't going *all out* on creating documentation to codify implementation strategies for particular goals. The reason for this is that it can be beneficial to undertake this process iteratively. Solutions you construct to support individual security goals can sometimes either synergistically help you achieve other goals, address multiple goals with the same strategy, or act to the detriment of other goals. By approaching this iteratively, you can fold in these other areas as opportunities arise.

A useful way to think about this is through the analogy of sound waves and constructive versus destructive interference. If you're not familiar with these concepts, one interesting property of waves (such as sound waves) is that they can move in such a way that the peaks of multiple waves are in sync and thereby become stronger. In this situation, the amplitude of the waves combine to make a result that is greater in amplitude than either would be individually. For example, a *sonic boom* that is made when an airplane travels faster than the speed of sound is caused by constructive interference. Likewise, when two waves are at inverse phases from each other, the amplitude is canceled out and the sound is lessened. This is destructive interference; many noise-canceling headphones work by harnessing this principle.

Just like sound waves can be constructive (each contributing to the other to make the end result that much louder) or destructive (each acting in opposition to the other to cancel each other out), so too can the solutions we create work synergistically together or in opposition. Ideally, we want to minimize our effort and maximize our resources by deriving the greatest benefit from our implementation strategies. This means that we need to select items, where we can, that are constructive (synergistic) rather than those that act in opposition.

As you went through the exercise in developing implementation strategies for each of the security goals that you identified, you probably noticed that there are areas where, in addition to the answers that you provide that impact other answers within the same goal, there are multiple goals that can be aligned in ways where the decisions you make influence other goals. As we outlined, these can align synergistically or non-synergistically. Therefore, it is useful to look for where you can align implementation strategies to find areas where actions you take can work together.

To see this in action, imagine that in addition to the goal of enabling SSO and identity federation with our SaaS application example, we are also looking to enable robust logging of user account credential usage. Perhaps we have a regulatory or compliance requirement that specifies that we record successful and unsuccessful login attempts made to the cloud provider by our employees. Assuming we are following the process listed previously, we might systematically work through the various interrogatives and arrive at a result for the enhanced logging implementation strategy that is similar to the following:

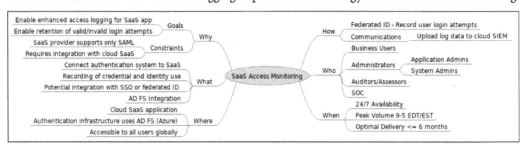

Figure 7.3 – Mind map – access monitoring

As you can see, the implementation strategies implied by both this goal and the identity federation (authentication) goal have some things in common. For example, they overlap in terms of user population, the location of various important elements, timing constraints, and so forth.

You'll notice that the requirements do not exactly overlap. There are also a few differences in how the same information is captured (note, for example, that administrators are listed as two peer items in the first example and child nodes under "Administrators" in the second example). We've done this on purpose to illustrate the fact that, in many cases, there might be natural deviations in the way that information is captured from analysis to analysis. Despite these small discrepancies, though, you will notice that they are potentially synergistic. For example, you might use ADFS in combination with the SaaS application to allow multifactor authentication. You may also enable the right logging features, both in the application and in Active Directory, to maintain the appropriate records of user authentication requests (both valid and invalid login attempts, as well as authorization and access).

In doing so, you will have potentially addressed the authentication requirement, potentially gone a long way to establishing the access monitoring and logging requirements for this second need, and laid the groundwork for authorization and access control goals. As you continue the analysis of your security goals, you might find others beyond these two where the same implementation can address multiple requirements. By noting these areas of synergy and iterating through your implementation strategies, you start to build a holistic picture. As this holistic picture comes into greater focus through your assessments of implementation strategies, you will find areas of overlap.

There are two different criteria to account for here. The first is **direct overlap**: situations where you can *kill two birds with one stone*, as in the preceding example. The second is **partial overlap**: situations where you can be more efficient if particular solutions are approached together. For example, you might discover, based on economic factors, resourcing/staffing factors, underlying technology stack requirements, or other factors, that there are areas where you can partially overlap. This is the rationale behind making note of estimates for this information early in the ideation process.

As you move through your implementation strategies with an eye toward creating a holistic picture, you may also discover areas where the implementation strategies you select are at odds with each other, or where constraints are created by virtue of decisions made due to selecting one approach over another; that is, where they require elements that are mutually incompatible or where solutions deviate from each other in ways that add unwanted complexity. In some cases, we will find situations where implementations might be related but practical reasons prevent cleanly addressing both goals with one implementation.

As an example, say that we had another application in the mix. Here, we want to update the identity management (specifically authentication), but the application also has a different set of constraints than the SaaS one we used as an example earlier. Perhaps we need to add support for external identity stores (for example, allowing the user to log into our application using their Google or LinkedIn credentials) in an application that our organization builds and provides to customers (perhaps hosted at an IaaS cloud provider). We therefore want to implement a customer authentication system that allows the use of OAuth to allow customers to authenticate via an identity provider outside our organization.

After analyzing these constraints, we might land with a result that looks something like the following:

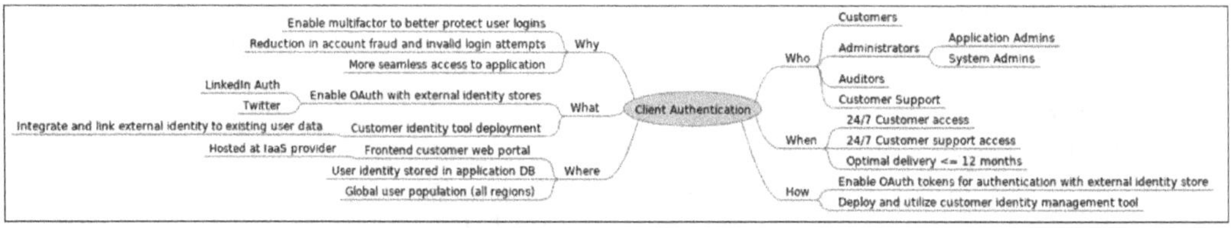

Figure 7.4 – Mind map – client authentication

As you can see, when viewed only cursorily, it appears that there might be some area of overlap: they are both related to authentication, they both will have similar utility in that they need to retain information about who is logging in (or attempting to), and they have similar needs around when and where users will need to gain access. At first, it might be tempting to attempt to manipulate the prior implementation in order to address this additional requirement through adaptation of the previous design strategy. In this case, though, by going through the full analysis, we realize that from a practical point of view, there is less overlap than what might appear on the surface.

You can also identify areas where the economics, staffing, or other factors potentially render an approach less compelling. Granted, at this stage, you will only have a vague idea of how true that is (after all, you won't know for certain until you bring the design down one level of specificity), but in many cases, you can get a good idea. Keep these factors in mind as you look for potential synergies or constraints. As always, don't be afraid to walk away from a design. Sometimes, the cleanest and most elegant solution isn't the one that is optimal based on these factors.

By holistically looking at the high-level implementation strategies for each of the goals that we addressed, we can strategically look for areas of synergy, as well as areas where we have inadvertently introduced additional constraints that weren't there before. This is the core reason why we approached the design of our implementation strategies iteratively and have saved documentation for the end – specifically so that we can refine and update our plans in light of situations like these. In some cases, you'll want to adjust how you address your goals in light of where you can address more than one goal with the same solution, where you can make partial progress on a given solution as a byproduct of satisfying another, or situations where you may need to update how you've solved a particular challenge in light of issues created somewhere else.

Next, we will validate our implementation strategies against the threat context, as well as start creating a solution document that documents our approaches for subsequent validation.

Validating against likely threat paths and creating a skeleton solution document

> *"In an ideal world, you should be aligned with two different north stars: one is what the business is trying to accomplish, what they're trying to protect, and what*

is important to them. The other is understanding what attackers are trying to do. Your best view of the latter is through your threat intelligence teams and the data that you have coming in about what attackers are doing and for what purpose. What good looks like will vary from organization to organization. There will always be some commonalities based on tools that attackers have available, what is cheap for them to buy on the dark web, the skills they have, the business model they have chosen (enterprise ransomware), and similar. But for the unique attacks – that is, those that are targeting you specifically – these are more likely to target those things that are most important to you."

– Mark Simos, Lead Cybersecurity Srchitect, Microsoft

At this point, you'll have a pretty good idea of what you will do to meet particular goals and how you'll do this. You won't have documented much beyond the barest, most high-level skeleton of it yet, but you'll have enough that, most of the time, you'll have a pretty clear idea of how you will accomplish your goal. However, we have yet to vet these implementation strategies with the SMEs and specialists to ensure that the designs work. Even if individual subject matter experts help with the creation of the design, there are usually multiple SME stakeholders, and it is rarely the case that all of them will be equally plugged into the solution design throughout. Therefore, it is valuable to explicitly re-engage to validate solution design. This is an important step, but doing so involves some work to get our thoughts in order and creating some documentation that we can use as a framework on which to base those discussions.

To begin this process, we'll want to do a few things. First, we'll want to record what we've gathered into a schematic or other technical drawing or document that concisely and unambiguously describes what we're looking to do. Because we're doing this before we have the group discussions with specialized engineers and SMEs, we do so knowing that this exercise will also be iterative. This means that the first draft of that document will likely have some issues that we will need to work on with the experts. However, to have a productive discussion with them about what we want to do, it's helpful to have something to work from. What we're putting together in this section is that initial baseline; that is, the baseline documentation that will allow us to work collaboratively with those engineers.

It's important to note here that we're not trying to do the job of these specialists for them or otherwise gainsay or obviate what they will tell us. In fact, it is neither required nor is it a good idea for us to try to design a solution in isolation from them. Instead, we want to enlist their support, get their buy-in and assistance on the implementation strategy, and ultimately – with their help – put together a solution that satisfies our security needs. To make it easy on them, though, we'll want to make sure that the strategy we have is as "baked" as it can be going into those discussions (if need be, by working individually with SMEs to formulate the proposal). This means that we have put as much productive thought into the solution as we can. This includes both making sure that we are satisfying the security goal and doing so in a way that minimizes potential threats.

To begin this process, it is valuable that you do two things:

- Validate that the implementation strategy addresses all relevant threats

- Create a document or diagram that encapsulates the implementation strategy

There's a bit of a "chicken and egg" problem associated with doing this. This is because in order to analyze the threats, you'll need a design to work from. However, to create a design to work from, you'll want to make sure you've addressed the threats to not waste effort. In practice, this often means doing these two things iteratively and contemporaneously.

We'll go through each of these processes in more detail, starting with threat validation.

Threat validation

> *"One mistake I see people make is not do any modeling or systematic analysis of threats. Building a program without awareness of the threats means what you're building won't align with what you will actually encounter. It also impacts your ability to measure. If you don't even know what you're protecting against, how can you possibly measure whether you are successful or not?"*
>
> *– Samantha Davison, Engineering Manager, Robinhood*

> *"Most systems don't get attacked by Adi Shamir. Instead, they get attacked by phishing or other less sophisticated attackers using less sophisticated tradecraft. Start with the most common scenarios and do what you can to cover the 90% of attacks – you can always go back and add complexity tomorrow."*
>
> *– Adam Shostack, President, Shostack & Associates*

Once you have reviewed each of the implementation strategies for areas of synergy and potentially adjusted them in light of additional constraints, you then refine the resilience of those implementations to threats that they might encounter. If you've followed our advice up to this point, you'll have some experience doing this from when you did your initial threat analysis back in *Chapter 5, Building an Architecture – Enterprise Blueprints*, and *Chapter 6, Building an Architecture – Application Blueprints*, (that is, in determining what your security goals were in the first place). We'll want to repeat this exercise but look at the threats as they pertain specifically to the areas involved in the implementation strategy (or strategies) under consideration.

To take this approach to a greater level of depth, it can be helpful to modify our approach somewhat. In the initial iteration of our threat modeling, we did one of two things:

- **Enterprise scope**: Used an asset view of the landscape to create a threat model, thus evaluating each asset through the lens of the kill chain

- **Application scope**: Used a decomposed component view of the application to create a threat model, thus evaluating each component through the lens of the STRIDE mnemonic

These approaches are great for their specific purposes, but as we build out the solution, it can be helpful to take them to a finer level of granularity and a higher resolution of detail. To accomplish this, we will alter the process somewhat. We'll do this by introducing a new tool to our threat evaluation: specifically, the tactics portion of the MITRE ATT&CK® matrix.

For those who are unfamiliar, the **Adversarial Tactics, Techniques, and Common Knowledge (ATT&CK)** framework is a catalog of tactics (goals/motivations) and techniques (methods) used by attackers to accomplish their objectives. It's a sort of database of how and why attackers take the actions that they take.

One of the ways in which this is useful is that you can use the ATT&CK tactics tables in the place of where you used either STRIDE (for applications) or kill chain analysis (for enterprises). Here, you start with a decomposed view of the application or segment of the environment that is in scope for the implementation strategies or solution areas that you are exploring and, for each element in that deconstructed view, you iterate through the tactic elements described by the ATT&CK framework.

You can, of course, use the same modeling technique that you employed earlier in the process – there is still value there. However, there are two primary advantages to using ATT&CK at this stage. The first is that the structure of ATT&CK correlates tactics to specific techniques employed by attackers. This means that, as you examine each of the tactical elements in your threat modeling, you can see a database of techniques that they use to accomplish that goal. This is advantageous because, while only rarely will all of the techniques be directly applicable to the particular situation that you are evaluating, you will find that looking through these techniques will cause you to start thinking about analogous methods that might be applicable to your particular use case. This is true because it describes both tactics and techniques generically without reference to particular implementations or specific attacker tradecraft, tools, or software.

The second reason why it's useful for this purpose is that it gives you a different window into analysis beyond the one you used in coming up with the goal in the first place. In many cases, you will find yourself thinking through similar threats as you did when coming up with your goals. That's to be expected. However, were you using the same approach, there would be a temptation to make assumptions based on the work that you initially did during goal formulation. A lot has changed since that first analysis, so by looking at things through a different lens, you have no option but to think this through differently – and analyze the threats objectively once again.

In using ATT&CK in this way, you'll want to select the tactics set that most closely aligns with the solution context that you are working within. In most cases, our approach is to start with the "enterprise" tactics; at the time of writing, they are cited by MITRE as follows:

- Reconnaissance
- Resource development
- Initial access
- Execution

- Persistence

- Privilege escalation

- Defense evasion

- Credential access

- Discovery

- Lateral movement

- Collection

- Command and control

- Exfiltration

- Impact

Note that the whole purpose of ATT&CK is to be a living, breathing ontology. Therefore, it is expected that these tactics will evolve in keeping with attacker activities. Because of this, while we have listed the current (at the time of writing) tactics, the best reference will always be the information on the MITRE ATT&CK website (`attack.mitre.org`).

Likewise, there are different categories of tactics based on context. The most generally applicable category for most business use cases will be enterprise tactics. That being said, there are others, including "pre-attack" categories (that is, what attackers do before they conduct a campaign) and mobile categories (for mobile attacks). Presumably, as researchers investigate additional context, others will emerge. Therefore, it is advantageous to utilize the context that makes the most sense for the type of usage and context in your scope.

Having walked through the method of threat modeling in prior chapters, we won't recap it here again. The important thing to note is that you should examine the implementation strategy that you come up with from a threat perspective once again, this time focusing particular attention on the components of the implementation, as well as the surrounding elements. Whether you choose to use the original approach (that is, STRIDE or kill chain) or ATT&CK is really a matter of preference. We prefer the ATT&CK approach at this stage because of the reasons that we set out, but either approach will work.

Skeleton solution document

> "What is architecture? Security architecture translates the organization's business and assurance goals into documentation and diagrams that guide technical security decisions. This is how I see it as a function within the organization itself. It is also the confluence of business requirements, risk, and the technical realities both for the current environment and what's available in the marketplace. The job of the architect is to take business and assurance goals – what the organization most cares about – and translate them so that the technical folks know how to bring them to life."
>
> – Mark Simos, Lead Cybersecurity Architect, Microsoft

The next logical question is in regard to *what* you are threat modeling; that is, how you can deconstruct the implementation strategies you're examining into the component parts for analysis. This is where the documentation for the implementation strategy itself comes in.

At this point, there are two things that you will need. First, you need to have a way to deconstruct what you are looking at into the component parts that will allow you to threat model the implementation strategy that you're considering. When we did this for our enterprise design scope, we used assets in the scope of the design domain; when we did this for applications, we used a component view of the application itself (that is, by deconstructing the application into the various components that comprise it). Ideally, we will want to follow a similar process here, but we need to know what those elements are. In the case of enterprise design, we will need to know what assets are involved, including the assets that exist in the landscape before we apply our implementation strategy (that is, what elements were in the landscape before we began thinking of solutions), as well as what elements are there once we've applied the solution to it. In the case of applications, the same principle applies; specifically, we want to know what components of the application are in place before and what will be in place after. It is against this superset that we will apply the threat modeling process to verify the solution.

The second thing that we will ultimately need is a document that outlines the implementation strategy in some level of formal detail. This will help us engage with subject matter experts and engineers to ensure that the strategy meets the following criteria:

- Technically and operationally feasible
- In line with existing technical strategies employed by other areas
- Free of unforeseen constraints that could impede implementation
- Viable within existing budgetary and resource constraints
- Culturally acceptable to the organization
- Satisfies the original goal, as documented and approved by stakeholders

Therefore, the document that we will create at this stage is, by design, a draft for discussion. Its purpose is to be refined and improved upon as we engage with the individuals and teams who will help us bring it to realization. We will need both these elements, and fortunately, we can satisfy both criteria with one work effort; that is, we can create the documentation strawman at the same time that we decompose the post-solution environment for the purposes of validating our threat coverage.

To do this, we will once again want to utilize the same language and mechanisms for documentation that are familiar to our target audience. This means that you will want to be adaptable here. If you are creating an implementation strategy that has a number of infrastructure or COTS components, but your organization is one where engineers are particularly used to looking at topological diagrams, then you should create a topological diagram to document and convey this information. If you are working in the context of an application and you're in an environment that is primarily used to dealing with UML 2.0 object interaction diagrams or sequence diagrams, use those.

Note that since it is useful to start with a diagram anyway for threat modeling, you can attempt to kill two birds with one stone by using the same document for both. Now, in saying this, we should note that we're not suggesting that you pigeonhole either your threat modeling process or your solution documents into a documentation format that makes it impossible. For example, if you are working in an environment where solutions are primarily expressed using a detailed hardware-level bill of materials, it would obviously be challenging to use that for a threat modeling exercise. While you could probably do so, it is likely not the most conducive format for it. In this case, you might choose to create intermediate documentation. That is, you'll create a version of the implementation strategy that you can threat model against and then, subsequently, create the model that you will use to present to technical teams for vetting, input, improvements, and (ultimately) concurrence. However, in most cases, the way those teams are used to receive and evaluate solutions will support the threat modeling process.

As an example, consider a relatively simple diagram that illustrates the multifactor SaaS hypothetical goal that we used earlier in this chapter. In this case, we have chosen a diagramming approach similar to that in use in many organizations. It is topologically structured and illustrates the system-level components involved in the solution:

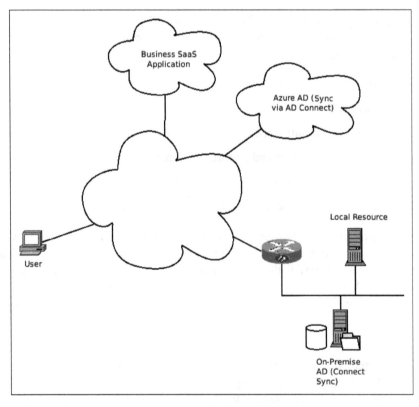

Figure 7.5 – Simple cloud topology

While this may not be the most sophisticated diagram ever, it should – when supported by verbal explanation or written documentation – be sufficient to illustrate what it is that you are hoping to accomplish.

If you are developing software – for example, software that integrates with a customer identity management platform as described previously – you will want to use the documentation method employed by the target audience for that as well. If your organization's *lingua franca* for conveying software solutions is UML 2.0, you might use a sequence diagram or interaction diagram. The point is twofold: you want to be versatile in the documentation elements that you create to be best understood, and you want to create something that you can use as input to the threat modeling process.

Validating implementation strategies

> *"The primary goal of a good cybersecurity architecture is to make the solution, whatever it may be, business enabling (or mission enabling). This is a little different from other architectural disciplines that might be more focused on enabling a given technology or capability (that is, ensuring it works) but less focused on the integration of that capability into the broader business and ensuring it operates in harmony with the broader context. Cybersecurity always needs to be focused on the business itself: the workflows, context, and processes in use. To ensure that the end result enables business, we need to understand how the business works in the first place."*
>
> *– Dr. Char Sample, Chief Research Scientist – Cybercore Division at Idaho National Laboratory*

At this point, you will have created a document that outlines the key elements of your solution and, along the way, validated the threat context that will be applicable after the solutions have been implemented to a set of security goals. It is important to stress that while many people think "diagram" when they think of architecture, the diagram piece is perhaps one of the less important parts of the process. It's a useful way to present a view or lens into an architecture, but it's only a part of a bigger whole. Nevertheless, because of the misconception that people have about these diagrams, it's useful to have one relatively ironed out as you start validating your work with others; they will expect to see one and many will discount your work if you don't have it.

From here, you will want to validate your work with technical stakeholders. You will want to be somewhat careful as you do this. When coming up with the initial set of goals, you likely spoke to a significant number of stakeholders, including individuals in the business, executives and managers, non-technology teams, and numerous others. They have validated the goals so that you have a pretty clear idea of what they want. However, it is important to recognize that not all of these stakeholders will have the technical skills to comment directly on the implementation strategy. Presenting them with a topology diagram or software engineering diagram might, instead of providing value to you and them, serve only to waste their time discussing details that they neither know nor care about.

Because of this, you will want to maintain a balance. You will want to communicate elements of the technical design back to the full body of stakeholders. This isn't so much so that they can provide input on the technical design (although sometimes you might be surprised) but more so that all stakeholders are invested in – and feel ownership of – the outcome. However, you will want to do this in such a way that you're not wasting their time having them look at materials that they won't understand. This is why it can be helpful to put together a high-level solution description that, in a few paragraphs, summarizes the approach that you intend to take and describes why you believe it to be the optimal strategy. This is best done after you have validated the approach with the technical stakeholders who can contribute directly to it (for example, by altering, providing feedback on, or directly improving the approach). Again, this is done to save everyone's time as it is quite possible (probable, in fact) that the approach will be altered somewhat upon discussions with the specialist engineers and subject matter teams who hold a stake in the design.

Therefore, the approach that we often use is to validate with these specialists first, where they exist, refine the design based on their input and feedback, work iteratively with them to reach a version of the implementation that all can agree upon, and then create a schematic, architecture description, or other technical documentation describing the solution in depth. Once that is agreed upon by all, we write up the high-level solution brief for consumption by all remaining, non-technical stakeholders.

As you validate this, you will want to increase the level of granularity and specificity around the practical elements of the solution. By this, we mean the following:

- Required budget to implement and maintain
- Operational impact on the existing ecosystem
- Staffing requirements to deploy and maintain
- Required infrastructure, hardware, software, and other technical substrate

Those individuals who work most closely with the functional areas that are being impacted are best positioned to provide this information. Therefore, as you meet with them to validate and improve what you came up with initially, gather and document as much information about these items as you can. Not only are they germane to the implementation itself, but also you will want to retain a record of this information for posterity and use it as a guide for implementation/deployment, as well as for future-proofing what you put in place.

Finalizing the documentation

"There is a continuum of mistakes people make. The first is not doing an architecture at all. This can be disastrous when it comes to a complex or high-risk system. On the other end of the spectrum, you have projects that are over-architected. They over-analyze everything but don't do a risk analysis to help define the focus with an understanding of what is most likely go wrong and cause

*material losses. They tend to generate lots of documentation, but don't actually
come up with useful output."*

*– Dan Blum, Cybersecurity Strategist, Security Architect,
and Author of the book Rational Cybersecurity for Business*

Once you have provided documentation back to stakeholders, iteratively incorporated their feedback, and refined it, you are left with a set of documents that describe the security goals and how to achieve them with a great deal of technical specificity. In terms of the actual implementation work itself, this will likely be sufficient enough to bring about the design. However, it can be extremely valuable to incorporate several artifacts from the technical design process back into the ADD (that is, the documentation we created in *Chapter 5, Building an Architecture – Enterprise Blueprints*, and *Chapter 6, Building an Architecture – Application Blueprints*). Specifically, you will need to incorporate the following:

- The end result technical specification (in whatever format is being used by your organization)

- Any solution briefs that you created for non-technical stakeholders

- Information about your budget, resources, operations, and hardware/software

- Any intermediate designs or approaches that were considered but were not included

The most important of these is the last item – what you considered but decided not to pursue, or determined (either based on threat analysis or on input from technical stakeholders) was infeasible or impractical. While you won't use this for the implementation process, it is extremely valuable for posterity. After all, consider what will happen down the road if this information isn't preserved. Others who are reviewing the goals and solutions might well hit upon that same approach and (in the best case) question why you decided to pursue the approach you did, instead of an alternate one, or (in the worst case) actually go down the path of pursuing a strategy that you considered but discounted, thereby wasting potentially significant amounts of their time and energy in the process. To help prevent this, keeping track of the solutions that you elected not to pursue (and why) is extraordinarily valuable. Likewise, because context can change, a solution that is non-viable today may become viable – perhaps even optimal – in the future should situations, technologies, business processes, or other factors change. Recording the rationale supporting the decision can help clue you into why it might be more viable down the road if circumstances change.

By combining these elements with the ADD, you now have a document that describes what you are trying to do (both in concrete, technical specificity as well as more business-friendly terms), why you are trying to do it, what risks the approach mitigates, how and why it is resilient against threats, who was consulted, and the dimensions by which success will be measured. In short, you have a fully formed design that is relevant to most stakeholders, regardless of their level of technical depth or where in the organization they sit. Pat yourself on the back. This is a huge milestone.

From here, let's look at how we can ensure that we have in place the operational framework for the design before we get into the nuts and bolts of execution.

Operational integration

> *"Imagine you have a Jenga tower comprised of everything required to support secure delivery. Each block in the tower adds weight, cost, and complexity to the Jenga tower of process that supports secure delivery. You want to remove every block you can while still allowing it to stand. There are three kinds of blocks: technical blocks (what logging system do I use?), soft skill blocks (how do I convince developers to do this?), and organization discipline (where does threat modeling fit? What are the escalation paths?). Breaking them out into the three types of blocks is useful and the belief that we want the tower to be both stable and light."*
>
> *– Adam Shostack, President, Shostack & Associates*

Reaching this milestone is huge in and of itself, but you'll notice that there are some areas that we haven't addressed yet. For example, we have developed implementation strategies to meet security goals that can be built and that have been vetted by technical stakeholders. This is important, but there are other factors to consider too. Chief among them are operational elements of the design. For example, what are the important operational elements that are required by the implementation strategies that you've selected and how will you address them?

Now, throughout the design process, any operational elements that are truly "game-breaking" will have been weeded out. For example, a process that requires a team of 1,000 analysts to operate will obviously have been discounted long since due to budgetary or personnel constraints, or have been decided against in favor of a more lightweight solution. But there are operational elements beyond those that would render a solution non-viable, such as the following:

- Changing context and evolution
- Monitoring execution

There are two primary reasons why we want to consider these things at this stage in the process. Specifically, at this point, we have a set of *potential* implementations; that is, we have designs that, should we execute them, will meet security goals and do so in a way that is cost-effective, and that are synergistic with each other to the greatest extent possible. This is a great start, but we actually have to build it and make it a reality. We need to actually do the work.

From a general point of view, pretty much all organizations have the capability to execute projects with various degrees of formality, success, and assumed risk. After all, any organization that was fundamentally incapable of project management would probably never have evolved past the start-up phase. Therefore, because project management approaches can be so different from organization to organization, we will assume that your organization has the capability to execute a project, but we won't delve into too many specifics or assumptions about what the process might be. Meaning, we won't talk at a high level of specificity about how to project manage the execution required to turn your designs into reality here, but will instead remain at a more abstract level.

While we're not going into the PM details, there absolutely are inputs into the project management phase and execution of the design that are relevant because they have a bearing on security. However, they are not always included as part of a "stock" project management approach. This means that they need to be injected into the project management approach we use to account for them.

This is also valuable for another reason, specifically because, in the next chapter, we will outline strategies about what to do next: how to implement and, ultimately, plan for what you will do as your organization changes, as business processes change, as technology changes, and as adversaries and threats change. In order to lay the groundwork to do that well, we will need to establish the operational foundation that will allow us to know when such changes occur and, to the best extent possible, future-proof our approaches. In the next chapter, we will build on this in more detail, but for now, it's important to note that the way in which we execute now will absolutely impact our ability to do that well.

To lay the groundwork, we'll want to account for two main factors as we implement the designs that we have so painstakingly put together. These are the operational elements of the design and telemetry (measurement). By *operational elements*, we mean those aspects of the implementation that will impact our ability to keep the solution running at optimum efficiency – and allow it to continue adding maximum value – over time. By *telemetry*, we're referring to those aspects of the design that allow us to collect the information that we will use to monitor the solution over time and, ultimately, that will provide feedback about future evolutions of the design. In this subsection, we'll walk through the operational elements and building the telemetry that we will require into the project.

Changing context and evolution

> *"Sometimes, assumptions can change. For example, an application might be designed for one purpose and used for other purposes later. An application designed for public data might be used to process PII once it is in production. In that case, the designers didn't bring in security professionals to layer in appropriate security. A security architect can be very helpful to find and address issues like these."*
>
> *– John Kallil, Chief Information Security Officer*

The first element that we will want to account for is how we might meet the challenge of growth or the evolution of what we've put in place. We put thought into what was needed to deploy the implementation strategy in the first place, but we also will need to think through what happens if major assumptions change. The most common assumption to change is the size of the implementation; that is, capacity, including volume of usage. However, there are other assumptions that could change as well. For example, consider the situation where we know our organization is early in the process of embracing a "cloud-first" strategy where they are externalizing (moving to the cloud) as many existing, on-premise technology components as possible. If we look solely at the landscape of today and do not plan for where the organization is going in the future, we may very well design something that works now but, in very short order (well before we've received the full return on our investment), will become out of step with the direction in which the organization is going.

Likewise, as we outlined in *Chapter 5, Building an Architecture – Developing Enterprise Blueprints*, there are situations where it might take you multiple evolutionary steps to get from where you are now to where you'd like to be. Each of these intermediate steps between where you are now and where you are going is itself something that (depending on the scope and context) will need to be defended along the way. It doesn't make sense to have a comparatively undefended interim state along the path. We needed to consider this back in *Chapter 5, Building an Architecture – Developing Enterprise Blueprints*, because we recognized that we might have a target state that will take some time to get to and we want to ensure appropriate protections as we transition to that state. These things are all still true now. Hopefully, when we were outlining the security goals, we accounted for these macro-level shifts. However, the same thing can happen at a micro level as well – for example, in the context of a subset of implementation strategies.

To see what we mean, consider an example. Say that we are writing software that will interface with a cryptographic module. Perhaps we would ultimately like critical cryptographic operations – for example, key generation – to take place on a **hardware security module** (**HSM**) that will have tamper evidence/prevention built into the hardware itself. However, we know that it might take some time before we can deploy that HSM – potentially months or years before it is universally fielded everywhere our application will run. Ideally, we would be able to put the HSM in place right away, but since we know that there will be an indeterminate period of time where we cannot, we might choose to implement the functionality in software as an interim step, transitioning to HSM hardware on a rolling basis as hardware is deployed and becomes ubiquitous.

In this case, if we think of the software functionality that we're implementing as an implementation strategy to support a larger goal (protecting user account data, for example), we can think of there being three distinct phases or iterations of the design:

1.   **Initial state**: The current state before addressing the security goal(s)

2.   **Intermediate (software-only) state**: The point in time where the software version of the cryptographic module is applied

3.   **Goal (HSM-enabled) state**: The point in time where the implementation strategy is fully realized

It bears stating that, since we are undertaking this for the purposes of meeting security goals, we will ideally want each interim state to provide security value as well. The particulars of each individual transition state to realize a solution will dictate how much of the goal we can address in that interim state. Sometimes, more can be addressed and sometimes, less – but it is important that we factor this into the execution process itself.

This is important for two reasons. First, logistically, we want to factor in these intermediate steps because we need to ensure they are accounted for in the project planning. Second, we want to make sure that we are realistic about how much risk – and how many threats – are mitigated at each stage and how many remain open. Except for very complicated projects, it is unlikely that you will have more than two or three interim evolutionary steps to deploy a given solution. It can happen, but as a practical matter, each interim step adds complexity to the project management, increases the time to achieve the ultimate goal state, and potentially adds expense. Therefore, a realistic upper bound (maximum number) of these transition stages is probably relatively low – and, since each stage has its own risk dynamics, it is advantageous to us that it stays that way.

Execution monitoring

> *"I don't believe that there's a difference between security metrics, operational metrics, and business metrics. For example, consider a typical exploit: very likely, it will show up in information that I'm collecting already: CPU has spiked, an OS crashed, an application went down, and so on. If I build an instance of a web application and am monitoring these things already, I can easily tie these metrics into security controls that I add. For example, if I introduce a web application firewall (WAF), I can correlate and tie the existing performance metrics into the data from the WAF, leading to more and better information. If you build a strong performance baseline where you are measuring things that matter to the business (uptime, performance, responsiveness, usage, access, and so on), you can often quickly detect security anomalies with those same capabilities. Take NetFlow, for example; even with something like NetFlow, if you're collecting that data and you see a quadrupling of connections, this could very well represent a security event. The trick is connecting the metrics you gather together, connecting the metrics to the business and operational context, and extending those to a security use case."*
>
> *– Anand Sastry, Director of Cyber Operations USA, Barclays*

The next area where we will want to provide input into the project management process is the arena of monitoring the execution progress. Note that this is different from the ongoing monitoring of the solution that we will do when it is in place (that is, the metrics that we identified and will further refine). Instead, we mean monitoring where in the implementation process the solution is as it is being put in place.

The reasons why this matters are twofold:

- First, we just went through how there can be multiple steps along the pathway to get from the current state to the desired future state. Since each of these evolutionary phases can have different risk dynamics and performance, we will want to ensure that we can measure risk as our implementation strategy is put in place.

- Second, in many cases, we may not be directly involved in the deployment process itself. In a smaller company or one where project management is very transparent and communicative, we might have some insight into the execution, but this is only sometimes the case.

Since the stage of execution impacts our risk (as you may recall, the ultimate driver for all of this in the first place was risk), it can be very important that we know where in the deployment cycle a project stands so that we can understand our risk profile at any given point in time.

Additionally, bear in mind that, in many cases, there will be multiple implementation strategies in the execution pipeline at any given point in time. Therefore, information about the state of each and translating that information back into a holistic risk picture means bringing the statuses of multiple projects together, understanding where they are, and integrating them into one view.

To accomplish this, and to ensure that you are getting the data that you need, you will likely need to establish a communication method and frequency with the project management team. Ideally, if you communicate why you need this level of transparency, they will be able to provide this level of reporting back to you. You will also need to collect data.

Case study – Operational integration

"In architecture, the most important thing is understanding the basics. If you don't understand the basics, you will never get to where you're trying to go. Things are very complex: how will you define architecture for a network or an application without the basics (putting aside cloud, IT, OT, and so on)? Even when you are just in technology and not necessarily cybersecurity, you need to understand how things are built and how they fit together. You need to understand what kind of technologies, tools, people you have access to -- and you need to understand who the stakeholders are. Once you have mastery of the fundamentals and can get the basic work done, nobody can beat you for sure. Our job ultimately is to fix the problems and to set up the right things so we help keep everyone else from getting into trouble."

– Vandana Verma, Security Relations Leader - APJ, BoD at OWASP & InfosecGirls

In an interview, we asked internationally recognized board member and speaker Vandana Verma about how best to operationally integrate architecture plans into the broader organization. We asked her for examples of when she's seen this occur successfully and when she's seen it transpire poorly. She responded by using two separate events in her career for us to compare and contrast.

First, she explained a "win" and what success factors were critical to the successful implementation of architectural planning. She teed this up by telling us about a problem situation she encountered at one point in her career: *"I'll explain a situation where I was working on setting up vulnerability management for an organization. Setting up a program like this is a big deal for any organization because it represents a culture shift – it can impact how people do their jobs and can cause the whole organization to shift in turn. When we started putting that program into practice, we noticed a concerning trend in the form of 'drift'. Meaning, everyone was drifting away from the original intent of the plan. They were saying things like 'this is not what we want' and 'this is not how it should be done.'"*

By now, you will realize exactly why this kind of situation is particularly concerning. Not only are stakeholders questioning the what, why, and how of the design (a truly suboptimal situation), but also, "group think" questioning of the design is starting to spread. How, then, can you contain this? Vandana explained how she leveraged the project management process in that organization to bring things back on track. She told us: *"What saved this was project management. The project managers made sure that the design that was there and the events transpiring – that everything was being communicated to everyone involved. The decisions ultimately came from leadership, so leadership really should know what is happening. Because of the involvement of the project management team and the solid communication, everything came back into alignment and the barriers became completely apparent. It took us six months to realize the outcome, but we ultimately got there. During the course of the journey, everyone realized that this effort was something important and needed for the organization and that the only alternative was we would be in trouble no matter what we did."*

In this case, project management saved the day, but we asked her about where she'd seen the opposite occur – where something interfered in a negative way. She told us a tale of a lack of stakeholder engagement; specifically, engineers hoping to completely bypass security: *"At one point, there was a critical release which was supposed to happen and there was a stakeholder meeting that was important to the release process. In this case, the engineers didn't invite either security or the project management team at all. In fact, they changed the meeting time and didn't relay that to either security or project managers so that by the time we reached the meeting room, it was almost over. Neither group had a chance to participate and as a consequence they were not able to release the project."*

Now, most PMs and security pros are familiar with teams who try to bypass process. But surreptitiously changing meeting times is unusual in the extremism by which it bypasses process. The important lesson to draw here? Vandana summarized it this way: *"For security, particularly when implementing a security architecture – trust, communication, and relationship building are incredibly important. In security, we often don't trust anyone – and if we're not careful, this can be reciprocated. It takes time to build trust. Project management can be key to building that relationship with different stakeholders, so it's important that we build a line of communication with them to assist in forging and maintaining those relationships."* To pave the way for collecting this data, next, we'll look at establishing telemetry – that is, metrics from both the execution and the implementation itself to fold into your overall picture.

Telemetry

> *"The 'right amount' of measurement for an architecture program is context-dependent, so there's no universal rule for measurement. However, without measurement, life is very difficult to lead. We measure things in almost every aspect of our lives. We measure time: how long will an activity take? How quickly can we get to a destination? We measure intuitively and innately. There are two key sets of metrics for pretty much anything: the rate of change (how will we transform over a period of time?) and the final endpoint of a change program (when will we get to where we want to be?). Both are critical to the architecture process."*
>
> *– John Sherwood, Chief Architect, Thought Leader, and co-Founder of The SABSA Institute)*

The second element that we want to account for as we execute is telemetry – that is, metrics. Now, keep in mind that we discussed metrics at length back in *Chapter 4, Building an Architecture – Your Toolbox*, as input to create our security goals. As a result, many security metrics will already be accounted for in the goal set that you are using to derive the technical implementation details.

In other words, we know what the solution is supposed to do and how/what we can measure to make sure that it is doing it (that is, that it is meeting the objectives).

While these metrics are incredibly relevant and important, they are not the only sets of metrics that will matter to you. There is other information that you will need, such as information about the technical operation of the solution that you field.

There are two reasons why this is important. In the next chapter, we will talk about constructing a *virtuous cycle*; that is, establishing a feedback loop that allows us to optimize the work that we do so that we can improve and develop our skills (and process) over time. To do that, we will need to set ourselves up to measure not only how well we are meeting the baseline goal, but how well our specific implementation performs technically, as well as other things about it that are difficult to accurately forecast prior to implementation (for example, the amount of staff time spent maintaining the technical solution elements).

Secondly, it is important that we understand other things beyond just the security of the solution during operation. We might want to become more efficient over time, improve our design process, or implement solutions faster or with less friction. If information about the technical operation of the solution forwards one of those goals, we will absolutely want to collect it.

As an example, to understand the economics of the solutions that we deploy over time and optimize for this purpose, we might want to keep track of the hours that are spent by personnel maintaining the solution. To do that, we will also want to understand how the solution performs operationally; for example, if it is a detective control designed to alert us when bad guys are taking action against us, how well does it do that? How many times does it alert us when there's nothing amiss (false positives) and how often does it not alert us when it should (false negatives)? This ties directly into the overall opportunity cost of the solution (since personnel responding to false positives are not available to do something more directly productive).

Because these items tie directly to the specific technical solution (that we selected after goals and such were initially identified), they may not be accounted for by the metrics that we decided upon and thought through in prior chapters. Therefore, during the execution – that is, as we implement the solutions that we have so carefully designed – we will want to account for any additional metrics that will help us understand the economic, technical, and operational profile of the solution over time.

It is advantageous to do this during the actual implementation phase itself. After all, common sense would suggest that measurement should be designed for inclusion (i.e., "baked in") before we actually start to bring about changes. Normally, this would be true. However, keep in mind what these particular metrics are. They're not the metrics that will help you understand whether your overall program is successful or not. Remember, these were captured and addressed before we even finalized the security goals. They're not the technical and operational metrics required to manage and maintain the solution either, since those will be addressed during conversations with stakeholders and, therefore, are optimally left to those individuals who will have direct oversight after deployment. Instead, what we're discussing here are the metrics that will give us the feedback that will allow us to improve over time, in combination with the information collection and telemetry that is already baked into the design.

Traditional wisdom holds that most technology teams don't have enough information. This is true, but for different reasons than many people think. Most people, when presented with that statement, tend to conclude that there isn't enough information being collected and that this is why there's not enough information available. However, often, the opposite is true – that is, organizations are collecting so much information that the most relevant data items become invisible due to the sheer volume of irrelevant and unnecessary information. Consider what information you are likely collecting right now. While the specifics will vary from organization to organization, most organizations collect most of the following:

- Firewall logs
- Router logs
- Application logs (including middleware)
- OS logs
- NetFlow and bandwidth usage
- IDS alerts
- SIEM reports
- Vulnerability alerts
- Cloud service provider logs
- Device telemetry

These are just a few of the pieces of information you are likely collecting. If someone told you that somewhere in that vast corpus of data there was an individual data point that was critical to you, how easily could you find it? For most of us, it wouldn't be very easy at all.

In fact, the volume of data for even a mid-size organization is overwhelming. Many metrics initiatives fail not because there's not enough data, but because there's too much. They fail because what data there is isn't actionable – because it's a drop of water in a sea of irrelevant noise.

As an analogy, say that a friend asked you for assistance preparing his or her taxes. You ask your friend to provide you with financial information so that you can help. If, in response, they show up at your house in a van filled with every receipt from every purchase they've ever made without any labeling or organization to help identify which are which, how likely is it that you would be able to find the particular items you'd need to complete their return? Not very, right? This is almost directly analogous to the situation that many organizations find themselves in when it comes to collecting telemetry about technology elements in their organizations. They keep so much information about everything under the sun that trying to distill down the actionable set of data elements is a significant undertaking.

Therefore, waiting until this phase is occurring means that you are forced to focus on the questions that you actually need answers to rather than collecting more information just for the sake of collecting it. A very natural and human temptation when addressing metrics is to gather information because you can, rather than because you have a specific question you want answered. You will want to avoid this.

This is one of the key reasons why it can be useful to wait until after you have a design in mind to systematically address operational metrics collection. By waiting until you are actually designing the solution, you will understand exactly what elements are involved in implementation. This means you can do two things. First, you can tie back operational data to the high-level goal. You already know what the goals are – you've mapped them out, documented them, and validated them at some length early on in the design process. Now that you have a solution in mind, you can translate the data from the technical implementation into a set of questions that inform and shed light on whether the solution meets the goals you've identified.

As an example, consider a problem that impacts many organizations: *phishing*. At the beginning of the design process, you might identify the goal of reducing the risk to the organization resulting from phishing. You might understand the phishing problem through an economic lens (that is, the financial and efficiency impacts associated with phishing), from a risk standpoint (that is, the risks introduced via successful phishing attempts), or through some other lens. If you've gone through this design process to create a solution, you should have an idea of what concrete information you will need (and ideally can collect) that helps answer the question of whether you are successful in accomplishing that goal. For example, if you deploy a mail filtering solution, you might track the rate of phishing attempts reported before and after the deployment of the solution; on the other hand, if you implement a phishing simulation, you might track how many phishing emails are reported. As you can see, the implementation strategy at hand dictates what information you want to collect to track progress against the original goal.

It is useful to do this here, at this stage of the process, because it gives you a chance to iterate; that is, you can start collecting metrics before you begin execution, building on and testing the data you collect while doing so (that is, while the solution is being deployed), and learn what questions are most relevant both to the higher-level security goals as well as to the ongoing operational management of the solution. As you learn which questions you most need answers to, you can begin to incorporate ways to answer those questions. As you validate empirically which metrics best answer the questions associated with the high-level goal (and how well you meet it), you can hone what you collect before the solution is even fully live.

Unfortunately, from our point of view, it is challenging to give specific advice about which metrics will be most valuable to you for a given set of circumstances. Much will depend on your goals and the implementation you select to reach those goals. But we should note that it is only when the implementation starts to become operational that you will know with certainty what questions are most relevant to you. And, if your environment is like 95% of others, chances are you are collecting much of that information already and just need to filter what you've already collected to answer those important questions.

Put another way, what you want to do at this stage is stay alert to questions; that is, as portions of the solutions you're implementing become operational, you will want to pay attention to what those questions are so that you can create strategies to answer them.

With that in mind, we've tried to spell out a few strategies that you can use to collect meaningful metrics as you go into the implementation phase.

Selecting strategic metrics

To begin, the most important thing you can do is ensure you take a metrics-eye view of the original goals. These are the "*strategic*" metrics that bear directly on the ultimate point and rationale for what you were trying to do with your solution at a high level. You might also call these "*goal metrics*" in that they relate back to the design goal of the entire solution. However, this term is a little confusing because it can imply metrics that speak to other goals above and beyond security goals (that is, business goals), which is why we've used the term "*strategic*" here.

To collect these, it is extremely important that you select metrics that inform the original purpose of why you began a security design effort in the first place. It might go without saying, but one way to do this is to go back to the ADD to ensure that you understand exactly what the original purpose was. Even if you think you understand it well, it's useful to revisit the ADD anyway. Why? Because at this point in the implementation, we can be so close to designing the solution that we lose sight of what was important when we started; that is, the high-level goal that caused us to go down the road we did in the first place. Going back to the original goal (and revisiting how it was derived) can be a useful refresher to help us combat this.

The next thing you will want to do is look for what information you can collect from the solution you envisioned that can help you answer those goal-related questions. You'll want to examine this through every lens that was important to the original goal. To illustrate this, let's consider two examples: one from an enterprise scope and one from an application scope.

Example 1 – privileged access management

For the first example, say that you were implementing a privileged identity management system to help reduce the risk associated with privileged accounts. If you're not familiar with the term, **privileged identity management** (**PIM**) refers to a category of tools that are designed to monitor or "gate" access to the use of privileged credentials, such as the "root" account in UNIX/Linux, administrator-level credentials in a Windows environment, and/or application-specific administrative credentials for the cloud and other important services.

In this example, you ultimately want to find the information that you can collect (ideally in an easy manner) from the solution you deploy that informs you of how well you are achieving your security goal in using the tool. To do that, you will want to know how well the solution succeeds at controlling the original risk area that you identified. Note that there are a few dimensions to this. In this case, you want to get information about the underlying risk "surface area," the control implementation and how effectively it succeeds at reducing that risk, the operational elements of the control (that might impact it operationally), and so on. There are any number of potential data points to collect here. Therefore, you will want to see what information you can collect – or that you already have available to you – that helps answer these questions. If you deployed a product as in this example, you might look to see what information the product provides. You might draw on metrics from other areas, such as number of logins or number of incidents associated with privileged credential use over time (to name just a couple of examples). Say, for example, you decide to collect and track the number of privileged accounts that are allowed access to the PAM versus the number denied per month per device as a starting point, based on what you need to measure success and what you think might inform your operational posture.

You'll notice that we've constrained the previous example in two ways: we've limited it by time (access attempts per month) and by machine (access attempts per machine). The first constraint (time) allows us to track improvements over time; by using a defined time period, we can see whether the number is increasing or decreasing. This gives us trending information that helps us track performance from time period to time period. But we also have an issue whereby the total population (in this case, of machines) can introduce changes in the observable metric that aren't relevant to the question that we're trying to answer. For example, if in one month we see a "spike" in successful access attempts, this is a lot less meaningful if I tell you that, over the same time period, a thousand new machines were introduced into the environment that weren't there before. By constraining the data in this way, we normalize both for time (by using time as an axis) and for population (by normalizing the rate per machine instead of a population of undefined size).

The aforementioned approach might be a reasonable starting point, but note that there are other things that we could track here depending on the specific goal(s) we have. For example, if we're an SSH-heavy shop and the solution we're deploying is designed to reduce SSH key *sprawl* within the environment, we might need to set up new measuring instrumentation specifically for gathering the information we want about proliferation and usage of SSH keys. In this example, we might write scripts to crawl through and flag any authorized keys on the filesystems of devices in scope, we might make SSHD configuration changes to limit what keys can get access, and so on. The specific telemetry we gather is tied together both to the goal and to the specifics of the implementation strategy we've selected.

This is getting better, but we're still not done yet. Say that we also identified that economic factors – and by extension, administrator efficiency – were part of the original goal. This means that to answer the original question, we'd also need to measure how much staff time is impacted by the solution's use. This is much harder to measure. Here, we'd have to define some way – an administrator survey, a timekeeping system, ticket resolution information, or another approach – to measure how much staff are impacted by the solution. This will likely be organization-specific (tying as it does into how the organization calculates the efficiency and economics of how staff time is employed), but is nevertheless important.

Example 2 – database encryption

For the second example, this time drawing from the application space, let's say that we identified a need to protect user data in a software package our firm is authoring. To help meet this requirement, we might have selected an implementation strategy for encrypting data within a database that the application uses to store application information, as well as encrypting communications between the application server and other devices (for example, the database server and user connections) to ensure that connections protect data in transit between these devices.

Once again, we will want to identify the specific metrics that support the purpose of the design in the first place. In this case, we are a bit hampered in our ability to do this in two ways. First, this is a new capability, which means we don't really have anything to compare it to in order to evaluate how well our strategy performs. Second, operationally, the information we have might be limited – in particular, information about the data in the database itself. In fact, we've picked this example deliberately because it is a challenging one. In such a case, it can often be helpful to build instrumentation of several related data points that help paint a broader picture.

The goal of *data protection* is one that has potentially major consequences if it's not performed. We might measure the number of application accesses (connections) that involve data from users, as well as the volume of database requests per unit of time. This is a useful starting point, but doesn't really tell us the risk reduction benefit. By collecting this, we know (in aggregate) the number of times that information would have been sent without protections had we done nothing. This provides one view into the control operation: the number of times the security measure was invoked relative to a baseline control (note that I mean "control" here in an empirical testing way – i.e., in the sense of a baseline, expected-output variable). Note that this example is subject to the implementation we select. In a full data encryption (i.e., **TDE** or **transparent data encryption**) model, the set of encrypted data access/connections would include any and all data access, while a narrower approach (e.g., encryption of only particular columns) would mean some data access/connections are encrypted while others are not.

This on its own is an imperfect measurement. It is perhaps useful for making the case to management or an auditor that we have taken action to protect the data – and in some cases, it might even provide information to help quantify that – but you'll notice that by itself it doesn't answer the original question (i.e., the effectiveness of the control and/or the risk reduced by it). It lends some perspective on that for sure, but on its own, it is not a complete answer.

This means we need to look elsewhere to supplement our understanding. We might supplement our understanding with information about the encryption of data in transit. Since the individual agents connecting to the database may vary in terms of the encryption methods (cipher suites) they support, we might choose to track the frequency of cipher suite negotiation with client browsers – that is, what protocols and ciphers are negotiated within a given time period. This tells us something about the degree of protection (of the transport layer connection specifically) as we can compare the relative strength and effectiveness of those connections compared to a baseline. Once again, this tells us something. Once again, it is not enough on its own to answer the original question.

We might still further supplement our view. For example, if we are applying encryption selectively (e.g., column-level encryption), we might utilize a DLP tool, regular expression processor, or similar search mechanism to iterate over data looking for unencrypted data elements. To illustrate why this might be useful, consider the situation where we have columns that are encrypted and those that are not in the same database. Perhaps we have columns that we know contain sensitive information (national identifiers, driver's license numbers, social security numbers, etc.) and we also have columns that can contain freeform, arbitrary text submitted by a user. In that case, if a user were to enter a social security number or other sensitive data into the freeform text field, this could put data at risk in unexpected ways. Therefore, we might periodically use a regular expression or similar method to search for unencrypted data elements and, when they are discovered, flag them for remediation (e.g., deletion).

Once again, this is a control with a performance we can measure, and that tells us something about the overall, high-level risk and exposure, but that does not (on its own) fully answer the question we originally had. There are, in fact, situations where nothing you can instrument will cleanly and directly answer the original question. In cases such as these, you must do the best you can. If you can't get to a full accounting using one metric, you might potentially implement several together that give you a fuller view (that, again, may still be incomplete).

Selecting operational metrics

Of course, there are other metrics that you may wish to collect that don't relate directly or indirectly to the original goal proposition, but that are nevertheless useful to you as you seek to optimize the performance of the solution that you're deploying. These are operationally important to the solution but aren't directly tied to the original goal.

It's a little hard for us to give you specific guidance about what to collect here because the specific data that you will be interested in will conform to exactly what the solution is for, how it's implemented, the processes that support it, and other factors unique to you. That being said, some items that you might want to account for include the following:

- Economics/cost
- Performance/throughput
- Accuracy
- Staff overhead
- Customer/staff impact
- Volume

Note that this is only a subset of the possible items that might be germane. The specific details of what you will collect relate to information about the solution as a discrete, contained entity. Just like you would collect data from any other solution or application that you field to help you optimize its use over time, do so here.

Summary

Throughout this chapter, we've progressed from high-level design goals to implementation strategies that address those goals. We've incorporated technical solution elements back into our architecture definition, and we've begun the process of building a framework to establish a *virtuous cycle*; that is, a feedback loop that will help us optimize and refine our efforts over time.

In the next chapter, we will build on this and discuss how to react in real time to events that arise, how to take note of and slot improvements based on information that you collect, and how to *future-proof* the work that you do to ensure that it stays relevant and useful over time.

Execution – Future-Proofing

In the last chapter, we went through the planning and execution of your security implementation strategies – that is, establishing what they are and laying the groundwork for putting the plans into practice. In doing so, we made a subtle but very important presupposition: namely, that things would go according to plan. Of course, in the real world, this will very seldom be the case. More likely, something will go wrong somewhere along the journey from the inception to the realization of the best-laid plans.

This chapter, then, is all about planning for the unexpected – both for unexpected events arising during the execution portion of the design implementation and situations that might arise in the future so that designs stay current over time. There are several strategies that you can use to make sure that your design goals remain achievable when these situations occur. We'll walk through several different types of events that can potentially impact your planning, how to avoid them in the first place, and (when you can't) what you can do to respond and recover from them.

The topics that we will cover in this chapter are as follows:

- Overcoming obstacles in project execution
- Future-proofing our designs

> **Note**
>
> Note that there are almost certain to be situations that will impact your planning that we won't cover explicitly here. For example, problems (or even just natural changes in business context) can come about based on your organization, industry, geographic location, culture, organization type (for example, governmental versus non-profit versus commercial enterprise), staff, or as a result of numerous other scenarios unique to you and your business. At a micro enough level, there is potentially a near-infinite array of things that can go wrong or that could change. However, by going through types of issues that can arise at a high level, our hope is that you can use the approaches for the high-level issue type and apply them to your particular set of circumstances. With that in mind, let's walk through these issues and explore what they are, how they arise, and what you can do about them.

Overcoming obstacles in project execution

> *"Extra complexity is often a mistake. People will sometimes gravitate to a 'safe' approach where they are implementing some control or security technology because everyone else is doing it – or in some cases because it's what they've seen before or done in the past. The trap in doing this is this doesn't require them to ask the bigger, harder, tougher questions. For example, just because something hasn't happened, that doesn't mean it won't happen in the future. Security architects need to answer the question of how controls they put in place add value – this requires change in attitude and approach."*

> *– Phoram Mehta, Director & Head of Infosec APAC, PayPal*

It's a truism of project management that unexpected events can bring about delays, budgetary shortfalls, resourcing challenges, and other unwanted outcomes. More rarely (though perhaps less rarely than we'd like), unexpected events can even put the completion of the project itself in jeopardy. If you've spent any time in a professional workplace, you will be used to these risks. In a security context, though, unexpected events can have an even broader impact than just deviations to the project schedule and budget. In fact, even complete failure to achieve the result isn't always the worst possible outcome. Rather, bringing about new risks to the organization or opening up attack pathways that make the organization subject to attacker activity are much less desirable outcomes than even the abject failure of the project.

For example, consider a situation where a failure – perhaps an unexpected event during execution, a change to underlying security controls, or new vulnerabilities – causes the security of the organization to be negatively impacted. This means that we, as drivers and champions of the implementation effort, need to be alert to these unexpected events, project failures, or other eventualities. We need to be prepared to respond to them when they happen and to make sure that the organization stays protected even when they do. Don't kid yourself: these situations will arise – and when they do, we need to be able to plan alternative strategies to reach our intended security goals.

Throughout the course of this section, we will go through some of the various challenges that can occur as you execute your plans. These obstacles can arise in any phase of project execution, and there are numerous and varied root causes of them. Some will just require us to address them at the point in time when we become aware of them; others may require us to go back to the drawing board and work through prior steps. We'll go through several different types of obstacles and discuss strategies for resolving them.

Scope and requirements

> *"Requirements should be a forward-thinking, collaborative discussion with stakeholders rather than a 'checklist.' Work with stakeholders to understand their needs and priorities and use this information to jointly discuss security requirements."*

> *– Dr. Richard Perez, vCISO*

First up are issues that relate to failures early in the design process. Generally, these fall into one of two categories:

- Scope failures
- Requirements

We'll go through both different types of issues, but you'll notice that the redress mechanisms for both are similar, which is why we're covering them both together in this section.

Scope failures

> *"The scope of any security activity is defined by the business, coming back to what the business is trying to do. It is further defined by the components and avenues for attack. Setting scope is an exercise in understanding what you're trying to build: your requirements, who are you trying to serve, and what it is that you absolutely have to do in the basic compliance requirements."*
>
> *– Phoram Mehta, Director and Head of Infosec APAC, PayPal*

First up is **scope**. Issues can and will arise that relate to how your design is scoped. These are often the most serious issues that you may encounter when it comes to barriers to executing your design. They are serious because, often, you will be faced with a choice of either allowing the design to run through implementation with the problem still there or to pull back and iterate through portions of the design process that you've completed already, thereby using resources such as time and budget in a suboptimal way.

You'll notice that early on in this book, we spent quite a bit of time talking about scope; in fact, if you recall the details of those chapters, you'll remember that we defined an initial scope, validated it, worked with stakeholders to craft our actual scope, and then refined and validated that. So, we've had at least two "bites of the apple" in terms of defining our overall architectural scope. There's a solid practical reason why we did it this way: scope is really, really important. And when you get it wrong, it can be very impactful on the execution process.

By the time we get to the execution of a given implementation strategy, it's important to recognize that we actually have multiple different implicit scope areas. Literally everything we do has a scope: the documentation we produce has a scope, discussions with stakeholders have a scope, reporting has a scope, interactions with executives have a scope, and so on. Ideally, we want to make sure that our architecture aligns with these smaller "sub-scopes." In cases where they don't align perfectly, we want to at least ensure that they are compatible. This is because when the scope becomes misaligned between those different areas, it can lead to issues. Or, in some cases, we might have just misjudged the scope early on and not had appropriate or sufficient feedback from stakeholders to be able to catch and resolve the scoping issue. Either too large or too small a scope is problematic to execution when it occurs. A larger architectural scope means there are areas where we don't have appropriate buy-in (leading to potential project delays or even project failure when stakeholders are antagonistic to what we're trying to do.) By contrast, if the scope is too narrow, we can create a situation where we cannot reach the target state effectively or where critical success targets are not achieved (which, in the case of security architecture, usually means risk to the organization).

There are two elements to scoping that are most likely to bring about an execution failure. First, there is the scope of the architecture domain itself – that is, the scope that we employed in the analysis portion and used as part of the prework that led up to the development of our implementation strategy. This is a failure of the fundamental scope upon which we completed our analysis and upon which the implementation of our security design was ultimately based. This represents a systemic failure to define scope appropriately from the beginning of the analysis and design. Scope failure at this level, while less likely if you've put in the time that we recommended for setting scope at the beginning, is the most significant and most impactful to us.

Second, there is the scope of the implementation that can potentially be at issue. This means the scope of the implementation strategies that we developed to meet the requirements (security and otherwise) that we want to achieve. In this case, we set the overall scope appropriately, but there is nevertheless a scoping issue in a document, in a conversation we had, in reporting, in metrics, or in some other supporting elements of the overall design. This is an example of **scope misalignment**, meaning we had the scope set appropriately somewhere in the process (either early or late) but set it wrong somewhere else. In this case, so long as we notice the misalignment, the obstacle can usually be recovered from with some effort.

If (or when) either of these situations arises, it's important that we remember first not to panic. Instead, recognize that scoping issues can be a natural and normal situation that we will need to respond to. From time to time, despite our best intentions, this can happen. When it does, we'll need to take active measures to understand and recover from those misalignments.

Note that by saying that "these things happen", we're not at all suggesting you be *cavalier*. Obviously, we always endeavor to take scoping seriously and do our best to avoid scoping failures where and when we can, and we encourage you to do the same. Instead, what we're saying here is that sometimes, despite our best efforts, we get something wrong about scope, and catching the scoping issue (regardless of whether we catch it earlier or later) is actually a good outcome. It's a "win" because catching it (no matter when in the process we do) means that we have an opportunity to address it. Despite what you might initially think, the "worst-case scenario" really isn't that you get the scope wrong somewhere. Instead, it's that a misaligned scope is allowed to persist into later execution phases or, worse yet, all the way through to delivery. In the former case, it can derail budgets and delivery dates, while the latter case can lead to the introduction of new risks into the environment (in many cases, making the overall organization's security posture worse rather than better).

There are numerous reasons why scope misalignment can happen. Perhaps we neglected to include an important business process because we didn't know about it. Perhaps we failed to respect an important organizational or political boundary. Perhaps we failed to take into account some critical factor that was unknown to us (and that wasn't picked up on by the stakeholders we engaged with). Perhaps we made assumptions that turned out later not to be true. Each of these things has happened to us and will almost assuredly happen to you as well. But even if we get everything right, there can still be misalignment brought about by elements outside our control – for example, changes in priorities among us or stakeholders, changes in the organization or management direction, changes in technology, or changes in business context. Any number of these (and dozens or hundreds more not listed) can cause scope misalignment.

Regardless of why it happened, a misunderstanding or mistaken assumption about scope means that we will need to address the issue, either by making adjustments during the execution phase or, where that isn't practical, iterating back through the design steps with the new scope in mind. By making adjustments during the execution phase, we mean attempting to reset or adjust the scope without entirely derailing the process. While difficult, this is sometimes possible. We will explain this in more detail when we talk about remediation of this type of issue. By "iterating through design steps," we mean temporarily pulling back on execution while we rework previous phases of the design process. While this might sound at first like an unnecessary hassle, it is actually less impactful than you might think; it's certainly less impactful than trying to move forward in the execution with a scope that is flawed or misaligned.

The second situation to keep in mind where we can face challenges is with the expansion of scope during the execution process itself – that is, **scope creep**. This means the scope expands during the analysis, design, or execution process. Scope creep is very common. In fact, controlling scope creep is another of the reasons why we were so careful about setting scope initially and also one of the key reasons why we documented scope so early in the process. Documenting the scope can help to ensure that a clear record of scope decisions is retained, meaning that if it changes, we have a higher chance of detecting that change and knowing that scope creep is happening.

The problem of scope creep is probably obvious. If we are in the throes of implementing a solution and the scope expands, this probably means that we are addressing areas outside of what informed our analysis. As an analogy, say that I wanted to build a sprinkler system to water my home garden. To do this, I might plan out the coverage area, investing time to measure the amount of coverage required, checking (and re-checking) the sprinkler placement to ensure that it covers the entire garden plot, planning water consumption requirements to make sure that the water supply (for example, a well) can handle the volume, and so forth. I might arrange plants in a certain way to ensure that each individual plant receives the right amount of water (neither too much nor too little). If, during the process of installing the irrigation system, my neighbor asks whether the irrigation could water their garden too and I say "Yes", this is scope creep.

There are a few problems that result from this:

- **Budget**: Even if I wanted to help by extending the system, it's not included in the budget, so additional materials such as piping and sprinkler heads would need to be ordered. This means unaccounted-for expenses that impact and expand the execution budget.

- **Resources**: The labor allotted to installing the system would be out of line with what's required to cover the new scope. Likewise, additional water would be required for operation and additional maintenance would be required to keep the solution operational. This means that we may not have sufficient resources to accomplish what we want or, worse yet, that we put something in place that cannot address the needs of what we intended due to the expanded resource consumption.

- **Optimization**: During the planning phase, you'll notice that careful planning went into ensuring the irrigation system meets the needs of the one single garden (not including the neighbor's). None of that planning was performed for the neighbor's needs. The neighbor might very well wind up with a solution that is suboptimal for their needs because the planning elements of the process didn't cover the additional usage.

In the context of our security planning, this expansion of scope has a similar effect. When we expand a solution beyond the scope of what was originally intended, we're basically skipping the analysis of much of the area that the solution needs to cover. This is obviously undesirable since we have spent so much time and energy doing a thorough analysis for the rest.

In fact, even scope contraction can be problematic when it happens. By this, we mean that the scope of an implementation effort is adjusted down from what was originally analyzed in the earlier phases of the design process. In general, this is a less common occurrence than its inverse (that is, scope creep), but it can and does happen. This too leads to suboptimal results and lost efficiency, specifically because the scope of the implementation strategy to meet the goals is less than the full set of goals that were analyzed. This creates a disconnect between what the organization and its stakeholders need and what is actually put in place. Put another way, the full scope of the analysis was completed as a way to design a solution to stakeholders' original requirements. When we adjust the scope of the implementation down afterward, we have not fully addressed those requirements.

This leads to one of two things happening:

- Stakeholders become aware of the disconnect and thereby realize that their needs were not fully accounted for. When this happens, it erodes confidence in the security team generally and the security architect specifically. In this case, stakeholders were honest about their needs, and the security team didn't deliver. This means that, in the future, they might be less willing to prioritize security activities – an undesirable situation, but certainly an understandable one from their point of view.

- Stakeholders are not aware of the disconnect, leading to false confidence about the security of the environment. In this case, because the disconnect is not communicated clearly or effectively back to those who helped define the scope in the first place, they may understandably believe that the implementation created does fully address the security concerns and requirements that they set forth; as they are not experts on the technical side of the solution creation, they may be unable to discern that the solution does not fully address their needs. This is a dangerous situation, as they might make mistaken assumptions about security or fail to look for other strategies to mitigate issues that they believe have already been addressed.

The point is, when scope is unexpectedly changed (whether increased or decreased over the lifetime of the design) or when it is wrong in the first place, this creates a situation that is important for us to address. Sometimes, this requires a full iteration of earlier analysis phases, while sometimes it does not. Later in this section (see the discussion in the *Resolution* section later in this subsection), we will discuss some options available to you on how to address this situation when it arises.

Requirements

> *"It's important to tie together solutions with the business goals they support. Consider a typical enterprise. At the highest level, there is the enterprise. Within that enterprise, you have business units and within that, business processes. The business processes are supported by technologies, in turn supported by infrastructure. If you start at technology or infrastructure, you potentially miss all the layers above it. But if you start from the business processes and work your way down, you understand how those technologies support those processes and, by extension, the business goals."*
>
> *– John Tannahill, a Canadian management consultant specializing in information security*

The second area that is important to be aware of is failure to appropriately set and keep to **requirements**. This means situations where key requirements are missed, requirements are miscategorized (for example, critical requirements being seen as optional), or where requirements are fundamentally misunderstood.

The first and perhaps least common issue that can arise in this regard is that requirements are fundamentally misunderstood at some point in the design process. The undesirability of this is probably straightforward: it means that the solution developed does not necessarily address what the organization needed it to in the first place. This would be analogous to an architect in the physical world being asked to design an airport and only realizing later that what the client really needed is an art museum. Could it happen? Maybe, but it'd be unlikely since a design that so fundamentally misunderstands the purpose would likely get caught before it got very far in the design process. For example, some astute observer or stakeholder would likely point out basic issues such as a lack of locations to display artwork, the inexplicable inclusion of runways (natural for an airport but extraneous for a museum), and so forth.

The same is, of course, true in a security design. If the requirements are just flat-out wrong, ideally, stakeholders – during the multiple verification steps and near-continuous interactions with them – would bring this to the attention of the design team and/or the architect. However, it is not unknown for them to miss something or to be disengaged or disinterested enough in the process for a misunderstanding this fundamental to slip through. When that situation occurs, we will need to take active steps to resolve the missing requirements and reincorporate them back into the design.

While a complete and fundamental breakdown of requirements understanding can occur as in the preceding example, the more likely situation is much more subtle. In this case, rather than requirements being fundamentally misunderstood or missed completely, there is instead a disconnect in prioritization. This means a requirement is of higher or lower criticality than we had assumed initially. Since it is a combination of risk understanding and threat awareness that is driving prioritization, this is most likely to occur when we misunderstand one of those two areas. It can also occur when stakeholders misunderstand the relative riskiness of business processes, technical implementations, and so on.

The reason that we address requirement-related failures together with scoping-related issues is that it can sometimes be challenging to determine which of these is responsible for a particular issue. For example, if we realize late in the process that our design doesn't account for an important element, is the issue that the important element in question was excluded from the scope? Or is it that the requirement to address it was misunderstood or not included? It can be challenging to tell until, and unless, we do some digging.

Resolution

As a practical matter, regardless of how the issue arises, we need to be prepared to address it. Resolving scoping and requirement failures can be challenging. First, we need to determine whether an issue has occurred in the first place. This is actually harder to do than you'd think. In the best case, you discover that the issue is there and can recognize it for what it is. In the worst case, you don't discover the issue (or discover it long after implementation strategies are implemented), introducing risk in the process while simultaneously spending resources suboptimally. We'll go through strategies and signposts as we discuss the resolution of these types of issues that will let you know that there's a problem. That will help clue you into what kind of issue it is when it does.

Once we determine that an issue exists, we need to determine what type of issue it is and where (that is, at what phase of the design process) the issue arose. These two pieces of information together will help inform us whether we need to reiterate – that is, whether we need to go back to the risk analysis portion of the process and proceed from there or whether we can potentially recover by updating the implementation strategy alone.

We've said this before, but dealing with issues such as these is exactly why we spent as much time as we did early in the process to fully document both the scope and the requirements. There are two reasons why it's valuable. First, by spending the time and doing it thoroughly early, you reduced the likelihood of having a failure such as this happen in the first place. But there's a second practical reason for spending time on these areas. Specifically, having a detailed record of the scope and requirements means that you will know (with at least some degree of precision) what the scope and requirements were at the outset. This means knowing what the scope and requirements were when you began the analysis and design phase. You can use this to help reverse engineer where in the process the disconnect occurred; if it's systemic, you will see that these important elements were misunderstood at the earliest phases, whereas if the situation happened later in the process, you'll see that these elements were understood correctly initially and can thereby infer that the disconnect occurred subsequently.

The point is that this documentation is helpful for both avoiding the problem in the first place and also being diligent about it to help you resolve it when and if it does occur.

Next, we'll look at how to address these issues should they occur and, equally importantly, discover that they're happening in the first place.

Requirement failure resolution

Let's look first at requirement failures before looking in depth at scoping. It's advantageous to do this because requirement-level issues will almost always require us to go back and iterate (repeat) some element of the design process. Scoping-related issues are often more "recoverable" since sometimes you can retroactively understand and synthesize scope changes without going back through a full detailed analysis. This will depend on where the issue is and when/how it arose. Requirement failures, because they are so fundamental to the design, are much harder to recover from without repeating some portion of the analysis that went into the solution design.

As outlined, perhaps the most difficult challenge in addressing a requirements-level issue is recognizing that it is happening in the first place. Once you've reached the point in the design process where you are actually executing a design, it is perhaps less "natural" for you to go back to the requirements to validate that the coverage of requirements is complete. In a software development context, this is exactly the reason why **user acceptance testing** (**UAT**) exists: it makes sure that requirements are met and that they account for what the users actually need. Consider what happens with a development project if the users don't discover until weeks or potentially months after a solution is delivered that important requirements are unaddressed. Internal development teams might already be reallocated to other projects, while contractors might have already concluded their engagement. This means that, in many cases, there won't be a development team in place to address oversights if they're not caught in time.

In a security context, a direct corollary to UAT is more complicated because many security goals are less directly visible to an end user or stakeholder. Said another way, a system that performs a task insecurely might look identical (from a user's point of view) to one that does so securely. This means that testing that we've delivered things appropriately is more complex and intricate than just asking stakeholders to test what was delivered.

It is possible, then, that a situation can arise where you miss a requirement entirely and that it will be less directly visible to the end user than would be the case if a user-driven requirement were missed. This can and does happen, but it is not the most common way that requirement failures occur. Instead, it is much more likely that a situation will arise where a requirement is misinterpreted and thereby only partially (but not fully) addressed. Likewise, it could be a situation where a requirement is addressed, but in the wrong context. Lastly, there could be other reasons why a requirement didn't totally "slip off the radar" but also still isn't satisfied fully. This will be the lion's share of the requirement failures that you encounter.

The most challenging part of requirement failures is knowing that you are facing one in the first place. There are three primary ways that you will notice it:

- Risk tracking
- Metrics
- Operations

Recognizing requirement failures – risk tracking

The first item, risk tracking, refers to a situation where you are tracking the organizational risk profile and, since the security requirements that define our architecture ultimately stem from risk management (remember that their ultimate purpose is to mitigate risk), the information we collect about risk, therefore, informs whether or not those requirements are satisfied.

This can happen in at least two different possible ways. First, since a well-founded security program will likely be conducting risk management activities anyway (regardless of the security architecture process), a risk issue may be flagged in the course of routine risk examination and analysis. In other words, information collected about risk (for example, assessments of the environment where a given requirement is applicable) may provide indications to us about an unaddressed or partially addressed requirement. Second, it can result from ongoing risk information, data collection, and analysis gathered pursuant to the architecture implementation, meaning mechanisms built into the design that allow us to realize that we aren't addressing the risks that we thought we would as we roll out an implementation.

In both cases, note that this implies that it's perhaps somewhat easier to identify requirement failures over a longer implementation cycle. In the first case, there is more time for someone external to the architecture to capture and notify us about the risk areas. For example, perhaps your organization performs an annual risk assessment activity, or perhaps there's a risk register that's kept updated on a monthly or quarterly basis. In the second case, we're more likely to track risk over time for a longer, more complicated deployment versus a short, relatively simple one.

Recognizing requirement failures – metrics

The second way to gain information about requirement failures is through metrics. It is in this arena that the high-level metrics we established in the early design phases really shine. Recall that, in the last section, as well as early on in the requirement gathering portions of the effort, we discussed strategies for metrics that answer the question of how well you meet the original purpose and security goals that necessitated an architecture effort in the first place. We talked about metrics twice: first, we tied specific metrics to security requirements – that is, ways to evaluate that you are meeting the overall goal (economics goals, risk reduction goals, compliance goals, and so on). These are the metrics that let you know whether or not you are achieving the original goal. Subsequently, we discussed operational metrics associated with the implementation itself.

The first set – those that address whether you are fulfilling the original purpose, requirements, and goals – are the most relevant for determining whether a requirements issue is in play. Why? Because they're the exact instrumentation we put in place for telling us whether or not requirements are being hit. If they are not, the whole purpose of those metrics is to inform us. If we have missed something at the requirement level, the metrics will highlight this. In the most extreme (and unlikely) case, they can tip us off to the fact that we've missed a requirement entirely. In the more likely case, our failure to fully satisfy a requirement will be pointed to if we review these metrics critically.

In the previous chapter, we created metrics for the implementation itself. These can play a role as well in ensuring that requirements are being met, and in many cases, can supplement higher level-metrics in a way that informs us about requirement failures. Consider two examples: one from the application world and one from a more enterprise-focused perspective.

For the first example, say that you are building a software application and you have outlined a goal of controlling defects (that is, software bugs that could lead to security vulnerabilities) within the final production output. To support this, perhaps you employ an implementation strategy that involves several elements: dynamic software testing (for example, as part of the release process), developer education/awareness, manual code review, and application-focused penetration testing. In the course of establishing these, you perhaps defined operational metrics such as information about how many defects per thousand lines of code (sourced, for example, from dynamic testing) and information about developer education coverage (for example, attendance records as a percentage of the total developer population).

By putting these two values together, you can derive objective feedback about how well the high-level requirement is being met. Because these metrics are specific to the implementation (they presuppose how we address the problem), they are unlikely to be reflected in the high-level metrics we defined at the outset. But yet, they directly inform whether or not the implementation is appropriately scoped. They don't directly provide data about defects per thousand lines of code, but they do provide information about how well and how thoroughly the mechanisms we put in place to hit that original goal are functioning.

We can build upon this to make it even better. For example, one of the limitations of the preceding is that the defect metric (defects per thousand lines of code) doesn't account for the severity of issues, which can be quite germane. Perhaps, for example, training reduces the criticality/severity of vulnerabilities, even though the defect rate remains more or less constant. This would be unaccounted for in the example metrics. To improve, we might factor in criticality into our analysis so that this conclusion isn't lost in the final analysis.

For the second example, consider that you have a requirement to support secure configuration management for production virtual environments. In this example, perhaps you employ hypervisor-focused tools along with asset-management tools for inventorying, group policy, and configuration management. You might have established operational metrics about the performance of each of these tools. For example, you might collect data on the scope of inventory coverage (as a percentage of all virtual images) and the degree of configuration drift from an established baseline (as reported by configuration management). Each of these feeds back into an understanding of how well you are meeting the original requirement (though indirectly).

In both of these examples, you'll notice two things.

First, they are focused on testing security parameters, specifically those that tie back to the original requirements by virtue of having been established to accomplish the original risk management goal. This will very often be the case since the whole purpose of the security design is to address risk, ensure appropriate resiliency, and enable appropriate security posture. It bears saying, though, that if you had other, non-security or risk-reduction goals at the outset as part of the requirements, you'd want to test those too.

Second, the operational metrics provide relevant information that ties back to the original requirements. Even though it would have been challenging for us to determine these ahead of time since they depend on the specifics of the implementation, they support those original requirements and provide data back about the degree to which they are met or unmet. Metrics such as these are some of the most valuable when it comes to finding requirements issues. Why? Because they tie together the goals with the implementation – they test that the implementation as built supports the requirements originally envisioned.

Now, you're likely thinking – and you'd be right – that by the time we are collecting operational metrics, we might be fairly far down the road with our implementation. This is true. It can be somewhat late in the process that our metrics tip us off on requirement-level issues. Being apprised (even if late in the game) is better than not being apprised, so this is still a win.

Remember earlier that we had said this kind of information is analogous to the function that UAT plays in the development of a software application. The function of UAT is to make sure that the application as it has been developed meets what the users need it to do. Is it possible that a developed application could go through development and get to UAT only for users to realize that some fundamental requirement was missed or that a requirement was misunderstood? Absolutely. Anyone who has ever been involved in application development knows that this can happen. While not exactly a cause for celebration, it's nevertheless worth having UAT built into the process since discovery of an issue such as this (even when it happens late in the process) is better than not discovering it at all.

Recognizing requirement failures – operations

The last way that we can become apprised of a requirement issue is via the operationalization of an implementation. This means that as we deploy it, we realize that the solution doesn't perform exactly the way we anticipated, such that some portion of the requirements are unmet or not satisfied completely. For example, say our implementation is supported by a particular product and that product doesn't provide the features we thought it did (or, perhaps more likely, those features don't perform as well as we thought they would). This is a much more "organic" method to discover the issue – it also requires that the people involved in the deployment know what to look for and apprise us. This is not always the case.

Regardless of how we discover it, we will need to address these requirement failures. Ultimately, we will need to decide whether we need to do another iteration of the design process or whether we can recover without doing so. Consider two examples to illustrate the difference.

In the first example, say that we have a requirement to support network security monitoring for a given environment, say an infrastructure as a service provider, and a set of applications in that environment. Perhaps one of the driving reasons for that requirement is that we need to maintain PCI DSS compliance. In planning out the implementation, perhaps we reviewed the default logging capability provided by the cloud service provider and concluded that this capability meets the requirements under PCI–that is, it satisfies the collection and storage requirements as well as the requirements for what specific information needs to be collected. So far, so good. Given this example, say that we discover that some critical piece of information—something required under the DSS—is left out of that default logging capability. Maybe we misunderstood how the logging worked until we actually saw it in practice, or perhaps there was a change in the cloud services provider logging facility where they no longer capture the information we need.

In this case, the unaddressed requirement is very specific and narrow in scope. The design is copacetic—that is, it addresses the requirements—in every respect other than with regard to this one particular missing data item from the logs. From a compliance perspective, we could, of course, seek alternative strategies in the short term, such as a compensating control to address the issue. However, in the long term, we will likely want to update that design to address the gap. In this case, because it's an issue with the specific implementation and because the requirement itself is well understood, we can choose to either iterate again over the entirety of the design process (that is, go back to the phase in the design process where we addressed the requirements in the first place and work forward) or, if time and/or resources usage is a factor, we might selectively alter the implementation to address just the one missing piece. In so doing, we leave the majority of the implementation, requirements, goals, architectural principles, and other foundational decisions intact. In short, we amend the implementation during or after the execution to address the missing piece.

But consider a more extensive example. In this second example, we will assume that we're working at application scope and that we've designed a billing application to support online payments. In this case, to keep the examples parallel, perhaps we missed a requirement entirely. Perhaps somehow we didn't realize that PCI DSS was in scope for the application during the design phase and only realized later in the process that it actually is. This could arise if we assumed that the billing application would not store, process, or transmit payment card information and would be logically separated from those system components that do (note that this is definitional for the scope of compliance under the PCI DSS standard), and it was only realized during the execution phase that our assumptions were invalid. In this case, while application logging for security purposes might be a known requirement of the application, the broader specifics of what that logging should entail would have been missed entirely.

In a case such as this second example, it is much harder to merely alter the implementation to address the oversight. In this case, the requirements are so foundational to the security model of the application that merely attempting to layer on the new requirements isn't realistic. Instead, we would need to address the overlooked requirement more systemically. In that case, our best option (impactful to the schedule though it may be) is to go back and iterate through the design process from the earliest phases—that is, from the definition of requirements and forward.

If this sounds extreme, think about what would happen in an analogous software development situation. Say, for example, that a development team had a requirement to develop a web-based mail client (for example, a webmail interface similar to Gmail). They design for this, and only when they get to UAT do they realize that they gravely misunderstood the requirements. For example, instead of a webmail system, what the users really wanted was an Android mobile application to check their corporate (Exchange) mail. Now, you're probably thinking that this is unlikely. After all, how could a disconnect such as this make it all the way to UAT without being caught? And you'd be right that this is an unlikely scenario—we're exaggerating to make the point. But unlikely though it may be, if such a situation should come to pass, how feasible do you think it would be to hit the original requirements (as intended by the users) without some major redesign work on the part of the development team? Not very, right? So, too, is it the case with security requirements.

Depending on the organization's risk tolerances, you might have some options available to you even if you do need to go back to a previous point in the design process. For example, if the risk is high enough, you might choose to do so immediately. This means rather than let the problematic design move forward, you decide to immediately go back to the point in time where the requirement was overlooked and proceed from there. Alternatively and depending on the specific situation, you might choose to allow the current implementation to proceed with a stopgap measure in place (such as a set of compensating controls) to address the risk in the short term while you begin the preliminary work of an additional redesign for future work. Again, the specific context, as well as your organization's risk tolerances, will dictate which is preferable.

The ultimate point of this is that the degree to which a requirement is misaddressed and the organization itself (that is, its risk tolerance, the threat landscape, the purpose of the assets in scope, and so on) will dictate the response.

Scoping failure resolution

Scoping failures can be addressed similarly to requirement failures. This means the mechanisms that we have for dealing with them are very similar. The key difference lies, though, in our mechanisms for determining that the issue has occurred in the first place. In the case of scope failures, ideally, one of two things will happen: 1) either stakeholders and subject matter or domain experts inform us of scope misalignment (as it can often be more obvious to them than to us given topics they are highly knowledgeable about), or 2) in the course of creating documentation and supporting execution plans, we become aware of scope misalignment. Barring those two things, our primary mechanisms for determining that a scoping failure has occurred include three other key mechanisms:

- Project management feedback and/or inability to realize implementation
- Organizational friction
- Operational gaps

The first clue we will have that our scope is awry will come from there being some logistical issue that prevents us from executing the implementation strategy as we've defined it. Generally, this occurs when the scope of the design is overly broad – for example, when it extends over an organizational boundary or beyond the workable limits of a solution domain. In this case, because our scope is broad enough to extend to an area that we can't influence (or can't easily do so), we are literally unable to put the implementation in place. This should tip us off that there is something wrong with the scope as we've defined it. In a best-case scenario, this will be flagged by project management prior to beginning the execution of the implementation phase. Only sometimes will this be true, however. In some cases, we may actually begin the execution only to realize later that some portion of the implementation strategy is impracticable due to scoping issues. In a situation where the scope is overly broad, it extends beyond the context within which we can bring about change and thereby becomes a very solid clue that something is amiss with the scope.

The second way that we can determine that the scope is inappropriate is through organizational friction. This is when we come up against a group that doesn't want to or won't help bring about the solution we've identified. In an ideal case, we will have involved stakeholders from the earliest phases, in which case those stakeholders will know (at least at a high level) what we are trying to do. It's possible though, that, for various reasons, we did not engage with those stakeholders early enough in the process and we only discover during execution that they are instrumental in effecting or championing the solution.

Now, you'll note that this is similar in many respects to the first mechanism we highlighted (inability to implement) as a way to inform us of scope issues. The biggest difference lies in the fact that the implementation isn't halted entirely, but rather becomes a source of friction or disagreement with other areas of the organization. In other words, while there may be a willingness on the part of other organizations to work with us toward putting in place the solution implementation, there is still hostility, incompatibility, or other tension introduced due to the solution's overly broad scope. If the scope is defined too broadly, it can bump into other areas of the organization and thereby bring about friction with teams operating in those areas. Note that not all organization friction is a result of scoping issues, but when you see friction that is a result of a design extending too far—or not far enough—it is a useful clue that scope could be at issue.

It bears saying that sometimes organizational friction brought about by a misaligned scope may seem preferable at first glance to a complete cessation of our ability to execute (i.e., the first warning sign we pointed to), but it can actually be much more subtle and insidious. Specifically, this is because we may not realize that our scope is overly broad until much later down the road. For example, we might only find out that we have traversed a relevant boundary when it comes time to put operational processes into place and we find that the relevant operations staff are unable or unwilling to support the solution.

The last tell relates to the inverse of the preceding two situations, both of which are typically indicative of an overly broad scope. This last one is more indicative of an overly narrow scope. Where scope is too narrowly defined, we may see gaps instead of an inability to execute. These gaps can manifest in one of two ways. Either the scope of the implementation is reduced from that used to do the solution analysis or the scope of the analysis itself was too narrow to address the requirements. Both are problematic. The symptom that we will most likely see when this is the case is one of two things. We might see gaps as we execute or we might see areas where critical security requirements go unmet.

For example, we might see places where important security goals are not being met and there is no strategy for them to be met. For example, consider a suite of related applications in a given environment, say an application built using a microservices design pattern. Perhaps you have architected a solution whereby all the services supporting that application employ a centralized state maintenance mechanism to ensure that only authenticated users can employ the application. As you execute, you discover that one critical service has been left out of the design. In this example, the scope of the implementation is too narrow; it leaves out a critical element of what is otherwise a holistic and unified system. In this situation, it is likely that the scope you set was too narrow.

Now, we should note again that it can be difficult to tell whether the underlying issue is a scoping problem or a requirement problem. Both are potentially grave, but it is advantageous to unpack which specifically is occurring because the manner in which you address it can vary depending on which type of problem it is.

Specifically, for a scoping issue, it is useful to first know the vector of the issue—that is, the direction in which the scope is misaligned. Is the scope too broad? Or is it too narrow? The second thing you will need to know is when in the design process the scope became misaligned. Was it wrong from the beginning? Or did it shift somewhere along the implementation path?

In a situation where the scope is wrong from the beginning, there can often be little recourse but to iterate. This means going back through earlier phases of the design process and adjusting each phase to the new, modified, and appropriate scope. Much like the example we used earlier of the software development team that fundamentally misunderstood their requirements, it is very difficult for us to recover without putting in the design legwork that we missed earlier in the process. In situations where the scope changed mid-stream (for example, if the scope of the implementation is too narrow while the original analysis was appropriate), you may need only revert to the prior phase where the contraction or expansion of scope occurred.

Likewise, it is actually easier to address an overly broad scope than it is to address an overly narrow one. A too-broad scope essentially means that you've done more analysis than you needed to. Perhaps you considered portions of the environment that are beyond your ability to change. In some cases, this will mean that you've introduced elements into your solution that are unnecessary or that satisfy requirements that are out of what the scope should be. In this case, it becomes a question of editing your work to meet the actual scope. Now, it probably goes without saying that the analysis and thought you've put into these broader areas of the environment can still be productively used at a future time and, therefore, are useful to retain.

By contrast, an overly narrow scope means that there are some areas that you should have addressed but didn't. If it is a matter of one or two systems or components, it might be possible (depending on the specific situation) to extend your solution to cover the missing portions. However, when multiple requirements are involved or when large portions of the environment are involved, it can sometimes be cleanest (painful though it may be) to rework the design from earlier phases to make sure that the solution you're building is the right one.

Next, we will look at another area that can be a source of concern or potential obstacles: those related to failure to obtain appropriate organizational backing for the architect's work.

Support failure and organizational issues

"I am a big fan of thinking about perspectives and lenses. The more that you can look at your current state or environment through other people's eyes, the better off you will be (as an architect or just as a human in life). Getting a 'no BS' perspective involves stepping out of your normal worldview and getting that true empathy with all the stakeholders: as a CEO, as a threat analyst, as a CIO, as the IT admin, as the CFO, as a support technician, and numerous others. This empathy should be informed by personal experience or listening to others and should be combined with technical data and metrics. The truth is most visible when you combine the subjective and objective where the subjective part is as rich in different perspectives as you can get."

– Mark Simos, Lead Cybersecurity Architect, Microsoft

The next area where we need to be alert for execution failure relates to the capability of the organization to support our designs. This can occur in one of two ways:

- Lack of management support
- Failure to achieve buy-in from key stakeholders

Both of these can be devastating when they occur. The reason is that they can completely stymie the architectural process at some point along the path to realization and bring everything to a complete halt.

To understand why this is the case is not difficult. In the first case, lack of management support, there are two possible ways that this can impact your efforts. The best case is that the point at which you fail to receive the support that you need is during the initial analysis phases before you get to actual execution. Why is this better? Because your effort will fail quickly and early on in the process. Frustrating as that may be, it's actually better than the alternative. The alternative to this is that the design gets through initial planning, through conversations and vetting by stakeholders, and through implementation planning. Only then does support evaporate.

The reason management support might evaporate partway through is that the cost and effort to execute tends to increase as you move down the deployment pathway. For example, consider that you're planning a renovation of your home. It costs you nothing to think through and imagine how you might change your home to accommodate different aesthetic goals or to change how you make use of your living space. You can solicit estimates from contractors to help you plan what you're going to do with little to no cost. But what happens when it's time to write the check to get them started doing the work? You have a significant expenditure of resources that hits you all at once. The same is true in many cases with our design plans. There are, of course, soft costs that go into staff time: time spent by the architecture team, stakeholders, and others throughout the initial phases of the project. However, the lion's share of resource expenditure (both in time and dollars) occurs once you start to execute.

It's understandable that this happens when it does. Organizations are naturally protective of their resources. In fact, recall that one of the main benefits of architecture in the first place is ensuring that organizations are using resources optimally and for the organization's maximum value. However, when support evaporates midway through the process, not only will you not be able to realize the design but you will also have wasted the time you spent planning an architectural vision that will never exist. Such an exercise in fact has negative value, as you'd have been better off doing nothing since you would not have invested the time in analyzing and building a design for something that will never happen. Said another way, you incur the entirety of the opportunity costs associated with planning but realize absolutely nothing of the value.

The second case, lack of buy-in from stakeholders, can arise when you have appropriate support from management but don't have the support and buy-in you need from other stakeholders. This is most likely to occur later in the cycle than earlier. The reason is that, while friction can arise early due to stakeholders who are unclear on the value provided by approaching cybersecurity architecture systematically—or in some cases, that fail to see the value of cybersecurity at all—such friction is relatively easily mitigated through discussions with those stakeholders, outreach, working with them to establish a sense of ownership in the process, and so on.

By contrast, when stakeholders are not included early in the process but only become aware of a design effort once that effort is already underway, it can be much more challenging to bring them into the fold. They might point out issues that, had we encountered them earlier, we might have been able to work through with them, but because they weren't included in the initial planning, there is much less flexibility to adapt to their particular needs or to account for their concerns. When the stakeholder in question is key to the effort's success—for example, if they represent an operational area critical to the success of the implementation or if they have ownership of a technical infrastructure that you need to make changes to for success to be realized—this can quite literally stall the effort mid-stream.

For both situations, recovery can be challenging. This is, in large part, why we tried so hard to make sure that you did have management support and that you were plugged into available stakeholders from early in the process. That said, should you find yourself in a situation where buy-in from one of these two groups is missing, there are some things you can do.

In the event that you suffer from a lack of management support, it is without doubt a difficult position to be in. Without management support, you might find yourself starved of resources or staff, find it hard to get commitment from stakeholders and peers, be encumbered by competing priorities, and numerous other constraints that limit your ability to be successful in realizing the design. In other words, you could come up with the most elegant design in the world, but it'll stay a design instead of a reality so long as there's no organizational will to implement it.

In the case of missing management support, there are a few strategies to try to help you (re)gain that support. The simplest and perhaps most effective strategy is through an executive champion. This means if you can win over just one person with a seat at the executive leadership table and impress them with the importance of what you're trying to do, they can help you win over the rest of the group. They can subtly reinforce the message with their executive peers, and (if need be) leverage their stored personal and political capital to help win support. In general, this is significantly easier to do before you've begun the analysis and creation of the design. However, if for some reason you find yourself later in the process and you don't have a champion, you do have some ammunition by virtue of where you are in the process that you can bring to bear on the problem.

For example, consider that at the stage of the process where you have already invested time and energy researching and crafting a solution, you have data that you would not otherwise have available to you. You have risk and threat information that supports why the organization's posture is outside accepted risk tolerances without the solution, you have information about the costs (in time and dollars) associated with putting the solution in place, and you have buy-in and support from all impacted stakeholders. In short, you should be able to create a very compelling business case solely on the basis of the information that you've collected to create your design. A solid, compelling, crisp, well-studied, and data-forward business case such as this can, when socialized appropriately with executive team members, make it almost a "no-brainer" for someone to want to help champion your efforts.

In fact, even just having a business case drafted to work from can often be useful even if you don't win over a champion right away. For any response other than a "hard pass," bear in mind that there can be room to negotiate and adapt the strategy to better align it with their goals or to overcome objections that they may have. You might, for example, need to reign in the spend of your design and alter it such that it helps to satisfy another goal (perhaps even a non-security goal) that the executive has, thereby using your design to help them solve problems they have and encouraging them to support the design. Of course, bear in mind that since the business case is reflective of the underlying design that it describes, changes and alterations made to the business case will require changes to the underlying design too. Depending on the extent of those changes, you might need to go back and reiterate through some portion of the analysis process and subsequent implementation design as well.

For stakeholders, the approach is similar. As with management support, we've tried hard to reinforce the message that avoiding altogether putting yourself in a position where you have resistant stakeholders is the most optimal path. This is for exactly the reason that a belligerent, resistant, or contrary stakeholder discovered late in the process can prove to be a major hurdle. However, we're all human, and, particularly in large organizations, it can be hard to ensure that we've found every stakeholder at the beginning of the effort.

Knowing then that this situation may arise, a useful strategy is to approach them openly and candidly about what you are trying to do and why. The interpersonal dynamics of this can be tricky because they very well could feel slighted in situations where they're being approached late in the design process. This means that approaching them from a position of being willing to explain, negotiate, and (most importantly) listen to their concerns and hear them out is much more likely to bring them around.

You should be prepared to spend your own personal or political capital if need be to accomplish this, and, as with gaining an executive champion, there may be ways that you can adapt what you're looking to do to help them solve challenges that they have. Although, as before, remember that the changes you make to accomplish this need to be folded back into the design.

You'll probably notice that these two elements—management support and stakeholder buy-in—interact with each other to a large degree. This means stakeholders are more likely to buy in when executive leadership supports what you're doing, and vice versa. Likewise, the strategies for doing both rely on the same core skill: consensus building. The greater the consensus you establish at the beginning of your efforts, the more the weight of organizational inertia will work in your favor to see it through. Therefore, anything you can do in the early stages to build that consensus is worthwhile.

Resource shortfalls

> *"There is a link between robust architecture and optimal use of resources. Having an architecture helps security programs focus on where they are investing and how they are investing. An architecture can give us a better selection of controls and a better arrangement of controls. It also lets us prioritize. There is an interplay between risk management and architecture; the union of the two lets us select the right controls and prioritize them appropriately."*
>
> *– Dan Blum, Cybersecurity Strategist, Security Architect, and author of the book Rational Cybersecurity for Business*

The next issue that can arise is resource gaps. This can happen in one of two ways. One way that it can arise is through budget overruns. For example, you've designed a solution that you think will cost x dollars to implement and you realize during the execution phase that the actual cost will be x plus some unacceptable overage. This can happen through no fault of your own, for example, in a situation where an external event or market conditions force organizations to reduce spending (budget cuts), reallocate critical staff (layoffs or reorganization), or otherwise constrain the resources necessary to complete the effort.

To overcome issues of this type, it is important to first understand what the limiting resource is that is no longer available. This is because the specific resource that is constrained will impact what strategies are open to you to resolve the situation. For example, if you have a solution that requires an external product or service to implement—for example, it requires you to purchase a software or hardware— your options for recovery are different than if staff with key skills are suddenly unavailable for your implementation efforts. Both are potentially recoverable (often without requiring a full iteration of the design process), but the strategies to recover will vary.

The easier situation (arguably) to recover from is a resource shortfall that impacts implementation alone. This is particularly true when the skills required for the implementation are still present within the organization but temporarily reallocated to something else, where their bandwidth is reduced, or where budget dollars are temporarily unavailable. In this case, the skills are still present in the organization to allow you to implement (though not necessarily to operate) the solution. This means you still have the capability to implement, even though you may need to make adjustments to the anticipated timeline for delivery. In this case, the solution is still viable as designed, the economics are relatively unchanged, and you can still execute the design; you will just need to adjust the execution timeline somewhat.

In this situation, it is valuable to revisit any documented time constraints built into the planning. This is to ensure that the delays don't create risk or leave it unaddressed. If the delay is significant, you may need to evaluate and introduce stopgap measures in the interim in situations where there would be open risk that would not be closed during the delay window.

This is less true, though, when the resources required to operate and/or maintain a solution once it's implemented are lost to the organization. For example, say the design involves deploying a Linux-based open source IDS system (Suricata, for example) and the organization lays off the entirety of the incident response team or lays off all Linux admins. Because these are the exact personnel that we had planned for to operate, administrate, and maintain the solution post-deployment, we no longer have those resources available, rendering the solution non-viable. It's a tricky proposition: if we proceed, we find ourselves with a suboptimal design because we no longer have the talent base to use it effectively. However, if we decide to redesign to accommodate the new reality, we need to adjust the implementation in ways that invalidate many of the key assumptions we made earlier in the design process.

In this situation, we might need to rework much of the design depending on what specific resources are no longer available. This is not always the case, though. For example, depending on what specific resources are unavailable, we might be able to make substitutions, realizing the same goal but shifting just the implementation of it such that the end state is operational within the capabilities and resources we have available. For example, in the case of the Linux IDS system, we might be able to deploy an appliance instead, consider a managed service, or employ other strategies that don't require the same skill base as the original design.

Note, though, that in evaluating this, there may be other impacts we will need to account for with a pivot such as this—for example, adjustment to the economics or budget of the project. In the preceding example, if we were to pivot from Suricata (an open source product) to Cisco IDS (a commercial one), we would need to factor in acquisition costs accordingly, as well as the operational approach that will be employed once the implementation is in place. If we were to pivot from an IDS to another monitoring strategy (an MSSP or other managed service, for example), there might be a very different timeline before we can have the capability operational.

As a general rule, permanent or longer-term adjustments to the budget are a little more challenging to recover from than staffing adjustments, though the dynamics are similar. Often, in the case of a budget overrun, we can petition to have additional budget made available to us to complete (or start, as the case may be) the execution. In many cases, this will be practicable provided that we have appropriate executive buy-in. This is yet another reason why it is a good idea to make sure that we have executive sponsorship and internal champions from early in the process. We will, of course, need to be prepared to provide an account of why our estimates were off in the first place. This can lead to some uncomfortable conversations, but ultimately, the execution is recoverable if additional budget can be made available.

Alternatively, there may be adjustments that we can make to the design that will bring the costs back in line with estimates—for example, perhaps by reprioritizing elements of the design, making targeted adjustments to scope, looking for efficiency gains in other areas, and so on. As with any project, sometimes smooth or efficient execution in latter phases of the process can help make up for hiccups in early ones. The same principle applies here.

It is possible, in some cases, that we need to scrap an implementation altogether depending on what resources are constrained, where, and for how long. In most cases, this is actually less problematic than it sounds. When this happens, several things are usually true. First, barring larger business-sweeping changes (such as the dissolution of a business unit or a radical shift in the underlying business), the requirements that drove you to design the solution you did will be largely unchanged. Second, the design principles are likely unchanged (again, barring large-scale "tectonic" shifts to the business itself). Third, the constraints have shifted in that now they preclude use of the resources that we thought would be available, but the other constraints (that we've meticulously identified, analyzed, and documented) are still there.

So, what this really means in practice is you'll need to find another implementation strategy, re-scope, or go back to stakeholders with data about the impact of the resource shortage on the requirement they were trying to hit. In fact, you can approach the analysis of it in exactly that order. First, look to see whether you can reiterate through the implementation design process and re-architect a solution that meets the new constraints while still addressing the requirements. In many cases, this will be possible if the resource reduction is minimal. If you cannot address the issue by re-examining the implementation, consider whether there are scope adjustments that you can make that will lead to the same result. In both cases, you will want to analyze and communicate back to stakeholders the trade-offs involved in making such a pivot. If the security goals are not met, communicate that. If they are met but at a reduced scope than what was planned originally, communicate that too.

If all else fails and there's just no way to adapt, you may need to pull back from the effort entirely. It's important to remember, though, that this is not necessarily your call to make. Recall that everything we do is in service to the business. This means that it should be the ultimate decision by the business— in our case, as personified by the executive champions and stakeholders—to objectively analyze the risks that will remain open should we be unable to effectively execute, evaluate the impacts of those risks, and ultimately decide whether or not they are tolerable. This means that, per the preceding, you will need to clearly and objectively communicate that risk back to those stakeholders so that they can make this determination in consultation with you. It is important that they understand what the risk is, why it exists, and understand the potential avenues available to close it should they choose to do so (for example, through reallocation of budget or personnel). It is also a good idea to formally and in writing obtain their directive should they choose to accept the risk on behalf of the broader business. Doing so serves two purposes: it ensures that they consider it carefully because they are taking on formal accountability for the decision, and it allows you to keep a record for future design efforts about why the risk continues to remain.

Communication failure

> *"Maintaining communication in teams is important, as an example, I was working on a large program for a client: a mission critical system that required 5 nines availability. The downtime for this system needed to be measured in minutes per year. From the architectural standpoint, we used a lot of forward-thinking approaches and tools but we never forgot the mission. The client was unfamiliar with the tools and techniques we were going to use. We trained them on the tools, developing a collegiate relationship with them in the process. Things were all going swimmingly and we had a mechanism where the whole team, including the client, could raise observations about any aspect of the project that went into a register and were subsequently reviewed and actioned. We were about 9 to 10 months in, and suddenly the rate of observations from the client started to increase dramatically. We realized that we had forgotten to maintain the strong client relationship that we had built at the beginning and we were not communicating effectively. After all of that early engagement, we had moved into a phase of going off and getting on with it. The client lost trust with us because they didn't really know what we were doing. The point of this is the importance of engagement. You need to engage—and stay engaged—all throughout the process."*
>
> *– Andy Clark, Founding Director, Primary Key Associates Ltd, Visiting Professor RHUL, Trustee of The National Museum of Computing, SABSA Coauthor*

Next are **communication failures**. The immediate effects of communication failures are—in and of themselves—less directly dangerous to the implementation than you might think. However, the secondary impacts of a communication failure can be deadly in the long run. Think about it this way: what is the logical end result of poor communication during the execution of your design? Obviously, either your team, stakeholders, or others required to make sure that everything is running according to plan are less effectively able to participate and do their part in seeing the design become a reality. But what happens next? It increases the likelihood of a host of very undesirable secondary effects.

For example, consider the following scenarios:

- If there is a lack of communication about the execution to executives, it can erode executive support

- If there's insufficient communication with stakeholders, it erodes their buy-in

- If there's ineffective communication with engineers and subject matter specialists, it prevents them from appropriately implementing the solution

- If there's poor communication with operations teams, it makes it harder to collect metrics, gather data, and prepare them for how to maintain the solution once fielded

What this means in practice is that the root cause for all the issues that we're working through in this chapter—as well as a host of other ones that might be idiopathic to your situation—can often be traced back to a root cause of communication failure. In other words, the symptom that you will observe directly is less likely the communication issue and more likely something else that can ultimately be traced back to a breakdown in communication. What this means is that it is particularly important to make an effort to ensure communications stay optimal throughout the entire process (and, in particular, during the execution phase itself) because failure to accommodate that is much more likely to bring about problems in other areas.

Fortunately, the way to remediate a communication breakdown is fairly straightforward: over-communicate. This means be as transparent as you can. For a longer effort, it is often valuable to put a communication plan together that addresses how you will communicate with key audiences such as stakeholders, technical specialists, executive team members, and other key demographics, as well as establishes a format and cadence by which that communication happens.

Also, don't forget to act as a pass-through to stakeholders and executives for information about design and execution that might come from outside the architect or architecture team. Keep in mind that stakeholders will most likely have been engaged with already by you and thus will look to you as the responsible party for delivery. As such, information about implementation status—and also information and metrics about the degree to which the requirements are satisfied (for example, information about risk offset)—may not be communicated to those stakeholders through any other channels other than by you. This means that, to provide information back to those audiences—and to ensure their ongoing support—the communication strategy should include those individuals as well.

Technical and environmental issues

> *"Common issues that can arise include network issues (failure to place systems securely on the broader network), application segmentation and design issues, and logging and monitoring capability (particularly in cloud). Very often, the root cause for these issues can be attributed to failures in the design process itself: for example, it can be easy to miss an important security element (e.g. logging) in the design of a given process or application. This is particularly true given that there may be minimal (or no) investment in security at the beginning of a project – where security is engaged, it may happen late in process. In this case, the overall design itself might be missing key security elements – finding those elements and ensuring they are addressed is where a robust architecture can play an important role."*

> *– John Kallil, Chief Information Security Officer*

The last item, a concern in pretty much any technical project, are technical and environmental issues. Specifically, we refer here to issues that can arise at a technical level that can impact your ability to execute your plan. Anyone who has ever undertaken a technology implementation of any size will likely know what we mean by this. In a network or enterprise context, it can include issues such as incompatibility between software and hardware and key systems that it needs to interface with, features in commercial products that don't integrate well or perform as expected, pre-existing issues that block successful implementation, and numerous other potential issues. In an application context, it can include integration between security-relevant components and business logic ones, API issues, bugs in the security logic or elsewhere in the application that prevent the security functionality from performing, and so on.

There is no single, unified, "one size fits all" roadmap that someone can provide to completely remove, troubleshoot, or otherwise mitigate all the technical issues you might encounter during the course of execution. To a large degree, this is because there are so many possible things that could go wrong. It's the same reason that nobody can give you a script that tells you how to address all the possible errors and anomalous situations that you might encounter in writing a piece of software, driving a car, or literally any other complex task. This means that you'll need to innovate solutions to these technical challenges as they arise in much the same way that you would for any other deployment or implementation.

In response to these issues, you may need to make adjustments to your technical strategies; you might need to look for workarounds, make configuration changes, or adjust elements of the implementation in order to successfully realize the intended outcome. The key thing to keep in mind as you do this is to evaluate each time the degree to which a change in the implementation necessitates a re-evaluation of the design. There is more art than science to this. A sweeping technical change that largely doesn't impact the security of the component(s) being altered might not cause you to re-evaluate the overall design, whereas a more modest change that does impact security—either the outcome of a security-critical feature or control or even the implementation of that feature or control—probably will.

You might be wondering, why not play it safe and just—as a matter of course— perform a design analysis and implementation review iteration each and every time something changes? Philosophically, this wouldn't be a terrible idea in and of itself. The problem, though, comes about when you consider the impact on a small team that is focused on agility (being nimble and moving quickly). In that situation, going back to the drawing board each and every time an adjustment is made in technical operation will add significant overhead in time and effort. Recall that we want to introduce just enough process to get to the outcomes we want without overburdening the effort and losing our ability to operate quickly and be nimble. Therefore, as a practical matter, it is often a much better strategy to have confidence in the metrics that you've established—and your own awareness— to guide you.

Ultimately, when it comes to issues of this type, it is hard to give specific guidance on how to resolve them. Organization-specific factors such as project management methodology and business context of course play a role, meaning that the organization itself and its approach to technology problem resolution will dictate how to proceed in part. Likewise, technology-specific factors such as what technology is in use, how it's planned and architected, and so on also impact this. And finally, since the universe of possible issues that might arise is so vast, the problem under consideration might be anything—as you know, it would be foolhardy to try to provide a one-size-fits-all solution for all technology challenges. On the bright side, though, these types of problems are ones that technology organizations have tremendous experience working through. So, for many problems of this type, solutions should be at hand using the same mechanisms that you employ for other technology-related issues that arise.

Now, let's turn our attention to strategies that we can use to "future-proof" our designs and ensure that they continue to stay relevant over time.

Future-proofing designs

> *"The future is data-centricity, not technology-centricity or network-centricity.*
> *Vendors have products focused on network security; they have engineers who know*
> *about networking. But that's only one aspect of the problem. For example, the*
> *emergence of cloud architecture is massive in its implications. People still do not yet*
> *appreciate how much cloud requires a change in architectural thinking.*
> *I think this tells us that the development of architectural ideas for security and risk*
> *management will always be changing because there's always new challenges coming*
> *along. It requires us to be agile and open-minded."*
>
> *– John Sherwood, Chief Architect, thought leader, and co-Founder of The SABSA Institute*

In planning out mitigation strategies for dealing with change, only one dimension of our change planning involves the potential issues and challenges we'll encounter during execution. We will also need to plan for future events that might impact how the solution performs over time post-implementation. This refers to what happens next once we implement. After all, we can't just walk away; today's new and shiny security capability can turn into tomorrow's burdensome and problematic legacy system.

This means that establishing the capability to ensure continued and ongoing value from the solutions we put in place is every bit as important to the architecture process as coming up with a solid and workable design. Throughout the process, we've put time and energy into planning out how the system will perform post-implementation. This is, after all, in large part the purpose of the metrics we gather, the planning that we do for what best meets the organization's goals, and so on. This means, along the way and during the planning, we've done the best that we can to account for the future and the full life cycle of the solution. However, this is not all there is to future-proofing our design.

In addition, there are three key elements that we should pay attention to when it comes to ensuring that our design stays relevant, useful, and valuable over time:

- Establishing a virtuous cycle
- Monitoring our landscape for changes
- Monitoring for external changes

We will discuss each of these areas briefly and continue the theme into the next chapter as we draw together all of the elements that we've discussed so far.

Establishing a virtuous cycle

*"To improve as an architect, I recommend that people spend more time thinking
through what is the true value of security for their organization. This could be
risk reduction for the business, trust for the end consumer, compliance for the
regulator, and so on. Incorporate this into how you architect your design. This
is more important than some other architectural disciplines. When defining a
network, architecture for example, you might primarily look at the firewalls,
routers, switches, etc. This lets you maximize network performance to provide the
best experience and bandwidth. But that on its own is not enough. If you don't
understand how threats are evolving and their impacts – for example, what a DOS
attack means to a software application or how it impacts customer experience
– it limits your ability to design."*

– Phoram Mehta, director and head of Infosec APAC, PayPal

Ultimately, at the highest level of maturity for any process, we reach a state where the processes we use are known and well understood, where we collect information about the ongoing performance of those processes, and where we use the information that we gather about the performance to improve it over time. This represents a virtuous cycle of continuous improvement, represented by the Shewhart cycle, or **PDCA** (**plan**, **do**, **check**, and **act**), as illustrated in the following figure:

Figure 8.1 – The Shewhart cycle (PDCA)

Essentially, what we are trying to do is develop a design (**Plan**), implement that design (**Do**), validate the design with metrics and information (**Check**), and then, based on what we learn from watching the solution in operation, take actions to improve (**Act**).

This of course isn't rocket science, nor is it the first time that you've probably heard of it. However, for many of us, the goal of employing a disciplined architecture process is to help us achieve this. We've talked about the first three of the four elements required for a virtuous cycle, but the last piece, the actions that we take to ensure continuous improvement, also needs to be thought about, and a framework must be put in place in order for it to come to pass.

We will discuss this concept of continuous and ongoing improvement more in the next chapter, but for now, there are three things about it that are useful to discuss here, as they tie into the other areas that we will discuss relating to future-proofing your design. Specifically, we need the following:

- The establishment of a cadence or frequency with which to refine and review
- The refinement of the metrics we gather so that they allow us not only to track performance but to improve it
- The establishment of barometers for contextual change

Each of these is important. Again, there is more to establishing a virtuous cycle of improvement than just these three things, and we will talk about why you might want to do this and how you might go about it in the next chapter. But whether or not you decide to push for this and increase your maturity to a point where you are seeing continuous improvement, these three elements are important.

The first element is essentially one where you establish an interval time along which you will review, re-assess, and potentially update designs in light of how those designs perform. Why define a specific interval ahead of time? It allows you to account for human nature. It's a fact of life that we will get involved in numerous other priorities over time; six months or a year after we've implemented a given design, we are likely to forget to revisit it or find that other events, such as new projects, cause what we've done in the past to fade into the background. Even assuming that we have perfect memories and won't forget, there is still the possibility that roles can change, meaning we might be in a new area, new position, or new firm in the intervening time.

The second piece involves reviewing and updating the metrics that we collect over time. As you recall, we were careful about setting up our metrics such that they answered questions that we could foresee about the degree to which solutions meet requirements and the degree to which implementation is successful. These were our best estimates about specifically what information we'd need, but as we all know, best estimates are not always perfect. We will need to refine and improve upon the metrics that we collect over time. We will need to have a plan and a pipeline in place to validate that the metrics we are collecting are the best ones to ensure that initial requirements are met, and also that they continue to be so as the business changes or when requirements evolve.

Lastly, this implies that you have a way to know when those requirements evolve. Businesses are not static. Processes change, technologies change, and the threat landscape changes. Changes to any one of these areas can have an impact on the relevance and operation of the solutions that we put in place. In essence, this means that the remaining two items that we'll discuss in this section are foundational elements to a continuous improvement virtuous cycle.

Monitoring our own environment for changes

> *"Expect your measurements to change throughout the architecture process. Galileo said 'measure that which is measurable and make measurable what is not so.' There are always things to measure, but you will need to be creative to find the things you*

want to know that are not yet measurable. Don't get stuck on measuring something just because you can: focus instead on measuring things that give you value. Be clear why you are measuring something and what value it provides to you for decision support."

– John Sherwood, Chief Architect, thought leader, and co-Founder of The SABSA Institute

The second element of future-proofing is establishing a mechanism to tell if things change in the first place. The reason why this is necessary is best illustrated by an example. Say, for example, that you have developed an implementation strategy for securing connectivity between two application components. Perhaps because of the nature of the data exchanged between the components in question, the encryption of data in transit between these two components was not in the original requirements set and you designed and deployed network-level controls (for example, network segmentation) to ensure that traffic between those two devices occurs only via a defined, protected internal channel.

This design might work for the particular context in which it was designed and fielded, but you will notice that there are two assumptions built into it:

- The two components live in close proximity to each other

- The data being exchanged between the components is such that encryption isn't required by policy or the reduction of risk

Both of these assumptions could change. For example, one of the two components could be moved to a new location, traversing an intermediate network along the way (such as would be the case if one of the components was relocated to a public cloud environment). Alternatively, a new version of the application could be released that introduces additional data exchanged via that same channel, such as social security numbers, financial account data, or personally identifiable information. Any assumptions about the internal environment could change, causing our assumptions to be invalid and introducing risk.

This means that we will want to ensure that, should these changes occur, we are alerted such that we can either extend current designs to stay relevant or iterate through the analysis process to address the new risks. Or, if the changes are extensive enough, initiate a new design process to create a new solution.

In general, there are three things that we will want to monitor for:

- **Business process changes**: Changes to how the organization conducts business. This can be literal changes to the business itself (for example, **Mergers and Acquisitions (M&A)**

- Apply P-Keyword (Bold) to the above. activity), changes in critical workflows, adaptations to what type of data is handled during existing processes, and so on.

- **Technology changes**: Changes to the surrounding technology within which a solution is designed to operate. This might include the introduction of new technology elements (for example, virtualization or containerization), changes to the environment (for example, the cloud), shifts in operational processes, or changes in the technology stack below.

- **Requirements changes**: Changes to the governing requirements. This might include policy changes, regulatory changes, and changes in organizational risk tolerances.

So, knowing what changes you are looking for, how can you gather information about them? There are a few different strategies to do this. First, we can leverage risk management—specifically, risk assessment activities—to provide information to us about these contextual changes. This is one of the many reasons why recording requirements (including supporting assumptions) and maintaining a record of them is valuable. Another approach is through opportunistic activities involving review that may be going on in parallel. For example, one strategy we've used with a great deal of success in the past is to make it a habit to participate in business continuity planning processes, such as **business continuity planning** (**BCP**) and **disaster recovery** (**DR**) plan creation and testing. Why? Because early phases of BCP and DR planning involve specific steps—such as conducting a **business impact assessment** (**BIA**)—that requires systematically and thoroughly gathering information about business processes.

Whatever strategy you choose, it is important that you set up a method to monitor for these changes in an ongoing way. As you discover changes occurring, ensure that the requirements that you've established for your designs are kept updated and, when those requirements change, that you revisit designs to ensure that they continue to best fit the organization.

Monitoring for external changes

"The time to begin your risk assessment is early and often. Meaning, begin as early as possible in the planning process. Do a risk assessment at the beginning of the design and revisit it throughout – in particular when there are major changes that occur. This gives you an ongoing feedback that can help guide the work that you do. Revisit the risk assessment periodically even if there are no substantive changes since threats, context, or how an asset is used can evolve over time."

– John Tannahill, a Canadian management consultant specializing in information security

Lastly, much like you keep track of changes that are made to the organization, its business/mission context, and how/what activities are performed, likewise do so with external events. The reason why this is important is that external events and conditions can impact requirements to the same degree that internal changes can. For example, consider how much time we spent in the early design phases evaluating the threat landscape. What happens to the threats that our solutions are designed to operate within as attackers innovate, pivot to address new targets that they haven't before, or otherwise gain in sophistication? Those threats will change over time, and as they do, the mechanisms that you have put in place to protect against them will need to change to stay current.

Now, you'll probably notice that this item is fairly similar to the previous one. The difference between them is what you're monitoring (in the previous item, you're monitoring changes in your own organization, whereas in this one, you're monitoring changes outside of it). There is a solid, practical reason for thinking about them separately, though: the methods that you can most effectively employ to maintain external versus internal situational awareness differ greatly.

For monitoring changes to the internal environment, you can use information-gathering tools, communication channels with peers inside the organization, and similar strategies to keep abreast. However, changes in the external environment require a different approach. You might, for example, leverage information such as threat intelligence reporting to keep pace with new threats or changes in how attackers operate. You might assign someone to systematically canvas and research attacker tradecraft—their tools, techniques, and procedures—to notify you when there's a significant change that will challenge or alter assumptions in ways that obviate or require adjustments to standing requirements.

The important part here is that ongoing situational awareness is a key part of establishing the capability to protect the value and utility of your solutions over time.

Specifics for machine learning projects

> *"The fundamental challenge that you have with building a proper ML model is that your organization is going to produce a colossal amount of data, most of which is probably useless. There's this iterative process of sifting through all the data you have, figuring out which of it can be framed as features for specific modeling outcomes.*
>
> *This is a 70,000-foot view, but it's important you start with this because the process starts with the need to have a broad group of people exploring the data. There are security controls implicit in and necessary for this. You can start by putting in appropriate permissions to access the data, log everything they're doing, making sure the access is temporary, to name just a very few. At the end of the day though, you're granting a lot of access – to a very large amount of potentially very sensitive data - to a few very trusted people for that data exploration. This is very different from a traditional software development model or a traditional application deployment model and therefore requires specific architectural approaches and an understanding of that process to account for these differences."*
>
> *– Chris King, Head of Product at Protect AI*

In our discussion of future-proofing, specific topics that bear discussion are machine learning, artificial intelligence, and data science. There are two reasons for this. First, the impact of machine learning on technology ecosystems is potentially significant. This is true in terms of the level of interest in machine learning by enterprises given their potential transformation impact on business and also because it involves new techniques, new technologies, new development methods, and numerous other potential ecosystem changes. Second, it potentially changes the underlying architectures as a consequence of delivering the capability.

As an example of what we mean here, in an interview for this book, Chris King, current Protect AI Head of Product and former AI Services Principal Architect for AWS, cited the challenges associated with the data exploration process (cited in the preceding quote.) He explained that one of the most important parts of the data analysis process (imperative to the machine learning development process) is "data exploration." This refers to a period of time where data scientists are allowed to freely explore, model, conduct experimental transformations, and other activities that allow them to figure out where connections are and what may be relevant for further analysis. The initial and surface impact of this is that the model by which a project such as this is developed has some very different development methodologies than we might be used to in a traditional deployment context.

The more subtle downstream impact of this though is more subtle; it takes some drawing out, but it has some very critical practical implications:

- The introduction of machine learning in many cases necessitates a revisiting of the underlying security requirements. If it's true that the development process is sufficiently different (as outlined in the previous example) and has unique properties that are dissimilar from development modes we may be more used to, it logically follows that these things would translate into security requirements that require being specifically addressed.

- If the previous point is true, this in turn implies that we may need to revisit requirements merely by introducing machine learning (or really any data science activities) into an existing solution or product. Since the harvesting of security requirements happens early in the architectural process, it is very important to understand this since it can require iterating through many of the earlier phases of the process to account for new and potentially ongoing new requirements in the development of that capability.

- Additionally, all of the previous points imply that we as architects understand the machine learning development and data science processes sufficiently to be able to account for these new requirements, to know that such adaptation is necessary, and so on. Currently, it is the rare security practitioner that understands these nuances. This, therefore, requires us to become educated on what they are doing and how so that we can make informed decisions about how, whether, and where to update these processes, address new requirements, and so on.

- Lastly, note that the preceding items all presuppose a new class of stakeholders that are currently unaccounted for in existing designs. Recall the importance of stakeholder engagement: unaccounted-for stakeholders are one of the most dangerous sources of friction in any architectural endeavor. They can literally derail entire efforts, foster strife, erode political capital, and engender long-term enemies. In a situation such as this, it is imperative that we find and engage with these new stakeholders at the earliest possible opportunity.

As you can see, these implications are pretty significant and can require some significant work to account for. Particularly insidious is the implication that architectural strategies need to potentially be revisited merely through the incorporation of machine learning into an extant solution just through the introduction of these techniques, and there's a lot of that going on in today's enterprises as organizations race to harness the value of machine learning. This is a pretty big deal (and the primary reason we're noting it here in its own subsection).

The good news, though, is that the architectural process itself doesn't change. All the same steps and techniques apply. For new projects, then, we follow the outlined process. For existing efforts, as well as efforts in flight, we may need to revisit earlier phases of the architecture development effort for the reasons outlined previously. While we might need to reiterate some of the earlier phases to account for the new requirements, stakeholders, and methodologies, we don't need to otherwise undertake any exceptional measures.

There is one important caveat that bears noting as we do this though. Specifically, it is tempting in the case of an existing project or product to merely iterate the architectural process with a heavily reduced scope as a strategy to minimize work. This means creating a piecemeal architecture that addresses only the machine learning and data science elements and excludes from the scope the pre-existing elements of the existing solution. This is a viable strategy in some situations, but bear in mind these capabilities can be very tightly integrated into existing solutions. The danger, therefore, is that there is a disconnect between the machine learning elements of the solution and the more traditional components. This means they can feed off, mutually support, and tightly integrate with each other in ways that lead to oversight if analyzed separately. If time, budget, and resource constraints allow, it can be valuable to analyze the whole thing together rather than attempting to conquer it piecemeal.

Next, let's examine some real-world implications of this.

Case study – future-proofing

"Security in a machine learning or artificial intelligence project is in some ways similar to traditional efforts: you make sure you have the right access controls, understanding of data flow and aggregation, data protection, etc. But there are some areas where architecture has to adapt.

For example, when you start talking to users. If I talk to a customer about a Postgres database, nobody becomes suspicious that I'm going to monitor that data – for example to build a better database and subsequently compete with them. It would seem paranoid and insane to ask whether I'd look at what's inside that database.

With machine learning though, you will often be called on to answer detailed questions about what you will use data for, how it will be accessed, when it will be accessed, etc. This means you often have to architect in specific transparency controls. Transparency can be just as important and data protection - and this in turn needs to be factored into the architecture process itself."

– Chris King, Head of Product at Protect AI

In an interview, we asked Chris King about situations he observed where differences between machine learning architectures deviated from more traditional approaches and where that led to unexpected architectural considerations. He outlined several instances where this was the case.

First, he relayed to us a situation that occurred in his former role as the Principal AI Services Architect, providing AI services. He told us, *"I was helping launch Customer Connectors for Lookout for Metrics— an anomaly detection service from AWS. It launched with DB connectivity that was far too broad, and as a consequence, customers were not adopting it. To help mitigate this, I worked to build a connector architecture first for Redshift (the biggest customer demand), but to make it generalizable enough for any SQL style-database later. The focus here was on isolating access to the source data, enforcing encryption constraints (KMS, etc.), and preventing DB access with higher permissions than needed."*

What's interesting about this example is the initial overly broad connectivity. This is a direct example of the considerations cited in the last section about how machine learning can require levels of data access that are unexpectedly broad and hence need to be considered directly as part of the architect's remit. From here, he went on to describe a related situation. He told us of another situation that also applied to Amazon Lookout for Metrics:

"A large fast casual food services organization was launching a new rewards program. Here, they were launching a loyalty program and needed to be aware of anomalous redemption data from the system within 24 hours of location. Essentially, they were looking to prevent viral coupon hacking-like behavior."

He then described the necessity of integrating the machine learning elements with the traditional environment:

"The initial ML bits weren't so complicated; instead, the complicated part was working out how to reliably get data from their franchise systems and how to securely aggregate it in environments with no direct access, only automation. We had to plan out every step first, code it, and then observe it running. This required digging into multi-account configurations, figuring out how to secure data at every layer, and how to bake in security of the data pipeline for production ML. Lastly, we had to apply security to the methods for delivering the insights, creating dashboards to report effectively, and to manage access to all these elements."

Of particular note in this example is the underscoring of new—and potentially unaccounted-for—security requirements and stakeholders by virtue of the machine learning-elements of the process. He told us, *"They wanted to bring in an external data scientist to help find this data and to figure out how to perform the transforms on the data. Their compliance department absolutely refused to share the sensitive retail data with a contractor. Therefore, they needed to provide sanitized versions of the data to the consultant to do the transforms."*

Likewise, he reported that there was an unexpected degree of automation required in the process:

"Everything for them was infrastructure as code, with no direct manual engagement allowed into any of their cloud environments. They were one of the best organizations I've ever worked for in terms of security, but it created some operational challenges. We needed to build out automation to work in each of development, QA, staging, and ultimately production environments. We ended up building custom connectors that allowed them to specify their own authentication system and create on-demand tokens. This allowed automation that would go out to the database, do the transformations we wanted, bring the data back to a very specific location in the cloud with all the controls desired, and do the transformations they needed there. Meaning, it involved writing specific automations to support that."

Implicit in this are a few things: the necessity of new architectural strategies, of course, but also the underscoring of the fact that these changes can bring in new requirements, new stakeholders, new techniques for releasing functionality, new types of controls, and so on.

Summary

Throughout this chapter, we've dealt with one important and key theme for both executing your solutions and ensuring that they stay current and valuable: managing change. In the first section, we talked about strategies to manage and mitigate change that can negatively impact the execution and practical implementation of solutions that you design, and in the second half, we talked about how you can monitor and manage changes that might impact the relevance of your designs after they're implemented.

In the next chapter, we will build on this, discussing how you can increase the maturity of your architectural approach and put everything that we've learned together to ensure that you are doing the best job you can in ensuring that your organization is appropriately safeguarded.

Putting It All Together

We've covered a lot of ground throughout this book. We've talked about the pre-work for solution building, how to determine and encapsulate important information about your organization that feeds into the design process, how to set the scope, how to derive solutions from risk and threat information (accounting for organizational needs and context along the way), how to craft technical solutions, how to implement them, and how to keep pace with unexpected changes and curveballs.

At this point, you have a solid understanding of a process that can help you get there, as well as a subset of the tools that you can use (or adapt) to do so. As you gain mastery, you will discover new tools, new techniques, new processes, and new approaches. You will build on the foundational principles to improve.

That's what this chapter is all about: how to take what we've covered forward and how to work to improve your skills over time so that you develop as an architect. Specifically, in this chapter, we'll cover the following topics:

- Virtuous cycles
- Tips and tricks
- Gotchas

This will help pave the way for you to expand your architecture efforts and tee you up to get better over time.

Virtuous cycles

> *"From my point of view, you need to align infrastructure and security design elements to the processes you have in place. For example, if your organization uses two-week scrums, align your architecture design and implementation process around that process. If you are using a different cycle or another approach, design around that instead. This is true both temporally as well as philosophically. Meaning, the cycle time should be aligned to best service their needs, but the design*

philosophy should be aligned as well: if the organization heavily leverages cloud, adapt – if it's DevOps and CI/CD, integrate into that. You want to be in sync with the environment around you not just to get buy-in and acceptance but also as a practical matter."

– Anand Sastry, Director Cyber Operations USA, Barclays

In the last chapter, we discussed the impact of change on the design process, both in dealing with unexpected change and issues that arise during the execution of a design as well as with strategies for laying a foundation for future-proofing – that is, managing changes that can arise post-implementation that impact the value and utility of the solutions we develop.

All of these things are necessary, and when taken together, they constitute a full iteration of an architectural design and implementation cycle. There is one thing to keep in mind though: there's more to the practice of architecture (both for you and for the organization you work within) than just one single iteration of the design process.

As an analogy of what we mean by this, consider baseball. From a batter's point of view in baseball, there is a lot involved and a lot to know; you need to know how to hit, which pitches to swing at, and which not to. Once you hit the ball, you need to know how to run the bases: when to steal, when to run, and when to slide. These are the fundamental mechanics of getting on base and then running the bases. By analogy, these things are akin to the skills that we've tried to give you guidance about throughout this book: the simple, fundamental skills involved in taking a "turn at bat" (i.e., iterating through the architecture process in this analogy).

But everybody who's ever played or watched baseball knows that you don't just hit the ball once and you're done. In each game, you'll have multiple turns at bat. If you want to play—whether recreationally or for the Yankees—there's more to it than just playing through one turn at bat, one inning, or even one whole game. You'll need to hit the ball and run the bases each and every time it's your turn at bat. You'll do this multiple times in each game. If you play professionally, you'll do it hundreds or thousands of times in a season and in every season over the course of your whole career. There are many, many iterations of your use of the same relatively simple skills. The difference, then, between playing poorly and playing well will come down to how well you can refine and improve your skills in executing these relatively simple actions over time.

The same is true of security architecture. The design process we've gone through in detail in this book represents one iteration: a single turn at bat. However, you will hone your craft—the process, the tools you use, your approach, your communication style, and much more—over the course of many iterations throughout your career. You'll need to know how to iterate effectively, meaning how to execute the design process so that each iteration gets better, becomes more efficient, and improves your outcomes.

In the last chapter, we brought up the idea of developing a "virtuous cycle" of continuous improvement. We discussed this through the lens of things that you can do within the context of a given iteration of the security design process. However, it's important that you understand how this plays out in a context that's broader than a given set of security solutions at a single point in time.

To illustrate what I'm talking about here, consider how you'd approach a routine task such as preparing meals. The first time you do it, maybe you follow a recipe and the meal you intended comes out just like the picture. It's a success! However, while you accomplished your goal, you still didn't perform quite as well as a trained chef would. If you prepare meals every day, maybe your skill level will improve. You notice things that hinder your ability to do it well and correct them. For example, maybe you notice that food sticks to your hot skillet unless you oil it first. You decide to try oiling the skillet to test your theory. Upon validating that the addition of oil or cooking spray helps prevent this, you add it to the process you follow. Perhaps you learn ways that could improve the efficiency of the process; for example, maybe you become more familiar with where the various tools (pots, pans, utensils, and so on) are located in the kitchen so that you can be much faster at finding them. Perhaps, as you learn this, you decide to adjust the layout and relocate items to allow you easier access to the items you need when you need them.

Now, this cooking metaphor might seem mundane, even trivial. But stop and consider what happened in those examples. You planned and executed a task. Based on observations you made while executing, you adapted the processes and environment to optimize what you are doing and yield a better result in less time. You posited hypotheses about how you could improve, you tested those hypotheses, and, after validating the assumptions, you put your optimizations into practice.

If you continue to perform the task of cooking, maybe you notice more things that you think can be improved. Maybe the cupboard where you store pans is disorganized, forcing you to stop and look for a given pan each time you go in there. Based on this, you might decide to organize that cupboard so that you don't have to spend as much time looking. Again, based on observations, you've refined the process—once again making the overall process more efficient.

In these examples, you've done a few things. First, by performing the task, you've established a framework within which you can continuously improve. You did the following:

- Planned out a task to the best of your ability
- Executed the task
- Observed the results of the task
- Based on your observations, you refined your process to get better results

This is exactly what we mean by a virtuous cycle. It is very important both to the architect over the course of their career, as well as to the organizations where they perform their duties. In fact, what separates the best security architects from the merely serviceable ones is the ability to establish cycles of improvement at two levels: creating the best designs that we can and building in mechanisms to improve each individual design over time. This means we plan out each design thoroughly and in as much detail as we can and create an implementation strategy to realize those goals. In doing so, we collect the metrics we will need to validate that we were successful in that implementation. Based on those metrics, we improve the design to optimize it and refine it over time and as opportunities allow.

But these all apply within one iteration of the design process. The second thing that the best architects do well is refine their *approach* and *process* just the same way that they set up the designs they create to allow optimizations over time. They build in metrics about the performance of individual designs, but they also build in metrics and performance at a *meta* level by keeping tabs on the performance of their design process itself. Like in the cooking example, each time we iterate the design cycle, we want it to become better optimized, better performing, and with better outcomes as we learn and adapt for efficiency, accuracy, and reliability.

Another way to think about the difference is through the lens of maturity. An architect might design a solution that has a target maturity baseline that they're trying to hit built into it. Say, for example, that as part of a design, they require a monitoring capability. They might set maturity targets around the underlying process that implements that monitoring—for example, they might have a requirement to ensure that the processes that drive that monitoring have consistent outcomes or that the process stays resilient in the face of attrition or other personnel changes. To accomplish that, they might plan an implementation that uses a qualitatively managed process (a high degree of maturity), for example, by ensuring that the process is well documented and validated using specific, concrete metrics.

You'll notice, though, that the maturity level of the design outcome (in this case, the monitoring process) is different from the maturity of the design process that is used to derive it. A quantitatively managed control could be conceived, designed, and implemented by a disorganized team following an ad hoc, unmanaged process or vice versa.

The point is that the most disciplined architects are willing to adapt their processes in a way that targets continuous improvement. They seek to understand the maturity of the designs they field, but they also seek to optimize and refine the methods that they employ to arrive at those designs too.

Adapting architectural processes

> *"A lot of architecture programs fail because they're too heavy weight. People will sometimes buy 'the book' and try to do exactly what the book says to do—but it's important to know how to take out the important bits based on what you are looking to do and applying those quickly. There's an old joke: 'if at first you don't succeed: try, try again... then stop since there's no use being a fool about it.' Meaning, there's value in perseverance – and don't give up on the first try—but also know when to adapt when what you're doing isn't working."*

> – Adam Shostack, President, Shostack & Associates

So, how do we do this? The first thing to note going in is that there's no perfect process. At least, there's no one-size-fits-all process that will work for every organization. Throughout this book, we've discussed reasons why this is. For example, some organizations have stakeholders that respond positively to communication in a certain way or in a certain context, other organizations might have different maturity targets, others might have contractual mandates that require them to adhere to a given formal architectural standard, others might operate in different industries or locations, have different needs, different cultures, and so on.

The obvious implication of this is that coming up with the optimal process for your organization will take refinement; you'll need to tailor and adapt your approaches based on the organization, its context, its mission, its culture, and numerous other factors. That's an important truism, but there's a more subtle implication as well, which is that inertia leads over time to suboptimal security architecture processes. This is because the organization is always changing, and, with it, so are culture, technology, personnel, and so on. This in turn means the design process will need to evolve and adapt over time to stay optimized. So even if you were somehow able to come up with the perfect design process out of the gate (which is very, very unlikely), it won't stay perfect for very long if you fail to adjust it to account for natural changes in the organization.

The point is that there are two key practical advantages of continuous improvement:

- It helps you adjust your process to be more valuable and efficient.
- Over time, it keeps the process performing optimally as the organization changes.

There are two keys to understanding how to bring this about in practice. The first is making sure that you fully understand what the goal is, and the second is to lean into human nature and interpersonal dynamics. We'll explain both in more detail.

First, let's be clear about what specifically we're trying to do. A lot has been written about process optimization and continuous improvement over the years, which can sometimes lead to misunderstandings. Someone looking to actually do this in practice is more likely to be challenged in refining available guidance and narrowing it down to a manageable subset than they are to be challenged with finding guidance about it in the first place.

Consider, for example, the Shewhart cycle, which we talked about in previous chapters:

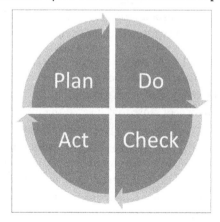

Figure 9.1 – Plan–do–check–act cycle (Shewhart cycle)

Under this approach, first you plan (**Plan**), then you execute (**Do**), then you validate and measure (**Check**), and then you act on those measurements to improve (**Act**). In terms of encapsulating the fundamental concepts of continuous improvement, this viewpoint has a few advantages. First, it's simple: literally anyone who's ever mastered any task (no matter how mundane) can understand it. Second, it's also the viewpoint espoused and embraced both in ISO 9001 and—more germane to our purposes—ISO/IEC 27001. This means that should you want to explore further how continuous improvement plays out in a security context, there's plenty of advice and guidance to choose from because it's codified in several international standards.

But understanding *what* it is represents something very far from understanding *how* to actually do it. Again, because every culture is different, there's only so much that someone else can tell you about what will work for you. However, fundamentally, it's about three things: practice, learning, and habit (or you might say "process"):

- **Practice**: Having something to improve that can be quantized or broken up into discrete iteration cycles

- **Learning**: Your ability to maintain situational awareness and distill that situational awareness into lessons learned

- **Habit**: Establishing habits and process frameworks that self-enforce (or reinforce) improvement throughout the process

The first key point is practice. What we mean by this is that there is something important that you will execute on that you will do multiple times over and over again. Earlier in this chapter, we used cooking as an example of a process that you might want to improve. The reason why we used this example is that it is iterative and occurs frequently. Something that isn't typically iterative is hard to optimize in this way because, though you may learn important lessons in your relatively few experiences performing the task, you're limited in how much you can change each time it happens.

As an example of why this is so, consider an example from everyday life: getting married. In this case, let's look at it from two different perspectives: the point of view of a participant (that is, the bride or groom) and the point of view of the officiant. From the point of view of the bride or groom, it's (for most) a once-in-a-lifetime experience, or close to it. Even if the marriage ends and they decide to remarry, it's still likely to occur only a few times in that person's lifetime. If they wanted to become an old hand at getting married, how could they do so given that (from their point of view) the process isn't iterative? By contrast, the officiant (the person conducting the marriage ceremony) may conduct thousands of weddings over the course of their career. They might learn by heart the words of the ceremony and they might learn about common issues that can arise during the ceremony and how to avoid or recover from them. From the point of view of the officiant, the process is iterative, so they can optimize and get better at performing the task.

Likewise, in the case when something is iterative but when the cycle time is very low (that is, when the frequency between iterations is very long), it becomes very hard to monitor feedback and plug lessons learned directly into the process to improve it. For example, in a security context, it can be very hard (for most of us) to optimize incident response or business continuity processes. Why? Because we typically only perform these processes rarely and sporadically. In fact, this is almost exactly the reason why conducting a tabletop simulation or other readiness exercises for both business continuity and incident response can be so valuable; these activities give you a vehicle to track, learn, and improve even though the event in question hasn't come to pass.

This introduces the second point: learning. By this, we're referring to two related concepts: the ability to monitor performance over time, typically through observation and metrics collection, and the ability to test potential optimizations and measure their impact.

When a process is very far from optimal, chances are you won't need quantitative metrics to know that it can be improved—you may even be able to suggest improvements and have high confidence in their success without specific metrics. As the process gets better and more streamlined, the improvements become more subtle. This is because you are getting closer and closer to optimum efficiency and performance. Think about it like a graph:

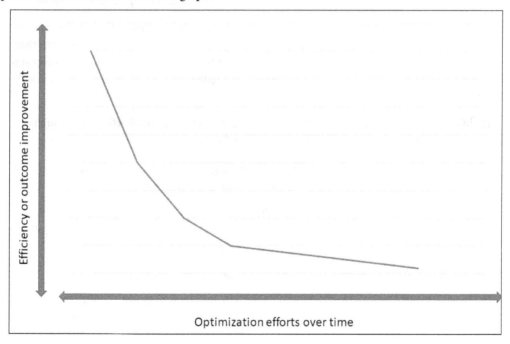

Figure 9.2 – Optimization diminishing returns

On the left side of the figure, you have a process that is so broken and ineffective that it doesn't perform the function at all. This means that changes to improve that process will likely be obvious, and it means that the improvements that you make are likely to have a tremendous impact on the quality of that process. Like Pareto's famous maxim, you can make significant improvements quickly at this stage with relatively little work. As you move toward the right side of the graph, you have processes that already perform fairly well but could still be improved. Here, what the specific changes are to bring about improvements are less obvious and, in order to spot them, you will likely need the assistance of data to evaluate how much or how little a given proposed optimization impacts the process. Additionally, each change that you do make will likely have a diminishing return. That's not to imply that the change isn't worth making; it's just that the impact of your change will likewise require measurement to be able to evaluate it. Again, keep in mind that we're referring here both to the metrics that you are establishing as part of the designs you build but also the metrics that give you insights about the design process itself.

The last key concept here is arguably the most important one: the ability to understand human nature and lean into it. At first, this might sound strange. After all, why would human nature be relevant to improving our architectural processes? The reason why it matters is that we want to use human nature as a way to make optimization and improvements of the architectural process self-reinforcing.

This is probably best illustrated through examples. To illustrate, consider two hypothetical architects, each one working in similar organizations and starting at more-or-less the same initial state with their architectural processes. They have a similar skill set and both intend to optimize their architectural process over time. They both establish processes where they gather metrics and make updates in light of those metrics to try to improve.

The only difference between the two is how they implement improvement efforts. The first architect in our hypothetical example adapts their process in the following way:

- The architect needs to remember to request a debriefing session with architects and stakeholders to capture lessons learned after implementation efforts are completed

- The process owner for the architecture process (for example, the architecture board, team, or owning individual) needs to remember to review the process in light of metrics on a quarterly or annual basis.

The second architect in the example adapts their process in this way instead:

- Before any implementation is considered complete, the team must perform an after-action review of how the process went. Projects are reported to management as incomplete until the after-action review is completed and filed.

- As a prerequisite to initiating a design cycle, the architecture team must meet to review current performance metrics and suggest process improvements.

What is the likely outcome of each of these approaches? Human nature suggests that three things are true:

- **Human memory is fallible**: People, no matter how well-intentioned, will forget things

- **People get busy**: Project teams focused on the final push to get something important done (such as implementing appropriate security controls and reducing risk areas) are likely to take shortcuts on things they consider to be lower priority

- **Humans respond best with feedback**: In the absence of direct feedback, people will often deprioritize improvement efforts

In light of these truisms about human nature, the first process—the one that relies on human memory and people's best intentions to function—is likely to come off the rails (that is, get deprioritized and as a consequence not be performed) as time goes by. The reasons why aren't hard to understand. Some teams will forget to complete the after-action review, meaning that lessons learned are only captured by the teams that remember to do it. Likewise, the periodic review of the architecture process can very well fall by the wayside as time goes by. For example, maybe whoever is responsible for that changes their job and the new person stepping in doesn't know how to do it, or perhaps it gets deprioritized during a busy period or is temporarily postponed (and subsequently potentially forgotten about.)

The second example is less likely to succumb to these situations. Why? Because the process itself enforces that the right steps are taken. Those working on a design will understandably be anxious to close out their design and implementation successfully (at least until the next design iteration begins in the future when the solution needs to be refined or improved). They are anxious to move on to the next task and to report their success to their management. Since a review where lessons learned are captured is required in order to do those things, they are highly incentivized to make sure the review happens. Likewise, rather than relying on individuals to remember to incorporate lessons learned back into the overall process, the process itself has that built in. That is, in order to bootstrap the cycle, participants must come to the table to discuss refinements and adaptations.

The point is that to make this a reality, you not only want to address the grievous errors that are the most obvious and that provide the most optimization, but you will also want to set yourself up to incorporate the more subtle lessons as well.

If you recall way back in the earliest chapters of this book where we discussed maturity, you'll recognize that this continuous feedback loop is the touchstone for a very mature and developed process. For example, Level 5 of the CMMI is *Optimizing*, which is characterized by moving toward optimization in much the same manner as we described earlier. In addition to incorporating measures from prior levels (for example, documentation and quantitative management), this stage is focused on making improvements over time based on the information you can collect and the improvements/lessons that you can distill from them.

While it is the case that continuous improvement and optimization in this way do correlate with a state of relatively advanced maturity, we should be clear that such a process does not have to be heavyweight. Likewise, we're not suggesting that every organization—regardless of context—should try to implement a process at a maturity level way higher than the rest of the organization or what they need. Instead, we're just trying to point out that you will want to improve over time, and one way to do that is by paying attention and putting yourself in a position to get better as you learn from the work you do.

Next, we will look at some tips and tricks that have worked successfully for us in the past to help align our processes toward continuous improvement.

Tips and tricks

"For the new architect, it is important to develop both technical and interpersonal skills. The technical skills are important, but you also need to listen, take inputs from a variety of sources (input from different people, different tools, and telemetry). The ability to understand, translate, and prioritize needs/wants between these stakeholders is important."

– Dr. Char Sample, Chief Research Scientist – Cybercore Division at Idaho National Laboratory

The second thing that we'll leave you with is a few things that have proven valuable to us in the course of our work. These are not the only things by any means that you can use to improve as an architect—in fact, because what is useful to each architect is subjective, there could be numerous techniques that we haven't thought to include but that you would find valuable. Likewise, these are not a retread of what we've already discussed. We've tried where we could to include advice throughout that has worked for us, as we've discussed scenarios that involve either the creation of a design, the documentation of it, or the execution of the implementation.

What we're covering here, then, are techniques that, while we've found them valuable, are not directly tied to any particular step of the design or implementation path. It's analogous to a baseball coach giving you advice to get a good night's rest before a game. That advice, while extremely useful, isn't tied to any particular aspect of your play. Since our approach throughout has been to walk you through how to perform the key tasks involved in iterating through an architecture cycle, there are some bits of advice that fall outside of that flow. We didn't want you to walk away without hearing them, though, so we are covering them briefly here.

There are five tips that we wanted to leave you with:

- Hone your ability to listen
- Cultivate empathy
- Have just enough process
- When in doubt, over-communicate
- Be ready to walk away

We'll outline what we mean by each briefly. Some of these might seem obvious, even trite, but you'd be surprised by how often these important elements are overlooked.

Hone your ability to listen

"An ex chief executive for whom I used to work once told me that in business, there are only three things you need to concentrate on: focus, focus, and focus. Sometimes architects seem to find it difficult to listen enough. At a point in my career, a very long time ago, I had planned on going into broadcasting. Initially, I worked as a freelancer for a local BBC radio station. A seasoned broadcaster explained to me how to ask people open-ended questions. I was very excited and I set out to ask the general public the open-ended questions I had prepared. In those early days, I was concentrating hard on asking the question, but I wasn't focused on listening to the answer. In the context of security architecture, when you engage with someone, they will have a series of things they want to say. Sometimes they don't always say them without encouragement. If you try to tease out what they want to say by asking open-ended questions, you can help them do so. From there, you can then learn more about not only about what they want but what they need."

– Andy Clark, Founding Director, Primary Key Associates Ltd, Visiting Professor RHUL, Trustee of The National Museum of Computing, SABSA Co-author

If there's one defining skill that all architects must have, it's the ability to listen. This is probably not rocket science, but it is very important and you'd be surprised how often even experienced architects struggle with it. There are two things that we mean by listening in this context: listening is both an active process and a strategy.

What we mean about it being an active process is that we need to seek out the right people and get them to tell us what's important to them. Sometimes, stakeholders and those invested in the process will tell us directly what is important to them, but often, they will not, or they will hold back important elements. This isn't from malice or an unwillingness to share—in fact, they often hold back just because they either don't know what's relevant or they are so close to the problem space that they thereby don't realize that fundamental assumptions wouldn't be known to others. This means that the architect needs to be an active participant in the listening process; they need to not only put themselves in a position to hear what is shared (that is, engage in conversations with the right people and pay attention to what they tell us), but to also ask the right follow-up questions to unpack what is underneath and driving what is being shared.

In addition to engaging actively to get to the root cause and ask probing questions, listening can also be a strategy that the architect can use to get better data. Sometimes, people have things on their chest that they are anxious to share with others. In a situation such as this, just providing them with a forum to say what they need to say will open a floodgate of additional information that might be relevant. Therefore, hearing these stakeholders out – by providing a forum for them to share what they feel is important – has the immediate impact of you potentially yielding data as they do so, and it helps you build rapport with them to allow you to ask more targeted questions.

It goes without saying that the opportunity is wasted if the listener can't (or doesn't) remember what is shared or they fail to capture and retain what they are told. So, while it's perhaps painfully obvious, a strategy to capture what is being discussed—either note-taking or (with permission) recording and subsequent transcription of interviews—can be the difference between making sure the information being shared is actionable versus a situation where it is not.

Cultivate empathy

"I went through a professional identity transformation about ten years or so ago. In my first architecture role, I realized that my job was no longer to be just a technologist but instead to be a storyteller. I strive to tell narratives that make sense to people and take them on a journey from where they are now to where they need to be. In effect, I'm a professional storyteller that tells technology and cybersecurity stories. Recognizing this has allowed me to be much more effective, to create better documents and drawings, and to communicate better."

– Mark Simos, Lead Cybersecurity Architect, Microsoft

The ultimate goal of the architect is to understand the viewpoints of those that will engage with the security elements of a system. Active listening (as described earlier) is a great way to put your finger on what the most important elements from their point of view are, but this only gets you halfway to where you need to be. The other half involves being able to understand their point of view and to envision what it is like to be in their shoes. In essence, this is to empathize with their position, understand their concerns based on what they share, and visualize the end state from their point of view.

It is the reality that some people are naturally better at this than others. While that's true, empathy is a skill that we can develop and hone just like any other. But what active measures can we take to improve our empathy when dealing with particular stakeholders? One strategy that can help us improve is to refine our knowledge of the organization itself and the stakeholder's role within it. Empathy tends to scale with knowledge. As you learn more about what stakeholders do, what their day-to-day experiences are, and the role they play in the organization, you become better equipped to understand what's driving them and why.

Understanding the stakeholder's viewpoint is important because it allows you to contextualize what they tell you about what's important to them: their motivations and goals. To help build that contextual understanding, obviously asking is a good first step. This means asking about the stakeholder's functional area: why it's important, what they do, how they do it, and what worries them. But this is just a first step. From there, it can also be helpful to gather data from other sources to round out your understanding. For example, if you are meeting with an executive stakeholder to talk about a team they manage, you might ask that stakeholder's permission to speak with members of that team to help build your understanding. You might review public materials on the company intranet (if there is one) or collaboration portals to better understand what the remit of the team is and how they work. Your goal is not to be intrusive or step on toes, but instead to understand where those individuals are coming from so that you can contextualize your discussions with them.

Additionally, building up a better understanding of the organization is valuable as it allows you to contextualize why a given stakeholder views certain things as important. Understanding the broader organization—its culture, business goals, activities, customer base, and so on—helps you contextualize the information you get back and also helps you ask the right questions to better get the information that will be germane to the design process.

Have just enough process

"For someone new, the value of following an established architecture process is that it helps you not reinvent the wheel every time you need to design. Existing frameworks that you can draw upon can take away some of the heavy lifting. This helps you focus on what fits best for your organization based on factors unique to you: company size, company stage, culture, and so on."

– Samantha Davison, Engineering Manager, Robinhood

In many smaller organizations, the default state is to start with very little in the way of architectural process. Consider a four-person startup: they have other fish to fry before their focus is likely to turn to building a formal, mature process around security architecture. This is both understandable and appropriate. In this case, existential concerns such as bringing in enough revenue to keep the lights on, bringing their minimum viable product to the marketplace, and other existential tasks take priority. As organizations get larger and more mature, though, their processes also mature; more individuals and stakeholders become involved, and other issues beyond the merely existential rise to the fore. In this case, process provides a context to work within—it acts like guard rails that keep everyone on the same page and makes sure that important tasks are completed.

The important thing to keep in mind about this is that architectural efforts can be stymied when the level of process or architectural rigor is out of sync with the organizational culture and needs. For example, consider what would happen if our example four-person start-up decided to implement every step—and create every deliverable—of the TOGAF ADM. On the surface, that might sound like a responsible goal; after all, who can't benefit from more discipline? But when you start to unpack the amount of work that would be required to do that and the opportunity cost of what that organization would have to sacrifice to achieve it, you'll find that, if this should be given top priority, the organization could very well go out of business before they ever complete just one iteration of the cycle. Likewise, imagine what a lightweight, streamlined process that could effectively support a small, agile organization such as this example one would look like. Now ask yourself if that process would be equally appropriate for a large, multinational bank. Probably not, right?

The point here is that the process itself needs to be tailored to the organization to best effect. Over the course of our preparation for writing this book, we talked to quite a few security architects. We were told again and again that the optimal amount of process is just enough to meet the needs of the organization and the players within it but no more. This means that you want to introduce as much process as needed for the output to be useful and to be consistent with organizational culture. Any more than that creates a drag on the ability of the organization to be nimble. When nimbleness/agility is reduced to a sufficient enough degree, the process starts to become actively counterproductive. When this happens, the best case is that you will get pushback from those with urgent needs. The worst case is that teams will attempt to bypass the process entirely.

The trap here, though, is that many generalize this point and start to equate process with a lack of agility, meaning they assume that just because there is a process, it has to be slow and detract from the ability of teams to react quickly. The truth is anything but. Recall again that the process provides a sandbox within which people can work. For a large organization, failure to implement enough process can be just as counterproductive as having too much is for a smaller organization. The goal instead, rather than concluding that "process is bad," should be to continuously evaluate and optimize how much process is enough as the organization evolves and matures over time.

When in doubt, over-communicate

> *"One of the biggest mistakes I see people make is insufficient attention to aligning with stakeholders. Security architects need to be security leaders as well as technologists; they must engage stakeholders on requirements, help them see the value, and understand the various people, process, and technology components. You need to make sure all stakeholders are on board with their security-related roles or duties. A successful architecture requires clear understanding of the risks, a thorough understanding of the subject matter, knowledge of the control set in scope, an open mind, and engaged, active communication with stakeholders."*
>
> *– Dan Blum, Cybersecurity Strategist, Security Architect, and Author of the Book Rational Cybersecurity for Business*

This one is almost the inverse of the first two items that we covered (that is, listening and empathy). Often, the trap that we can fall into is to assume that others—for example, stakeholders, executives, champions, project managers, engineering teams, and so on—are equally as invested in the outcome of the security design process (as well as the logistics involved in completing it) as we are. This is only rarely the case.

Other teams have other things on their plate beyond security architecture—they have work to do that doesn't have anything to do with our efforts (or, in fact, with security more generally). In general, we can rely on them to want us to be successful in our efforts and (for the most part) do their best to help us, but the fact that they are at one remove from the design process (they participate in it but are not responsible directly for it) often means that we are the de facto broker of status and logistical information back to the broader team.

Likewise, sometimes there can be an unwillingness to divulge detailed information about specific security measures. Even seasoned security practitioners can fall into the security by obscurity trap—that is, believing that, because security measures are non-public, this will somehow present an additional obstacle for attackers. It would be folly to suggest that there's not some truth to that. There are, after all, a whole category of issues—information disclosure issues—that represent security issues specifically because they leak information about the details of security-relevant controls to attackers. However, bear in mind the opportunity cost that comes with keeping all implementation details to yourself, even when they intersect with other teams.

In this case, by keeping that information to ourselves, not only do we lose out on the opportunity to refine the design in light of what other functional areas can tell us (since they can't provide feedback on what they don't know), but we also potentially make enemies internally or lose political capital. Neither outcome is desirable. In general, therefore, a useful way to approach it (at least with internal teams) is through the lens of *Kerckhoff's principle*. Dutch cryptographer Auguste Kerckhoff posited that a cryptographic system should be secure even when everything about that system other than the key is public knowledge. In the words of cryptographer Claude Shannon in his famous maxim, as outlined in his 1949 paper, *Communication Theory of Secrecy Systems*, "*…one ought to design systems under the assumption that the enemy will immediately gain full familiarity with them.*" In other words, design systems with the mindset that information about the implementation will become public. This is both a useful security approach and reduces the barriers that would preclude others from systematically examining the design and providing feedback.

The point is that there are times when it is natural that we will feel a natural shyness when it comes to communicating, and there are other times when we might not do so for the simple reason that it will not occur to us that additional communication is necessary. In either case, don't fall into the trap. It is almost always better to overshare (again, at least internally to the organization) than it is to undershare. This means that actively espousing a position of sharing and communicating that's more than we feel is necessary can often be beneficial. We should keep this in mind during conversations we have, in creating the documents and deliverables we produce, and in the metrics and data we share as output. In fact, assuming we have a sufficient amount of process to hang it on, including points along the pipeline whereby we communicate information to the broader team is valuable. You can create a communication plan (in fact, frameworks such as TOGAF and SABSA specifically advocate this), or you can do something less directly formal but that ensures the same result. In short, keep communication in mind as you design and alter your processes where possible so that doing so is unavoidable.

Be ready to walk away

The last point that we'll bring up is to retain a willingness to walk away from a design. It is human nature that we become attached to our designs. In fact, we would probably make poor architects if we didn't feel passion about our designs. Esteem for elegant design and a passion for turning those designs into reality means we're looking to do the right thing for our organization and our investment in the outcome is a barometer for how seriously we view the value provided. It means we're invested.

Therefore, it is natural to feel a sense of ownership over a design and also to want to fight for that design to see it realized. However, there are times when for a variety of reasons—cultural, economic, technical, and so on—a given design isn't viable. We should of course do the work to verify the assumptions about why it isn't viable (perhaps instead of true roadblocks, they are merely hurdles to be overcome), but there comes a time when we need to go back to the drawing board.

We should be willing—even eager—to do so when this situation arises. Why eager? Because determining that a given solution isn't viable before you start to implement it is a win. This represents time, energy, and expense that you don't have to invest in order to cross the idea off the list of potential strategies to accomplish a security goal. Therefore, even by walking away, you're still being efficient.

Sometimes, you can be faced with a choice of walking away from a design or adapting it in light of feedback in a way that wins you political or social capital with other teams. Remember that ultimately you are operating in service of the broader business; if you can work collaboratively with other teams (including what might otherwise be an elegant or even optimal design to foster that give and take), this is often a useful strategy. Why? Because in the future, this group will see you as a reasonable, adaptive, and helpful problem-solver.

Of course, you don't want to leave the organization hanging either when (as is sure to happen) you discover late in the process that you can't proceed down a direction that you thought was already settled. Don't forget that even if you do need to walk away from a design for whatever reason, you can put in place temporary measures or stopgaps to keep the organization protected in the interim as you design a better solution.

Gotchas

> *"At the core of architecture, I think there's two fundamental principles. First, there is architecture as a philosophy of how you think about a [security] function (a core component within an organization) in a way that understands and interprets the requirements for what it needs to perform. The second is the ability to communicate why that function is important. Using the example of a physical building, the architecture describes the safety aspects of why you need to build something in a particular way; for example, the assumptions of why having x number of bolts in a certain place makes the building more safe. It's the same with security: if you understand the business you are in, and what safety means in that context, and clearly understand what security means to that business, architecture is about making that clear and describing it to others."*
>
> *– Phoram Mehta, Director and Head of Infosec APAC, PayPal*

As helpful as the preceding tips and tricks can be, there are also some potential traps and gotchas to be on the lookout for that can introduce tremendous difficulty into the architecture process when they arise. As with the tips and tricks, this isn't an exhaustive list of all the possible things that could go wrong. Instead, it's a targeted subset. These mistakes are ones where many architects struggle and that can (and do) lead to potentially negative situations. They are also easy to fall into: it can take even seasoned architects years to internalize how to avoid them.

Note that in laying these out, these gotchas represent issues that can arise that aren't directly tied to any particular step along the design path. Throughout earlier chapters, we tried to outline potential traps and pitfalls that can occur at individual steps as we went through the design iteration phases.

There are many things that can go wrong though, and these are the items that we've learned (in most cases, the hard way) are best avoided.

To keep it simple, we are focusing on five potential gotchas here:

- Be aware of (but don't play) politics

- Don't shirk the preparation

- Stay engaged until the end

- Leave ego at the door

- Use a multidisciplinary approach

We'll walk through what we mean briefly in the remainder of this section.

Be aware of (but don't play) politics

> *"The architect needs to understand politics. There is going to be politics in whatever environment you are working in. For example, these may influence how their client contacts careers will be affected according to the outcome of the architect's work. The architect naturally needs to think about these politics, understand them, and find guides who can help them navigate them."*
>
> *– Andy Clark, Founding Director, Primary Key Associates Ltd, Visiting Professor RHUL, Trustee of The National Museum of Computing, SABSA Co-author*

Most of us hate corporate politics. In a perfect world, we would be able to do our jobs well, perform our work in an efficient and timely manner, and everything would work out. This, however, is often not the world we live in. Organizations are made up of individuals, and it would be foolhardy to assume that the personal and/or career aspirations of those individuals don't ever play a role in helping or hindering us from realizing a successful outcome.

What this means in practice is that we should retain a healthy awareness of politics in the organization. This speaks directly to our ability to empathize with others in the organization. In other words, if we empathize with others and understand their point of view, we will (and should) naturally gain some understanding of their interests and thereby the political situation surrounding them. We should and will gain some understanding of how those individuals are measured and evaluated, what interests their organization (or them as individuals) might have, and what motivations (political motivations included) help drive them. The better we can understand these, the better we can empathize with them and see things from their point of view.

A useful corollary to this is the observation that, while the political reality is one that we should understand and stay alert to, it's also safer if we don't play the political game ourselves. This means that, to the extent practicable, it's advantageous to stay as neutral as we can be. Now saying that, it is true that our function will report to some management chain in the organization. Our management, being human, may have political interests, and therefore sometimes politics in the work that we do will become unavoidable. But in most situations, staying clear of politics is advantageous; it allows us to remain an unbiased advocate for all stakeholders, it cultivates a reputation for impartiality that in turn leads to enhanced trust from those whom we will need to engage with, and it helps us refrain from accidentally making enemies of the very people whose trust we will require in the future.

Don't shirk the preparation

One particularly nasty trap that many fall into is rushing directly into creating technical designs for things without following through on preparation. You'll notice that in this book, there was quite a bit of pre-work that we did before we actually started creating and documenting the technical design aspects of our solution. This is by design, and the pre-work is important.

No matter how aware you remain of the importance of these earlier phases of the process, it is a near-certainty that you will at some point fall into this trap (just like we all have). At some point, you will be faced with a problem that you've seen a hundred variations of before and where the solution seems so profoundly obvious that you'll be tempted to skip directly to the technical design. Sometimes you'll be right and save some time by doing this. However, there's a danger in doing this, even when you're right. The dangers are twofold:

- If you're wrong (even by a little), you waste more time than you save

- Whether you're ultimately right or wrong about the solution, less preparation means less defensibility

The first one isn't hard to understand. It's like driving double the speed limit to get to work. If you don't get caught, you get there a little bit faster… but if you get pulled over by the police, you'll lose all the time you would have saved and then some.

Analogy aside, think about it this way. The temptation to skip prework is highest when time is a factor. After all, if you didn't have a deadline, the little bit of extra time doing the preparation work wouldn't be missed. When you have a deadline and the pressure is on, it is exactly the wrong time to get caught out by a simple, easy-to-avoid issue. For example, what if you assume the wrong scope or misunderstand a requirement? This is more likely to happen when you assume you fully understand what the problem is without either documenting it or validating it with the stakeholders requiring the solution in the first place.

If that happens, you'll have two choices: 1) you either try to recover and adjust the technical design based on the new requirements or 2) you reiterate through the whole process anyway. In the first case, the error means you've already obviated the time you "saved" by failing to be thorough in the first place, and since you're still not analyzing it thoroughly in recovering, you could be wrong again. In this case, you're worse off than you would have been if you had not skimped on the preparation. And if you need to go back and reiterate, you've now made the process longer because you've had to go back and redo what you missed the first time through.

The upshot is that very rarely do you save time by skipping preparatory steps. Since you're only likely to be tempted by this the most when time is already a factor, these are exactly the projects for which you want to avoid the extra delays likely to be brought about by taking the shortcut.

But even when you're right and you don't cost yourself extra time (though most of the time you will), there is still the problem of defensibility. What happens when someone down the line questions why you did something the way you did? If you followed a disciplined, thorough process in creating the design, you can tell them exactly why you did what you did. You can point to the many alternatives you considered and why you (in collaboration with others) decided to select one approach over another. This is all valuable information. Two years down the line, you will absolutely not remember the many possible solutions that were floated and ultimately shot down when thinking through your solution. This makes it very easy for others to second-guess your design decisions or to question whether the solution you selected was in fact the optimal one. This, in turn, can lead to friction between you and other teams down the line, questions of confidence with key stakeholders, and potential lost time, as already-discussed solutions are relitigated.

The purpose of much of the work you've done in the early phases, in addition to gaining feedback and concurrence, is to establish defensibility. Why did you choose option instead of B? It's spelled out right there in black and white. Why are you measuring this metric and not some other one? Again, the decision is transparent. Context or situations might change to make other solutions more compelling than the one you ultimately went with, but there is zero ambiguity why you (in lock step and documented full agreement with all the other stakeholders) made the choices you did. If you bypass the early stages, you're left without any of this defensibility. It might not bite you right away, but it can (and often does) lead to issues down the road if you don't do a thorough job documenting how the sausage was made.

Stay engaged until the end

"I think it is immensely valuable to have your subject matter experts engaged early and to carry them with you throughout a project. If as well as being a subject matter expert, they have an interest that is broader than their subject matter area, they will be interested in what you're doing and how you're doing it and may well provide valuable input outside their primary expertise for which you engaged them. You might find someone who is the greatest subject matter expert in all the world, but if you find it very difficult to communicate with them and it doesn't feel comfortable, find someone else. What is critical is that you have someone you can ask questions of, you can trust the answers, and trust that they will put their hand up and say when they got something wrong."

– Andy Clark, Founding Director, Primary Key Associates Ltd, Visiting Professor RHUL, Trustee of The National Museum of Computing, SABSA Co-author

Sometimes during a project, we can reach a rhythm where it seems like we're firing on all cylinders. In moments like these, it can be natural to disengage somewhat from important elements of the project. For example, maybe we took significant time to establish an initial rapport with stakeholders so we deprioritize our communications with them because the relationship is so firmly established. Perhaps we do the same thing with the internal champions of our efforts. We might have a project manager who is so on the ball that we stop monitoring progress as closely as we might otherwise.

The specific situation will dictate when this disengagement might arise, but the thing to note is that there will be times when it is a natural temptation to take our eyes off the ball before the effort is complete. Don't fall for it. It is imperative that we stay engaged—with specialist engineers, champions, executives, business teams, and all other stakeholders—all the way through the design and implementation process. It will often take active measures set up in advance to ensure that we do so. In fact, this is one of the key benefits of establishing and sticking to a communication plan from the earliest phases of the design process. Even something informal such as a calendar reminder to periodically (every week or two) check in with these individuals throughout the process can serve as a reminder to make sure that it gets done. The situations where it seems most unnecessary are when it's most valuable, specifically because it is under these circumstances that we might be tempted to become complacent.

Leave ego at the door

"I believe that humility is an important characteristic of successful people. Take John Harrison, he's the creator of the clock used to solve the longitude problem – the first marine-capable chronometer. He was not a clockmaker but a carpenter, he thought diligently over many years about how to create the best marine chronometer that would enable mariners to navigate on the great oceans of the world. He succeeded by listening to others who understood how to realize his designs in metal, even though they dismissed him at the time as being just an amateur. When we look at designing systems – creating our architecture – we are looking at systems of systems and cannot be expert in all areas that they encompass. If we are humble and encourage everyone in the chain to consider everyone else's capability and input that plays to each individual's strengths, we wind up with better results."

– Andy Clark, Founding Director, Primary Key Associates Ltd, Visiting Professor RHUL, Trustee of The National Museum of Computing, SABSA Co-author

This is an important one. We all want to feel like we are performing well in our jobs and that we have something valuable to contribute to the organization. In fact, projecting confidence can be a great tool in our toolbox. Recall that most of the stakeholders that we work with will not have a background in security. Therefore, they will judge our output (at least in part) by the confidence that we project to them in how we present ourselves and our ideas. If we present a design in a furtive, non-confident way, they are likely to view the output with skepticism. Therefore, confidence (even when it's slightly affected) can be a good thing.

However, there is a difference between healthy confidence and an unhealthy ego. By this, we mean an unwillingness to revisit designs in light of input, unwillingness to reconsider or scrap non-viable ideas, or other situations where our own personal self-view colors the work that we do. We should expect to be wrong and be willing to question assumptions at any point along the design process. Likewise, we should know our own limits. It's not expected that we will know everything about all topics, so when we're not on firm ground or if our knowledge of a given topic is limited, that is the time to admit our limitations and seek outside help. If the skills we need are in-house, this means engaging the subject matter experts to help. If we don't have the skills in-house but need them, we may need to look outside the organization. There is no room for ego if our ultimate goal is to best protect our organization. This means not being overconfident in our own skills, being willing to admit ignorance, and also being willing to understand when we don't have the right folks with the right skills within our own organizations.

Use a multi-disciplinary approach

> *"Security architecture is an interdisciplinary approach. It requires key skills from across technology disciplines and the business. There are multiple domains that you will need to draw upon to build and maintain a robust architecture. For example, a chief security architect should have people from multiple domains that don't often fall under the architecture function: the threat hunting team, identity management, and numerous others with operations or specialized expertise report into him. In turn, he would be paired up with the line of business folks so that solutions tie directly back to the business need. This gives him access to disciplines and expertise that might not be usually a part of the security architecture discussion and keeps his focus on what the business itself directly needs."*
>
> *– Steve Orrin, Federal CTO at Intel Corporation*

In keeping with this point, no one person will have all the skills required to look at every solution from every angle. You will absolutely need the involvement of those with experiences and specializations different from your own. While this is obvious, the same is true when it comes to other skills; for example, soft skills, non-technical skills, communication skills, organizational skills, and others.

The more diversity of thought and perspective that you can bring to the design process, the more efficient the work will be and the better quality the output will be. There are a few reasons why this is so. First, when thinking through risks and threats, different perspectives will lead you to consider different types of threats. For example, if a project team contains someone with a social engineering background, they will likely raise different scenarios of how humans in a given process could be manipulated into providing access to critical data. Someone with a physical security point of view might suggest physical-based threats.

Second, people with different skills will add value when it comes to the socialization aspects of the effort, for example, in performing important elements of the process such as communication or requesting support. They might have different styles of communicating, different communication skills, or other unique traits that assist in gathering support, relaying feedback, or otherwise interacting with all the various stakeholders and interests in scope.

Lastly, different points of view will add value just by people asking questions and providing input. Very often, just having someone ask the right question can open up discussions and lines of thinking that would have never occurred had you employed only one perspective. Ask a group of engineers how to solve a problem and you will likely get an engineering-focused answer. If you invite business teams and others into the conversation, it's more likely that someone will see the problem in a different way and lead you down paths that you wouldn't have thought of.

In a large organization, it can be easier to find a diversity of skills in-house. In a smaller organization, though, sometimes you will need to be creative to get access to a diversity of skills. This might require engaging with others outside the organization through social media or groups, it might require that you turn to trusted advisors and mentors for help, or it might require you to bring in external talent (for example, consultants) to help.

Case study: gotchas

> *"People are still thinking about architecture without embedding resilience in a way that can lead to security problems. By not thinking about remaining resilient comprehensively, you risk a) increasing the blast radius of vulnerabilities, b) expanding the volume of both unintended information sharing and intentional, nefarious information sharing, and c) increasing susceptibility to malicious reconfiguration.*
>
> *Think about it this way. If am making a holiday meal, I take an architectural approach but build resilience around the goal of feeding people. My implementation plan would then include the use of 2 ovens, and I put lasagna in one and turkey in another. If one fails, I may lose the turkey, but I still have lasagna to serve. We would do well to plan for resilience in a structured way. I think that's in large part because you need a blending of skills from software architects, cloud architects, and networking architects sitting in a room together and thinking through in detail how customers will use the things being built. Moreover, that conversation needs to happen at a very high level of detail and specificity and in the context of a particular community or set of stakeholders."*
>
> *– Edna Conway, CEO and Founder of EMC Advisors*

In an interview for this book, we asked former Chief Security and Risk Officer for Microsoft Cloud Infrastructure and former Cisco Global Value Chain Chief Security Officer, Edna Conway about where and how security architects can improve and where she's seen things to watch out for or strategies that can add significant value to the architecture process.

She began by illustrating the importance of the interdisciplinary approach and the value of differing perspectives on the same problem.

"In my personal life, I use two financial planners because I am wired for resilience. Among the accounts directed by these planners and accounts that I manage myself, I can leverage diverse models. While all three areas have one unified goal, this segmented approach can deliver resilience despite a failure or loss in one of the architecturally aligned systems."

From here, she expanded to consider the importance of a baseline understanding of security principles and finding the patterns for how those play out even in more complicated architectures. She highlighted that a resilient approach ensures the security architecture is designed for all the environments that enable our digital experience.

"Take, for example, the implementation of network segmentation. How do you achieve the benefits of segmentation when your workflows are in a cloud environment? Hardware architectural controls are simply not adequate when operating in the cloud. Consider how users access the cloud—via browsers. Browser security and, dare I say it, web isolation, are a key part of a resilient security architecture. And finally, always layering identity and access management and the long-standing principle of least privilege into your architecture enables resilience in the face of an intrusion."

"Let's look at how that plays out using integrated circuits as an example. Does the supplier of a CPU need to know in detail what graphics controller manufacturers are doing? New architectural models built for resilience require that we take the same fundamental models of segmentation and least privilege and wrap protections around who can access what, who can manipulate what, and who can work with what is being protected. To me, this means that every enterprise today must devise its own plan for how to effectively utilize things like cloud capabilities. The network we protect architecturally is no longer just the physical or virtual routers, firewalls, or switches, but instead a complex network of business processes."

"Let me offer an example of what I mean here. In the course of working with third parties, I've seen knowledge of architectural changes (in this case hardware architectures) leading to a subversion of the security model. In one case, a particular supplier was able to intuit the direction of an organization's plans based on required underlying changes. Specifically, that supplier correctly concluded that a move from an x86 to ARM architecture was being planned. This knowledge led to consequences down the road in terms of the business relationship."

"This example is particularly interesting to me because it opens the aperture on what security really means in the first place. What lies at the core is the confidentiality and integrity of information and the ability to operate undisrupted. We reflect that in simple assertions like, 'I don't want you changing this information', or 'You do not need to see this information', or 'You may not share this information other than with those identified as legitimate recipients. In this case, by sharing access to planned hardware architecture changes

too broadly, unintended parties were able to make conclusions about broader business ramifications. This is a glaring business example of how architectural decisions—if not approached cautiously, carefully, and purposefully—have the potential to cause havoc and set you back from delivering what you want to your customers. This can limit the movement forward of the innovation that lies at the heart of your technological progress."

This example is interesting because it speaks to the core of what the practice of architecture even is in the first place: understanding the problem space, understanding the risks, understanding the potential business impacts of architecture decisions (both pros and cons), and purposefully communicating information based on context.

Summary

In this chapter, we've covered how you can extend your architectural design process into a broader program – that is, how to create a virtuous cycle whereby your process reinforces itself to achieve greater efficiency and better outcomes. We've also covered some of the best advice that we've received from the architects we interviewed to give you insight into what you can do to improve as an architect, and also what common missteps and pitfalls to avoid as you do your work.

Throughout this book, we've tried to map out a process that you can follow to create a cybersecurity architecture for the systems, applications, hosts, processes, and other elements of your technology ecosystem. We've tried to emphasize how to do this in an adaptive, flexible, and nimble way, both to help you tailor existing architectural frameworks to models such as DevOps and Agile, but also so that even if you're not following an architectural framework, you can hit on all of the important elements of solid and repeatable design.

We hope you find this information to be valuable and that you are able to grow as an architect by looking through the combined experiences and insights of the many individuals from all segments of the industry who have provided their counsel throughout, and also make use of the techniques that we've employed successfully throughout our careers as security architects. Just remember that security architecture is a craft, and like any craft, it involves skills you can learn and improve upon. With diligence and practice, these skills can be picked up by anyone with a willingness to learn.

Also, like any craft, your skills will continue to grow for as long as you practice them; you will be improving your skills and honing your techniques each and every day. This also means that the best way to grow is by doing. The more you apply your skills, the better they will become. So, much like learning to play a musical instrument, the single most important thing you can do to improve as a cybersecurity architect is to practice.

Index

A

S

Packtpub.com

Subscribe to our online digital library for full access to over 7,000 books and videos, as well as industry leading tools to help you plan your personal development and advance your career. For more information, please visit our website.

Why subscribe?

- Spend less time learning and more time coding with practical eBooks and Videos from over 4,000 industry professionals
- Improve your learning with Skill Plans built especially for you
- Get a free eBook or video every month
- Fully searchable for easy access to vital information
- Copy and paste, print, and bookmark content

Did you know that Packt offers eBook versions of every book published, with PDF and ePub files available? You can upgrade to the eBook version at packtpub.com and as a print book customer, you are entitled to a discount on the eBook copy. Get in touch with us at customercare@packtpub.com for more details.

At www.packtpub.com, you can also read a collection of free technical articles, sign up for a range of free newsletters, and receive exclusive discounts and offers on Packt books and eBooks.

Other Books You May Enjoy

If you enjoyed this book, you may be interested in these other books by Packt:

Fuzzing Against the Machine

Antonio Nappa, Eduardo Blázquez

ISBN: 978-1-80461-497-6

- Understand the difference between emulation and virtualization
- Discover the importance of emulation and fuzzing in cybersecurity
- Get to grips with fuzzing an entire operating system
- Discover how to inject a fuzzer into proprietary firmware
- Know the difference between static and dynamic fuzzing
- Look into combining QEMU with AFL and AFL++
- Explore Fuzz peripherals such as modems
- Find out how to identify vulnerabilities in OpenWrt

Windows Forensics Analyst Field Guide

Muhiballah Mohammed

ISBN: 978-1-80324-847-9

- Master the step-by-step investigation of efficient evidence analysis
- Explore Windows artifacts and leverage them to gain crucial insights
- Acquire evidence using specialized tools such as FTK Imager to maximize retrieval
- Gain a clear understanding of Windows memory forensics to extract key insights
- Experience the benefits of registry keys and registry tools in user profiling by analyzing Windows registry hives
- Decode artifacts such as emails, applications execution, and Windows browsers for pivotal insights

Packt is searching for authors like you

If you're interested in becoming an author for Packt, please visit `authors.packtpub.com` and apply today. We have worked with thousands of developers and tech professionals, just like you, to help them share their insight with the global tech community. You can make a general application, apply for a specific hot topic that we are recruiting an author for, or submit your own idea.

Share Your Thoughts

Now you've finished *Practical Cybersecurity Architecture, 2nd edition*, we'd love to hear your thoughts! Scan the QR code below to go straight to the Amazon review page for this book and share your feedback or leave a review on the site that you purchased it from.

https://packt.link/r/1837637164

Your review is important to us and the tech community and will help us make sure we're delivering excellent quality content.

Download a free PDF copy of this book

Thanks for purchasing this book!

Do you like to read on the go but are unable to carry your print books everywhere?

Is your eBook purchase not compatible with the device of your choice?

Don't worry, now with every Packt book you get a DRM-free PDF version of that book at no cost.

Read anywhere, any place, on any device. Search, copy, and paste code from your favorite technical books directly into your application.

The perks don't stop there, you can get exclusive access to discounts, newsletters, and great free content in your inbox daily

Follow these simple steps to get the benefits:

1. Scan the QR code or visit the link below

https://packt.link/free-ebook/9781837637164

2. Submit your proof of purchase
3. That's it! We'll send your free PDF and other benefits to your email directly